The fall of Man
Keys to rise above

The Awakening

Bruce k Deodat

ISBN:
ISBN-13: 9781729420485

DEDICATION

Dedicated to friends and relatives

- *The people of the Caribbean and the West Indies,*
- *The people of South America, and North America*
- *The people of Africa, Asia and also to the people of Europe*

The book and material dedicated to the lost generations: The young generations of today who do comprehend the effect and actions of the past generations have on the present generations such as the lifestyle, problems, and issues they are facing. A very brief overview to understand, comprehend and make changes that will be of benefit for the present and future generations to come. Many are living a good life because someone in our ancestry, father, mother, grandparents have prayed and broken all bondages from the past and cater for the future generations to be free, and free indeed.

It is up to us to make that reservation for future generations and to make a difference in the world today.

Romans 8: 28   And we know that all things work together for good to them that love God, to them who are the called according to his purpose.

29   For whom he did foreknow, he also did predestinate to be conformed to the image of his Son, that he might be the firstborn among many brethren.

30   Moreover whom he did predestinate, them he also called: and whom he called, them he also justified: and whom he justified, them he also glorified.

31   What shall we then say to these things? If God be for us, who can be against us?

We are losing our young generation to everything else except religion, spirituality, and GOD; politics internationally are creating divisiveness and division leading to brother hating brother and family division due to the mixed message from the various sources. Our leaders are aware of it all but are not making an effort to change or save the next generation to teach them and lead them to let the chain of Knowledge continue especially in spirituality and building self-image.

> **Joel 2: 28** *And it shall come to pass afterward, that I will pour out my spirit upon all flesh; and your sons and your daughters shall prophesy, your old men shall dream dreams, your young men shall see visions:*
> **Acts 2:16** *But this is that which was spoken by the prophet Joel; 17 And it shall come to pass in the last days, saith God, I will pour out of my Spirit upon all flesh: and your sons and your daughters shall prophesy, and your young men shall see visions, and your old men shall dream dreams:*

It is a calling for young people to take up the Mantle and lead the world through the coming age of chaos and tumultuous times towards the elimination of the dust of war, rage and humanity's created storms.

> *1 Kings19 So he departed thence and found Elisha the son of Shaphat, who was plowing with twelve yokes of oxen before him, and he with the twelfth: and Elijah passed by him, and cast his mantle upon him.*

> *Isaiah 61:3 To appoint unto them that mourn in Zion, to give unto them beauty for ashes, the oil of joy for mourning, the garment (MANTLE) of praise for the spirit of heaviness; that they might be called trees of righteousness, the planting of the LORD, that he might be glorified.*

CONTENTS

The Awakening

AUTHOR'S NOTE

This book was written for the enlightenment of man's quest for freedom, understanding the unseen, free from the turmoil's of life we are facing in the present physical world. Many do not understand the concept of the different multiplicity of dimensions in existence. They do believe in phenomena and miracles that take place in our societies and do find events in the supernatural but are unaware of how and why it affects us. We need to understand our bodies, our mind, our soul and how our bodies work in sync with the main components that affect our mental and physical health. We need to be in control of our inner-self and outer environment, our physical and our spiritual makeup and the forces around us for the betterment of our health and prosperity. We are a very complex organism; human beings far more sophisticated and complex in comparison other living being, yet built with a similar molecular structure and atomic format that is too close to each other to differentiate our wellness and the reasoning for our breakdown and traumatic circumstances that haunts us daily. We roam from depressive emotional valleys to joyful emotion mountains, up and down and far too wide for our stability and control. We lack the connection of perfect relationships with our kind and everything around us and influenced by a quest we do not understand fully, though many try to find the answers and drive themselves to understand who we are and what we are, where we are going and what our destiny is. What is the purpose of our lives and why we can or cannot achieve what we are ordained to be? Where do we come from and why are we moving in this direction? What is our physical makeup and why it is disintegrating so rapidly? Why are we not balanced? The imbalance overwhelms our sustenance, our endurance, and our physical self; it is far stronger, more overwhelming than our being can withstand, the severe battering of all environmental, climatic, mental and physical stress is a constant push to the fall, we spiral downwards towards extinction. Why our lifespan is reduced to just about 70 years rather than nine hundred as we were created to live according to ancient scriptures

In the beginning, penning this material on paper and electronic format, the wrath of the dark world and the persecution began in all directions, the evil influences; loss of job, sicknesses, and emergencies, breakages in the house that takes up financial resources: a crashed car which was totaled, weaknesses, visitation from people who are nonbelievers and have an evil aura, encounters, dreams and visions, arguments, and a whole lot of negativity. It is proof that what I am putting down in writing affects Satan and the dark world, demons and devils are looking into this material that it will make a vast change in the world and the young generation of today. People are going to learn what they need to do to sever all ties to the dark world that was binding them and putting them into this little box. A box where life has become difficult and everything seems to go the wrong direction, where parents will allow their children to read the material and become more investigative and research more into spirituality and the connectivity to God (for it is real and GOD is real, and so is Satan).

*Daniel 10:10 A hand touched me and set me trembling on my
ands and knees.*

11 *He said, "Daniel, you who are highly esteemed, consider carefully the words I am about to speak to you and stand up, for I have now been sent to you." And when he said this to me, I stood up trembling.*

12 *Then he continued, "Do not be afraid, Daniel. Since the first day that you set your mind to gain understanding and to humble yourself before your God, your words were heard, and I have come in response to them.*

13 *But the prince of the Persian kingdom resisted me twenty-one days. Then Michael, one of the chief princes, came to help me because I was detained there with the king of Persia.*

14 *Now I have come to explain to you what will happen to your people in the future, for the vision concerns a time yet to come."*

20 *So he said, "Do you know why I have come to you? Soon I will return to fight against the prince of Persia, and when I go, the prince of Greece will come; 21 but first I will tell you what is written in the Book of Truth. (No one supports me against them except Michael, your prince.*

The material is not designed to convert anyone to any specific belief system or religion or draw into a state of realization and wonder, exposing chaos and confusion. It is intended to open up the inner mind and drive curiosity to find out more on the why's, how's, where's, what's, and ultimate quest, knowing and learning how to manage our being internally, mentally and spirituality towards the greater good and understanding why we are here. We are human; we have one life to live, we waste time in living a life of risk, engaging in acts that we should not be involved in, eat the foods that bring about an imbalance. We follow the displays of media full of positive and negative information and digest much negativity that gets ingested in our subconscious mind and acts out what we have ingested. We need to know our body and learn how to take care of this one body that belongs to us and learn what to focus on to keep us physically healthy, mentally original and enhance our spiritual state that influences our well being.

It brings together the various religious studies and utilizes the popular doctrines to open up the mind to figure out what should pay more attention to, to build the mind and psyche to resist the adverse actions, negative forces of nature and various dimensions. To understand that we are not alone and we need to "Subdue" our dominion and "replenish" our environment as ordained for our betterment and prosperity in life, to live a life of abundance. We need to understand why we follow a specific religious path, the reasons why we choose that path and what good do we achieve by following that path. It is designed to enlighten our understanding of the communication with divine forces and what is the importance of that divine force in our makeup and our life journey.

Written in a common language that any person would understand and not misinterpret its word or ideas and will cause a tickling of your minds and emotion to either put down the thought and the book or delve deeper to get a better understanding, better knowledge and interpretations of the message it is meant to deliver. Waking up that inner sleeping powers of our gifted body, mind, and soul, "understand me "it asks, "seek me" it begs, "find me "it quests and "keep me" it demands and "I will make sure you are well" it states.

The intent is not to inject feelings of despair, hate, prejudices of any negative traits, but to touch on a few subject lines and make us understand more of why we do the things we do, and why we behave in a manner, we do. Why we hate, why do we see the differences and indifference and to draw attention that the problems we all face today caused not by one source, but by a multiplicity of actions that were influenced by unseen forces, powers and principalities of the air and other dimensions? Some of us may not even comprehend the meanings, some will and the many that do get the gist of the pointers in this book will tempt and create an unction to delve deeper do more research and see what is behind generational curses, bondages and actions, and the influences our ancestors have on our present situations and our world. Some may have fallen into the trap of being forced into bondage, and many have been the ones to inflict such bondages upon others and have resulted in critical sinful actions that caused bondages more overbearing than on those that they have inflicted pain and made others into bondsmen.

During specific periods in time, there was quite a lot of self-absorbed superiority which causes many to become murderers, rapist, serial killers, the vision of which lived with them ingrained into their DNA and passed down to their offspring and possibly injected into the minds of the next generations.

Do we know what our forefathers have done in the past that may affect our present live, whether it is spiritual, emotional, psychological or physical? Some of it may be the cause and effect of us being under the influence of spiritual bondage, forbearance of a sin we are paying for according to scriptures that sin pass down to four or seven generations and a result of curse or curses, sicknesses or illnesses, bondages or mal-effects in life today? There may be records, and there may not be records, but we all need to break off any negativity that came from yonder past, any curses, hexes, cults, and activity tied to the occult or demonology that may have been performed in the past that is unknown to our awareness.

God loves all people, and God loves all faith, and a reminder he did not create religion but deliver messages, doctrines, rules regulations and commandment that all should learn and benefit from which leads to one vertex – GOD. God incarnates himself time and time again to bring the man a more in-depth explanation of the old text, laws, and commandments. Therefore, Study the old for knowledge and lessons from the past and acknowledge the new as it is relevant to the times, the present era and the times to come –recognize the spiritual guidance.

Every Human being should understand their physical make-up as well as their spiritual ability and divine connection, what are the factors that make us what we are and why we do the things we do, why we do always look for solutions from a higher intelligence. We need to understand the physical connection to the spiritual and how we physical responds to the spiritual. How are we connected to the supreme divine entity of the Universe and how the connection established? The context of this book will enable all to get a grasp and a broad spectrum and view of these questions and answers. There is still an unexplored phenomenon of the Supernatural and the various dimension that exists that we are not able to see, hear, feel, or experience because of our limitations. There are sounds that our ears cannot understand, listen, because of the limitations of our ear, same goes for the eyes, not being able to see beyond our boundaries. However, putting it all together, between seeing, hearing, feeling, experiencing and spiritual, mental synapses of the brain and mind, we can experience much supernatural, and God is allowing us to be able to do so if we have the desire and drive to do so. Therefore, after the full read, it will be necessary to re-read and do more in-depth investigation until I come out with the second part of this book. Until then enjoy the broad spectrum of knowledge I am sharing and become an investigative reader to find out whatever you so desire to know. The philosophy is out there, be careful what is input into the mind and what to put fingers on to read.

The Major downfalls in a person's life: Listing 7 significant areas only

- Spiritual defeat, being disconnected from the Divine

- Physical downfall – Sicknesses, disability, terminal Sickness, Loss of vision

- Mental Downfall: Depression, loss of psychic abilities, confusion, Grief

- Financial downfall – Loss of Job, investments, property, legal related issues. It is the worst area of affliction and is a method used by the enemy to affect all other areas in a person's life.

- Loss of Family – Death of family member or being deserted by family

- Losing Dominion – Overcome by the Spirit of Ahab and Jezebel

- Falling to The Immoral Woman – getting involved and trapped

Job 12:12   Is not wisdom found among the aged? Does not long life bring
Understanding?
Proverbs 1:7 the fear of the LORD is the beginning of knowledge, but fools despise
wisdom and instruction
Hosea 4:6 ESV, My people, are destroyed for lack of knowledge; because you have
rejected knowledge, I reject you from being a priest to me. And since you
have forgotten the law of your God, I also will forget your children.
"This person is my relative, and that person is a stranger, says the small minded one,
for the one who knows the truth, the whole world is a family." -Maha Upanishad

"For the one, who has conquered his mind, the mind is best of friends; but for one who
has failed to do so, his very mind will be his greatest enemy." -Bhagavad Gita

"Who truly knows, who can honestly say where?
This universe came from
And where it will vanish to at the End?
Those godlike wise men who claim they know were born long
After the birth of Creation.
Who then could know where our universe really came from?
And whoever knows or does not know where Creation came from,
Only one gazing at its vastness from the very roof of the final Heaven
Only such a one could possibly know,
But does even He know?" -Rig-Veda, creation verse.

Written in dedication to all friends, family, and many who inherited Generational curses and bondage of their ancestors being in bondages from indentured-ship, slavery, Slave masters and plantation owners and those who were vested in the act of the old trade of humankind and putting them under the subjection of bondage. There is light at the end of the tunnel, Ask, and it shall be given to you; seek, and ye shall find; knock, and it shall be open unto you: For every one that asketh receiveth; and he that seeketh findeth, and to him that knocketh it shall be opened. Look back at the past and find out where the mark missed or where we tripped and aim forward towards the target. Return to spirituality as your mind and spirit guides you and as you pray, let your mind be opened up to receive the truth. Do due diligence and justify what is right and do not be followers of doctrine that are in no way beneficial to you or but be driven by the spirit of God and God will direct you towards the mark and what is right. If you have gained some knowledge or at least learn a few subject matter form this writing, I will feel accomplished that my message was delivered and received well. Pastors and Priests preach the Gospel to people who already know the Bible and Christianity and to those found, this book dedicated to those who are lost and not yet discovered.   The reference of "Man" in the context refers to "Mankind, "Male and Female" "Man and Woman" and can be applied while reading to the appropriate gender.

Spiritually Inspired   ***Bruce K Deodat***

Introduction

The basic understanding of Religion and its role with Humanity

The context covers a variety of subject matter that brings an understanding to humanitarian physical, mental and spiritual awareness and the spirit minded individual, witnessing the confusions and turmoil that faces the general public in the world and the chaos that exists, especially under religious divide. It keeps them bonded into a Unitarian belief system not allowing them to venture into the understanding and reasoning of why people are bent within the tracks of the culture, beliefs, and religion and tied to their native tongue, native ancestral practices: the cultural system specially designed behaviors and practices, worldviews, literature (Doctrine), ethics, principles, spiritual laws, documented messages to coax and teach humanity of the supernatural and transcendental existence of everything brought about by supreme divinity and paranormal activity from Supreme entity. We are still trying to understand, know, build a relationship with and induce into our mind towards a belief system of its existence – known as GOD. Religion is a belief system where worship of superhuman controlling power, a shared collection of the belief that was passed down for generations to generations as claimed it was the divine word from GOD. Tracing the foundation of the origin goes to the Far East where the practice of religion in the various classifications Polytheistic, pantheistic and monotheistic belief in many Gods, all is God, God is everything, and everything is God and finally, the belief system that God is One.

The context focused on understanding the belief systems and patterns administered through culture as integrated into the various religious sect giving the audience a general feel for the connection and the interaction between the human body, mind, soul and spirit and the faith and believe in culture and religion. How they are intertwined and the influences religion and spirituality have on the effect on the human well being and their spirituality. The latter part will define the roadmap to spirituality in various ways.

A brief and comprehensive definition of the critical organs and glands we need to pay attention, understanding spirituality, how the body, mind, and spirit associated with divinity. Please pay attention and research more on the following, The human body, the blueprint of man, Brain, mind, body , spirit, pineal gland, laminin, Gluon, blood, baptism, the "God Particle", The forces of nature that influences our body and our daily functions are essential to our well being in every aspect, including our health and spirituality (our walk with God). These are the reasons for the definition of our physical body and the parts of the body that are important for our well being. The introduction of the glands that helps our physical body ward off radical infections and viruses and protect our bodies from diseases and sicknesses and connecting us in the spirit (spirituality) in man that controls our mental and abstract being. The being that gives us the ability to think and reason as well as utilize our psyche, psychic abilities, and phenomena to connect with the Universe and the Supreme Entity to condition us physically to be in tune with Nature and the laws of godliness.

Some of it may be very confusing, but as you read, stop to ponder what is the "Brain"? "How does it function?" What is the "Pineal Gland? What is the thymus? Moreover, what is its purpose in our bodies? How do we function and why are our bodies are always in a state of imbalance that influences us to get the feeling of sickness or weakness or depression, fatigue. How do we maintain this body and keep a balance so that we are in good health and a sound mind?

The importance of maintaining a healthy body is to focus on specific body parts that may be influential in enhancing our spirituality and those that influence our body, mind, and spirit. People sometimes believe they can separate part of their lives from their emotional and physical self. The cause of struggles overall, and when we divide them and keep the thought factors separate, the body itself struggle to maintain a proper balance and affects the emotional self. Be observant and use your own judgment, look at some Pastors, preachers, Pundits and other religious men and leaders, spends more time in their spiritual quest and not their physical well-being and their physical self are left in a state of neglect due are losing physical form, opening the door for other elements to come in. This statement applies for only a small percentage and is not a blanket statement, but it needs to be investigated and remedied. The relationship between physical and spiritual is a balance, and the mind plays the part to keep that balance, we must attend to the physical body and the need to keep that physical body healthy, it is the only one you have and if it becomes unhealthy, could handicap your performance and delivery of your spiritual message.

Check: How is my emotional Health? Am I depressed? Do I have fears and anxiety, so I sleep well? What are my dreams/ how am I feeling during the Day? Do I get enough sleep? Am I exercising? What kinds of ailments are in me? What are the sicknesses that are haunting me or on my borderlines? How about Diabetes, Cancer? High Blood Pressure, Low Blood Pressure? How is my heart's health? How are my organs such as lungs, liver, kidneys, Colon, Stomach, Eyes, hearing and sense of smell? What do I need to do to fix my health, emotion and well being?

Can I pray and meditate effectively? Am I able to focus without interruption or having to shift? What are my thoughts? Do I get upset too often, or angry, what are the ideas that are ingrained in me and raise most that bother me mentally? Why do people snap and commit the various form of sin? We are a three dimension being of Body, Mind, and spirit and we possess a tripartite nature, we think and act in this manner wherever we are or in whatever we do. Trying to satisfy the physical and ignoring the other parts are not only dangerous but creates an imbalance within and affects us in more ways than we can imagine or even fathom.

1 RELIGION I

Some important dates in the history of religion and the creation of thereof, link below has a concise detail of timelines
https://www.allaboutreligion.org/origin-of-religion.htm

https://en.wikipedia.org/wiki/Timeline_of_religion

- **40,000 BCE** The remains of one of the earliest anatomically modern humans to be cremated was buried near Lake Mungo
- **38,000 BCE** The Aurignacian, Löwenmensch figurine, the oldest known zoomorphic (animal-shaped) sculpture in the world and one of the oldest known sculptures in general, was made.
- **25,000–21,000 BCE** Clear examples of burials are present in Iberia, Wales, and Eastern Europe.
- **9130–7370 BCE** This was the apparent period of use of Göbekli Tepe, one of the oldest human-made sites of worship yet discovered
- **7500–5700 BCE** the settlements of Catalhoyuk developed as a likely spiritual center of Anatolia. Possibly practicing worship in the communal shrine
- **5500–4500 BCE** The Proto-Indo-Europeans (PIE) emerged, probably within the Pontic-Caspian steppe (though their exact urheimat is debated). The PIE peoples developed a religion focused on sacrificial ideology, which would influence the religions and cultures throughout Eurasia
- **3750 BCE** The Proto-Semitic people emerged from a generally accepted urheimat in the Levant. The Proto-Semitic people would migrate throughout the Near East into Mesopotamia, Egypt, Ethiopia and the eastern shore of the Mediterranean
- **3300–1300** The Indus Valley Civilization (IVC) was a Bronze Age civilization (3300–1300 BCE; mature period 2600–1900 BCE) in the northwestern region of the Indian subcontinent, noted for its cities built of brick, roadside drainage system and multi-storeyed houses, as well as for creating artifacts which could be linked to pre-Vedic religions.
- **3200–3100 BCE** Newgrange, the 250,000 ton (226,796.2 tonne) passage tomb aligned to the winter solstice in Ireland, was built
- **3100 BCE** The initial form of Stonehenge was completed.
- **3000 BCE** Sumerian Cuneiform emerged from the proto-literate Uruk period, allowing the codification of beliefs and creation of detailed historical religious records.
- **2635–2610 BCE** The oldest surviving Egyptian Pyramid was commissioned by Pharaoh Djoser.
- **2600 BCE** Stonehenge began to take on its final form. The wooden posts were replaced with bluestone. It began taking on an increasingly complex setup (including an altar, a portal, station stones, etc.) and shows consideration of solar alignments.
- **2560 BCE** This is the approximate time accepted as the completion of the Great Pyramid of Giza, the oldest pyramid of the Giza Plateau.

- 2494–2345 BCE The first of the oldest surviving religious texts, the Pyramid Texts, was composed in Ancient Egypt.
- 2200 BCE The Minoan Civilization developed in Crete. Citizens worshipped a variety of goddesses.
- 2150–2000 BCE The earliest surviving versions of the Sumerian Epic of Gilgamesh—originally titled He who Saw the Deep (Sha naqba īmuru) or Surpassing All Other Kings (Shūtur Eli sharrī)—were written.
- 1700–1100 BCE The oldest of the Hindu Vedas (scriptures), the Rig Veda was composed.
- 1600 BCE The ancient development of Stonehenge came to an end.
- 1500 BCE The Vedic Age began in India after the collapse of the Indus Valley Civilization.
- 1351 or 1353 BCE The reign of Akhenaten, sometimes credited with starting the earliest known recorded monotheistic religion, in Ancient Egypt.[citation needed]
- 1300–1000 BCE The "standard" Akkadian version of the Epic of Gilgamesh was edited by Sin-liqe-unninni.
- 1250–600 BCE The Upanishads (Vedic texts) were composed, containing the earliest emergence of some of the central religious concepts of Hinduism, Buddhism, and Jainism.
- 1200 BCE The Greek Dark Age began.
- 1200 BCE The Olmecs built the earliest pyramids and temples in Central America.[12]
- 877–777 BCE The life of Parshvanatha, 23rd Tirthankara of Jainism.[13][14]
- 800 BCE The Greek Dark Age ends.
- 8th to 6th centuries BCE The Chandogya Upanishad is compiled, significant for containing the earliest to date mention of Krishna. Verse 3.17.6 mentions Krishna Devakiputra (Sanskrit: कृष्णाय देवकीपुत्रा) as a student of the sage Ghora Angirasa.
- 6th to 5th centuries BCE The first five books of the Jewish Tanakh, the Torah (Hebrew: תורה), are probably compiled.[15]
- 6th century BCE Possible start of Zoroastrianism; however some date Zarathustra closer to 1000 BCE. Zoroastrianism flourished under the Persian emperors known as the Achaemenids. The emperors Darius (ruled 522–486 B.C.E.) and Xerxes (ruled 486–465 B.C.E.) made it the official religion of their empire.[16]
- 600–500 BCE The earliest Confucian writing, Shu Ching, incorporates ideas of harmony and heaven.
- 599–527 BCE The life of Mahavira, 24th and last Tirthankara of Jainism.[17]
- c.563/480–c.483/400 BCE, [18] [19] [20] Gautama Buddha, founder of Buddhism was born.
- 551 BCE Confucius, founder of Confucianism, was born.[12]
- 399 BCE Socrates was tried for impiety.
- 369-372 BCE Birth of Mencius and Zhuang Zhou
- 300 BCE The oldest known version of the Tao Te Ching was written on bamboo tablets.
- 300 BCE Theravada Buddhism was introduced to Sri Lanka by the Venerable Mahinda.[citation needed]
- c.250 BCE, The Third Buddhist council, was convened by Ashoka. Ashoka sends Buddhist missionaries to faraway countries, such as China, mainland Southeast Asia, Malay kingdoms, and Hellenistic kingdoms.
- 140 BCE The earliest grammar of Sanskrit literature was composed by Pāṇini.[citation needed]

- **100 BCE–500 CE The Yoga Sūtras of Patañjali, constituting the foundational texts of Yoga, were composed.**
- **BCE–c.30/33 CE The life of Jesus of Nazareth, the central figure of Christianity.**
- **570–632 The life of Muhammad Ibn 'Abdullah, the Prophet of Islam.**
- **650 The verses of the Qur'an were compiled in the form of a book in the era of Uthman, the third Caliph of Islam.**

Above brings the Dateline to most of the religious dateline of Importance as it is related to the great conquest of modern times. The timeline above depicts the worship and recognition of a Form of prayer to deities and supreme entities and God or Gods

Religion designed to get people into a state of focused attention, energy and belief towards a Supreme Being, a force that is above all and creator of all we have and to live within, an authority with great compassion and sharing of Love for us because of his creative power. It is written and found that we were all created beings, created by a supreme authority, a creature that from out of this world created in this world to honor, love, worship, fellowship and tune our inner self towards this entity. On the one hand to pattern our thoughts and minds to be engaged entirely within ourselves and devotion towards the agape love of our creator, on the other side, to live in fear being under a divine command and following all instructions and commandments that were given onto us to adhere and live by. The opposite of these laws will lead to sin and sin is not adhering to God's commandments, being disobedient can result in receiving penalties and punishment in many forms. The payment for being insubordinate and rebellious is death, spiritual death.

It is difficult to trace the origination of many ancient religions, but the new era discovered to proximity in the timeline. They are relative to each other in the search and findings of the objectives, God, The purpose of life, the present life, the biggest issue of life itself, and the presence of the spirit of God, the afterlife and what becomes of us after this short lifespan and the many similarities in the various religion in their individual quest. This quest for God has a significant impact on the life of every human being as reflected in history, and as a reflection to history, its effect on each experience, the culture, the doctrines and scriptures, the rituals and purpose, the footprints left on the face of the earth in the form of artifacts, constructions and buildings, temples. Most of all the inspirations and the faith in the supreme that all is left to be carried into the future from generations to generations. Religion has played an essential role in society; it tends to deliver from teachings the way to a good life or to be an excellent Godly person, doing good deeds. Helping organization build the bridges of unity and thrashing out the divide and segregation, living a life full of purpose, influencing their subliminal, subconscious mind into grooming the conscious being to robotically follow principles and processes set in as an example for humanity to follow as set by deities and pious men. The common theme is spirituality, connectivity or communion with the Supreme entity and divinity. The way human can encounter spiritual dimensions in a heightened state of consciousness that enhances the mind to develop the mental faculty of man towards being godlike or as it is written "in the image of God" for God has given humanity the power to be like him on the face of the earth. The collective nature in a religious community becomes the meeting of the minds where praying and meditating together can result in creating a powerful force of shared spirituality and spirit within, for the good of individuals and the overall goodness of the people and world. Such is the invention of Festivals and occasional celebrations, such as marriages, weddings, special occasions, even at a funeral.

The push for recognition internationally, mass conversion in building the largest sector of a specific religion is the new drive. Religion is becoming and, playing a more prominent active role in politics and world government. The two put together has the most significant influence on the minds and actions of the mass and each. The ultimate purpose has occasionally shifted from the spiritual to political and power control of masses for power and wealth gain of a few. Individuals or groups who study the sacred texts become the knowledgeable spokesperson to deliver clarity of holy books to the most straightforward interpretation for the individual or groups, thus becoming a school for educating people in general and spreading the faith.

The interpretation of the sacred doctrine, texts and, writings sometimes leads to misinterpretations and disagreements between scholars of the faith. The distortions or humanistic interpretations (based on the education or knowledge of the scholar) and the disputes in these interpretations lead to division. Each believes their comprehension is correct and others are wrong or incorrect resulting in the rise of religious organizational split and the forming of a new sector of the same religion with a small twist of, maybe one line of interpreted text that differs from the other individuals leads to the diversity of worship and a new denomination of believers who follows one interpretation over another.

The quest to understand man, religion and belief system in GOD, we must understand the functionality of the human being and how his system operates. What happened to the man in the course of history that caused the creation of Religion and belief system he has to maintain to manage and govern his actions towards a good nature and the resulting goodness in his life? A karmic action as one sow, one will reap and will receive what they have put out.

There is much controversy on the existence of God, the creation of the universe, the creation of man, how, where, when and why? The Bible does not try to prove the existence of God; it leaves it to the believer to know by faith that GOD existed, allowing the scriptures to speak to them through the religious medium of Pastors and Ministers and the Holy Spirit to be the counseling agent of the existence. God's presence is fundamental to man, through experience, literature, doctrine, reflection, faith and discovery, teaching and preaching.

Matthew 19:26 "*But Jesus beheld them, and said unto them, with men this is impossible, but with God all things are possible." So how do you connect to God to make all things possible? It stated that God will not fill an unclean vessel, meaning that if you are unclean, full of sin and have no characteristic of God, how can he be with you, or how can he enable your spirit. God can very well communicate and send messengers with messages, but still need you to clean up your act to be clean, pure and holy so that he can do works in you and with you. We are missing this area in our lives, we are missing the message, and we fail to comprehend the true message of God. Clean up your act, make your mind and body clean so that "all things can become possible."*

Let's stress the effect religion had on this planet, Religion created most wars and continued to create more hatred, separation, and segregation than anything else. The most battles in history fought over religion and religious beliefs, and men and people are getting brainwashed by the wrong concept of morality. Every religious doctrine, GOD teaches "LOVE," "Love as the key to human bonding and integration of spirituality. We harbor hate and anger rather than love, we are becoming more corrupt to negative thoughts as they grow and produces more children thoughts, it becomes injected subliminally fused in our mind and possibly transferred into our genetic code and DNA, which may pass on to our seeds as they are all born with the corruption and anger, hatred and confusions that you have harbored in your mind.

Church, synagogue, mosque, temples spend a great deal of time to educate us with the knowledge of the scripture and what the scripture represents. The message from the divine for all mankind needs to be delivered in relations to modern times as it was in ancient times. Every religion teaches to respect others, love thy neighbors as thyself, and love your children, wife, father, mother, friends, families, and strangers. God did not create a religion and the multiplicity of faith. Man created religion of various denomination, because of interpretations, misinterpretations and translating the doctrines, thereby applying it into the minds of others and creating a split in belief system, they produce several secular religion which they believe is the truth of their interpretations and cause a division, which further leads to separation and non-communication later to separation and hatred against the very own people that they were once brothers. Spirituality can sometimes be a farce and the motives may be different versus teaching and preaching the truth, like the Sadducees and Pharisees. These are very similar to today's televangelists who are throwing around their jackets, selling water, handkerchiefs, sprinkling water with a well-paid crowd of actors to throw themselves to the ground pretending to be filled with the Holy Spirit. In **Acts 5** Peter told Ananias that Satan filled his heart with greed and he lied to the Holy Spirit (The spirit of GOD). It is proof that you do not lie to God for Greed. There are many living examples of these incidents and those who lie to the Holy Spirit, but we cannot judge them, it is for God to decide. These are the situations we have to discern and be wary of otherwise we fall into the rut of following the wrong crowd and getting engaged with the crazy people, whose motives may be miss-guided or for personal reasons. Many religious leaders in many parts of the world, indulge in the materialistic values , sold their soul to the devil for money, wealth, power and status in this carnal world and have sold out their faith in Christianity defying religious laws, giving in to Satan's whims and preaching against the doctrines, preaching what the Politician wants them to teach, recognizing the evil traits of people in high positions as they are promised and paid off. Their failure to accept lies, adultery, Sinicism, lust, avarice and all kinds of illegal, uncultured and unscriptural actions and behaviors as justifiable, an act that takes us back to the old testament and the seven sins that are an abomination to God and what God hates the most as being scriptural.   Men fell into self-desire they stand on the pulpit and preach to an audience that has the very same mentality, the same arrogance, lust for money, power and fame, self-preservation more on the recognition of politics rather than stand their grounds on what the scripture states:

> *(Revelations 12:9 And the great dragon was cast out — that serpent of old called the Devil and Satan, who deceiveth the whole world. He was cast out onto the earth, and his angels were cast out with him). (Revelations 13:3 And I saw one of his heads as it was wounded to death, and his deadly wound was healed: and all the world wondered after the beast. 4 **And they worshipped the dragon** which gave power unto the beast: and **they worshipped the beast**, saying, who is like unto the beast? Who can make war with him? 5. And there was given unto him a mouth speaking great things and blasphemies and power was given unto him to continue forty and two months.)* BUT what is about to happen be that all the Saints will rise up as Ezekiel and prophesy unto these false Christians:

> *Ezekiel 34.1 And the word of the LORD came unto me, saying, 2. Son of man, prophesy against the shepherds of Israel, prophesy, and say unto them, Thus saith the Lord GOD unto the shepherds; Woe be to the shepherds of Israel that do feed themselves! Should not the shepherds feed the flocks? 3. Ye eat the fat, and ye clothe you with the wool, ye kill them that are fed: but ye feed not the flock.4. The diseased have ye not strengthened, neither have ye healed that which was sick, neither have ye bound up that which was broken, neither have ye brought again that which was driven away, neither have ye sought that which was lost; but with force and with cruelty have ye ruled them.*

The promises, the covenant were released to the Gentiles, caused a great envy and the gentiles are taking advantage of the opportunity they were given and becoming more spirit filled and greater worshippers and have accepted the new covenant for 'the cup' is the new covenant where the Blood of Jesus Luke 22:20 shed through his death for those who have accepted the Christ in his time and all the gentiles received mercy for it was extended to them.

Cosmology: Creation itself defines and bears witness that there is a supreme intelligence, omnipotent, loving being as the creator of all things, the existence of the Universe and the power within, and energies emitted. All in all whichever belief system you have on the creation of the Universe, whether it was self-created, always existed or created by God, it takes great faith and belief to accept that it does exist and there are abundance of mysteries about it and it is alive, growing and expanding, producing and creating constantly. Cosmologists now believe that our universe evolves by long slow processes.

Teleology: Derives from Greek word "telos" (end, goal, purpose) and logos (reason, explanation) its design, the orderliness, and perfect design requires an architect and a designer like everything else. The complexity of the purest form of material in life shows that all did not happen or evolve by accident.

The explanation of phenomena by the purpose they serve rather than by postulated causes, the doctrine of design and use in the material world

Ontology: How can we as ordinary human beings with a finite mind ever conceive an infinite, omnipresent, omnipotent, omniscient, and perfect supreme being (GOD), unless this knowledge was given or passed down from the existence itself?

The ancient indigenous people came to have the same belief, and their knowledge was limited in comparison to what we have today, the oldest of all religion and scripture tells of Supreme beings or an incarnation of One Supreme entity.

So, leave it to your very own belief system and be convinced through teachings that there is an existence of a supreme being, and intelligence that is above and beyond all, a creative force that exists and we call that being "GOD" in many languages and all types of phonetic sounds. It is a human factor to possess a critical mind that leads to constructive critical thinking and question every aspect of theory and facts of the unseen, supreme divine existence and the scientific definitions related to the same – "the Existence of a Supreme Force in the Universe and the World."

For all humanity to know if this is real, God will have to display himself and show himself to Man, thus confirming that he does exist. He must reveal himself to man and have done so through multi-faceted means, nature, conscience, feelings, mental phenomenon, miracles, prophecy, and history and through messengers from Heaven in the form of Angels and even in man. The Bible is the sole authority for the doctrine and instruction in salvation and Christian living. It provides the complete revelation of God's nature and his will for all in the world. The idea of religion is to give man knowledge to live a better life, peaceful, harmoniously with each other and the environment. It does not seem to be too successful today as the train of thought is lost and segmented; only a tiny portion of the population maintains the tradition of old and spreads the teachings to the particular audience. Sacred texts and doctrines are full of moral instructions from early examples, leaders and prophets and the venue and channel of God messages and form a very intricate, rich and even complex framework of values by which followers should adhere and live within. The bottom line the God experience is an individual experience and can experience by each worshipper, the lessons are not the same, and this is the only real connection a person can have with the Supreme Being or Entity and God.

As we strive to connect to the Divine God of the Earth and Universe, we tend to go back in time and research, relate to the Old texts, scriptures, Doctrines, and texts to find the Truth. Since we are going back in time and looking at the creation of man going forward, we also need to acknowledge the ethnicity of our heritage and admit that we are also not as perfect in color class or creed as we are claiming to be today. We come from one root ADAM & EVE as per scripture; we carry the same DNA and the same contents, the same makeup, the same material. As time rolls by and we replenish the earth in humanity, there were an intermix of people from various parts of the world, some dark, some light, some of the diverse culture, tradition and thought patterns, But the DNA remains the same. God did not create prejudices in our hearts to look upon another man as a lower being, even though after the blood contamination, he decided to choose a tribe of people so he can preserve the blood and the originality of his creation and venture to use various tribes to wipe out the contamination. Thus, the Blood today is critical and essential in any religious rituals and ceremonial cleansing.

The list of attributes for the nature of God, a brief bullet point: Per Scriptural Doctrines
- God is a living Being and the source of all life
- God is an individual being with unique qualities, characteristics, and personality
- God is an Intelligent being with reasoning ability, emotions and will
- God is a spirit, not made of a material of the body
- God is invisible to the human eye
- God has an independent existence
- God is eternal, immortal, everlasting, with no beginning or ending
- God is omnipresent and can be anywhere at any time and all places at the same time
- God is Omnipotent, all-powerful, unlimited
- God is omniscient, all knowledge
- God is unchanging, but responds in whatever way or manner depends on his objective
- God is Transcendence and beyond comprehension
- God is one, in oneness, he is self-existent, eternal
- God is Holy, which is a fundamental moral characteristic

- God is fair and impartial
- God is Love
- God is merciful and gracious
- God is unfailing in faithfulness
- God is truth
- God is virtuous

We must understand the essential components of the body that plays the most crucial role or roles in the interconnection of the physical material man and the physical material earth and environment and how the interaction and integration through the spiritual body, mind and soul and communication with the spiritual domain of the planet and its religious atmosphere. It leads to the understanding of how we communicate and interconnect with the various forces that play significant roles in our lives, how we connect to the divinity of good forces and evil forces. How we connect with GOD (the Supreme Entity) and integrate our being into a higher interconnection and communication from an earthly physical domain to a spiritual dominion. The greatest secret is that the knowledge and wisdom of the gospels and scriptures and God is already in man. Man is seeking god all over the world in many forms, ways and, methods except looking for God within himself. God is already there and is waiting for a man to discover all these secrets within. The human body is so complex; it would take about 10 Acres of land space to fit and create a replica of the Human being in machines and machinery. The mind of man is so vast that the entire Human race of intellect cannot comprehend or understand One human brain, the spirit of man is a great mystery, and it boggles the thought of all scientist and medical professionals. The healing power of man is already in man, the enlightenment and knowledge of God is already him. The super infinite intelligence, strength, wisdom and, solutions to all issues is already in man; it within the most extensive library of books and materials all enclosed into each human being, and have not tapped into it yet or may never get to know it all. We are only utilizing or using ten percent of our brain. What are the possibilities for using 100% of our brain; this is what God meant to produce by creating us in his image. Man is a God within himself, the perfect image of God, but we got beat down after the fall. The man was beaten down by evil, cursed, driven out of his comfort zone, ordained to experience sorrow and pain, insulted for listening to the voice of his wife, cursed with hard work. Now It is time to rise again, remove all the obstacles and shut all negative doors to the dark world and rise above, soar like an eagle and create your destiny with the guidance of your spirit and the spirit of God.

Genesis 3: 15   *And I will put enmity between thee and the woman, and between thy seed and her seed; it shall bruise thy head, and thou shalt bruise his heel.*

16   Unto the woman he said, I will greatly multiply thy sorrow and thy conception; in sorrow, thou shalt bring forth children, and thy desire shall be to thy husband, and he shall rule over thee.

17   And unto Adam he said, Because thou hast hearkened unto the voice of thy wife, and hast ate of the tree, of which I commanded thee, saying, thou shalt not eat of it: cursed is the ground for thy sake; in sorrow shalt thou eat of it all the days of thy life;

18   Thorns also and thistles shall it bring forth to thee, and thou shalt eat the herb of the field;

19   In the sweat of thy face shalt thou eat bread, till thou return unto the ground; for out of it wast thou taken: for dust thou art, and unto dust shalt thou return.

But the next verses are clear what took place in the eyes of God

Genesis 3: 22 And the LORD God said, **Behold, the man is become as one of us, to know good and evil:** and now, lest he put forth his hand, and also take of the tree of life, and eat, and live forever:

A few interpretations: man, after the 'eating of the apple', knew 'good and evil' and the differences, he felt 'guilt and shame', he understood 'disobedience and sin', lost his innocence, lost the favors of God for he was the object of God's favor and even his delight. The man lost all dominion over the Earth and all living beings.

Adam created in the Image of God (spirit) with the intent of the physical image of Jesus Christ, which was to come, the second Adam. The scriptures define that Jesus Christ was the creator at the beginning as per John 8: 58 Jesus said unto them, "Verily, verily, I say unto you, Before Abraham was, I am." Romans 5:14 "Nevertheless death reigned from Adam to Moses, even over them that had not sinned after the similitude of Adam's transgression, **who is the figure of him that was to come.**

The image of Adam, which is the image of Jesus, a description we do not find anywhere in the scripture. The only portrait of Jesus was in Revelations for his vision in heaven, Hair and head white like wool, face shining like the sun, eyes like a flame of fire, sword coming from his mouth, seven stars, golden sash around his chest, feet like burning brass.

Adam created from red dust in the image of God which was and is and to come – Jesus. According to Daniel's vision Jesus body looked like Beryl Daniel 10: 5 "His body also was **like the beryl**, and his **face as the appearance of lightning**, and **his eyes as lamps of fire**, and his arms and his feet like in color to **polished brass**, and the voice of his words like the voice of a multitude".

Because Jesus was among the crowd and many times use the group to escape, he is very similar to the Jewish people of the Middle-east in appearance; other scriptures state "wheatish complexion, long straight hair"

another "a man of brown complexion and lank hair."
Adam had gained Knowledge f Good and Evil by eating from the tree, his eyes were opened, and he can see and envision more than in his created state. The Serpent was the instrument to lead humanity to knowledge and wisdom he is not capable of handling for the moment and now can see things as God did, without the ability to decipher and manage the differences.

2 FORCES IN THE UNIVERSE

Align with the energies of the Universe

The five fundamental forces that exist are Gravity, Electromagnetism, the weak force, the strong nuclear power and the X and Y Boson (unknown hypothetical elementary particles). The smallest units of matter are particles called Quarks and leptons which seem to be the fundamental building blocks.

> *The Higgs Boson field: - Particle which permeates all of space-time and helps to give all another particle their mass – called "the GOD Particle." These are the subatomic particles which provide different matter properties such as mass, protons, and neutrons, etc. Gravity pulls you down into your seat; toward the Earth's center thus we can stand on the earth and not fly up into the Sky. Electromagnetism, another force, holds the atoms of your seat together, preventing your molecules from intruding on those of your place. The* **strong force** *holds the nucleus together. The weak force is responsible for radioactive decay, beta decay where a neutron within the nucleus changes into a proton and an electron, ejected from the core. These are the forces that hold the Universe together or at least these are the forces that the scientific man can define as existing. I am sure there are tons of other powers which we have not been able to detect, identify or even unaware.*
>
> *"The Higgs field is a field of energy that is thought to exist in every region of the universe. The field is accompanied by a fundamental particle known as the Higgs boson, which is used by the field to continuously interact with other particles, such as the electron. Particles that interact with the field are "given" mass and, similarly to an object passing through a treacle (or molasses), will become slower as they pass through it. The result of a particle "gaining" mass from the field is the prevention of its ability to travel at the speed of light."*

Gravity holds the Stars, moon, Sun, earth and galaxies and tons of heavenly bodies that make up the universe.

Why should we understand the forces of nature? They have a significant influence to our bodies and can be a negative force to us that can cause an adverse effect on our physical and mental self or positive energy that either takes us to a more positive nature and a healthy, sound mind and influences our well being. Our body is a replica of the universe and operates in the same manner. Therefore we do not want to go against the forces of nature but align our physical self to be in tune with nature
Visualize how water flows, the wind and wind force that can cause tornado and hurricanes, volcanoes, lightning and fire, thunder and thunderstorms, earthquakes and earth movements. Take a look at or review the effects that change the face of the earth

and the dynamic ever-changing planet itself due to the wind, water, fire, ice, erosion, volcanic activities, floods, earth movements. Alter the earth surface on a daily basis, some noticeable and some not noticeable immediately bit over time. Weathering, farming, deforestation, mining, construction, population growth, road building, and accessibility causes a great deal of Erosion which creates rivers to buildup sediments and the riverbed rising. Glacial shifting cause's erosion and surface changes that affect nature differently, the earth's soil is moving into the riverbeds and the ocean beds.

Visualize the body and what happens in the various situations like swinging a rollercoaster, driving over a river on a bridge, winter, summer, spring, and fall. Not to go deeper into nature itself, but to relate it to your body, mind, and life.

Religion has a few main features. First, it is on doctrine; second is the stories and mythology of Gods and Angels and heavenly beings and beautiful stories of their history, action, and role towards and in a relationship with humanity. Third, comes the concepts of excellent religious ideas and experiences, how a human can encounter the Gods and the divine in knowledge, accomplishments, consciousness, and copycat. Next (fourth) is organizing group and groups into communities and eventually globalization of the ideology, building a temple or building as host of the organization and the body. Then comes (fifth) the created by-laws and rules and regulations, either depicted from the doctrine of created by the group of principles to follow and live within. Practices follow (sixth), a way to worship, ceremonial, sacrifices, offerings and methods to practice in the invocation of religiosity and spirituality devoted to divinity –GOD, whether by name or object, whether by image or visualization. The teachings and preaching's pulled from doctrines that were translated from old parchment, stone, palm leaves, artifacts, drawings, symbols etc are interpreted into modern language to the closest possible meanings and read, sang or passed on by songs from one to another as it becomes from a broken un-deciphered language to what we think it means in modern literature. So, we get the meaning as close as possible, and after years of repetition, it becomes real, the truth and a solid doctrine until more archeological discovery is uncovered.

I am not knocking down religion; I am addressing how it has gotten us tainted mentally from old to now. The point here targets the opening of the notion and thinking that "Each one of us has to know GOD and religion for ourselves" we can very well learn from the scholars, but GOD has instructed us to discern and gain the knowledge of the truth. Now we have many "Tom, Dick and Harry 's "interpreting in their very own fashion and twisted understanding of religious scriptures and uses it for their selfish purpose or rather led blindly in teaching others their misguided understanding, as many follow Jesus' warnings and teachings of "Wolves in Sheep clothing."

For us to appreciate humanity in its fullest, we must try and gather the concepts of religion from every major religious group, to understand what their beliefs are and what makes them choose to worship God in the way they do. What keep them bound into the faith, trust, ceremonies, and rituals they perform under their religious umbrella convincing them that their belief system is real and the truth or their God is different and delivers different laws and rules and regulations, laws and commandments and require a particular type of worship and offering? It enables us to understand the other person, his feelings, ways, and manner of living and we can very well build a bridge, at least of communication and discussion about God, the promises, the history, the mythologies, and doctrines. Not to overwhelm the other person to be converted over to religion or being encouraged to convert over his belief. The discussion will have to be mutual, for we all understand Who God is and has been through Doctrines that were written thousands of years ago by other men, inspired by the Spirit of God. What will be the chances if "Those men – prophets of old were 'beguiled' by Satan in the manner Eve was deceived and tricked? Even if done to part or parts, small part or small parts of the doctrine "God Said DO NOT" "Did God Say DO."

"I am A Christian" a claim made by many just because they go to Church and read little parts of the Bible, praying with the congregation, fellowship and bible studies. Being a Christian is not a simple act, it is a way of life, living Gods way, knowing the doctrines and doing God's work. Renew the mind and the way to think and act towards all living beings act and replicate the word of God.

>*Ezekiel 33:31 ESV* *And they come to you as people come, and they sit before you as my people, and they hear what you say, but they will not do it; for with lustful talk in their mouths they act; their heart is set on their gain.*
>*Romans 16:17-18 ESV* *I appeal to you, brothers, to watch out for those who cause divisions and create obstacles contrary to the doctrine that you have been taught; avoid them. For such persons do not serve our Lord Christ, but their own appetites, and by smooth talk and flattery they deceive the hearts of the naive.*
>*James 1:26 ESV* *If anyone thinks he is religious and does not bridle his tongue but deceives his heart, this person's religion is worthless.*
>*Luke 6:46 ESV* *"Why do you call me 'Lord, Lord,' and not do what I tell you?*
>*Matthew 7:1-29 ESV* *"Judge not, that you be not judged. For with the judgment you pronounce you will be judged, and with the measure, you use it will be measured to you. Why do you see the speck that is in your brother's eye, but does not notice the log that is in your own eye? Or how can you say to your brother, 'Let me take the speck out of your eye,' when there is the log in your own eye? You hypocrite, first take the log out of your eye, and then you will see clearly to take the speck out of your brother's eye.*

For those who claim "I am a Hindu," first and foremost, Hinduism is not a religion; it is a culture of the people who lived on the banks of the Sindhu River, Indus Valley civilization. The word Hindu misunderstood and misused. Hindu and Hinduism refer to a set of people belonging to a definite religious system. The Indus River was called Sindhu, and due to pronunciation syllables of the Persian language, the word became "Hindus" and "Indos" by the Greeks. Hinduism is an Indian Dharma or a way of life, the religions of Hinduism are

Sanatan Dharma ((Sanātana Dharma) Hinduism is the world's third most popular religion, with around 750 million followers. The doctrine of Hinduism originated in Northern India, near the river Indus, about 4000 years ago and is the world's oldest existing religion. Hinduism practiced by more than 80% of India's population.),

Vedic Religion (Vedism) - {Vedism is the earliest stratum of religious activity in India for which there exists any Material. It was one of the major traditions that shaped Hinduism. Knowledge of Vedic religion is derived from surviving texts and also from certain rites that continue practice within the framework of modern Hinduism}.

Jainism - traditionally known as Jain Dharma, is an ancient Indian religion. Followers of Jainism are called "Jains," a word derived from the Sanskrit word Jina (victor) and connoted the path of victory in crossing over life's stream of rebirths through an ethical and spiritual growth.

Sikhism from Sikh, meaning a "disciple," or a "learner"), is a religion that originated in the Punjab region of the Indian subcontinent about the end of the 15th century. It is one of the youngest of the major world religions

3 THE SOUND OF NATURE AND GOD

Vaishnavism (Vaishnava dharma) is one of the major traditions within Hinduism along with Shaivism, Shaktism, and Smartism. It is also called Vishnuism, its followers are called Vaishnavas, and it considers Vishnu as the Supreme Lord.

Shaivism (Śaivam) (one of the major traditions within Hinduism that reveres Shiva as the Supreme Being or its metaphysical concept of Brahman. The followers of Shaivism are called "Shaivites" or "Saivites."

The syllable "Om" or "Aum" described as an all-encompassing mystical entity in the Upanishads. Hindus believe that as creation began, the divine, all-encompassing consciousness took the form of the first and original vibration manifesting as sound "OM."Before creation began, it was "Shunyākāsha," the emptiness or the void. The vibration of "OM" symbolizes the manifestation of God in form ("sāguna Brahman"). "OM" is the reflection of the absolute reality, it is said to be "Adi Anadi," without beginning or the end and embracing all that exists. The mantra "OM" is the name of God, the vibration of the Supreme. When taken letter by letter, A-U-M represents the divine energy (Shakti) united in its three elementary aspects: Bhrahma Shakti (creation), Vishnu Shakti (preservation) and Shiva Shakti (liberation, and destruction).

Be proud of your history and scriptures. The Vedas is being deciphered by scientists and Theologians for its values and input into science today. It is a reality that the Higgs Boson (the real name of God's particle) is an Indian discovery as mentioned in the Vedas as "the Hiranyagarbha" or "The Golden Embryo," "Creator"; Vishwakarma imaginary primeval man Purusha and Prajapati Lord of Beings.

https://en.wikiquote.org/wiki/Vedic_science
Huston Smith, A Tribute to Hinduism, page 58

> *"The Indians came closest to modern ideas of atomism, quantum physics, and other current theories.*
>
> *The Rig-Veda is the first Indian literature to set down ideas resembling universal natural laws. Cosmic law is connected with infinite light, with gods, and, later, specifically with Brahman. It was the Vedic Aryans who gave the world some of the earliest philosophical texts on the makeup of matter and the theoretical underpinnings for the chemical composition of minerals. Sanskrit Vedas from thousands of years before Christ implied that matter could not be created and that the universe had created itself.*

Two thousand years before Pythagoras, philosophers in northern India had understood that gravitation held the solar system together and that therefore the sun, the most massive object, had to be at its center." "Twenty-four centuries before Isaac Newton, the Hindu Rig-Veda asserted that gravitation held the universe together. The Sanskrit speaking Aryans subscribed to the idea of a spherical earth in an era when the Greeks believed in a flat one. The Indians of the fifth century A.D. calculated the age of the earth as 4.3 billion years; scientists in 19th century England were convinced it was 100 million years".

Pierre-Simon Laplace the Celestial Key to the Vedas, page 61.

Hindu is more exact in astronomy and astrology than any other people.
Tarikh al-Yaqubi, the Foundations of the Composite Culture in India, page 59
It is the clearest image of the activity of God which any art or religion can boast of. Modern physics has shown that the rhythm of creation and destruction is not only manifest in the turn of the seasons and in the birth and death of all living creatures, but also the very essence of inorganic matter.

For modern physicists, then, Shiva's dance is the dance of subatomic matter. Hundreds of years ago, Indian artist created visual images of dancing Shiva's in a beautiful series of bronzes. Today, physicists have used the most advanced technology to portray the pattern of the cosmic dance. Thus, the metaphor of the cosmic dance unifies ancient religious art and modern physics. The Hindus, according to Monier-Williams, were Spinozists more than 2,000 years before the advent of Spinoza, and Darwinians many centuries before Darwin and Evolutionists many centuries before the doctrine of Evolution was accepted by scientists of the present age.

The Hindu religion is the only one of the world's great faiths dedicated to the idea that the Cosmos itself undergoes an immense, indeed an infinite, number of deaths and rebirths. It is the only religion in which the time scales correspond, no doubt by accident [this part of the quote is often left out], to those of modern scientific cosmology. Its cycles run from our ordinary day and night to a day and night of Brahma, 8.64 billion years long. Longer than the age of the Earth or the Sun and about half the time since the Big Bang. And there are much longer time scales still.
Jean-Sylvain Baily, World as Seen under the Lens of a Scientist, page 460
Religious faith in the case of the Hindus has never been allowed to run counter to scientific laws. Moreover the former is never made a condition for the knowledge they teach, but there are always scrupulously careful to take into consideration the possibility that by reason both the agnostic and atheist may attain truth in their own way. Such tolerance may be surprising to religious believers in the West, but it is an integral part of Vedantic belief.

Today this knowledge is partially contained, the teachings are not spread widely across the world and Hinduism is losing its grip on its very own people for the sake of "Lack of Knowledge"," Lack of Faith", "Illiteracy", "Engagement of cultural cults rather than the more in-depth focus of the literature that exists.

Matthew 2: 4	*And when he gathered all the chief priests and scribes of the people together, he demanded of them where Christ should be born.*
5	*And they said unto him, In Bethlehem of Judaea: for thus it is written by the prophet,*
6	*And thou Bethlehem, in the land of Juda, art not the least among the princes of Juda: for out of thee shall come to a Governor, that shall rule my people Israel. Mic 5:2*
7	*Then Herod, when he had privily called the wise men, enquired of them diligently what time the star appeared.*
8	*And he sent them to Bethlehem, and said, Go and search diligently for the young child; and when ye have found him, bring me word again, that I may come and worship him also.*
9	*When they had heard the king, they departed; and, lo, the star, which they saw in the east, went before them, till it came and stood over where the young child was.*
10	*When they saw the star, they rejoiced with exceeding great joy.*
11	*And when they were come into the house, they saw the young child with Mary, his mother, and fell down, and worshipped him: and when they had opened their treasures, they presented unto him gifts; gold, and frankincense and myrrh.*
12	*And being warned of God in a dream that they should not return to Herod, they departed into their own country another way.*
13	*And when they were departed, behold, the angel of the Lord appeareth to Joseph in a dream, saying, Arise, and take the young child and his mother, and flee into Egypt, and be thou there until I bring thee word: for Herod will seek the young child to destroy him.*
14	*When he arose, he took the young child and his mother by night, and departed into Egypt:*

The wise men (There were no numbers mentioned, But magi are usually a group of 12) who came from the east, names were not mentioned, but the three names mentioned:

Melchior – Melchior as a king of Persia, the Parthian Empire, which is the center of Persia, the dominant religion was Zoroastrianism, with its priestly Magos Class and there is a root heritage here.

Caspar or Gaspar - Gaspar as a king of India, Caspar is old, generally with a white beard, and gives the gold; he is "King of Tarsus, land of merchants" on the Mediterranean coast of modern Turkey (ancient Indo-Asian subcontinent), and is first in line to kneel to Christ.

Balthazar or Balthasar is the king of Arabia,
Many Chinese Christians believe that one of the magi came from China
These wise men were highly educated scholars in science and astrology of noble birth, wealthy and politically influential. They were the philosophers, counselors and very spiritual men. As they saw the great light in the sky and the Star

that lit up and from their scripture of old knew that the King is born, the Savior is born and they will have to come and pay their respect and obedience.

The point here is to demonstrate that the three major regions of spiritual and cultural recognition of God and the presence of God, with all promises and prophecy, have embarked on the journey to the truth, for they knew the scriptures and the prophetic word and the religious texts. These are the regions where the world's religions of Islam, Hinduism, and Zoroastrianism were predominant, and they knew the truth. It is believed and found in some texts that Jesus escaped to Egypt and dwell the land where these wise men came from fro the age of twelve to thirty before returning to start his ministry. Multiple images and paintings are on display in India, and other eastern countries of the presence of Jesus dated to those time.

Islam has 1.6 billion Followers, almost a quarter of earth's population; Islam is the second-largest and the fastest-growing religion in the world. If the drive is to make every soul a Muslim, and then Islam is very successful, but if the drive is towards divine spirituality, power, peace, love, and harmony, then Islam is a failure, for, in every part of the world where the religion thrives, there is more turmoil, unrest, hatred, cruelty, inhuman activity, child marriages, and female suppression. Not that I am comparing it to other religion and places, if the faith can spend more time in developing the spirituality and powers that lie in belief, then there would be more love and forgiveness within the humanity of the gospel, leading to more peace, tolerance, more zakat and giving off more (this is not just about money) love. "Allah" is an Arabic word meaning 'GOD" and agreed that everyone worships "GOD" whether his name interpreted in Hindi as "Bhagwan" "Parmeshwar", "Ishwar, Devata, Deva" or Spanish – "DIOS", Urdu "Khuda', Japanese "kami", Chinese "Shen", Russian "Bog", Portuguese "Deus", Italian "Dio", Greek "Theos". There is a great worshipping of God, in the various languages and culture. ALL religious text defines that one of the greatest commandments from God is "Love" Love thy neighbor, Love Thy Brother.

> *Islamic Text on the Golden Rule: The Quran:*
> *"Serve God, and join not any partners with Him; and do good- to parents, kinsfolk, orphans, those in need, neighbors who are near, neighbors who are strangers, the companion by your side, the wayfarer (ye meet), and what your right hands possess [the slave]: For God loveth not the arrogant, the vainglorious" (Q:4:36)*
> *The Golden Rule: "Return evil with Kindness." (13:22, 23:96, 41:34, 28:54, 42:40).*
> *Prophet Muhammad (PBUH):* **"None of you have faith until you love for your neighbor what you love for yourself."**

Therefore if not following the commandment or the laws as given to the Prophet, and just a few mentioned above "You are not a Muslim" but a part of a social gathering in a Pharisee-*tical manner.*

Your task is not to seek for love,
But merely to seek and find
All the barriers within yourself
That you have built against it.
– Rumi
Ya Haqq!

The "Jihad" is not to fight against other human beings but to fight the fight within you. Scholars of Islam are spreading the wrong message for Control and gathering of masses. They create confusion and hostility, cause violence and rebellion against GOD, for God did not ordain any Jihad against any other Man. Jihad is a fight against the sinful flesh of man himself, his free will and desire to sin himself and others.

Definition of jihad: https://www.merriam-webster.com/dictionary/jihad
1: a holy war waged on behalf of Islam as a religious duty; also: a personal struggle in devotion to Islam especially involving spiritual discipline
2: a crusade for a principle or belief

The term derives from Jahada, an Arabic word meaning to labor, struggle or exert effort
The Three Jihads: The jihad against yourself, the jihad against Satan and the jihad against an open enemy (When in danger)
It is the Struggle to conquer the inner self against the contamination and confusion of "The Whisperer" who speaks to your mind and creates confusion
Jihad should be purposeful for your upliftment and the upliftment of your family for peace, education, and protection of people of all religion and faith and especially for those who are without faith or have "No Faith". According to Islam the four fulfillment of 'jihad' is through, the heart, the tongue, the limbs (hands) and the other is through the Sword.
Jihad through the heart is a Spiritual purification of the soul and fighting penetration of the evil into the center.
Jihad through the tongue, the most froward part of the body, to control and speak good things, and pray consistently without ceasing, the hand are the good works and giving.
Jihad of the sword has a modern definition of war, but according to scripture and the Quran it is an offensive war and not an aggressive war, it is to defend the faith. The interpretation of the 'sword' is the scripture, and if interpreted as the scripture, then you should spend the time to read and gain the knowledge of your scripture. **Most of the Muslims** who claim and utilized 'jihad by the sword' do not

know the Quran; they use parts and pieces of the Quran to satisfy their evil ways and their twisted minds and their hatred for a specific people or nation. They are vengeful over the things they do not know or understand and uses the Quran to create hatred against each other (Muslim against Muslim). They do not know the Quran period, for one of the most important verses in the Quran

Quran 2:255: Surat Al-Baqarah Known in Arabic as Ayah al-Kursi: "Allah: there is no true God but Him. The Ever-Living, the Eternal Master of all. Neither drowsiness nor sleep overtakes Him. His is all that is in the heavens and all that is on earth. Who is there that can intercede with Him, except by His permission? He knows all that lies open before them and all that lies hidden from them; whereas they cannot attain to anything of His knowledge save as He wills. His Kursi extends over the heavens and the earth, and the preservation of both does not tire Him. He is the Highest, the Most Great."

Everyone must submit to "GOD" (Allah means GOD and if that is not so then what is the meaning of Allah? this is the first, we must understand what and who is GOD). The same definition for God in all religions, The only difference is that it is another language, which means someone does not understand GOD [[Allah is the name of the only God in Islam. Allah is a pre-Islamic name coming from the compound Arabic word Al-ilah which means the God, derived from al (the) ilah (deity)]. Today we are all fighting for a name of a pre-Mohamed name of a Chief God over 360 Gods for the name "Allah" which means "God' unless it is the name of 'the moon God. The fight is not carnal, but against principalities and powers of the air, which we are allowing for overtaking us into the twist of hatred and war over the unseen (God)against what is the 'seen' (family), yet the way to God's heart is to Love your neighbor as yourself and do good unto others.

Then, on the other hand, why does ISLAM claim the Hindu prophesy of the return of the tenth incarnation of Hindu God Vishnu in the form of Kalki (which is the same description and purpose as Jesus Christ in Revelations) as their Prophet.

*Prophet Muhammad (PBUH): "**None of you have faith until you love for your neighbor what you love for yourself.**"*

Exodus 32: 7	*And the LORD said unto Moses, Go, get thee down; for thy people, which thou broughtest out of the land of Egypt, have corrupted themselves:*
8	*They have turned aside quickly out of the way which I commanded them: they have made them a molten calf, and have worshipped it, and have sacrificed thereunto, and said, These be thy gods, O Israel, which have brought thee up out of the land of Egypt.*
9	*And **the LORD said unto Moses; I have seen this person, and, behold, it is a stiff-necked people:***
10	*Now, therefore, let me alone, that my wrath may wax hot against them, and that I may consume them: and I will make of thee a great nation.*
11	*And Moses besought the LORD his God, and said, LORD, why doth thy*

wrath wax hot against thy people, which thou hast brought forth out of the
land of Egypt with great power, and with a mighty hand

For this same reason, there has been a curse upon the Seeds of Abraham as they fail to carry out the Laws and Commandments of GOD, they keep facing disaster and destruction at intervals, whether it is caused by man or by Nature or by Divine forces. Take some time to look back into history and see the suffering that was faced and is facing; some will be in the fate to come; it does not justify that some nations or people are prosperous and mighty now. The curse and the wrath of God have no respect for the man, fame or fortune, wealth and riches, physical or mental ability. He will discipline those who do not adhere to his commands and rebel with Disobedience. This is what's happening today?

God will not allow humanity to destroy this world or for any nation to destroy the other country. He is a Just God and will Judge those who persecute the poor and the innocent.

The enemy of God is not Lucifer , Satan or the Devil or Demons, It is Man and Man's free-will to choose whether to stick with GOD and be obedient and Live the holy life and replenish the earth and its kind, be a child of God or want to follow the evil path influenced by Evil beings for the purpose of earthly materialistic things, powers that he cannot control and lust of his very own flesh. The enemy that God is facing, because of his kindness, he does not want to destroy man but to wait for him to turn from his wicked ways back to God. The battle between the various dimensions can be a win by the winning of the souls of the mortal man and mortal beings. Spirits and demons can operate through a medium of bodies. Thus they fight to possess human beings, animal beings, etc., this is how demons operate.

God in his wrath can use his ultimate power and zap the demons, spirits, Lucifer, Satan, the Devil, and all his emissaries either into oblivion, Hell or thin air, but the battle focused on how many souls of human beings can they win over, and we (humans) are becoming the playground for this battle. Why are we focused on the Armageddon? The Rapture? The End Times? Is there anything anyone of us can do to change the outcome? The prophetic end of the world? The answer is "yes," yes, we can, and that is the quest of the Supreme God, to get humanity to reject all the evil that surrounds them and refuse to be a vessel for the Devil, his demons and all that follows him. If we resist and purify ourselves and lean towards God, they (the Demons) will have no place and will have to seek the bodies of other living beings such as the animals.

2 Chronicles 7:14   King James Version (KJV)

14   *If my people, which are called by my name, shall humble themselves, and pray, and seek my face, and turn from their wicked ways; then will I hear from heaven, and will forgive their sin, and will heal their land.*

15:   *Now **mine eyes shall be open**, and **mine ears attent unto the prayer** that is made in this place.*

HOW MANY COUNTRIES IN THE WORLD ARE SUFFERING FROM FAMINE, NATURAL DISASTERS, AND OUTBREAK OF DISEASES, GENOCIDE, TRIBAL WARS AND NEEDS HEALING?

2 Chronicles 7:19 But if ye turn away, and forsake my statutes and my commandments, which I have set before you, and shall go and serve other gods, and worship them;

2 Chronicles 7: 20 Then will I pluck them up by the roots out of my land which I have given them; and this house, which I have sanctified for my name, will I cast out of my sight, and will make it be a proverb and a byword among all nations.

2 Chronicles 7: 21 And this house, which is high, shall be an astonishment to every one that passeth by it; so that he shall say, Why hath the LORD done thus unto this land, and unto this house?

Confused yet? Where do I stand now? Who do I worship? Am I going to be persecuted if I do, or don't worship God?

We do need to get a personal connection to God and let the spirit lead to righteousness and do not lean unto the other man understanding; you must be filled with the spirit of God.

We are different, and we take those differences and make it into a weapon, which we use against other person or persons that do not have the same belief that we have. Thereby create enmity against each other and eventually fight great wars against our fellow man because of these twisted, demented, humanistic flaws and the battles make us sinners beyond the acceptance of Gods order and thus God twists his face in disgust of what we have become in the eyes of each other and the eyes of divinity. We are no longer the man created in the image of God. But are the children of the "evil one' who now claims you as sons, and your rage, anger and despair, your heart full of fire and hate, contaminated by the fiery darts of Satan, embedded in your flesh, fused into your DNA. Ready to be passed on to your children in that little sperm/Ovum you bear, into the nuclei (embryo) of your offspring and the world becomes into the pre-Noah state once again doomed for all mankind as God himself gets disgusted once again with the Human race, even though he swore not to flood them out .

The Idea here is to understand all the various aspects of religion, how they were created and how it affects us on a daily basis and has designed us in a manner that we are stuck in the phase of understanding what we choose to believe and dedicate our faith and abilities.   It is good to have knowledge of all aspects of religion and what others think or feel, not to be convinced, convicted or change our very own beliefs, but to understand what is involved that causes another person or individual be hardcore stuck in their very own belief system, without being deterred from changing or accepting any other belief. "Knowledge is Power', a proverb inscribed into the order from old.

I added the footnote to email address quote "Knowledge is power, only and only when utilized appropriately and applied congruously." I believe possessing all the knowledge in the world is good, but if it sits in our head and not utilized, it all goes to waste.

If 1.6 Billion Muslims, 2.5 Billion Christians, 1.0 Billion Hindus, Millions of Jews , Buddhist, and all the other religions and religionists diligently pray for Peace and the blessings of God upon the earth, Stop the violence, stop the persecution, break the yoke of the Devil, make provisions, feed the hungry, fight against crime and violence, eliminate racism and hatred. It will surely bring about miracles and wonders, but if we trample on each other, then thy will be done on thyself and by others. We focus on religion and dogmas rather than what the religion is teaching us to be and how to act towards the calling of God and what God wants us to be, and we allow ourselves to become led by the bullring (nose ring) and be separated from God's true nature and not getting into the realm of God's spiritual dominion, we neglect the humanitarian aspect of the duties of Man as designed by God and becomes self-centered, egocentric, egoistic and selfish in our thoughts and deeds. The most important message from God is "to love thy neighbor as thyself' which is ignored as we become selfishly super-spiritual. All religions acknowledge Jesus Christ and his existence as God Incarnated in these latter days, a common understanding that in every religion Jesus is a major character that is spiritually connected to God and is part of God, the Prophet of God, The Son of God and God himself manifested in the flesh as Jesus Christ, then I am sure that there will be some growing spiritual peace that will spread like wildfire in the hearts of all people. God himself said in the scriptures that "My People are a stiff-necked people" and their hearts are hard and commonly disobedient, no matter how many times they were saved from persecution, they will always be a Stiff-necked people with a hard heart. Why do they possess a hard heart? It is because they are still falling prey into the hands of the Devil in the various forms, even in their worship. The reason why many nations suffer at certain intervals every 100 years or 40 years, or at the specific biblical numerical, symbolic era, it may look as though they are prospering and getting more powerful and wealthier, but come a time when God himself puts them under persecution and puts them into slavery and bondage.

Knowledge is Power

*"It is commonly attributed to Sir **Francis Bacon**, although there is no known occurrence of this precise phrase in Bacon's English or Latin writings. However, the expression "ipsa scientia potestas est" ('knowledge itself is power') occurs in Bacon's **Meditationes** Sacrae (1597)."*

*'**Knowledge is power**' is a famous **proverb**. It **means** that **knowledge** is more powerful than physical strength and no great work can be done without **knowledge**. **Knowledge** is a powerful factor that empowers people achieves great results. The more **knowledge** a person gains, the more powerful he becomes. **Knowledge is power definition**. The more one knows, the more one will be able to control events.*

Knowledge is one of the most valuable of all attainments. Happiness and usefulness depend upon it. Knowledge is the apprehension of facts and application of them to life.

Knowledge Biblical

Proverbs 1: 7   *the fear of the LORD is the beginning of knowledge, but fools despise wisdom and instruction.*

Isaiah 11: 2   *the Spirit of the LORD will rest on him — the Spirit of wisdom and of understanding, the Spirit of counsel and might, the Spirit of the knowledge and fear of the LORD—*

There is a spirit of Fear, and we need to get rid of it altogether, which is difficult but acomplished through prayer, commitment to GOD and dedication to God. Get rid of all bitterness, unforgiveness, selfishness, rejection, self-pity and stinking thinking

Get Rid of Fear:

2 Timothy 1: 7   *For God hath not given us the spirit of fear, but of power, and of love, and of a sound mind. 8 Be not thou therefore ashamed of the testimony of our Lord, nor of me his prisoner: but be thou partaker of the afflictions of the gospel according to the power of God;*

2 Corinthians 10: 3   *For though we walk in the flesh, we do not war after the flesh:*

4   *(For the weapons of our warfare are not carnal, but mighty through God to the pulling down of strong holds ;)*

5   *Casting down imaginations, and every high thing that exalteth itself against the knowledge of God, and bringing into captivity every thought to the obedience of Christ;*

6   *And having in a readiness to revenge all disobedience, when your obedience is fulfilled.*

7   *Do ye look on things after the outward appearance? If any man trust to himself that he is Christ's, let him of himself think this again, that, as he is Christ's, even so, are we Christ's.*

James 4: 1	*From whence come wars and fightings among you? Come they not hence, even of your lusts that war in your members?*
2	*Ye lust, and have not: ye kill, and desire to have, and cannot obtain: ye fight and war, yet ye have not, because ye ask not.*
3	*Ye ask, and receive not, because ye ask amiss, that ye may consume it upon your lusts.*
4	*Ye adulterers and adulteresses know ye not that the friendship of the world is enmity with God? whosoever, therefore, will be a friend of the world is the enemy of God.*
5	*Do ye think that the scripture saith in vain, The spirit that dwelleth in us lusteth to envy?*
6	*But he giveth more grace. Wherefore he saith, God resisteth the proud, but giveth grace unto the humble.*
7	*Submit yourselves therefore to God. Resist the devil, and he will flee from you.*
8	*Draw nigh to God, and he will draw nigh to you. Cleanse your hands, ye sinners; and purify your hearts, ye double minded.*
9	*Be afflicted, and mourn, and weep: let your laughter be turned to mourning and your joy to heaviness.*
10	*Humble yourselves in the sight of the Lord, and he shall lift you up.*
11	*Speak not evil one of another, brethren. He that speaketh evil of his brother, and judgeth his brother, speaketh evil of the law, and judgeth the law: but if thou judge the law, thou art not a doer of the law, but a judge.*
12	*There is one lawgiver, who is able to save and to destroy: who art thou that judgest another?*
13	*Go to now, ye that say, Today or tomorrow we will go into such a city, and continue there a year, and buy and sell, and get gain:*
14	*Whereas ye know not what shall be on the morrow. For what is your life? It is even a vapor, that appeareth for a little time, and then vanisheth away.*
15	*For that ye ought to say, If the Lord will, we shall live, and do this, or that.*
16	*But now ye rejoice in your boastings: all such rejoicing is evil.*
17	*Therefore to him, that knoweth to do good, and doeth it not, to him it is a sin.*

4 THE HUMAN

THE HUMAN MIND

We must understand how our Mind works and what influences our body, mind, spirit, and soul

A mind /maɪnd/ is the set of cognitive faculties that enables consciousness, perception, thinking, judgment, and memory—a characteristic of humans, but which also may apply to other life forms. - Wikipedia

[Mīnd]

1.   the organ or seat of; the faculty by which one is aware of the surroundings and
        by which one can experience emotions, remember, reason, and make decisions.
2.   The organized totality of an organism's mental and psychological processes, conscious and unconscious.
3.   The characteristic thought process of a person

One of our greatest quests in this life is to find out who we are. Moreover, why are we here? Understanding self is one of our great pursuits.

Who am I? What is my relationship with this world? What is my purpose?

We are curious about our origin and our existence, where are we heading and what our purpose is?

One observation is that we are the highest of all animal species and our accomplishments enhanced due to our ability to communicate at a higher level through sound, words and created language.

We have seen the human growth from conception to fetus development, deliverance into the world by birth process and as we grow, we experience aging.

We become addicted and experience addiction, feel pain and witness our body heal, we experience moods, depression, and action of anger, violence and various mental feelings that reflect in our efforts.

Our quest to know and understand ourselves is complicated and very difficult to put into perspective of what is real and what is not.

The mind does not age or grow old; it gains more and more ability, knowledge through experience, available studies and acquired knowledge. The creation of new Synapses

We can be as young as our mental self as long as we harbor love and love only and do not entertain anger, hate and any negative traits.

Life of the mind is a symphony, or rather the harmony of life is the limitations of the brain. Your mind is the key to everything you do in life, once you can think and conceive the idea in your mind, it can materialize as your mind begins to work on the senses (ideas are children of the mind) and defines methods, ways, pathways, solutions, possibilities of, making plans into reality. Put together the pieces, the patterns, view the boundaries and the abilities bring knowledge into the Calderon of the mind and expand the resources, delve and investigate everything the mind is telling and giving. It will develop your wisdom and knowledge of nature and everything around.

> *Michio Kaku wrote "The universe is a symphony of strings, and the mind of God that Einstein eloquently wrote for thirty years would be cosmic music resonating through **eleven-dimensional** hyper space"*

The idea is to utilize your mind effectively and waste not your mind it can discern thoughts and filter good productive thoughts, filter out the negative thoughts and cast them aside.

The mind ties together a three-dimension consciousness, unconsciousness, and subconsciousness, intertwined together to form the reality that was conceived.

So, what is the Mind? Was it ever born? Was it created? Alternatively was in inherited?

How does the mind play a role in what and who we are? What do we do? How do we act?

All these answers lie not in science, Psychotherapy or Physiology, but in mind itself. All knowledge lies therein and can acquire like a computer connected to the internet by a Network cable or a wireless device; the Human MUST be connected to access the university and library within the minds and get access codes with the connection.

The mind does not know the age or grows old; it gains more and more ability through experience, knowledge and the creation of new synapses. The mind searches to identify itself and to associate itself with the spirit of human being. It becomes a learning experience for the mind and the brain; it takes harmony between all three to complete perfection and functionality within the human being. The mind is the God part that is abstract has no physical mass on and initially have the element of GOD in our conception, as we grow and develop the enhancement all the details is crucial to our ability, spirituality, and physical empowerment.

Our minds remain in a state of the present; we constantly battle with our thoughts on a daily basis in the present and stay disturbed and preoccupied with problems, tasks, and people throughout the day. It holds us stagnant in the present and the flesh and not allows us to move in the spirit. Discipline is required to cultivate equanimity of the mind and control it in mind and body, the senses and ability to detach and disassociate our mental self from the physical and multi-task with the mind/thought/spirit working in the background while we deal with life in the foreground. This cause and effect changes reality and makes life grow and reveal itself for your benefit and fits into your creation.

GOD created man in the Image of GOD (Likeness of GOD, therefore we already have the particle of GOD in us), some may be physical, and because God is a spirit, in depth, it means we – the spirit- is created from the spirit of GOD and in the likeness of GOD the spirit.

If we allow the external world to grab hold of us and cultivate an environment for us, we will be lost in the outer. We will not be utilizing the gift of our psychic ability, our spirituality and our GOD given talent to create a world in which we want to live and will live, but will be lost in the external world of which others have built, and becomes part of that world, rather than our own.

The Human Being is made up of replication of trillions and trillions of tiny cells/atoms and molecules that are a replica and mirror image of each other. Humankind is a Universe within a universe, within a world, within a planet to infinity. To see the Universe, what it looks like, what it feels like, what it smells, taste like, look within. Look at the inner you from an external view, a whole picture and go deeper layer by layer into the minutest physical and spiritual parts of you to experience the Universe and what it is. The Powers that exist in the Universe are the combination of the Powers of Supreme entity and supreme powers we know as GOD and what we can define as GOD. This power creates, programs, change and deliver what we desire as Human beings as a creation of GOD.

Evolution theory states that Man evolves from age to age, era to era, from Ape to Standing Man, but not accurately and scientifically proven as hard evidence that the Human Being is a being that came from one single cell in water or any other form. It does not answer the question of why are there still Apes. Are the present Apes a being transformed from another way?

The one fantastic addition given to man is the ability to communicate, a language, a communication tool that he can have a high level of discourse with his fellow man and his creator GOD. This is why Man is the highest form of animal and was given dominion over all other creatures. Given the power, he was ordained with through God in his creation.

5 BODY SPIRIT AND SOUL

The power of belief can influence the mind to change our lives, including heal the body

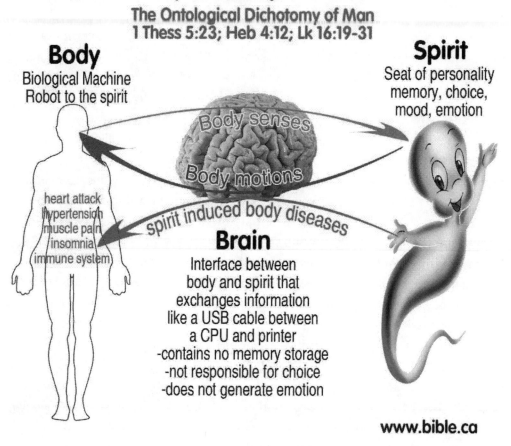

Biblical Psychiatry's view of man
The Ontological Dichotomy of Man
1 Thess 5:23; Heb 4:12; Lk 16:19-31

Body
Biological Machine
Robot to the spirit

Spirit
Seat of personality
memory, choice,
mood, emotion

Body senses

Body motions

heart attack
hypertension
muscle pain
insomnia
immune system

spirit induced body diseases

Brain
Interface between
body and spirit that
exchanges information
like a USB cable between
a CPU and printer
-contains no memory storage
-not responsible for choice
-does not generate emotion

www.bible.ca

The Body (Greek, "soma")

Here is the entire material or physical structure of a human being -- it is the physical part of a person.

The Apostle Paul, writing to the Romans again connects the body, the mind (soul) and the spirit.

(Romans 12:1-2 NASB) *Therefore I urge you, brethren, by the mercies of God, to present your bodies a living and holy sacrifice, acceptable to God, which is your spiritual service of worship. And do not be conformed to this world, but be transformed by the renewing of your mind, so that you may prove what the will of God is, that which is good and acceptable and perfect.*

(1 Cor. 6:20) *For you have been bought with a price: therefore glorify God in your body.*

<u>The Soul (Greek, "psyche")</u>

Genesis 2:7 states Man created as a "living soul." The soul consists of the mind (which includes the conscience), the will and the emotions. The soul and the spirit are mysteriously tied together and make up what the Scriptures call the "heart." It is the spiritual or immaterial part of a human being as the immortal embodiment of the human being, the mental abilities of reason, character, consciousness, and feelings.
 Genesis 2:*7 Then the LORD God formed man of the dust of the ground and breathed into his nostrils the breath of life, and man became a living soul.*
> *"I am seated in everyone's heart as the all-pervading Super soul and from me come remembrance, knowledge, and forgetfulness." ~ Bhagavad Gita 15:15*
> *"For the soul, there is neither birth nor death at any time. He has not come into being, does not come into being, and will not come into being. He is unborn, eternal, ever-existing and primeval. He is not slain when the body is slain." ~ Bhagavad Gita 2.20*

The writer of Proverbs declares, *"Watch over your heart with all diligence, for from it flows the springs of life."* (Prov. 4:23). We see here that the "heart" is central to our emotions and will.
But a natural (psuchikos -- soulish) man does not accept the things of the Spirit of God, for they are foolishness to him; and he cannot understand them, because they are spiritually appraised (1 Cor. 2:14).

Paul, looking intently at the Council, said, *"Brethren, I have lived my life with a perfectly good conscience before God up to this day"* (Acts 23:1).

The Spirit (Greek " Pneuma")

In Numbers 16:22, Moses and Aaron, "...fell upon their faces and said, *'O God, God of the spirits of all flesh, when one man sins, will you be angry with the entire congregation?'*" This verse named God as the God of the spirits that are possessed by all humanity. Notice also that it mentions the flesh (body) of all humanity, connecting it with the spirit. The human spirit is the spiritual part of man. *"Then the LORD God formed a man from the dust of the ground and breathed into his nostrils the breath of life, and the man became a living being"* (Genesis 2:7), the very breath of God, the intangible, unseen spirit that manages our mental and emotional being.

Another critical verse that describes the separation between soul and spirit is Hebrews 4:12:
For the word of God is living and active and sharper than any two-edged sword, and piercing as far as the division of soul and spirit, of both joints and marrow, and able to judge the thoughts and intentions of the heart (Heb. 4:12).
We see in this passage of Scripture that the soul and spirit can be divided -- and that it is the Word of God that pierces our heart to bring the division of soul and spirit, something that only God can do.
As human beings, we live eternally as a spirit, we have a soul, and we dwell in a body. We can rejoice with the Psalmist and declare,
For you formed my inward parts; you wove me in my mother's womb. I will give thanks to you, for I am fearfully and wonderfully made; Wonderful are your works, and my soul knows it very well (Ps. 139:13-14).
Hebrews 4:12, *"For the word of God is living and operative and sharper than any two-edged sword, and piercing even to the dividing of soul and spirit and of joints and marrow, and able to discern the thoughts and intentions of the heart."*

For we are a complex being that is created by a supreme divine entity we call GOD, same can be easily destroyed and can separate from GOD through the powers of the free will given onto man. Where the Spirit and Soul concerned only a supreme entity can divide and destroy these as such, we can see the great battle to covet our "SOUL" by the devil. Our spirit is of two folds, the spirit of the man and the integration of the Spirit of GOD which takes the forefront by connectivity to GOD via worship, devotion, Dedication, Submission, baptism by the Holy Spirit. The destruction on the entirety of a man **is easy** for the DEVIL, the reasons why the Apostles offered much warning to Guard your mind.

6 THE HUMAN MIND

Mind: scriptural quotes to safeguard your mind

Romans 8:5-6 - *For they that are after the flesh do mind the things of the flesh; but they that are after the Spirit the things of the Spirit (Paul divides people into two categories – this who let themselves be controlled by their sinful nature (carnal minded) and those who follow after the Holy Spirit)*

Romans 12:1-2 - *I beseech you therefore, brethren, by the mercies of God, that ye present your bodies a living sacrifice, holy, acceptable unto God, [which is] your reasonable service (God has good, pleasing, and perfect plans for his children. He wants us to be a new people with renewed minds, living to honor and obey him)*

Colossians 2:8 - *Beware lest any man spoil you through philosophy and vain deceit, after the tradition of men, after the rudiments of the world, and not after Christ. (Paul writes against any philosophy of life-based only on human ideas and experiences. He is not condemning philosophy, but that which puts humans above the Christ)*

2 Corinthians 10:5 - *Casting down imaginations, and every high thing that exalteth itself against the knowledge of God, and bringing into captivity every thought to the obedience of Christ; (We are weak humans when it comes to the carnal ways and fighting against powers and principalities. God's mighty weapons are available to fight against Satan's strongholds. God's strong weapons are faith, love, prayer, and belief)*

2 Timothy 1:7 - *For God hath not given us the spirit of fear; but of power, and of love, and of a sound mind.*

Isaiah 26:3 - *Thou wilt keep [him] in perfect peace, [whose] mind [is] stayed [on thee]: because he trusteth in thee.*

Philippians 4:6-8 - *Be careful for nothing, but in everything by prayer and supplication with thanksgiving let your requests be made known unto God.*

2 Corinthians 5:17 - *Therefore if any man [be] in Christ, [he is] a new creature: old things are passed away; behold all things become new.*

1 Peter 5:8 - *Be sober, be vigilant; because your adversary the devil, as a roaring lion, walketh about, and seeking whom he may devour:*

Joshua 1:8 - *This book of the law shall not depart out of thy mouth; but thou shalt meditate therein day and night, that thou mayest observe to do according to all that is written therein: for then thou shalt make thy way prosperous, and then thou shalt have good success.*

1 John 4:18 - *There is no fear in love; but perfect love casteth out fear: because fear hath torment. He that feareth is not made perfect in love.*

Philippians 2:5 - *Let this mind be in you, which was also in Christ Jesus:*

7 THE HUMAN BODY

An authoritative knowledge of the body and making sure the body is kept as per created

1 Corinthians 6:19-20 - *What? Know ye not that your body is the temple of the Holy Ghost [which is] in you, which ye have of God, and ye are not your own?*

1 Corinthians 3:16-17 - *Know you not that ye are the temple of God, and [that] the Spirit of God dwelleth in you*

Leviticus 19:28 - *Ye shall not make any cuttings in your flesh for the dead, nor print any marks upon you: I [am] the LORD.*

Romans 12:1-2 - *I beseech you, therefore, brethren, by the mercies of God, that ye present your bodies a living sacrifice, holy, acceptable unto God, [which is] your reasonable service.*

1 Corinthians 10:31 - *Whether therefore ye eat, or drink, or whatsoever ye do, do all to the glory of God.*

1 Corinthians 9:27 - *But I keep under my body, and bring [it] into subjection: lest that by any means when I have preached to others, I myself should be a castaway.*

1 Corinthians 6:19 - *What? Know ye not that your body is the temple of the Holy Ghost [which is] in you, which ye have of God, and ye are not your own?*

Matthew 6:22 - *The light of the body is the eye: if therefore thine eye be single, thy whole body shall be full of light.*

1 John 2:15-17 - *Love not the world, neither the things [that are] in the world. If any man loves the world, the love of the Father is not in him*

Jeremiah 1:5 - *Before I formed thee in the belly I knew thee; and before thou camest forth out of the womb I sanctified thee, [and] I ordained thee a prophet unto the nations.*

Matthew 10:28 - *And fear not them which kill the body, but are not able to kill the soul: but rather fear him which is able to destroy both soul and body in hell.*

8 THE SPIRIT OF MAN

Man is a living being, connected with physical, mental and spiritual abilities and components able to be walking, talking, and thinking and be a man of action. Lose your spirit, and you will become a zombie, a living dead, a walking dead, a cabbage, mindless and just a physical mass of flesh and bones.

Job 32:8 - *But [there is] a spirit in man: and the inspiration of the Almighty giveth them understanding. (The recognition of the truth that God is the only and ultimate resource for wisdom and should be used as part of our life continuously)*

Proverbs 20:27 - *The spirit of man [is] the candle of the LORD, searching all the inward parts of the belly. (God has given each of us a conscience to tell us the differences of right and wrong. The conscience searches us and exposes our hidden motives. This is assisted with the wisdom and knowledge and the word of GOD to carve the righteous ways that help us to identify the wrong motives and ways.)*

Ecclesiastes 12:7 - *Then shall the dust return to the earth as it was: and the spirit shall return unto God who gave it. (Strip off the spirit of God, our bodies return to dust. A strip of God's purpose, our work is in vain. Strip off God's love; our service is futile. We must put God first. Without God we have nothing).*

Romans 8:16 - *The Spirit itself beareth witness with our spirit, that we are the children of God: (here it declares the spirit of God bears witness to the spirit of man which is us. Those who let themselves be controlled by their sinful nature to be Carnally minded is to have a mindset confirmed by their sinful nature and those who follow after the Holy Spirit. Once we have confirmed and agreed to follow Jesus, we will want to continue following him. When the Holy Ghost defines what is right, we should do it eagerly.*

1 Corinthians 6:17 - *But he that is joined unto the Lord is one spirit.*

Zechariah 12:1 - *The burden of the **word of the** LORD for Israel, saith the LORD, which stretcheth forth the heavens, and layeth the foundation of the earth, and formeth the spirit of man within him. (This siege against Israel is defined).*

1 Thessalonians 5:23 - *And the very God of peace sanctify you wholly, and [I pray God] your whole spirit and soul and body be preserved blameless unto the coming of our Lord Jesus Christ. (The spirit, soul, and body referred not so much too distinct parts of a person as to the entire **being** of a person. This expression is the Apostle Paul's way of saying that God must be involved in every aspect of our life. It is wrong to think we can separate our spiritual life from everything else, obeying God only in some sense or leaving for you one day*

John 4:24 - *God [is] a Spirit: and they that worship him must worship [him] in spirit and in* *truth.*

Genesis 2:7 -   *And the LORD God formed man [of] the dust of the ground, and breathed into his nostrils the breath of life, and man became a living soul.*

1 Corinthians 2:11 - *For what man knoweth the things of a man, save the spirit of man which is in him? Even so, the things of God knoweth no man, but the Spirit of God.*

Luke 24:39 -   *Behold my hands and my feet, that it is I myself: handle me, and see; for a spirit hath not flesh and bones, as ye see me have.*

Romans 8:10 -   *And if Christ [be] in you, the body [is] dead because of sin, but the Spirit [is] life because of righteousness.*

1 Corinthians 6:19 - *What? Know ye not that your body is the temple of the Holy Ghost [which is] in you, which ye have of God, and ye are not your own?*

The understanding and knowledge of the Body/Spirit/Soul of man and how they integrate with the Mind of a person give higher wisdom and awareness. What we are and what we are ordained to be and the ability that has been given to us by the father of Heaven and Earth, Yet it is also effortless to lose it all and be under the control of the dark worlds and its emissaries

Human Kind is a three-dimensional being of Body, mind, and spirit. **The body,** formed by God from the dust of the ground (Earth – Hebrew: Adamah – Red earth). We are created from the elements of the planet otherwise we will not survive the physical components and nature of the Earth, same as if we were to be transported to Mars or Jupiter our physical bodies will not be able to withstand and be compatible with the elements of those planets. **The Spirit,** which was the breath from the spirit of God into the nostrils of Adam, therefore we are a part of God, from God's spirit. Endowed by God to us and will return to God at the end of life. **The Soul**, which was created by the uniting of the spirit of God (and our Spirit) with the material body, and is the real personality of the man, containing all that he is, his reality and character. These three elements of man are sense-consciousness (body), self-consciousness (soul) and God-consciousness (Spirit). We as human beings are the only animal category that received the Spirit of God and gave the ability to communicate via language, because of specially dedicated to God for his glory and worship, fellowship, and communion with God.

9 THE HUMAN BRAIN

The Brain, a 3lb mass is the embodiment of the mind, as the mind is abstract. The human brain is the command center of the entire human nervous system, receiving inputs and sends outputs to muscles. Most brain cells are made up of Glia (means Glue) which holds 10% neurons together. ***The male and female brains (and brain-power)*** are similar with minimal differences in internal masses of each region, which is influenced by environment and patterns in life. These small differences in size and masses do make many differences in functionality of both male and female humans. Men have stronger connections between **brain** areas for motor and spatial skills. That means **males** tend to do a better job at tasks that need hand-eye coordination and understanding where objects are in space, such as throwing a ball or hammering a nail. On average, **male brains** are about 10% larger than **female brains**. Men tend to use one side of their brain (particularly the **left** side for verbal reasoning) while women tend to use both cerebral areas for visual, verbal and emotional responses. These differences in brain use cause a difference in behavior between men and women. The right and left hemispheres of the male and female **brains** are not the same way. For instance, females tend to have verbal centers on both sides of the **brain**, while males tend to have oral centers on only the left hemisphere a significant **difference.**

Hormones influence the brain development in the womb, and at about age 13 the brain for both boys and girls remain the same. During and after puberty hormones again influences the development of the brain and starts to create different programs and the circuitry internally adopts a separate architecture building "Brain roadmaps" called "The connectome" which influences the difference in performance and thinking. The connecting bands between the left half and the right half for women are broader and can access both sides simultaneously back and forth while men are more left-sided which is the logical thinking half of the brain, the right associated with intuition.

Studies revealed that men require more brainpower than women when multitasking, this is related to the effort it takes to switch from left brain to right brain and back to left brain across a thinner band that connects both sides of the brain for men

The idea of this discussion is to understand the physiology of our makeup so as not to be fuzzed out by when your performance may be challenging versus another individual and for you to focus on putting effort towards building and faster interconnect in your brain cells. Defined that the average human only utilizes about 10% of our brains. What happened to the other 90% of the gray matter in our brain that remains underutilized? We need to open up your mind to thinking and assessing the Whys of our limitations. Are we dumbed down over time by the environment, food, social and environmental influences? Or are we using lesser and lesser of our brain cells or brain capacity because we are not exercising the faculty of the brain? Or are we under the influence of the 'death of the spirit' of divinity as spelled out in the bible and other religious texts. This is food for thought and opening the curiosity of the mind to think it through. Revisit the Movie "Lucy" to give ideas on one version of a chemically enhanced brain capacity. Go back to scriptures and understand our creation, we were created to live eternally (forever) with the spirit of God (divine spirit) within us and reproduction was not in the picture of creation yet when Adam was created.

Later was the instruction and command from God *"to Replenish the earth"* in *Genesis 1:28,* which could include simply mead "to fill."

> ***Genesis 1:28***   *"And God blessed them, and God said unto them, Be fruitful, and multiply, and replenish the earth, and subdue it: and have dominion over the fish of the sea, and over the fowl of the air, and over every living thing that moveth upon the earth."*

> *The Bible in Genesis 1: 2 states*   *"And the earth was without form, and void; and darkness was upon the face of the deep. And the Spirit of God moved upon the face of the waters." Genesis 1:6 "And God said, Let there be a firmament in the midst of the waters, and let it divide the waters from the waters." Which means that the entire earth was under water for according to Genesis 1: 2? "And the earth was without form, and void, and darkness was upon the face of the deep. And the Spirit of God moved upon the face of the waters."*

The integration of electric, electrostatic and kinetic energies from the brain cells and fibers create and keep creating thus the combination of the creative force that ties into the spirit of the body.

Internally communication is electric, electrostatic and kinetic flows through the fibers and cells and body fluids.

The mind instigates and creates thoughts that convert into energy transmitted through the brain fibers, bands and mass through fluids and matter in the little 3 lb mass of "The Brain," which becomes the console and control room of large universe-like dimension of the Human Being.

Neurotransmitters send instructions across the entire body, triggering action, influenced endocrine enzymes and transmuted nothing that contains ideas into something that affects activity. Chemical messengers from in the internal membranes,

Chemical messengers produced by nerve cells and released from the axonal endings usually act in endocrine or paracrine fashion. When the neural signaling molecules are released into the synaptic gap to activate receptors on the adjacent cell **membranes**, they are called neurotransmitters.

BRAIN: neuroscience:

The Brain is one of the most important organs in our bodies, without a Brain we matter (flesh, bones, water, and molecules). The importance in the study of the Brain is growing and getting more intensified in the eyes and mind of Scientists, Doctors, and about everyone in all industry. People are getting more conscious and want to know more about the brain, its functions, how to keep it healthy, clean and clear not get it clogged up.

It is difficult to stay in layman's language and terminologies when writing about these subjects, but I will put it as simple as possible. The brain is and related to our Health, Personality, sanity, social and environmental well being, love, mood, physical and mental stability, intuition, behavior, and mental process, memory and stored information and so on and so on.

The brain – an amazing and powerful tool that allows us to function in every mental and physical faculty, learn and see, remember, communicate and comprehend, controls every other organ in the body and the body itself, our taste, smell and feel. Not only an amazing and powerful organ that we are in possession of, but it also can fail, and when there is a failure, but we also panic and want to know what? How? And fix? Its failure can lead to the terminal or long-term hardcore suffering that may or may not be reversible.

Bottom line, without a functioning brain and the network of nervous system we would not be able to function, we could not walk, talk, breathe, our heart would not perform in the rhythm and performance. We would have no emotions, no abilities, no sense of smell, taste or touch. The brain in conjunction with our nervous system and blood vessels are the life source of the human body; the rest our bodies, glands, and organs that process and works in harmony with the central controller - the Brain. The Brain has an abstract connection to the Spirit of the Man, and the spirit of the man is connected to the universe and the forces of nature which in turn is an unexplained divine force that caused the creation, maintenance and directs the function of the whole Human being. This source we referred to as the Supreme entity, or supreme authority of the Universe and called GOD Complex.

This complex structure of the brain is so intricate it is still not explored by scientists and Doctors or medical intellects, they can explain the physical masses and structure, but cannot tell the harmony and how and why each part keeps its rhythm and harmony with each other. They all function with a precision that if there is a split second miss or misalignment in timing, the body reports a malfunction, and the results slowly starts to deteriorate, and other factors play a role in the body's breakdown and generate atoms and particles that do not belong to this perfect human building. The brain is the control center of the nervous system; it receives and sends messages to every tiny part of the body in an ideal communication that is un-deciphered by human intellect. It includes consciousness and unconsciousness, language – verbal and non-verbal, triggers such as fear or flight, responses to temperature – hot or cold, only to be protected by a helmet of a healthy bone shell with intricate padding to avoid the shock and shaking which can shatter its soft tissues.

The idea of this simple definition is to allow the understanding of the correctly built human being that is tougher than many elements of the earth and yet vulnerable to the tiniest invisible particle. It must be a unique creation, and it cannot be just something that has been formed out of nothing or from a single atom and generated into this vast complex unexplainable being that has no purpose but to live. It is a question that has to be answered by something more significant that MAN.

How do we maintain its perfection? How do we keep it in perfect form? How can we avoid it from getting damaged or deteriorate into a few pounds of dust (elements of the earth)?

A high percentage of wars in the world are affiliated to religion and from some religious cause, where man due to a belief system and territorial dominion wants the ownership of others and their values. These are led by thoughts that overcome the emotions and created by negative influences in the Brain

"Religion is excellent stuff for keeping common people quiet." — Napoleon Bonaparte

"Emotional excitement reaches men through tea, tobacco, opium, whiskey, and religion." — George Bernard Shaw (1856 – 1950)

Religion has a very similar effect on the brain as some narcotic drugs and other chemicals

There are about 10,000 religions, and each one believes they possess the keys to the truth or to have the fact that the rest of the world does not possess, own or understand.

Belief and religion have such an effect on the brain that it is controlling and free will is gone, dissipates into oblivion after the consistent pounding into the subliminal the doctrines of culture and scriptures. It functions like drugs and has a very similar effect and sometimes suppresses the brain network used for analytical thinking that engages nervous system for emotions, empathy, love, and feelings of mental and emotional control. Submission and fear of GOD take its place, and we became complacent in our belief system of self and lost into the abstract of the Spirit of God being in control and hopeful dependency in faith and belief that we are under control, governed and taken care of by God. We focus our human drive forwards from the ego and self-preservation, self –sustenance, and determination to do and make do the things we want to do to strive and achieve greatness as a human being an inbuilt system was instilled since creation. The leap of faith to the belief in the supernatural severs the critical and analytical manner of thoughts and thinking that pushes us to achieve and achieve greater things in our life socially and emotionally.

There is that 'God Spot" in the brain dedicated to this type of experiences, whether it is religious, spiritual or phenomenal and that links to the Pineal gland and a few other regions in the brain that connects to the feelings, belief system, and cognitive functions. Humanity was always aware of the supernatural, the divine existence whether he believes it is ancestors of another form of spiritual life form, but since creation, it has been embedded into the mind of human beings and engrained into their ego and system of awareness cognizance of the existence. This belief in the super supernatural has an effect on our very own personality, physically, mentally and spiritually and drives us to further greatness and physical enhancement to perform amazing feats; it also can tear us down if it has an adverse effect. This brief overview and a much more in-depth study can give better enlightenment if needed.

We live in a sea of germs and viruses; they are in the air we breathe, the water we drink, foods, on our skin, in our hair, mouth, and body. These germs are in the rivers, oceans, in the ground and everywhere can possible can travel or be. Our only shields are our skin and the virus-fighting antibody's cells and white blood cells and the body's strange, complex immune system. Our bodies are in constant attack from these viruses and germs, and we put up a good fight until one germ may penetrate our system and create chaos, multiplying it and weakening our defense system, causing sickness to overtake and bring us down by making us weaker and weaker. We must understand the body's amazing immune system and how it operates in our defense; this fantastic biological army is more powerful and sophisticated than any army that man can put together. The body encountered these disease and viruses over the years, learned of their strategies and how to counter-attack and mobilize these viruses and maintained a memory of each infection, thus building resistance to each one. Our skin and mucous membranes are our first line of defense and protect us from these viruses penetrating our bodies if they do penetrate through cuts and bruises, the blood cells (neutrophils) are the secondary attack system that attacks the cells of the bacteria or germ. We also have a type of blood cell called Macrophages that patrol the body through the bloodstream and attack all unknown cells that do not belong in the body and eating them. As these cells fight against other virus cells, the T-Cells and B-cells define previously take up the big challenge to be the powerhouse cells in the immune system to back up and take over the fight against viruses that are stubborn and more powerful. These fighter cells:

The Helper cells

Cytotoxic T-Cells

Suppressor T-Cells produces the antibodies that are the destroyer of viruses. The body also creates B-Cells daily that comes from bone Marrow into the lymph nodes that fight against viruses and bacteria.

Mitochondrion: an arganelle found in large numbers in most cells, in which the biochemical processes and energy production occurs. They have a double membrane; the inner being folded inwards to form layers (cristate). Function: The most prominent roles of mitochondria are to produce the energy currency of the cell, ATP (i.e., phosphorylation of ADP), through respiration, and to regulate cellular metabolism. The central set of reactions involved in ATP production is collectively known as the citric acid cycle, or the Krebs cycle. The chemical reactions occur and the complex matrix where the fluid is stored. This cell main job is to perform cellular respiration, breaking down of nutrients and turn it into energy.

A brief definition of the complexity of the body and how it operates against sicknesses and illnesses, and as the Bible states "**I Corinthians 6:19: [19] Do you not know that your bodies are temples of the Holy Spirit, who is in you, whom you have received from God? You are not your own;**"

There is a smart brainiac inside the body that creates the skills and abilities to educate the body to maintain its purity and perfection by designing this army of cells to defend it. Therefore, there is a divine connection between our body and the divine (God), and he has also designed ways and means of defending and preparing our bodies for this defense. Back to the biblical passage of

Hosea 4:6 – My people are destroyed for the lack of knowledge". You must get the knowledge of your body's parts, essential organs, the body's function and maintaining our body's health and physical form. There are ways and means to tie it all into the spiritual connection and how the religious aspect of our mind and spirit controlled our consciousness and regulated all functionality of our body, mind, and spirit.

Many scriptures tell us to "Guard our Heart" Proverbs **4:23 "Above all else guard your heart, for it affects everything you do."**

Understand your heart, its functionality, how it works, what its purpose is and how to keep it healthy and protected.

Hosea 4:6.   *My people are destroyed for lack of knowledge: because thou hast rejected knowledge,*

And right above the heart is the Thymus gland that produces the T-Cells that protects the body. Thus God is continually warning us to **"Clean up our heart."**

Psalms 51:10   *Create in me a clean heart, O God; and renew a right spirit within me.*

Matthew 6: 21   *for where your treasure is, there your heart will be also.*

Proverbs 3: 5   *Trust in the LORD with all your heart and lean not on your own understanding;*

Proverbs 4: 23   *Above all else, guard your heart, for everything you do flows from it.*

Romans 12: 2   *Do not conform to the pattern of this world, but be transformed by the renewing of your mind. Then you will be able to test and approve what God's will is—his good, pleasing and perfect will.*

Matthew 5: 8   *Blessed are the pure in heart, for they will see God.*

10 BLUEPRINT OF A MAN

For a man to survive on planet earth, his physical body had to be from the components of the planet in precision, a precise percentage of each chemical component. If the percentage lapse or changes, the Physical man will be off balance and susceptible to physical changes affecting his equilibrium and full functionality of all organs.

https://en.wikipedia.org/wiki/Composition_of_the_human_body

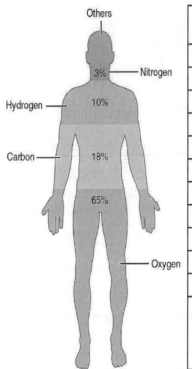

Element	Symbol	Percentage in Body
Oxygen	O	65.0
Carbon	C	18.5
Hydrogen	H	9.5
Nitrogen	N	3.2
Calcium	Ca	1.5
Phosphorus	P	1.0
Potassium	K	0.4
Sulfur	S	0.3
Sodium	Na	0.2
Chlorine	Cl	0.2
Magnesium	Mg	0.1
Trace elements include boron (B), chromium (Cr), cobalt (Co), copper (Cu), fluorine (F), iodine (I), iron (Fe), manganese (Mn), molybdenum (Mo), selenium (Se), silicon (Si), tin (Sn), vanadium (V), and zinc (Zn).		less than 1.0

DNA

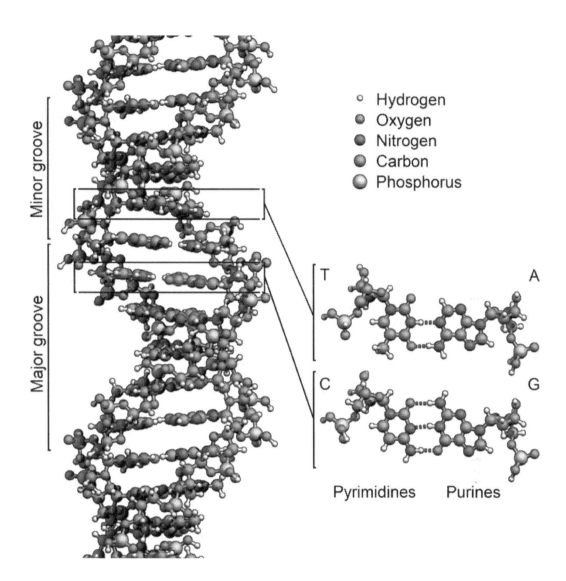

Https://en.wikipedia.org/wiki/DNA

Deoxyribonucleic acid (Listeni/diˈɒksiˌraɪboʊnjʊˌkliːɪk, -ˌkleɪɪk/; DNA) is a molecule that carries the genetic instructions used in the growth, development, functioning, and reproduction of all known living organisms and many viruses. DNA and RNA are nucleic acids; alongside proteins, lipids and complex carbohydrates (polysaccharides), they are one of the four major types of macromolecules that are essential for all known forms of life. Most DNA molecules consist of two biopolymer strands coiled around each other to form a double helix.

The two DNA strands are termed polynucleotide since they are composed of simpler monomer units called nucleotides. Each nucleotide comprises of one of four nitrogen-containing nucleobases—either cytosine (C), guanine (G), adenine (A), or thymine (T)—and sugar called deoxyribose and a phosphate group. The nucleotides are joined to one another in a chain by covalent bonds between the sugar of one nucleotide and the phosphate of the next, resulting in an alternating sugar-phosphate backbone — the nitrogenous bases of the two separate polynucleotide strand bound together (according to base pairing rules (A with T, and C with G) with hydrogen bonds to make double-stranded DNA. The total amount of related DNA base pairs on Earth is estimated at 5.0 x 1037 and weighs 50 billion tonnes. In comparison, the total mass of the biosphere has been determined to be as much as 4 trillion tons of carbon (TtC).

DNA stores biological information. The DNA backbone is resistant to cleavage, and both strands of the double-stranded structure store the same biological information. This information replicated as and when the two strands separate. A large part of DNA (more than 98% for humans) is non-coding, meaning that these sections do not serve as patterns for protein sequences.

The two strands of DNA run in opposite directions to each other and are thus antiparallel. Attached to each sugar is one of four types of nucleobases (informally, bases). It is the sequence of these four nucleobases along the backbone that encodes biological information. RNA strands are created using DNA strands as a template in a process called transcription. Under the genetic code, these RNA strands are translated to specify the sequence of amino acids within proteins in a process called translation.

Some additional relevant information about your body essential to your knowledge base and critical to your healthcare and to taking care of your physical health which has a chain reaction towards your mental health

11 LAMANIN

Laminin is a protein that is part of the extracellular matrix in humans and animals. The extracellular matrix (ECM) lies outside of cells and provides support and attachment for cells inside organs (along with many other functions). Laminin has "arms" that associate with other laminin molecules to form sheets and bind to cells; Meaning Laminin and other ECM proteins essentially "glue" the cells (such as those lining the stomach and intestines) to a foundation of connective tissue that holds all our cells together and our body tissues together. It has been described as the protein equivalent of glue, though it functions differently than actual chemical glue will. The cells in place and allows them to operate correctly. The structure of laminin is essential for its function (as is true for all proteins). One type of **congenital muscular dystrophy** results from defects in laminin.

Excerpts from the Internet: Wikipedia - https://cn.wikipedia.org/wiki/Laminin
Read carefully to gain knowledge of how they are connected and the importance of their matrix

(1) "The **laminins** are an important and biologically active part of the basal lamina, influencing cell differentiation, migration, and adhesion. ... They secrete and incorporated into cell-associated extracellular matrices. **Laminin** is vital for the maintenance and survival of tissues."

(2) "**LAMININ**: a **cell adhesion protein molecule** that holds the body together.'He is the image of the invisible God, the firstborn over all creation."

(3) "The **trimeric** proteins intersect to form a cross-like structure that can bind to other cell membrane and extracellular matrix **molecules.** The three shorter arms are particularly good at binding to other **laminin** molecules, which allow them to form sheets."

(4) In blood cells, as we have seen, **integrins** also serve as cell-cell adhesion molecules, helping the cells bind to other cells, as well as to the extracellular matrix.

(5) The long arm is capable of binding to cells, which helps anchor organized tissue cells to the membrane. The **laminin** family of glycoproteins is an integral part of the structural scaffolding in almost every tissue of an organism. They secrete and incorporated into cell-associated extracellular matrices.

(6) The **basal lamina** is a layer of extracellular matrix secreted by the epithelial cells, on which the epithelium sits. It is often incorrectly referred to as the basement membrane, though it does constitute a portion of the basement membrane.

(7) **Collagen IV** (CollV or Col4) is a type of **collagen** found primarily in the basal lamina. The **collagen IV** C4 domain at the C-terminus not removed in post-translational processing and the fibers link head-to-head, rather than in parallel.

(8) **Collagen fibrils** are semi-crystalline aggregates of **collagen** molecules. These are bundles of **fibrils**. Each of the tissues has a different arrangement of these **fibrils** to give it different structure, shape, and tensile strength

What holds cells together in the human body?
Each tissue is an organized assembly of **cells** held **together** by **cell-cell** in epithelial tissue; by contrast, **cells** are tightly bound **together** into sheets called epithelia. The extracellular matrix is scanty, consisting mainly of a thin mat called the basal lamina, which underlies the epithelium.
How important is laminin?

The long arm is capable of binding to cells, which helps anchor organized tissue cells to the membrane. Secreted and incorporated into cell-associated extracellular matrices. **Laminin** is vital for the maintenance and survival of tissues.

Forms a complex network and extracellular matrix, where the secretions of extracellular macromolecules build a support framework, holding cells together. The lack or loss of Lamanin within the body is closely related to some specific illnesses, tumor growth, muscular dystrophy, aggressive cancers, the breakdown of the nervous system, the rupture of the skin membranes. Krabbe (crab-ay) `Disease, also known as Globoid Cell Leukodystrophy, is a genetic disorder that affects the central and peripheral nervous systems results by a deficiency of an essential enzyme called Galactosylceramidase (GALC). Krabbe Disease also is related to Lysosomal Storage Disorder (LSD) and the progressive disorder that affects the white matter in the brain.

The long passages of medical definition and lingo are to give you an idea of the essentials of the body that affects on a daily bases and may lead to the long list of sicknesses and diseases that may change us that sometimes doctors and medical experts find it hard to diagnose when someone gets sick. It is a chain reaction within the body as we lose essentials. The body tries to fight and build up an active immunity to the specific disease and gets trapped by the multiplicity of infection that develops and becomes an army to fight against our immune system. Most of the time the Anti-bodies sustaining the immune systems gets defeated, and we begin to dive deeper and deeper into various ailment beyond recovery.

Role in peripheral nerve repair: Laminin enriched at the lesion site after peripheral nerve injury secreted by Schwann cells. Neurons of the peripheral nervous system express integrin receptors that attach to laminins and promote neurodegenerations after injury.

Dysfunctional structure of one particular laminin, laminin-211, is the cause of one form of congenital muscular dystrophy *(Congenital muscular dystrophies are autosomal recessively-inherited muscle diseases. They are a group of heterogeneous disorders characterized by muscle weakness which is present at birth and the different changes on muscle biopsy that ranges from myopathic to overtly dystrophic due to the age at which the biopsy takes place.)*

Lamanin in cancer pathophysiology can create or destroy cancer cells based on the direction, strength or weakness of the physical body and the cells itself, but if we can command these cells to work positively for our health, then "yes" why not gives it a try. Laminin: Evidence of Divine Creation the cross-like shape of the laminin molecule is evidence of God's hand in the creation of the human form.

Thus, we come to the definition of this intricate design and architecture of the body, and its creation that cannot be recreated by any human (I may be in a state of "stand corrected" with the cloning technology). The cell itself is shaped like a T or a Cross and has the same effect within the body as the molecules and elements that hold the world and the universe together. The body itself built like the Universe and functions as the universe. Sending most of you into research and new read on the purpose and operations of the Universe.

https://answersingenesis.org/biology/microbiology/laminin-and-the-cross/

How Has Laminin become an Icon of Christianity? This vague resemblance to a cross is the reason for the surge of interest in laminin in some Christian circles.

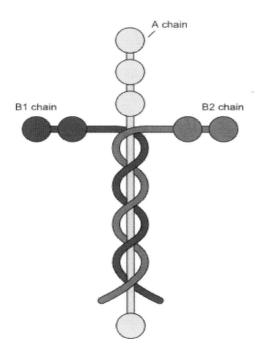

Sticking in these scriptures as a read that will be referenced later as per the connection between the perfect creation of the Body of humanity and the contamination that cause it to break down and lose its purity, strength, and resistance to the elements of the world

> *Colossians 1:15–17, which, speaking of Christ, says, "In Him, all things hold together."*
> *This is about the equivalence of Jesus Christ and God, being the same in spirit and flesh*
> *since God came down to earth in the flesh, Jesus body was the vessel that hosted the*
> *spirit of God from the Womb through his years on earth*

Jesus is the image of the invisible God, and through him, all things were created, visible and invisible, in heaven and on earth. In relating this to physics, applied to the structure of the smallest atom, with a nucleus held together by the forces of Nature and the Universe is held together by the very same forces of nature, biblically created by God or is GOD.

Hinduism

Hindus believe that there is one true God, the supreme spirit,
*called **Brahman**. **Brahman** has many forms, pervades the whole universe, and*
symbolized by the sacred syllable Om (or Aum). Most Hindus believe
*that **Brahman** is present in every person as the eternal spirit or soul, called the*
Atman."

***Brahma** is the Hindu god (deva) of creation and one of the Trimurti, the others*
*being **Vishnu** and **Shiva**. He is not to be confused with the Supreme Cosmic Spirit*
in Hindu Vedanta philosophy known as Brahman.

The collective Hindu scriptures are the Vedas and documented in the ancient Sanskrit,
which is still undeciphered, the "Vedas" means "Knowledge" consists of 4 Vedic
Collections called "Samithitas": Rig Veda, Yajur Veda, Sama Veda, and The Atharva
Veda.
These texts were initially passed down by Brahmin priests who sang the entire millions of
Verses to students, which put into writings in the original Sanskrit language. Sanskrit
Supposedly is a language that only the Priests spoke and understood and was
Interpreted as the language God chose to communicate with his priests, a Language not
Commonly understood by any other person or persons. The similarities between them

Sanskrit and the Ancient Hebrew (possible Ancient Aramaic) are remarkably close and
Like the Psalms carries much of the very similar stories, including the breakdown of
tribes
And their roles versus the Caste systems were identical. All the Scriptures delivered
Through revelation, and the Vedas are without beginning and end provided through
Vedic vibrations [(sound) reverberates and Echoes of vibrations and tones through sine
Waves and the air to create] in the form of Amkara directly to and through living beings.
According to Hindu scriptures, the entire Vedas are already within the Human Psyche
And mind, same should be for the Word of God in Judaism and Christianity, through
The breath of life the entire knowledge was transferred and needs to be tapped into or
Discovered by every individual through various forms, prayer, and meditation,
Teaching and preaching, Dreams and visions and from messengers of God (angels and
Prophets) for no man – no man has the ability to deliver through his ability except
through God.

By God's power, believers are sanctified, made holy. Meaning we are set apart from sin **enabled** to obey and to become more like Christ. When we are growing in our relationship with
Christ, the Holy Spirit frees us from the demands of the Law and fear of judgment.
Because we are free from sin's control, the Law's demands, and fear of God's punishment,
We can grow in our relationship with Christ. By trusting in the Holy Spirit and allowing him to
help us; we can overcome sin and temptation.

God oversees and cares about his people, past, present, and future. God's ways of dealing with people are always and entirely in charge of all creation; he can save whoever is within his will. Because of God's mercy, both Jews and Gentiles are saved through his mercy, grace, acceptance, and forgiveness. Because he is sovereign, let him rein in your heart.

When our purpose is to give credit to God for his love, power, and perfection in all we do, we can serve him properly. Helping him unifies all believers and enables them to show love and sensibility to others. None of us can be entirely Christ-like by ourselves; it takes the entire body of Christ to express Christ fully. Christians can be a symphony of service to God by actively and vigorously building up others believers.

Romans 1: 18   For the wrath of God is revealed from heaven against all ungodliness and
unrighteousness of men, who hold the truth in unrighteousness;
19   Because that which may be known of God is manifest in them; for God hath
shewed it unto them.
20   For the invisible things of him from the creation of the world are clearly seen,

being understood by the things that are made, even his eternal power and Godhead; so that they are without excuse:

21 *Because that, when they knew God, they glorified him not as God, neither were thankful; but became vain in their imaginations, and their foolish heart was darkened.*

22 *Professing themselves to be wise, they became fools,*

23 *And changed the glory of the incorruptible God into an image made like to corruptible man, and to birds, and four-footed beasts, and creeping things.*

24 *Wherefore God also gave them up to uncleanness through the lusts of their own hearts, to dishonor their own bodies between themselves:*

25 *Who changed the truth of God into a lie, and worshipped and served the creature more than the Creator, who is blessed forever. Amen.*

26 *For this cause God gave them up unto vile affections: for even their women did change the natural use into that which is against nature:*

27 *And likewise also the men, leaving the natural use of the woman, burned in their lust one toward another; men with men working that which is unseemly, and receiving in themselves that recompense of their error which was meet.*

28 *And even as they did not like to retain God in their knowledge, God gave them over to a reprobate mind, to do those things which are not convenient;*

29 *Being filled with all unrighteousness, fornication, wickedness, covetousness, maliciousness; full of envy, murder, debate, deceit, malignity; whisperers,*

30 *Backbiters, haters of God, despiteful, proud, boasters, inventors of evil things, disobedient to parents*

31 *without understanding, covenant breakers, without natural affection, implacable, unmerciful:*

32 *Who knowing the judgment of God, that they which commit such things are worthy of death, not only do the same but have pleasure in them that do them.*

12 THYMUS GLANDS

The **thymus** gland, containing glandular tissue and producing several hormones, is much more closely associated with the immune system than with the endocrine system. The **thymus** serves a vital role in the training and development of T-lymphocytes or T cells, a fundamental type of white blood cell.

What is the role of the thymus in the body?
The **thymus gland** plays a vital **role** in the development of a regular, healthy immune system. The **function of the thymus gland** is to generate mature T lymphocytes (white blood cells that help the immune system fight off illness).

> **Cytotoxic T cells** - directly terminate antigens.
> **Helper T cells** - precipitate the production of antibodies by B-cells and also produce substances that activate other T-cells.
> **Regulatory T cells** - also called suppressor T cells, these cells suppress the response of B-cells and other T-cells to antigens.

The thymus gland regulates the immune system by developing anti-bodies immunity cells influences and protects many bodily organs such as the kidneys, spleen, reproductive system, nervous system, circulatory system, cardiovascular organs (heart, blood vessels), lymphatic organs, digestive systems, endocrine systems, muscular systems, respiratory systems and even the bone structures. An essential component of the immune system, which as we grow older starts to diminish in size and functions resulting in the body break down and losing its guard against disease. The thymus is supposedly the key to aging and the gradual loss of the cells ability to protect itself and repair any damages to our DNA which is the foundation and structure of our self and inheritance for our parents. The primary function of the thymus gland is to release thymosin hormone that will stimulate the maturation of T cells (Thymosin stimulates the development of T cells, in childhood years. At the age of 50, despite its importance to the immune defenses, only about 15 percent of the thymus remains) which migrates into the Lymph nodes, which are storage for immune cells, are prepared ready transforming them into T-Cells, transported to the medulla prepared to attack any foreign antigens or Pathogens or bacteria. Therefore, it is essential to pay attention to the Childhood years and your children's health so that they can develop these hormones for future long-term health care and longevity. The immune system has many vital functions. One of its components generates the antibodies and other protectors that defend against infections

Can we communicate with these Cells? Can we use the Holy Spirit, Our Mind to command this part of the body to function more efficiently to produce of introducing means and methods of protecting our body? It' time to research and read more about these organs, for we only have one body and one life and one of each of these glands, another part of the body careful attention is needed such as the reason the scripture

Proverbs 4:   *22 for they are life unto those that find them, and health to all their flesh.*

23 Keep thy heart with all diligence; for out of it are the issues of life.

13 PINEAL GLANDS

The **pineal gland** (also called the **pineal** body, epiphysis cerebri, epiphysis or the "third eye," or conarium) is a small endocrine **gland**. It produces melatonin, a hormone that affects the modulation of wake/sleep patterns and photoperiodic (seasonal) functions. Melatonin hormone is responsible for sleep /wake patterns (circadian rhythms). The pineal gland activated by darkness and inhibited by Light is also known as "the Mind's Eye" or Inner eye, giving us the hindsight, hunch, psychic ability, abilities to discern, foresight and hindsight. Considered in the ancient religions as the gateway to heaven, the third biological eye or "The Seat of the Soul," "The Epicenter of enlightenment."

Matthew 6:22   *the light of the body is the eye: if therefore thine eye be single, thy whole body shall be full of light.*
But be careful of the second verse Matthew 6:22 But if thine eye is evil, thy whole body shall be full of darkness. If therefore the light that is in thee be darkness, how great is that darkness!

The shape of the Pineal Gland is a small cone shape, which influences historical uses of the pinecone to symbolize human consciousness and pathways to enlightenment. The pinecone was used throughout history by Egyptians, Indians, Greeks, Romans, Asian Subcontinent, Catholics, Freemasons, and listed in almost all ancient scripture. The Hindu God of Shiva depicted with a Physical Third eye, and the Pine Cone symbol exists virtually everywhere in every religious building and site.
The Egyptian Staff of Osiris, Statue of Mexican God "Chicomecoati"
The Roman and Greek Dionysus carrying "thyrsus' staff woven with leaves and topped with a pinecone.
The Roman 'Pigna,' The temple of Isis, The Pope Staff, Assyrian Palace carvings and paintings, The Ruins of Angkor Wat, The Buddha Crown, The Pinecone symbol is in every ancient Temple, In the Vatican Museum and even on the US One Dollar bill.

The Eye is the Lamp of the Body, The seat of the Human Soul, The connection between the physical world and the spiritual world

What is the function of the pineal gland in the endocrine system?
The **pineal gland** is a small, pea-shaped **gland** in the brain. Its **function** isn't fully understood. Researchers do know that it produces and regulates some hormones, including melatonin. Melatonin is best known for the **role** it plays in regulating sleep patterns. Sleep patterns are also called circadian rhythms.

What is a pineal gland and what does it do?

Of the endocrine organs, the function of the **pineal gland** was the last discovered. The Pineal gland is located deep in the center of the brain, was once known as "The Third Eye." The Pineal Gland produces melatonin, which helps maintain circadian rhythm and **regulate** reproductive hormones.

What is the location of the pineal gland?

The **pineal gland**, also known as the "**pineal** body," is a small endocrine **gland**. Located on the back portion of the third cerebral ventricle of the brain, which is a fluid-filled space in the brain. This **gland** lies in-between the two halves of the brain.

What is your third eye?

In certain dharma spiritual traditions such as Hinduism, the **third eye** refers to the ajna, or brow, chakra. The **third eye** sees to the gate that leads to inner realms and spaces of higher consciousness.

The pineal gland develops from the roof of the diencephalon, a section of the brain, and located behind the third cerebral ventricle in the brain midline (between the two cerebral hemispheres). Its name derived from its shape, which is similar to that of a pinecone (Latin pinea). In adult humans, it is about 0.8 cm (0.3 inches) long and weighs approximately 0.1 gram (0.004 ounces).

The ancient religion is aware of the links between the physical and spiritual world, the pineal gland a tiny gland in the center of the brain is the source of this connection and is also the source of the internal Para-phenomenal supernatural powers within any human being that radiates that power. This gland that gives someone the physic abilities and talents and also associated with divine connectivity. In Hinduism it is said to be the Third –eye and was visible on the God Shiva, most of the drawings and paintings of Shiva displays his third eye. According to ancient doctrines, the pineal gland possesses the ability to empower a person to experience and see visions beyond the norms and see beyond space and time and linked to the Chakras

The pineal gland is a small pine shaped gland displayed as the "All Seeing Eye" on the US Dollar bill and in many historical and religious sites, symbolic and a representation of its existence and in the belief system of many religious organizations

The pineal gland (also called the pineal body, epiphysis cerebri, epiphysis or the "third eye") is a small endocrine gland. It produces melatonin, a hormone that affects the modulation of wake/sleep patterns and photoperiodic (seasonal) functions. Located near to the center of the brain between the two hemispheres, tucked in a groove where the two rounded thalamic bodies join. Unlike much of the rest of the brain, the pineal gland is not isolated from the body by the blood-brain barrier system. It is reddish-gray and about the size of a pea (8 mm in humans).

https://en.wikipedia.org/wiki/Pineal_gland#/media/File:Gray715.png

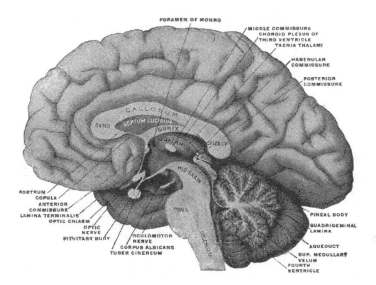

The pineal gland, also known as the conarium or epiphysis cerebri, is a small endocrine gland in the vertebrate brain. The pineal gland produces melatonin, a derived serotonin hormone which modulates sleep patterns in both circadian and seasonal cycles. The shape of the kidney resembles a pine cone, hence its name. The pineal gland located in the epithalamus, near the center of the brain, between the two hemispheres, tucked in a groove where the two halves of the thalamus join.

Nearly all vertebrate species possess a pineal gland. The most important exception is the hagfish, which often thought of as the most primitive extant vertebrate. Even in the hagfish, however, there may be a "pineal equivalent" structure in the dorsal diencephalon. The lancelet Branchiostoma lanceolatum, the nearest existing relative to vertebrates, also lacks a recognizable pineal gland. The lamprey (considered almost as primitive as the hagfish), however, does possess one. A few more developed vertebrates lost pineal glands throughout their evolution.

The results of various scientific research in evolutionary biology, comparative neuroanatomy, and neurophysiology, have explained the phylogeny of the pineal gland in different vertebrate species. From biological evolution, the pineal gland represents a kind of atrophied photoreceptor. In the epithalamus of some species of amphibians and reptiles, linked to a light-sensing organ, known as the parietal eye, which is also called the pineal eye or third eye.

René Descartes believed the pineal gland to be the "principal seat of the soul." Academic philosophy among his contemporaries considered the pineal gland as a neuro-anatomical structure without unique metaphysical qualities; science studied it as one endocrine gland among many. However, the pineal gland continues to have an elevated status in the realm of pseudoscience.

Structure: The pineal gland is a midline brain structure that is unpaired. It takes its name from its pine-cone shape. The pineal gland is reddish-gray and about the size of a grain of rice (5–8 mm) in humans. The pineal gland, also called the pineal body, is part of the epithalamus and lies between the laterally positioned thalamic bodies and behind the habenular commissure. It is located in the quadrigeminal cistern near to the corpora quadrigemina. It is also located behind the third ventricle and bathed in cerebrospinal fluid supplied through a small pineal recess of the third ventricle which projects into the stalk of the gland.

Blood supply: Unlike most of the mammalian brain, the pineal gland is not isolated from the body by the blood-brain barrier system; it has profuse blood flow, second only to the kidney, supplied from the choroidal branches of the posterior cerebral artery.

Nerve supply: The pineal gland receives sympathetic innervations from the superior cervical ganglion. Parasympathetic innervations from the pterygopalatine and otic ganglia are also present. Further, some nerve fibers penetrate the pineal gland via the pineal stalk (central innervations). Furthermore, neurons in the trigeminal ganglion innervate the gland with nerve fibers containing the neuropeptide PACAP.

It's about the Eye, Zero Point, focusing your consciousness and trusting what you see. You do it all the time and may not beware of the difference between your thoughts and those from higher frequency. The third eye has a lens that opens to see behind physical reality, so you might want to relate to that theory. The third eye opens it can feel like pressure at the base of the brain. We all want to be more psychic and increase the connection with the other side as our Consciousness Hologram closes and souls return to the light. We want to empower and most of all to understand beyond the physical. Meditation, Visualization, Yoga, and all forms of Out of Body Experiences help.

Do not be fooled by all the various discussion of paganism and the third eye/pineal Gland discussion of occultism. This is a part of your physical body and intertwined into the brain and works closely with the mind. This is one gland that you need to pay attention to in your spiritual walk and spiritual enhancement for spiritual enlightenment. Why would anyone not want you to be aware of a gland in your body that is so important to your spiritual development?

In this age and time where we are suffering from brain changes, causing more brain trauma such as Alzheimer's disease, Parkinson's disease, Dementia, Mental Disorder, Brain Tumor, Neurological Disease, Encephalopathy, Neurodegeneration, Multiple Sclerosis, Epileptic seizure, Epilepsy, Amyotrophic Lateral Sclerosis –ALS or Lou Gehrig's disease and a rise in multiple brain-related illness, even though through faith and belief we lean on to God, It states that God will also need your help to help you. You cannot sit down and do nothing and expect God to be the sole provider of health. You need to work in every direction, find the necessary knowledge and understand whatever possible cure there is to get you out of the dilemma, for it is your life and you only have one. There is an abundance of information on the pineal gland and the ability to achieve enhanced pineal Gland functionality. The possibility of getting the help necessary through methods of activating the Pineal Gland, the God particle, the T-Cell and mental, spiritual warfare against this disease could be a win and successfully overcome and conquer many sicknesses, illnesses, and terminal diseases. Change your mind and change the way you think and it will change your life. Spend the time to understand you, your life and what it would take to secure a healthy life.

14 PSYCHO-SPIRITUAL

Psycho-Spiritual is an integrated approach taking into account body, mind, emotions and **spirit**. **Psycho-Spiritual** Healing is an approach that works "outside the box" of set procedures. Adding Psychologically to things spiritual and spiritual beliefs. It is the area where some religions discard as mystical and condemn as occult, but most of the writings are by men who used their interpretations of doctrines to streamline the belief system of others and discard the powers and abilities that are inborn and given by God.

The discipline attempts to describe and integrate **spiritual** experience within the modern **psychological theory** and to formulate a new **method** to encompass such expertise. Transpersonal **psychology** has made several contributions to the academic field, and the studies of human development, consciousness, and **spirituality**.

Mind and Body were considered to be two different entities, but there is an interconnection between the mind and body which has a significant effect on our well being as well as our not-so-well-being. It plays a very significant role in health, healing, and longevity. Spirituality is within the range of our belief system and not associated with 'religiosity' which is man's display of false spirituality, showing how religious a person is when displaying a physical demeanor of spirituality. It can be seen in the Church, Mosque, temples, and synagogues, where many pretend religiosity but do not fully understand divine spirituality and the actual connection to divinity or God.

Psycho Spirituality is the merging of the body, mind, and spirit to create the new man, changing the mind frames of the old man and altering the states of consciousness into the new man. This science is used extensively in Eastern religion and is utilized unwarily in modern religions, including Islam and Christianity. Inner transformation is one of the first steps in the spiritual journey as we reach out to live our lives to the full potential which we are not at this time and era. We are becoming dependent to unknown rather than our very own God-given spirit that connects us to the spirit of God, which is the path to enlightenment and true spirituality. We have been born with a pure spirit and taught that we are born in sin and born contaminated, but we are born pure, and as we grow we encounter all form of positive and negative influences and experience that shifts our thinking. Affects our mind to a negative mental state, resulting in a more corrupt spiritual state further affects our physical state. Religions teach us to get into a state preparedness for a mind change, which trickles into our mental state and enhances our physical state. Man is three dimensional – body, mind, and spirit and for the Human being to be in perfect harmony with the universe and its energy. Man must be able to bring his body, mind, and spirit into subjection and balance with each other, thus becoming a single unit that can be in tune with nature, the physical world and the spiritual world and further delve into more enlightenment towards a spiritual dimension and divine nature. The big debate between religions and the religious variances between multiple belief systems. The Great War to conquer the ego and self and the physical, the mental and spiritual person of man to bring into unison with each other and become ONE – A new MAN, A divine Man, an enlightened man, or a God-man (being connected to God)

Not being able to streamline the three dimensions of man, causes a tearing away or pulling apart or creating conflict within the various entity of man resulting in negative forces pulling apart or pushing apart. Meditation, for example, is a good thing for being able to achieve that goal of Oneness of One-self, but it can also cause a more significant negative influence where the forces and energies from outside can enter the Body causes a fluctuation of energy levels and changes within the physical, mental, electrical, electromagnetic and static energy flow of the body. It can also have a devastating effect, leading to a lost mind, and physical injury and sicknesses that may not be from this dimension and the diagnosis will be incorrect, such becomes a forgotten man, a lost soul, a lost person, where your mind and spirit lives in a different dimension, and the body lives in another.

Many ancient teachings and doctrines – Considered mystical teachings by others – are the root and soul of the spiritual quest related to Psycho spiritual enlightenment – Moksha, Nirvana, spiritual enlightenment, the many names and words used to try and establish a name for the technique, commonly called 'interfaith' Spirituality.

You now have a clear understanding of the components and makeup of man, next is the pathways of the interconnect and how they are meant to perform to the abilities are given by the Divine Supreme being, become like him and to be what he had created us to be, to grow and to live according to commandments, laws, and doctrines provided for man's benefit.

Bear in mind that men also manipulated the doctrines and had taken God's divine teachings and word and twisted it for their very own benefits for higher power, their prosperity and to subdue other to become followers be put under submission for political power. Even unto today there are preachers and teachers who twist the word of God, whether it is deliberate or due to their misunderstanding and misinterpretations of the Scripture or even for personal power, it could also be because they strayed away from God's word by the Whisperer, the Serpent, the Devil, the negative forces of evil. The world is full of preachers who feast on the impoverish and build their empire and kingdom with mansions, planes, billions of dollars and holds under subjection hundreds, thousands and even millions of followers through legalism and even subliminal trances, hypnotism and other authoritarian methodologies to keep followers under their subjection. Twisting the word of God and injecting into their sub-conscious mind to bring all their wealth and possessions to the Church and giving it to God.

There are new consciousness studies that document the positive effect of psycho-spiritual healings, it related to being more than the normal, by utilizing more than the five senses and diving deeper into the body, mind, spirit therapy, where healing takes place in a deeper dimension of the human being than just physical. It takes place in the mind and soul level in believing and telling your body to heal and telling the cells to fight and be healthy rather than abnormal. We know that fear and worry causes stress which put pressure on the human mind and transferred to the human body. Therefore it will be a venture to be able to communicate to your very own mind and your very own subconscious mind to robotically adjust all your organs to function efficiently and produce all fluid and immunity necessary to heal yourself. Fear is one of the most dangerous and negative emotion to the human being, and every religious doctrine speaks out against it. Therefore renewing your mind to be strong and healthy is not confirming to worldly facets, but is in conformation to God's message to us in the multiple ways and there is plenty of healing in the Bible to support the definitions.

> *Romans 12:2 And be not conformed to this world: but be ye transformed by the renewing of your mind, that ye may prove what is that good, and acceptable, and perfect, will of God.*

> *Joshua 1: 9 Have not I commanded thee? Be strong and of good courage; be not afraid, neither be thou dismayed: for the Lord thy God is with thee whithersoever thou goest.*

> *Deuteronomy 31: 6 Be strong and of good courage, fear not, nor be afraid of them: for the LORD thy God, he is that doth go with thee; he will not fail thee, nor forsake thee."*

The battle is very much in mind, yet we have to be cautious that we are not taking away the glory of God for it is God that gives us a sound mind

> 2 Timothy 1:7: *For God hath not given us the spirit of fear; but of power, and of love, and of a sound mind.*
> 2 Corinthian 10: 2 *But I beseech you, that I may not be bold when I am present with that confidence, wherewith I think to be bold against some, which think of us as if we walked according to the flesh.*
> 2 Corinthian 10: 3 *For though we walk in the flesh, we do not war after the flesh:*
> 2 Corinthian 10: 4 *(For the weapons of our warfare are not carnal, but mighty through God to the pulling down of strong holds;)*
> 2 Corinthian 10: 5 *Casting down imaginations, and every high thing that exalteth itself a*

against the knowledge of God, and bringing into captivity every thought to the obedience of Christ;

2 Corinthian 10: 6   And having in a readiness to revenge all disobedience, when your obedience is fulfilled.

2 Corinthian 10: 7 Do ye look on things after the outward appearance? If any man trust to himself that he is Christ's, let him of himself think this again, that, as he is Christ's, even so, are we Christ's.

Ephesians 6:12 "For we do not wrestle against flesh and blood, but against the rulers, against the authorities, against the cosmic powers over this present darkness, against the spiritual forces of evil in the heavenly places.

Matthew 21:21-22:   Jesus answered and said unto them, Verily I say unto you, If ye have faith, and doubt not, ye shall not only do this which is done to the fig tree, but also if ye shall say unto this mountain, Be thou removed, and be thou cast into the sea; it shall be done. And all things, whatsoever ye shall ask in prayer, believing, ye shall receive. Jesus gave us the power to do as he has done – heal the sick

3 John 2:   Beloved, I wish above all things that thou mayest prosper and be in health, even as thy soul prospereth.

Proverbs 4:20-22 -   My child, pay attention to what I say. Listen carefully to my words. Don't lose sight of them. Let them penetrate deep into your heart, for they bring life to those who find them, and healing to their whole body.

Isaiah 58:8:   "Then your light will break forth like the dawn, and your healing will quickly appear; then your righteousness will go before you, and the glory of the LORD will be your rear guard."

2 Timothy 3:16-17   All Scripture is breathed out by God and profitable for teaching, for reproof, for correction, and for training in righteousness, that the man of God may be competent, equipped for every good work.

Proverbs 11:14 Where there is no guidance, a people falls, but in an abundance of counselors there is safety.

15 THE FALL OF SATAN

The fall of Man

Begins with the fall of Lucifer

The fall of humanity has been the highest goal of Satan to regain his kingdom (Earth), where he fell after being thrown out of heaven. To begin, we must understand the creation of man and the purpose for the creation of man.

Lucifer (Hebrew: Helel – " Morning Star," "Bright Star") was a heavenly being the top ranking Angel, according to Ezekiel, Lucifer was " an Anointed Cherub," the seal of perfection, the highest creature that God had created. Full of wisdom (The wisest creation of God), perfect in beauty, beautiful beyond description, highest of being, Cover the Mercy Seat, given free will thus his thoughts and iniquity found in him *(Isaiah 14: 12-14 "I will ascend to heaven; I will raise my throne above the stars of God; I will sit on the mount of assembly on the heights of Zaphon; I will ascend to the tops of the clouds, I will make myself like the Most High.")*

Revelation 12:9, which reads, "The great dragon was hurled down—that ancient serpent called the devil, or Satan, who leads the whole world astray. He was hurled to the earth, and his angels with him."

Lucifer, just another name for Satan, leader of evil, is the real, though invisible, the power behind the successive rulers of Tyre, Babylon, Persia, Greece, Rome, and all many evil rulers in nations of the world. Satan is the principality behind the powers of this corrupt world system, the very fall of Satan in the pristine, sinless spheres before the creation of man.

John 12:31 declares Lucifer to be the ruler or "god" of this world,
2 Peter 2:4, "For if God did not spare angels when they sinned, but cast them into hell and committed them to chains of gloomy darkness to be kept until the judgment...");

https://en.wikipedia.org/wiki/Satan

Satan is a malevolent figure in the Abrahamic religions, who seeks to seduce humans into falsehood and sin. In Christianity and Islam, he is usually seen as a fallen angel, or a jinn, who used to possess great piety and beauty but rebelled against God out of hubris. God allows Satan temporary power over the fallen world and grants him a host of demons.

A figure is known as "the Satan" first appears in the Tanakh as a heavenly prosecutor, a member of the sons of God subordinate to Yahweh, who prosecutes the nation of Judah in the heavenly court and tests the loyalty of Yahweh's followers by forcing them to suffer. During the intertestamental period, possibly due to influence from the Zoroastrian figure of Angra Mainyu, the Satan developed into a malevolent entity with abhorrent qualities in dualistic opposition to God. In the apocryphal Book of Jubilees, Yahweh grants the Satan (referred to as Mastema) authority over a group of fallen angels to tempt humans to sin and punish them.

The Book of Revelation describes a war in heaven between angels led by the Archangel Michael against those influenced by "the dragon"—identified as "the devil or Satan"—who were defeated and thrown down to the **_earth_**.

Isaiah 14:

12   *How art thou fallen from heaven, O Lucifer, son of the morning! how art thou cut down to the ground, which didst weaken the nations!*

13   *For thou hast said in thine heart, I will ascend into heaven; I will exalt my throne above the stars of God: I will sit also upon the mount of the congregation, in the sides of the north:*

14   *I will ascend above the heights of the clouds; I will be like the most High.*

15   *Yet thou shalt be brought down to hell, to the sides of the pit.*

16   *They that see thee shall narrowly look upon thee, and consider thee, saying, Is this the man that made the earth to tremble, that did shake kingdoms;*

17   *That made the world as a wilderness, and destroyed the cities thereof; that opened not the house of his prisoners?*

18   *All the kings of the nations, even all of them, lie in glory, everyone in his own house.*

19   *But thou art cast out of thy grave like an abominable branch, and as the raiment of those that are slain, thrust through with a sword, that go down to the stones of the pit; as a carcass trodden under feet.*

2 Corinthians 10:3-5.   "For though we live in the world, we do not wage war as the world does. The weapons we fight with are not the weapons of the world. On the contrary, they have divine power to demolish strongholds. We demolish arguments and every pretension that sets itself up against the knowledge of

God, and we take captive every thought to make it obedient to Christ."

Isaiah 14:12   *"How you have fallen from heaven, morning star, son of the dawn! You have been cast down to the earth, you who once laid low the nations! You said in your heart, 'I will ascend to the heavens; I will raise my throne above the stars of God; I will sit enthroned on the mount of assembly, on the utmost heights of Mount Zaphon. I will ascend above the tops of the clouds; I will make myself like the Most High.' But you are brought down to the realm of the dead, to the depths of the pit. Those who see you stare at you, they ponder your fate: 'Is this the man who shook the earth and made kingdoms tremble, the man who made the world a wilderness, who overthrew its cities and would not let his captives go home?'"*

The Earth was under the feet of God for God made the earth his footstool

Isaiah 66:1 1   Thus saith the LORD, The heaven is my throne, and the earth is my footstool: where is the house that ye build unto me? And where is the place of my rest?

God gave dominion of the Earth to Adam with all power and authority over all living creatures, problem is God did not give Adam authority and control of all spiritual being, but God did ask them to bow down to MAN for he, created in the Image of God (which gives man the qualities, characteristics, and attributes of GOD)

Eve did not understand the Goal of Satan neither was she in any way full of a spirit of discernment to be able to see within the underlying motives, actions and words of Satan as such she was fooled (Beguiled) as it is written that the Devil would deceive the world. Here is the first Human being that the Devil has applied his cunning, devious and figurative language to bring Eve the illusion of the effect of the spoken word. Satan used God's words and changed the context by adding a simple "not" in between the lines, and includes "Surely" to reaffirm that he is telling the truth in a similar manner Jesus used "Verily" in the New Testament.

"Did God say you WILL die, or did he say you will NOT die"? To ordinary Human Being it is an offset to put them in a state of recollection and if the memory does not serve well, can be confused and convinced that whatever this Heavenly being is saying now may be true, for the words used to describe Satan at that present was "serpent" which could be a figurative language for the forked tongue, or the characteristics defined. Satan could have presented himself in any form, he would have chosen a better-looking form, more handsome, more physically good looking than Adam, which could also be an influence over Eve's visual image for Satan made the Apple look Good as well, Even knowing that it was not GOOD to eat was "beguiled" by illusion that it looks good.

His first method of approach was to question the word of God and the knowledge of Eve if she was acclimated with the word of God. This defines that we should have the greatest quest to know, understand and memorize God's word and embed it into our hearts and mind so as not to be deceived or fooled. Similarly, Satan is using all the methods that exist in the world today to fool everyone and getting them to doubt the word and authority of God, from social media, movies, films, TV, Social Clubs, various secular organizations, Psychology, books, educational institution, Governments and Earthly laws, occult and paganism. A human being do not have the knowledge and spirit within to be able to discern, gets bombarded with all of the various methods of information fed into the ears, sight, and minds on a daily bases causes subliminal confusion, and the mind starts to wonder what is really the truth, could it be this or could it be that. Therefore, it is always good to know the word of God and allow the Holy Spirit to be the great counselor and guide towards the understanding of God's word.

Eve was approached in a threefold manner to make it more convincing. First, through LUST of the eyes, Lust of the flesh and also EGO and PRIDE for this was a warning from Jesus in the New Testament as referred to in *1 John 2:16 For all that is in the world, the lust of the flesh, and the lust of the eyes, and the pride of life, is not of the Father, but is of the world.* Eve wondered if their eyes would open and they will become like God and make them wise.

Therefore, going back into the discussion if the fall of humanity, here are the three areas where we are the weakest. The flesh will always be the toughest to control for it is still in want of whatever feels right and whatever makes it more comfortable and being influenced by the Lust of the Eyes as we see everything that looks good may be good for the body as well.

Our Ego and pride do not come from GOD; this is related to the first Sin created in heaven. Lucifer was the fairest, most handsome, and most decorated archangel, He was the leader of the choir, and a great musician as such had great pride in himself and very egoistic due to these characteristics. The carnal ego of man that appeared in the form of the Serpent and has been either injected into a man since the beginning of time or at the fall

> *Luke 10:18 and he said unto them, I beheld the EGO of Mankind as lightning fall from heaven. This is related to the creator of Ego – The Devil, Satan or Lucifer.*

Pride: High *or inordinate opinion of one's dignity, importance, merit,*
or superiority, whether as cherished in mind or as displayed in bearing, conduct, etc.,
a becoming or dignified sense of what is due to oneself or one position or character; self-respect; self-esteem.

Proverbs 16:18-*19 Pride goes before destruction and a haughty spirit before a fall. It is better to be of a lowly spirit with the poor than to divide the spoil with the proud.*

James 1:14   *but every man is tempted, when he is drawn away of his own lust, and enticed.*

Satan used this same method in the temptation of the Jews and Jesus in

Matthew 4 1- 10

1   *Then was Jesus led up of the spirit into the wilderness to be tempted of the devil.*

2   *And when he had fasted forty days and forty nights, he was afterward a hungered.*

3   *And when the tempter came to him, he said, if thou be the Son of God, command that these stones be made bread.*

4   *But he answered and said, it is written, Man shall not live by bread alone, but by every word that proceedeth out of the mouth of God.*

5.   *Then the devil taketh him up into the holy city, and setteth him on a pinnacle of the temple,*

6   *And saith unto him, If thou be the Son of God, cast thyself down: for it is written, He shall give his angels charge concerning thee: and in their hands, they shall bear thee up, lest at any time thou dash thy foot against a stone.*

7.   *Jesus said unto him, it is written again, Thou shalt not tempt the Lord thy God.*

8.   *Again, the devil taketh him up into an exceeding high mountain, and sheweth him all the kingdoms of the world, and the glory of them;*

9.   *And saith unto him, all these things will I give thee, if thou wilt fall down and worship me.*

10.   *Then saith Jesus unto him, get thee hence, Satan: for it is written, Thou shalt worship the Lord thy God, and him only shalt thou serve.*

Many challenges set forth and many flowery language and terms that would become a tool to use to Beguile: "If thou art the son of God."

16 SATAN'S ROLES

Satan can manipulate truth and be able to mix it with lies (untruth); some calls it "alternative truth," making it sound convincingly truthful. The Fall of Satan has influenced him to make sure that Man also falls from his authority and dominion given to Adam in the beginning. The reason why faced with the so many difficulties and obstacles in life, from sicknesses, financial loss, and loss of family, loss of security, loss of spirituality, and loss of connectivity to God.

Satan's plans including the creation of false religions that will draw people into believing that he is God and indeed can be the one true God, he will lead millions into thinking in these new faiths and will display miracles and wonders to convince them. These newly developed religions governed by men of high status and global recognition, voices that have the charm and eloquence that will subliminally be their tool to Inject doubt on one side and alternative truth (lies) on the other hand. It is important to know that many who are scholars and deeply spiritual in Christianity and other religions will be deceived, without knowing that they are deluded and will follow like a bull led by the nose ring (bullring) as the deception seems more real than they were ever familiar with and will shun words of the Gospels and scriptures. God has mentioned that Satan is God of this world (Earth) and people are going to be deceived by the Satan falsely replicating and displaying his form as the angel of light and perform many miracles and wonders. Satan is the God of most global organizations and has placed his highest-ranking demons in high places as a means of having his will done and controlling the masses as he will display himself as 'Jesus.' Counterfeit religions created by splitting up of many religions where believers will take online of the Gospel to make it a major case against the other side of the very same congregation. Today there are over 43,000 different denominations of Christian churches, each using alternative terms to describe themselves, with different mission statements and different views of the Bible. Believing this is part of the role Satan played in the minds of religious men and their religiosity, twisting and whispering into their minds, causing conflict and confusion, especially to those who are weak spiritually and are victims of Satan's whims.

There are about five main denominations in Hinduism and another ten to fifteen other faiths with different school of thoughts and selective doctrines that they follow. But there are many counts of cults that are related to Hinduism and the dark side of Hinduism, where many of these cults openly follow and worship specific deity or groups of deities for particular benefits and specific cultural practices that are adaptations from their ancestry.

Islam has three main sects: Sunnis, Shi'as, and Kharijites, all following different schools of thoughts, worship, and practices all linked to the Holy Quran, but there are over seventy different schools of jurisprudence, sub-denominations, and schools of theology, which totals over 1.5 Billion Muslims. Practices based on local ancestral traditions and interpretations of the Quran as well as other Islamic doctrines.

The three major religions of the world, which consist of and includes most of the world's population, even though they are from one root, one source, also though all the primary religious scripture and doctrine defines creation in the same way, with little variances, and from the same source, they all have different opinion of where each one came from and their existence in the world. They see each other differently and with a multi-multi definitive manner rather than one spirit. The works of the "God of This World," so yes you are a victim if you see a fellow man and view the indifference or inferiority in comparison to yourself and looking upon you as superior mentally, physically, spiritually and in color, class, and creed. The limitations of man and his ability to only be able to use a minute fraction of his brain for that is all his ability that the Devil allowed him to envision out of the 100 percent of the brain that God gave to him. Prejudice and discrimination linked to a demonic trait and a special gift given to that specific man from the 'God of this world – the Devil or Satan.' Unison according to Satan's methodologies comes through war, war for another man's possession and domination over another or the masses. Satan is a mighty being, a personality that has the highest of Spirituality and knowledge of the Doctrines, since he was one of the highest of the Angels, meaning that he knows the scripture more than we do, but we have been created and given dominion over the living beings of the earth. Therefore any one of us can pray against Satan and save even a fly, an ant, a bird or any other human being and take the authority away from him. In the chapter with Job God gave Satan permission to cast his effect on Job. Therefore Satan needs permission from God to interfere with us physically, maybe not mentally, spiritually or environmentally.

Genesis 3

1   Now the serpent was more subtle than any beast of the field which the Lord God   had made. And he said unto the woman, Yea, hath God said, ye shall not eat of every tree of the garden?

2   And the woman said unto the serpent; we may eat of the fruit of the trees of the garden:

3   But of the fruit of the tree which is in the midst of the garden, God hath said, ye shall not eat of it, neither shall ye touch it, lest ye die.

4   And the serpent said unto the woman, ye shall not surely die:

5   For God doth know that in the day ye eat thereof, then your eyes shall be

opened, and ye shall be as gods, knowing good and evil.

6 *And when the woman saw that the tree was good for food and that it was pleasant to the eyes, and a tree to be desired to make one wise, she took of the fruit thereof, and did eat, and gave also unto her husband with her; and he did eat.*

7 *And the eyes of them both were opened, and they knew that they were naked, and they sewed fig leaves together and made themselves aprons.*

8 *And they heard the voice of the Lord God walking in the garden in the cool of the day: and Adam and his wife hid themselves from the presence of the Lord God amongst the trees of the garden.*

9 *And the Lord God called unto Adam, and said unto him, where art thou?*

10 *And he said, I heard thy voice in the garden, and I was afraid because I was naked, and I hid myself.*

11 *And he said, who told thee that thou wast naked? Hast thou eaten of the tree, whereof I commanded thee that thou shouldest not eat?*

12 *And the man said, the woman whom thou gavest to be with me, she gave me of the tree, and I did eat.*

13 *And the Lord God said unto the woman, what is this that thou hast done? And the woman said, the serpent beguiled me, and I did eat.*

14 *And the Lord God said unto the serpent, Because thou hast done this, thou art cursed above all cattle, and above every beast of the field; upon thy belly shalt thou go, and dust shalt thou eat all the days of thy life:*

15 *And I will put enmity between thee and the woman, and between thy seed and her seed; it shall bruise thy head, and thou shalt bruise his heel.*

16 *Unto the woman he said, I will greatly multiply thy sorrow and thy conception; in sorrow, thou shalt bring forth children, and thy desire shall be to thy husband, and he shall rule over thee.*

17 *And unto Adam he said, Because thou hast hearkened unto the voice of thy wife, and hast eaten of the tree, of which I commanded thee, saying, Thou shalt not eat of it: cursed is the ground for thy sake; in sorrow shalt thou eat of it all the days of thy life;*

18 *Thorns also and thistles shall it bring forth to thee, and thou shalt eat the herb of the field;*

19 *In the sweat of thy face shalt thou eat bread, till thou return unto the ground; for out of it wast thou taken: for dust thou art, and unto dust shalt thou return.*

20 *And Adam called his wife's name Eve; because she was the mother of all living.*

21 *Unto Adam also and to his wife did the Lord God make coats of skins, and clothed them.*

22 *And the Lord God said, Behold, the man is become as one of us, to know good and evil: and now, lest he put forth his hand, and take also of the tree of life, and eat, and live forever:*

23 *Therefore the Lord God sent him forth from the Garden of Eden, to till the ground from whence he was taken.*

24 *So he drove out the man, and he placed at the east of the garden of Eden Cherubim's,*

And we have had a pleasant view of the holiness and happiness of our first parents, the grace and favor of God, and the peace and beauty of the whole creation, all good.

Satan uses various methods to deceive humanity, trickery, doubt, distraction, conviction, guilt, arguments, Media, TV, Radio, Internet, thoughts and through others, etc. It is difficult to list and analyze all the methods Satan uses to deceive Mankind, even as well educated and knowledgeable in scripture and Satan himself. One of Satan's most significant accomplishments is to convince the world that he does not exist.

The fall of man in the beginning with Adam and Eve was a Primeval Event, in the beginning, that caused a domino effect on all of humanity, contaminated by the Original Sin of Man. This affected Man to become a physical human subjected to ignorance and transformed to just an abandoned being by GOD. This Sin became the inheritance that caused humanity to be subjected to physical and spiritual death, suffering and lack of knowledge of divinity. Disobedience to the commandment of GOD resulted in a protective response from GOD and his warning of seeing what could occur if he continues to acknowledge man as "The Dominant Species" in the world, the hierarchy of values and the values of man in the belief of GOD and his ordinance. Adam was given charge over the Garden (world) to look after and take care of the world. Originally ADAM as a Human Man should not be subjected to Death but will live to be as Guardian of the World, the generations of humanity, the animal kingdom, plants and trees and everything in this physical and spiritual world that will be here for millions and billions of years. The God-given ability, intelligence, free will, knowledge, and responsibilities that make him higher than all animal species on the planet. His duties were to be dominant over all life form and also be "the steward" of all life form. This ability was induced into his body, mind, and spirit from his creation by GOD, and given knowledge, wisdom and in-born God-given ability to represent GOD on Earth. Some of these characteristics include the ability to develop our spirituality and connect to the divine for greater knowledge and wisdom, for guidance and direction, to develop our mind and aptitudes in an evolutionary process to become more advanced in physiological and psychological processes to be what God ordained a man to be. The age of the Earth cannot be proven, and we cannot predict how long it will exist, as such GOD created Man to be the guardian over it and take care of represented in the Bible as "The Garden."

The original sin is Man *missing the mark of being* obedient and on a secondary level, to be led astray or influenced, beguiled by illusions and lust of the flesh (eyes, ears, taste, touch) figuratively "Eat the Apple from the Forbidden tree" that made him *miss the mark.*

Genesis 2: 15	**And the LORD God took the man, and put him into the Garden of Eden to dress it and to keep it.**
16:	**And the LORD God commanded the man, saying, of every tree of the garden thou mayest freely eat:**
17	**but of the tree of the knowledge of good and evil, thou shalt not eat of it: for in the day that thou eatest thereof thou shalt surely die.**

Genesis 1:	*And every plant of the field before it was in the earth, and every herb of the field before it grew: for the LORD God had not caused it to rain upon the earth, **and there was not a man to till the ground.***

Genesis 3: 6	**And when the woman saw that the tree was good for food, <u>and that it was pleasant to the eyes, and a tree to be desired to make one wise</u>, she took of the fruit thereof, and did eat, and gave also unto her husband with her; and he did eat.**
Genesis 3: 7	**And the eyes of them both were opened, and <u>they knew that they were naked</u>; and they sewed fig leaves together, and made themselves aprons.**

Man created physically from the elements of the Earth (dust re the blueprint of Man – below)) and was given "The breath of Life" (spirit of GOD), "Free will" (a Mind) combined together becomes a three dimensional being, thus is "naturally Good-perfect" and spiritual, connected to divinity, full of Love (mirroring the IMAGE of GOD). Disobedience has caused a turning away from what is ordained and becomes a consequence of lust, greed, anger, illusion, and delusion, which led to suffering and death. Reality consists of spiritual and physical entities, and man created in the God-like attributes and characteristics, and Man is to be a replica of his actions, deeds and thinking, performing duties as assigned by God. Many called it a rebellion that caused a man to miss the mark and other listed it as disobedience, but we have in-built characteristics to think and act upon what flows into the thoughts and minds. With the innocence of not knowing the differences between the evil beguiling and disguised statements of the Serpent, a free-willed mind deceived into thinking that 'it is good,' but the disobedience involved not adhering to 'Specific instruction" DO NOT EAT from the tree. Evil had a field-day with Eve and their innocence of not knowing what Evil is and can be, such as the word "Beguiled" used, Eve was charmed and attracted to the verbiage used and became delighted by the twist of meaning to the instruction from God.

Eve did admit to being fooled, *"And the Lord God said unto the woman, what is this that thou hast did? And the woman said, the serpent beguiled me, and I did eat." (Genesis 3:13)* ". The Hebrew word was "Nasha" which was 'to lead astray,' or "morally seduce "or the Greek word is "expattio" meaning " deceived into illusion" therefore the Serpent influenced the mind of Eve and her thoughts. It is a rare Hebrew word and carries an intense experience which evokes an emotional, psychological and spiritual trauma", which means it, was not only trickery but more of a spell or putting her into a trance. The word "Serpent" is used as a characteristic rather than a physical form.

Genesis 3:4-5   *"And the serpent said unto the woman, ye shall **not** surely die for God doth know that in the day ye eat thereof, then **your eyes shall be opened**, and ye shall **be as gods**, knowing good and evil."*

Genesis 3:6   *"And when the woman **saw** that the tree was good for food and that **it was pleasant** to the eyes, and **a tree to be desired** to make one wise, she took of the fruit thereof, and did eat, and gave also unto her husband with her; and he did eat."*

Here is the flaw of the man:

> **Genesis 3:12-13** *"And the man said, **the woman** (shift of blame) whom thou gavest (It is like saying I did not ask for this) to be with me, **she gave me** (being beguiled himself by his wife) of the tree, and **I did** (he should not have eaten, but repeated the command that God gave to him) eat. And the Lord God said unto the woman, what is this that thou hast done? And the woman said, the serpent beguiled me, and I did eat."*

It is considered a wrong to be disobedient, and disobedience is a sin, sin is a turning away, this missing the connectivity to GOD (The Mark). A defilement of the mind which led to disconnection to the spiritual and even the physical as initially planned. God did give Adam a set of laws, a set principle and instructions with a specific command "Do not eat from the Tree of Knowledge of Good and Evil" (a symbol for knowledge, immortality, temptation, the fall of man and sin.)

> **Genesis 1:29**   *And God said, Behold, I have given you every herb bearing seed, which is upon the face of all the earth, and every tree, in the which is the fruit of a tree yielding seed; to you, it shall be for meat.*

> **Genesis 1:30:**   *And to every beast of the earth, and to every fowl of the air, and to everything that creepeth upon the earth, wherein there is life, I have given every green herb for meat: and it was so.*

> **Genesis 1:31.**   *And God saw everything that he had made, and, behold, it was very good. And the evening and the morning were the sixth days.*

The most excellent majesty of GOD's creation on Earth is "Man," simple because Gods took the time and discussed the image that he wanted for man… What a great honor created in the image of GOD. What can be more special than being a mirror image and likes of the God who created us? And thus, God is a spirit, and the image of GOD is a spirit and MAN created in the image of GOD "a Spirit" housed in a body made from the 'dust of the earth,' thus "Man- the physical body of Dust' became a 'living being. '

The man had to be created with the elements of the Earth so that he can survive on the face and atmosphere of the earth. Man possesses within his very own physical body all the features of the planet in different percentage as per the same proportion that existed on the Planet.

Satan used many methods to make sure this does not go according to plan, due to his jealousy of this new creation, knowing this new creation is overtaking his dominion and given the authority belonging to Satan. The anger and resentment against this new creature multiplied exceedingly, and Satan was bent on spoiling the perfection that God Created.

Not only was the world Dominion given away, he made this new creature in his image, gave this new creature the breath of Life", Language, speech to communicate, a well-fortified garden and spends the time to teach the Man 'Wisdom of God', made him a little lower than angels, but given more power more than angels. *"Be fruitful and multiply, and fill the earth, and subdue it; and rule over the fish of the sea and over the birds of the sky, and over every living thing that moves on earth", "Behold I have given you every plant yielding seed that is on the surface of all the earth, and every tree which has fruit yielding seed; it shall be food for you; and every beast of the earth, and to every bird of the sky and to everything that moves on the earth which has life, I have given every green plant for food".* The man has a purpose; he was to exercise his given dominion over **all living** creatures. So, Adam was King and Eve was the Queen, they were initially given a task to view and acknowledged each creature and gave each an identity and name, done. They were given free will and a commandment, to obey *"Be Fruitful and multiply, and fill the earth."* A second command was to eat of every tree in the garden; a third commandment was "Do not eat of the tree of knowledge of Good and Evil" for it was not good for man to consume as commanded by GOD.

God had put MAN under a test of his free will to verify that what he created in his image would indeed be "Good," which happen to turn out he (GOD) had to repent a few generations later for the creation of Man. Man's divinity reversed, and the order and dominion lost. The domino effect is what we are experiencing today in the present time, The Chain of command and order lost, and MAN is becoming rather than a leader and KING of the earth has become a slave and a beast under his actions. The Fall of Man has been a slow and a surely downhill effect of his authority and establishment. He is slowly losing his Name as Man and becoming what he was not created to be or become. The free will given to both angels and Man had been proven to be disastrous in its order and ordination, to the human beings given free will. This free will has led to separation, and the downward spiral of a divine being into a creature that is existing in confusion and an abyss lost connectivity to GOD and harbors anger that is endowed by the Devil to hate and be repulsive not only to self but to GOD and all others.

Lost is his Divinity, immortality, connectivity to the Supreme, Salvation,

Both Adam and Eve were in a state of humility, love, providence, and unison with each other, with God and with creation. When God finished the creation of Man, he saw that "it was GOOD." Adam had dominion over ALL LIVING CREATURES, BUT not all spiritual beings, in our world this is certainly a place for corrupt thinking and creation of jealousy that comes out of free will. It means that Satan as Lucifer had "Free will" as well.

Thus, he is full of the evil trait passed it over to Eve, for Adam at that time was not susceptible to his deceit. Satan full of "Lust" "Lies "and "Pride" used these characteristics to pass it over to Eve in a subliminal manner.

Satan: As described in Isaiah 14:12-15 and Ezekiel 28:12-19.

> *Satan was a spirit being, a heavenly being that was cast out to the Earth and had dominion over the earth which was dark and void, an abyss of a kingdom under Satan until GOD created man. Satan was the highest rank of all Angels. Satan is primarily understood as an "accuser" or "adversary" in the Hebrew Bible*

> *Satan in the form of a beast was very "crafty", Biblical definition of Lucifer; he was the greatest of all of God's creation (heavenly Creation). He was above all Angels and THE most powerful of them all including the Earthly creation of MAN. He was the most beautiful, the fairest; nothing in the universe is of comparison. The highest of all Angels was filled with iniquity of Sin in the form of Pride and jealousy. Heaven is a Holy Place and Iniquity cannot survive or find any place there.*

Psychologist agree that the human being does not have any instincts for evil and 'evil is inherent in human nature,' the sin as per the doctrine of the original sin is the only doctrine that is valid to Christian faith. Therefore the original sin has been transferred possibly through subliminal processes through the DNA. Later Jesus defines the sin as the works of the flesh sexual immorality, impurity, sensuality, idolatry, sorcery, enmity, strife, jealousy, fits of anger, rivalries, dissensions, divisions, envy, drunkenness, orgies, and things like these. I warn you, as I warned you before, that those who do such things will not inherit the kingdom of God."

Galatians 5:19   *Now the works of the flesh are manifest, which are these; Adultery, fornication, uncleanness, lasciviousness*

     20   *Idolatry, witchcraft, hatred, variance, emulations, wrath, strife, seditions, heresies,*

     21   *Envying, murders, drunkenness, revellings, and such like: of the which I tell you before, as I have also told you in time past, that they which do such things shall not inherit the kingdom of God.*

     22   *But the fruit of the Spirit is love, joy, peace, longsuffering, gentleness, goodness, faith*

     23   *Meekness, temperance: against such there is no law.*

This definition from God' Mouth reveals how mighty Satan was before he fell from Heaven or instead before being cast out of heaven to Earth. Therefore, he cannot live in heaven any more but can undoubtedly visit Heaven as defined in

JOB 1:7 -   *And the LORD said unto Satan, Whence comest thou? Then Satan answered the LORD, and said, from going to and fro in the earth, and from walking up and down in it.*

The existence of Satan was defined and found in Genesis 3:1-16, Isaiah 14:12-15; Ezekiel 28:12-19; Matthew 4:1-11. Even Jesus testified the existence of Satan whom he faced during his ministry, whereby details of people possessed by Demons and Satan, and the war in heavens between God and Satan, and are labeled devils, demons, evil and unclean spirits.

Satan is the leader of the fallen angels, and 1/3 of the heavenly angels fell with Satan (at that time he was Lucifer). The Bible teaches that fallen angels are invisible, supernatural, angelic, spirits created by God.

Ezekiel 28: *12:*	*Thou sealest up the sum, full of wisdom, and perfect in beauty*
13:	*Thou hast been in Eden the garden of God; every precious stone was thy covering, the sardius, topaz, and the diamond, the beryl, the onyx, and the jasper, the sapphire, the emerald, and the carbuncle, and gold: the workmanship of thy tabrets and of thy pipes was prepared in thee in the day that thou wast created.*
14	*:Thou art the anointed cherub that covereth; and I have set thee so: thou wast upon the holy mountain of God; thou hast walked up and down in the midst of the stones of fire.*
15:	*Thou wast perfect in thy ways from the day that thou wast created, till iniquity was found in thee.*
16:	*By the multitude of thy merchandise they have filled the midst of thee with violence, and thou hast sinned: therefore I will cast thee as profane out of the mountain of God: and I will destroy thee, O covering cherub, from the midst of the stones of fire.*
17:	*Thine heart was lifted up because of thy beauty, thou hast corrupted thy wisdom by reason of thy brightness: I will cast thee to the ground, I will lay thee before kings, that they may behold thee.*
18:	*Thou hast defiled thy sanctuaries by the multitude of thine iniquities, by the iniquity of thy traffick; therefore will I bring forth a fire from the midst of thee, it shall devour thee, and I will bring thee to ashes upon the earth in the sight of all them that behold thee.*
19:	*All they that know thee among the people shall be astonished at thee: thou shalt be a terror, and never shalt thou be any more.*

> **Ezekiel 28:14** *"You were the anointed Cherub." "Anointed cherub who covers"*
> 15:   Thou wast perfect in thy ways from the day that thou wast created, till iniquity was found in thee.
> 16:   By the multitude of thy merchandise they have filled the midst of thee with violence, and thou hast sinned: therefore I will cast thee as profane out of the mountain of God: and I will destroy thee, O covering cherub, from the midst of the stones of fire.
> 17:   Thine heart was lifted up because of thy beauty; thou hast corrupted thy wisdom by reason of thy brightness: I will cast thee to the ground; I will lay thee before kings, that they may behold thee.
> 18:   Thou hast defiled thy sanctuaries by the multitude of thine iniquities, by the iniquity of thy traffick; therefore will I bring forth a fire from the midst of thee, it shall devour thee, and I will bring thee to ashes upon the earth in the sight of all them that behold thee.
> 19:   All they that know thee among the people shall be astonished at thee: thou shalt be a terror, and never shalt thou be any more.

Satan was created by God as Lucifer, "The Day Star" or "Light-Bearer," the "morning star" or "star of the morning" or "bright star" Perfect. *Lucifer is one of three archangels mentioned in Scripture. He was created by God just as all angels were, but his role was different from the other angelic hosts. Lucifer referred to as the 'covering angel.' Only as the cherubim covered the mercy seat of the Ark of the Covenant, Lucifer was established by God to be the angel of worship, one whose ministry surrounded the heart of heaven. Lucifer was created to dwell eternally in the throne room of heaven, in the very presence of God (Ezekiel 28:14).*

Lucifer, also known as The Devil, Light Bringer, The Morning Star, and **Satan**, is the second of the four Archangels created by God and is his favorite son. He is also a fallen archangel and the first fallen angel. **Satan** in Job and Zechariah translated by the Greek **word** diabolos (slanderer), the same **word** in the Greek New Testament from which the English **word devil** derived. Satan (Hebrew: שָׂטָן Satan, meaning "enemy" or "adversary"; [1] Arabic: شَيْطَان shaitan, meaning; "astray", "distant", or sometimes "devil")

Satan is the principality power behind the corruption in the world system. Therefore it is vital to understand who and what he is and his abilities, his works, his methods, and his plans. We need to know and understand the enemy; whether it is human or spirit, we must understand the traits, characteristics, motives and how they can interfere with our family and us. We are always tempted to blame "the Devil" for any mishap or negativity in our lives, but we must first and foremost look deep into our inner self and figure out if we have open doors to the darkness, did we allow wicked thoughts, evil lustful and devious ways to become part of us. Just like the Spirit of God can manifest into the hearts, body, and minds of humanity, the same way wicked spirits can follow suit and possess your mind, body, and spirit, they can influence your environment and or people around you. We must be able to develop the 'gift of discernment.'

Isaiah 14:12-17 New King James Version (NKJV)
The fall of Lucifer

12 :   "How you are fallen from heaven, O Lucifer, [a] son of the morning!
     How you are cut down to the ground,You who weakened the nations!

13:   For you have said in your heart:'I will ascend into heaven,
     I will exalt my throne above the stars of God;I will also sit on the mount of
     the congregation
     On the farthest sides of the north;

14:   I will ascend above the heights of the clouds,I will be like the Most High.'

15:   Yet you shall be brought down to Sheol,To the lowest depths of the Pit.

16:   "Those who see you will gaze at you,And consider you, saying:
     'Is this the man who made the earth tremble?Who shook kingdoms?

17:   Who made the world as a wilderness?And destroyed its cities,
     Who did not open the house of his prisoners?

Isaiah 14:12-23   "How you have fallen from heaven, morning star, son of the dawn! You have been cast down to the earth, you who once laid low the nations! You said in your heart, 'I will ascend to the heavens; I will raise my throne above the stars of God; I will sit enthroned on the mount of assembly, on the utmost heights of Mount Zaphon. I will ascend above the tops of the clouds; I will make myself like the Most High.' But you are brought down to the realm of the dead, to the depths of the pit. Those who see you stare at you, they ponder your fate: 'Is this the man who shook the earth and made kingdoms tremble, the man who made the world a wilderness, who overthrew its cities and would not let his captives go home?'"

Ezekiel 28:12-14
Ezekiel 28:12   "You were the seal of perfection, Full of wisdom and perfect in beauty.
Ezekiel 28:13   You were in Eden, the garden of God; every precious stone was your covering: The sardius, topaz, and diamond, Beryl, onyx, and Jasper,

Sapphire, turquoise, and emerald with gold. The workmanship of your timbrels and pipes was prepared for you on the day you were created.

Ezekiel 28:14   *You were the anointed cherub who covers; I established you; You were on the holy mountain of God; You walked back and forth in the midst of fiery stones."*

We must be very careful when we express prejudices, especially of ethnicity, color, class or creed for we may possess the characteristics and possible a mutation of the DNA because of our thoughts and mental states, which may be instilled or "beguiled" into our spirit by Satan, for this is one method of creating corruption, animosity, division and divisiveness among men

JOB 1:20   Then Job arose, and rent his mantle, and shaved his head, and fell down upon the ground, and worshipped, 21 And said, <u>Naked came I out of my mother's womb, and naked shall I return thither</u>: the LORD gave, and the LORD hath taken away; blessed be the name of the LORD

http://www.markbeast.com/satan/names-of-satan.htm
Satan has many names. He is also called the devil, **Dragon, Serpent, Beelzebub, Abaddon, Apollyon**, and many other names. Lucifer referred to this angel when he lived in heaven. Satan and the Devil are named for this angel after he became evil and came to our earth.

Abaddon: Hebrew name for Satan meaning "Destruction."
Revelation 9:11 *"And they had as king over them the angel of the bottomless pit, whose name in Hebrew is Abaddon, but in Greek, he has the name Apollyon."*

Accuser: *Revelation 12:10 "Then I heard a loud voice saying in heaven, 'Now salvation, and strength, and the kingdom of our God, and the power of His Christ have come, for the accuser of our brethren, who accused them before our God day and night, has been cast down.'"*

Adversary: *1 Peter 5:8 "Be sober, be vigilant; because your adversary the devil walks about like a roaring lion, seeking whom he may devour."*

Angel of light: *2 Corinthians 11:14 "And no wonder! For Satan, himself transforms himself into an angel of light."*

Angel of the bottomless pit: *Revelation 9:11 "And they had as king over them the angel of the bottomless pit, whose name in Hebrew is Abaddon, but in Greek, he has the name Apollyon."*

Anointed covering Cherub: *Ezekiel 28:14"You were the anointed cherub who covers; I* *established you; You were on the holy mountain of God; You walked back and forth in the midst of fiery stones."*

Antichrist: *1 John 4:3 "And every spirit that does not confess that Jesus Christ has come in the flesh is not of God. And this is the spirit of the Antichrist, which you have heard was coming and is now already in the world."*

Apollyon: *Revelation 9:11 Greek name for Satan meaning "Destroyer." "And they had as king over them the angel of the bottomless pit, whose name in Hebrew is Abaddon, but in Greek, he has the name Apollyon."*

Beast: *Revelation 14:9"Then a third angel followed them, saying with a loud voice, 'If anyone worships the beast and his image, and receives his mark on his forehead or on his hand, Revelation 14:10 he himself shall also drink of the wine of the wrath of God, which is poured out full strength into the cup of His indignation. He shall be tormented with fire and brimstone in the presence of the holy angels and in the presence of the Lamb.'" Who is the beast?*

Beelzebub: *Matthew 12:24 "Now when the Pharisees heard it, they said, 'This fellow does not cast out demons except by Beelzebub, the ruler of the demons.'"*

Belial: *2 Corinthians 6:15 "And what accord has Christ with Belial? Or what part has a believer with an unbeliever?"*

Deceiver: *Revelation 12:9 "So the great dragon was cast out, that serpent of old, Called the Devil and Satan, who deceives the whole world; he was cast to The earth, and his angels were cast out with him."*

Devil: *1 John 3:8 "He who sins is of the devil, for the devil has sinned from the beginning. For this purpose, the Son of God was manifested, that He might destroy the works of the devil."*

Dragon: *Revelation 12:9 "So the great dragon was cast out, that serpent of old, called the Devil and Satan, who deceives the whole world; he was cast to the earth,and his angels were cast out with him."*

Enemy: *Matthew 13:39 "The enemy who sowed them is the devil, the harvest is the end of the age, and the reapers are the angels."*

Evil one: *John 17:15 "I do not pray that You should take them out of the world, but that You should keep them from the evil one."*

Father of lies: *John 8:44 "You are of your father the devil, and the desires of your* *father you want to do. He was a murderer from the beginning and does not stand in the truth, because there is no truth in him. When he speaks a lie, he speaks from his own resources, for he is a liar and the father of it."*

God of this age: *2 Corinthians 4:4 "Whose minds the god of this age has blinded, who do not believe, lest the light of the gospel of the glory of Christ, who is the image of God, should shine on them."*

King of Babylon: *Isaiah 14:4 "That you will take up this proverb against the king say: 'How the oppressor has ceased, The golden city ceased!'*

King of the bottomless pit: *Revelation 9:11 "And they had as king over them the angel of the bottomless pit, whose name in Hebrew is Abaddon, but in Greek, he has the name Apollyon."*

King of Tyre: *Ezekiel 28:12 "Son of man, take up a lamentation for the king of Tyre, and Say to him, 'Thus says the Lord GOD: "You were the seal of perfection, Full of wisdom and perfect in beauty."'"*

Lawless one: *2 Thessalonians 2:8-10 "And then the lawless one will be revealed, whom the Lord will consume with the breath of His mouth and destroy with the brightness of His coming. 9. The coming of the lawless one is according to the working of Satan, with all power, signs, and lying wonders, 10. and with all unrighteous deception among those who perish, because they did not receive the love of the truth, that they might be saved."*

Leviathan: *Isaiah 27:1 "In that day the LORD with His severe sword, great and strong, will punish Leviathan the fleeing serpent, Leviathan that twisted serpent; And He will slay the reptile that is in the sea."*

Liar: *John 8:44 "You are of your father the devil, and the desires of your father you want to do. He was a murderer from the beginning and does not stand in the truth, because there is no truth in him. When he speaks a lie, he speaks from his own resources, for he is a liar and the father of it."*

Little horn: *Daniel 8:9-11 "9 And out of one of them came a little horn which grew exceedingly great toward the south, toward the east, and toward the Glorious Land. 10 And it grew up to the host of heaven, and it cast down* *some of the host and some of the stars to the ground and trampled them. 11 He even exalted himself as high as the Prince of the host, and by him, the daily sacrifices were taken away, and the place of His sanctuary was cast down."*

Lucifer: *" Isaiah 14:12   How you are fallen from heaven, O Lucifer, son of the morning! How you are cut down to the ground, you who weakened the nations! Isaiah 14:13   For you have said in your heart: 'I will ascend into heaven, I will exalt my throne above the stars of God;I will also sit on the mount of the congregation On the farthest sides of the north; Isaiah 14:14   I will ascend above the heights of the clouds, I will be like the Most High.'*

Man of sin: *2 Thessalonians 2:3,4 "3 Let no one deceive you by any means; for thatDay will not come unless the falling away comes first, and the man of sin is revealed, the son of perdition, 4. who opposes and exalts himself above all that is called God or that is worshiped, so that he sits as God in the temple of God, showing himself that he is God."*

Murderer: *John 8:44 "You are of your father the devil, and the desires of your father you want to do. He was a murderer from the beginning and does not stand in the truth, because there is no truth in him. When he speaks a lie, he speaks from his own resources, for he is a liar and the father of it."*

Power of darkness: *Colossians 1:13 He has delivered us from the power of darkness and conveyed us into the kingdom of the Son of His love, 14 in whom wehave redemption through His blood, the forgiveness of sins."*

Prince of the power of the air: *Ephesians 2:1,2 "1 And you He made alive, who were dead in trespasses and sins, 2 in which you once walked according to the course of this world, according to the prince of the power of the air, the spirit who now works in the sons of disobedience."*

Roaring lion: *1 Peter 5:8 "Be sober, be vigilant; because your adversary the devil walks about like a roaring lion, seeking whom he may devour."*

Rulers of the darkness: *Ephesians 6:12 "For we do not wrestle against flesh and blood, but against principalities, against powers, against the rulers of the darkness of this age, against spiritual hosts of wickedness in the heavenly places."*

Ruler of demons: *Luke 11:15 "But some of them said, 'He casts out demons by Beelzebub, the ruler of the demons.'"*

Ruler of this world: *John 12:31 "Now is the judgment of this world; now the ruler of this world will be cast out. 32 And I, if I am lifted up from the earth, will draw all peoples to myself."*

Satan: *Mark 1:13 "And He was there in the wilderness forty days, tempted by Satan, and was with the wild beasts; and the angels ministered to Him."*

Serpent of old: *Revelation 12:9 "So the great dragon was cast out, that serpent of Old, called the Devil and Satan, who deceives the whole world; he was cast to the earth, and his angels were cast out with him."*

Son of perdition: *2 Thessalonians 2:3, 4*
"3. Let no one deceive you by any means; for that Day will not come unless the falling away comes first, and the man of sin is revealed, the son of perdition, 4 who opposes and exalts himself above all that is called God or that is worshiped, so that he sits as God in the temple of God, showing himself that he is God." Star: "Then the fifth angel sounded: And I saw a star fallen from heaven to the earth. To him was given the key to the bottomless pit." Revelation 9:1

Tempter: *Matthew 4:3 "Now when the tempter came to Him, he said, 'If you are the Son of God, command that these stones become bread.'"*

Thief: *John 10:10 "The thief does not come except to steal, and to kill, and to destroy. I have come that they may have life and that they may have it more abundantly."*

Wicked one: *Ephesians 6:16 "Above all, taking the shield of faith with which you will be able to quench all the fiery darts of the wicked one." Ezekiel 28:17"Your heart was lifted up because of your beauty; you Corrupted your wisdom for the sake of your splendor." Ezekiel 28:6 "You have set your heart as the heart of a god."*

He fell and took with him one-third angels his replication of the fall focused on God's created beings. We must understand that this is not only for humanity, but all living creatures that were created by God on Earth also faces the wrath of Satan and are experiencing "the Fall" in their ways. Understand that the verdict was initially under the **authority of Satan and his sins and his angels as such the fall cause such great catastrophe.** The reason for the fall was due to pride, ego and the self-centeredness which led to disobedience disrespect and loss of authority. Lucifer's rebellion attributed to some motives, all of which stem from his great pride. These motives include: A refusal to bow down to humanity on the occasion of the creation of man

Ezekiel 28:12-18 you will find God describing him: *"Thus says the Lord GOD, you had the seal of perfection, Full of wisdom and perfect in beauty. You were in Eden, the garden of God; every precious stone was your covering: The ruby, the topaz, and the diamond; the beryl, the onyx, and the jasper; The lapis lazuli, the turquoise, and the emerald; And the gold, the workmanship of your settings and sockets, was in you. On the day that you were created, they were prepared. You were the anointed cherub who covers, and I placed you there. You were on the holy mountain of God; you walked in the midst of the stones of fire. You were blameless in your ways from the day you were created. Until unrighteousness was found in you."*

1 Chronicles 21:1,"Satan stood up against Israel" (KJV) or "And there standeth up adversary against Israel."

Psalm 109:6   "and let Satan stand at his right hand" or "let an accuser stand at his right hand."

The other eight instances of Satan without the definite article are traditionally translated (in Greek, Latin, and English) as "an adversary," etc., and taken to be humans or obedient angels:

Numbers 22:22, 32 "and the angel of the LORD stood in the way for an adversary against him."32   "Behold, I went out to withstand thee,"

1 Samuel 29:4   The Philistines say: "lest he [David] be an adversary against us."

2 Samuel 19:22 David says: "[you sons of Zeruaiah] should this day be adversaries (plural) unto me?"

1 Kings 5:4   Solomon writes to Hiram: "there is neither adversary nor evil occurrent."

1 Kings 11:14   "And the LORD stirred up an adversary unto Solomon, Hadad the Edomite"[12]

1 Kings 11:23   "And God stirred him up an adversary, Rezon, the son of Eliadah."

1 Kings 11:25   "And he [Rezon] was an adversary to Israel all the days of Solomon."

John 8:44   Satan is a Murder, Satan is a Liar

Matthew 13:19 Satan is a Thief

II Corinthians 11:3 Satan is Subtle

Revelation 12:9Satan is a deceiver

Satan is a Roaring Lion and a serpent

***According to Revelations one-third of the angels fell with Lucifer and was cast down to earth Revelations**: 12:4. And his tail drew the third part of the stars of heaven, and did cast them to the earth: and the dragon stood before the woman which was ready to be delivered, for to devour her child as soon as it was born.*

Categories of Angels:

Seraphim: *A member of the highest order of angels, one of the 6-winged angels standing in the presence of God*

Cherubim: *The mighty angels, protector of the throne of God*

Thrones: *Celestial beings that are the carrier of the Throne of God*

Dominions or Lordships: Celestial beings" Lordships." Divinely angel's human looking with feathered wings regulating the duties of lower angels

Virtues or Strongholds: the angels that deliver signs, wonders and miracles on Earth

Powers or Authorities: Supervise the works of heavenly beings and bodies to keep the cosmos in order

Principalities or Rulers: The educators and guardians, protectors of nations and rulers, groups, church, and congregations.

Archangels: Chief Angels and Chief Princes

The number of Angels in Heaven per
Revelations 5:11 "And I beheld, and I heard the voice of many angels round about the throne and the beasts and the elders: and the number of them was ten thousand times ten thousand and thousands of thousands";

Scriptures related to Lucifer in the King James Bible:

Isaiah 14:12-15 -   *How art thou fallen from heaven, O Lucifer, son of the morning! [How] art thou cut down to the ground, which didst weaken the nations!*

Revelation 12:7-9 - *And there was war in heaven: Michael and his angels fought against the dragon, and the dragon fought and his angels,*

Isaiah 14:12 -   *How art thou fallen from heaven, O Lucifer, son of the morning! [How] art thou cut down to the ground, which didst weaken the nations!*

Corinthians 11:14 - *And no marvel; for Satan himself is transformed into an angel of light.*

Ezekiel 28:17 -   *Thine heart was lifted up because of thy beauty, thou hast corrupted thy wisdom by reason of thy brightness: I will cast thee to the ground, I will lay thee before kings, that they may behold thee.*

Luke 10:18 -   *And he said unto them, I beheld Satan as lightning fall from heaven.*

John 8:44 -   *Ye are of [your] father the devil, and the lusts of your father ye will do. He was a murderer from the beginning, and abode not in the truth, because there is no truth in him. When he speaketh a lie, he speaketh of his own: for he is a liar and the father of it.*

Ezekiel 28:14 -   *Thou [art] the anointed cherub that covereth; and I have set thee [so]: thou wast upon the holy mountain of God; thou hast walked up and down in the midst of the stones of fire.*

1 Peter 5:8 -   *Be sober, be vigilant; because your adversary the devil, as a roaring lion, walketh about, seeking whom he may devour:*

Jude 1:6 -   *And the angels which kept not their first estate, but left their own habitation, he hath reserved in everlasting chains under darkness unto the judgment of the great day.*

Ezekiel 28:15 - *Thou [wast] perfect in thy ways from the day that thou wast created, till iniquity was found in thee.*

Revelation 12:9 -   *And the great dragon was cast out, that old serpent, called the Devil, and Satan, which deceiveth the whole world: he was cast out into the earth, and his angels were cast out with him.*

Genesis 3:1-24 -   *Now the serpent was more subtil than any beast of the field which the LORD God had made. And he said unto the woman, Yea, hath God said, Ye, shall not eat of every tree of the garden?*

2 Peter 2:4 - *For if God spared not the angels that sinned, but cast [them] down to hell, and delivered [them] into chains of darkness, to be reserved unto judgment;*

Ezekiel 28:16 - *By the multitude of thy merchandise they have filled the midst of thee with violence, and thou hast sinned: therefore I will cast thee as profane out of the mountain of God: and I will destroy thee, O covering cherub, from the midst of the stones of fire.*

Ezekiel 28:13 - *Thou hast been in Eden the garden of God; every precious stone [was] thy covering, the sardius, topaz, and the diamond, the beryl, the onyx, and the jasper, the sapphire, the emerald, and the carbuncle, and gold: the workmanship of thy tabrets and of thy pipes was prepared in thee in the day that thou wast created.*

Hebrews 2:14 - *Forasmuch then as the children are partakers of flesh and blood, he also himself likewise took part of the same; that through death he might destroy him that had the power of death, that is, the devil;*

Matthew 4:3 - *And when the tempter came to him, he said, If thou be the Son of God, command that these stones be made bread.*

1 Timothy 3:6 - *Not a novice, lest being lifted up with pride he falls into the condemnation of the devil.*

Job 1:6 - *Now there was a day when the sons of God came to present themselves before the LORD, and Satan came also among them.*

Revelation 20:10 - *And the devil that deceived them was cast into the lake of fire and brimstone, where the beast and the false prophet [are] and shall be tormented day and night forever and ever.*

Assumption:

Daniel 7:10 *A fiery stream issued and came forth from before him: thousand and thousand ministered unto him, and ten thousand times ten thousand stood before him: the judgment was set, and the books were opened.*

Revelation 5:11 And I beheld, and I heard the voice of many angels round about the throne, and the beasts and the elders: and the number of them was ten thousand times ten thousand, and thousands of thousands;

In mathematical equations, the number of angels as seen in John's vision in heaven is 10,000 x 10,000 x 1,000 x 1,000 (and I am using the number One for the last two). Adds up to 100,000,000,000,000 angels in heaven at the time John spiritual visitation in revelation And stated that 1/3 angels fell with Lucifer, so that equates to 3,333,333,333,333 angels That fell to Earth. If the numbers that John saw in his vision were the remaining 2/3 Angels, it would compare that we have to exist on Earth 5,000,000,000,000 We have more fallen angels that Human and Living beings on Earth. It is so very crucial to understand and know; we are at the mercy of Satan, and his emissaries outnumbered, outwitted and under armed, ill-prepared. The numeric assumption does not include the billions of lost souls and spirits that were from the days of Noah that died in the flood and those from the beginning of time that were lost and were in a state of wondering the earth trying to get back into their body or a body to replicate their death instance to undo that death, and /or gather a few companion, for wandering spirits moves in groups.

Species on Earth: Excerpts from the Internet

 https://www.livescience.com/54660-1-trillion-species-on-earth.html

About 8.7 million (give or take 1.3 million) is the new, estimated total number of species on Earth -- the most precise calculation ever offered -- with 6.5 million species on land and 2.2 million in oceans. Announced by the Census of Marine Life, the figure is based on a new analytical technique Indiana University researchers Kenneth Locey and Jay Lennon analyzed data sources that sampled 20,376 sites for bacteria, Achaea and microscopic fungi, and 14,862 sites for trees, birds, and mammals. Using the total abundance of individuals, the researchers were able to work out the scaling rules that linked the number of individual organisms to the number of total species.

> *The method led to an estimate of between 100,000,000,000 (that's 100 billion) and 1,000,000,000,000 (that's a trillion) species of microbes on Earth.*

The Largest Study of Life Forms Ever Has Estimated That Earth Is Home to 1 TRILLION Species

There are more species on Earth than stars in our galaxy.

PETER DOCKRILL- 3 MAY 2016 States:
The largest scientific study of its kind estimates that Earth could play host to more than 1 trillion different species, which means we've probably only identified a vanishingly small proportion of them – only about one-thousandth of 1 percent.
To figure this out, biologists in the US combined more than 35,000 separate analyses of microscopic and non-microscopic species. This massive compilation of documented life forms covered 5.6 million species sampled from locations across all the world's oceans and land masses (excluding Antarctica), and if the

scientists are correct in their estimates, we've got a long way to go before we have seen all that Earth has to offer.

This fall of Mankind has affected the entire generation of humankind, for just falling by disobedience and personal lust is not only limited to our physical self and disconnected from God but also spiritual isolation and detachment from God. It also led to our eternal life and lifespan for the result of this disobedience classified as a sin and under the sin rules of God, leads to death, natural lifespan and death, and spiritual death as well. The age of Innocence is gone, and the awareness of sin and evil has infiltrated the human body, mind, and life. Their well being and comfort of the Garden of Eden taken away. This Garden of Eden represents all physical, moral and physical pleasures, Adam job was to take care of the garden, which was a flourishing land of Providence. As shame and guilt of the sin committed by Adam now aware that he had to hide his sinful nature from God, and as we can observe this is an adaptation or a contamination that infiltrated Oman's mind and psyche that he is now aware of his uncovered self, he no longer had the covering of God with him, he is left alone uncovered and filthy in sin. Fig leaves were not adequate to cover man's nakedness and shame, God, had to reach out and seek him out from hiding and performed the first service of redemption by sacrificing a Lamb and shedding the blood to try and redeem Adam and Eve from the human nature that has overcome them.
The first rejection of God for man's works; He sewed Fig Leaves as covering and god rejected that covering, thereby making a covering of Lamb Skin, a representation of the robe of righteousness.

There were additional repercussions from the results of this Sin and fall; the earth cursed with the hard produce of thorns, the woman cursed with pain and Adam was cursed with hard labor for his sustenance by God. Even further we lost the connection and ability to be living in Paradise, next to the tree of Knowledge and the Tree of Life

Romans 6:23 *for the wages of sin is death, but the gift of God is eternal life through Jesus Christ our Lord.* All in all, God has a heart for man for he had created man in his image and decided to create a plan for the salvation of Man after all. As such was the Sacrifice of the Lamb and the clothing made of lambskin, but man had to go through the karmic routine of his penance and dharmic duties to return to god in faith, trust, and submission, in devotion, prayer, fasting, and sacrifice.

Humanity created out of divinity; human nature composes of A body, spirit and soul and the most complex and intricate components that are superior to any other living form on Earth *(Psalm 139:14).* Human beings had to be created from the material of the earth so that they can exist in the atmosphere and plains of the planet to be able to survive, live and exist, utilizing the compound and materials of the earth to feed and fuel its body and be able to breathe the air without issues and complications.

God breathes the breath of life in the nostrils of man, which makes him a living being, thus the breath from GOD is the living spirit from GOD , it also carries all the material and spiritual values of GOD, therefore man was created Like GOD, to be the GOD of earth, but the spiritual death has caused man to lose those abilities and GOD is leading man back to the knowledge and skills to become like GOD again, and gains salvation to be able to survive in another plain and dominion called the heavenliest.

Nowhere in the Bible does it mention that GOD will take the man to heaven, suggested that Jesus will prepare a place for us, NOT IN HEAVEN (well it is a kind of heavenly home).

Understand that after the breath of life into Man "Man Became a Living Soul," this tells you that the soul is the God particle that given to man from the divine, and this soul does not die, it lives on and goes back to GOD. The jewel and pearl of the Human Being, the most treasured aspect of a human being, thus the fight that the devil created to win your soul. The Body returns to the earth as dust; the Human spirit is the spirit of the man that the Holy Spirit enters when there is a union with GOD.

Emphasis must be made to SATAN and THE DEVILS only fight to take your Soul; they are not interested in your Body or your spirit. they can enter and possess your body and control your spirit. Satan's demons can own your body and push out your spirit, which is the spirit of MAN, **but as you conjoined with the spirit of GOD, the void filled, and the spirit of Man and the spirit of GOD becomes conjoined as one. Ecco 12:7**

Hebrews 4:12   *"For the work of God is quick, and powerful and sharper than the two-edged sword, piercing even to the dividing asunder of soul and spirit, and of the joints and marrow, and is a discerner of the thought and intent of the heart."*

This thought became part of Man and man's quest for power and might and recognition and to exalt himself above the Stars (angels). These thoughts were subliminally injected into the minds of mankind from the inception of his creation, and the illusion of "the Apple" "Beguiled" through the eyes to see the Kingdoms of Earth which was an illusion to the sight and mind eye. The quest for power over kingdoms has been one of the ultimate desires of Satan, injected into the minds of person or persons who are under the influence of Satan, as the quest for mankind from Adam, Cain, the Carthaginian Empire, Ancient Egypt, Sumer and Akkad, Mitanni, Babylonia, Assyria, Hittite Empire, Phoenicia, Ancient Persia, Ancient Sub-Saharan Africa, Ancient India, Ancient China, Ancient Europe and Ancient Indigenous empires

"...I WILL ascend into heaven; I WILL exalt my throne above the stars of God: I WILL sit also upon the mount of the congregation, in the sides of the north." (Isa. 14:13).

Bible verses related to *Lucifer* from the King James Version

Isaiah 14:12-15	*How art thou fallen from heaven, O Lucifer, son of the morning! [how] art thou cut down to the ground, which didst weaken the nations!*
Revelation 12:7-9	*And there was war in heaven: Michael and his angels fought against the dragon, and the dragon fought and his angels,*
Isaiah 14:12	*How art thou fallen from heaven, O Lucifer, son of the morning! [How] art thou <u>cut down to the ground, which didst weaken</u> the nations!*
2 Corinthians 11:14 -	*And no marvel; for Satan himself is transformed into an angel of light.*
Ezekiel 28:17 -	*Thine heart was lifted up because of thy beauty; thou hast corrupted thy wisdom by reason of thy brightness: I will cast thee to the ground; I will lay thee before kings, that they may behold thee.*
Luke 10:18 -	*And he said unto them, I beheld Satan as lightning fall from heaven.*
John 8:44 -	*Ye are of [your] father the devil, and the lusts of your father ye will do. He was a murderer from the beginning, and abode not in the truth, because there is no truth in him. When he speaketh a lie, he speaketh of his own: for he is a liar and the father of it.*
Ezekiel 28:14 -	*Thou [art] the anointed cherub that covereth; and I have set thee [so]: thou wast upon the holy mountain of God; thou hast walked up and down in the midst of the stones of fire.*
1 Peter 5:8 -	*Be sober, be vigilant; because your adversary the devil, as a roaring lion, walketh about, seeking whom he may devour:*
Jude 1:6 -	*And the angels which kept not their first estate, but left their own habitation, he hath reserved in everlasting chains under darkness unto the judgment of the great day.*
Ezekiel 28:15 -	*Thou [wast] perfect in thy ways from the day that thou wast created, till iniquity was found in thee.*
Revelation 12:9 -	*And the great dragon was cast out, that old serpent, called the Devil, and Satan, which deceiveth the whole world: he was cast out into the earth, and his angels were cast out with him.*
Genesis 3:1-24	*Now the serpent was more subtil than any beast of the field which the LORD God had made. And he said unto the woman, Yea, hath God said, Ye, shall not eat of every tree of the garden?*
Ezekiel 28:16	*By the multitude of thy merchandise they have filled the midst of thee with violence, and thou hast sinned: therefore I will cast thee as profane out of the mountain of God: and I will destroy thee, O covering cherub, from the midst of the stones of fire.*
Ezekiel 28:13	*Thou hast been in Eden the garden of God; every precious stone [was] thy covering, the sardius, topaz, and the diamond, the beryl, the onyx, and the jasper, the sapphire, the emerald, and the carbuncle, and gold: the workmanship of thy tabrets and of thy pipes was prepared*

in thee in the day that thou wast created.

Hebrews 2:14   *I likewise took part of the same; that through death he might destroy him that had the power of death, that is, the devil;*

Matthew 4:3   *And when the tempter came to him, he said, if thou be the Son of God, command that these stones be made bread.*

Revelation 12:4   *And his tail drew the third part of the stars of heaven, and did cast them to the earth: and the dragon stood before the woman which was ready to be delivered, for to devour her child as soon as it was born.*

1 Timothy 3:6   *Not a novice, lest being lifted up with pride he falls into the condemnation of the devil.*

Job 1:6   *Now there was a day when the sons of God came to present themselves before the LORD, and Satan came also among them.*

Revelation 20:10   *And the devil that deceived them was cast into the lake of fire and brimstone, where the beast and the false prophet [are] and shall be tormented day and night forever and ever.*

Gen. 3:4-6. "And the serpent said unto the woman, Ye shall not surely die: For God knoweth that in the day ye eat thereof, then your eyes shall be opened, and ye shall be as God, (Heb. omits "as") knowing good and evil. And when the woman saw that the tree was good for food, and that it was pleasant to the eyes, and a tree to be desired to make one wise, she took of the fruit thereof, and did eat, and gave also unto her husband with her; and he did eat. In Adam's mind and also in the Mind of Eve "They will be like Gods, knowing good and evil

---

Isaiah 14: 13   *For thou hast said in thine heart, I will ascend into heaven, I will exalt my throne above the stars of God: I will sit also upon the mount of the congregation, in the sides of the north: (this man has been trying to do since the beginning*

Isaiah 14: 14   I will ascend above the heights of the clouds; I will be like the most High.

Isaiah 14: 16   *They that see thee shall narrowly look upon thee, and consider thee, saying, Is this the man that made the earth to tremble, that did shake kingdoms; (isn't this what some men do in the history of mankind?*

17 PRAYERS

Prayers: Getting answers

What are Prayers? It is communication between Man (Spirit, Body, mind, and soul) and the Supreme Entity – GOD, where the conversation is bi-directional where Man speaks and makes his request, deliver what's in his mind. It is similar to a father and child conversation, where the child is talking to the father and relaying all that he has in his heart, including all complaints, requests, wants and needs. It is a request for intervention from a divine source as you voice your innermost feelings, there is no specific formula or methodology, but according to scripture the better order as defined in the bible when the disciples asked Jesus on how to pray.

- Acknowledge who you are referencing (God), where (in Heaven)
- Acknowledge his supremacy and give him glory (Hollowed be your name)
- What would you like (Thy kingdom come to earth as it is in heaven)?
- Your requests (give us this day our daily bread –sustenance)
- If you flawed in any way (forgive us our trespasses), Karma (as we forgive those who trespass against us)
- Asking for direction (lead us NOT into temptation, but deliver us –from evil)
- Acknowledge whose dominion it is (for thine is the kingdom, the power, and the glory

Most Christian organizations define a pattern as follows:

Prayer begins with Praise, and ends with praise, forgiveness and Confession of all wrongdoings and sins committed that are known and those that are even unknowns, making your petition, wants and needs, reading and quoting specific scriptures (especially what holds God to his word for God does not lie and cannot turn back his word or commitment), Intercession –(best results is to pray for someone who is going through the same as you, pray for others, financial, physical, mental and spiritual needs). Give thanks for listening to the prayers and give thanks for expectations getting them answered and finally do some meditation and look; surprisingly people do hear the quiet voice or gain insight in their mind or thoughts as a response, God does answer. When all done, sing some songs of praise as you believe and have faith that you will get the answer, solution or find a way out.

Praying is also therapeutic as you release what's inside of you, for according to scripture

Proverbs 23:7 *"As a man thinketh in his heart, so is he,"* what he thinks, he becomes. Prayer is a phenomenon that is universal, it exists in all walks of life and all religious affiliations, whether there is a belief in God, self or any other form. It is a natural part of human living and is part of daily communication, whether your focus is on the divine or another object or person, it is a form of expression, thoughts, and emotions where you believe that your communication heard, acknowledged and addressed. The controversial phenomena come to play as you talk to a stone, object, idol or anything material, you cannot expect an answer for these are objects and have no life or spirit unless you are internalizing in the form of psychoanalytic conversations, where they are used as focal points or objects to divinity. Many religions have Idols and Objects on their alter and wonder why there is no response from any spiritual divine source, the reason is that your focus is on the object and not the spirit of divinity – GOD, having installed an Alter of objects or representations of God, your attention must be on GOD and not the objects. Prayer brings humility, reduces stress, brings your body, mind, and spirit into subjection of altered state that influences changes into your character, physically, mentally and spiritually. Altered states that balances the alpha state, slowly into a beta state and can also put you into a theta state, which is the state used by Psychotherapist, psychoanalysis and Clinical Hypnotherapist, to induce changes and reference neurolinguistic programming patterns that may have been injected, instilled or programmed into your subconscious minds in an earlier time, anchored into your memory such as abuse, accidents, danger, an incident, a traumatic situation a memory that may be affecting your reflections.

Christianity does not recognize or acknowledge any methods that influence altered state as an acceptable and labeled them as an abomination unto GOD, but there is little mentioned biblically about altered states, for there are many events in the Bible where people drawn into altered states and either received the Holy Spirit, go into a trance or receive healing. Being possessed by a demon is an altered state that is negative; therefore I believe utilizing prayer and clinical psychoanalysis for healing or removing the negatives are not an abomination. The difference is getting into a drunken state where you cannot control your actions and mind. The variances (differences) are whether the experiences are objective, subjective, intuitive, mentally conscious, or subconscious or a natural event or sickness, faith, and belief is your strength, tool, power and intellectual ammunition utilized to overcome, thus the new science in prayer. The words "hypnosis," "psychoanalysis," "psychotherapy" did not exist in the days of biblical times, but the methodology existed since the beginning of time. The occult science is an abomination, divination, and worship of spirits and anything that is apart from GOD is an abomination.

Christianity started as a profound spiritual, supernatural practices in the Middle-east, where there were all kinds of ghostly encounters and physical and mental altered states, including supernatural healings, visions, experiences, transfigurations, ghostly appearances. It reached the West and morphed, edited and tuned by the elect to what it is today and continues and Religion gets intertwined with Politics and Government (as was in the early days). Even in the Church Gathering as we worship with song and music, it eventually turns into the altered states of closed eyes, lifted hands and a focus to Divinity and chanting the name of God and releasing praises and passionate love towards the divine God.

Genesis 2: 21 *And the LORD God caused a deep sleep to fall upon Adam, and he slept: and he took one of his ribs, and closed up the flesh instead thereof;*

1 Corinthians 3: 16 *Know ye not that ye are the temple of God, and that the Spirit of God dwelleth in you?*

1 Corinthians 3: 17 *If any man defiles the temple of God, he shall God destroy; for the temple of God is holy, which temple ye are.*

Acts 10: 1 *There was a certain man in Caesarea called Cornelius, a centurion of the band called the Italian band,*

Acts 10: 2 *A devout man, and one that feared God with all his house, which gave much alms to the people, and prayed to God alway.*

Acts 10: 3 *He saw in a vision evidently about the ninth hour of the day an angel of God coming into him and saying unto him, Cornelius.*

Acts 10: 4 *And when he looked on him, he was afraid, and said, what is it, Lord? And he said unto him, Thy prayers and thine alms are come up for a memorial before God. And he said, The God of our fathers hath chosen thee, that thou shouldest know his will, and see that Just One, and shouldest hear the voice of his mouth.*

Acts 22:15 *For thou shalt be his witness unto all men of what thou hast seen and heard.*

Acts 22:16 *And now why tarriest thou? arise, and be baptized, and wash away thy sins, calling on the name of the Lord.*

Acts 22:17 *And it came to pass, that, when I was come again to Jerusalem, even while I prayed in the temple, I was in a trance; On the morrow, as they went on their journey, and drew nigh unto the city, Peter went up upon the housetop to pray about the sixth hour:*

Acts 10: 10 *And he became very hungry and would have eaten: but while they made ready, he fell into a trance,*

Acts 10: 11 *And saw heaven opened, and a certain vessel descending upon him, as it had been a great sheet knit at the four corners, and let down to the earth:*

Acts 10: 12   *Wherein were all manner of four-footed beasts of the earth, and wild beasts, and creeping things, and fowls of the air.*

Acts 10: 13   *And there came a voice to him, Rise, Peter; kill, and eat.*

GOD is a jealous god and will not heed the prayers of anyone who is not praying directly to him and have a full dedicated faith and heart towards acknowledging his presence. Therefore give up all other devotion that is away from GOD and dedicates you wholeheartedly to him, your mind, body, spirit, and soul. Be diligent and steadfast praying to the one true God in the right way.

Luke 11: 9   *And I say unto you, Ask, and it shall be given you; seek, and ye shall find; knock, and it shall be opened unto you.*

Luke 11: 10   *For every one that asketh receiveth; and he that seeketh findeth, and to him that knocketh it shall be opened.*

Luke 11: 11   *If a son shall ask bread of any of you that is a father, will he give him a stone? or if he asks a fish, will he for a fish give him a serpent?*

Luke 11: 12   *Or if he shall ask an egg, will he offer him a scorpion?*

Luke 11: 13   *If ye then, being evil, know how to give good gifts unto your children: how much more shall your heavenly Father give the Holy Spirit to them that ask him?*

First and foremost, be convinced the true God is the Real God, and as we research the facts, the GOD of the Bible has living proof that he is the TRUE God of Heaven and Earth, who reveals himself to humanity in every creation and incidents. GOD is a plural word and is a word of Plurality, but it is stated and prophesized in the Bible that "The GOD of the BIBLE is the One True GOD." Not defined in religions, there is a great hatred among the billions of religious people as per the truth of a REAL TRUE GOD.

ISLAM: *The 99 names of Allah and most are hidden from Mankind. "The Greatest Name of Allah is the one which if He [Allah] is called (prayed to) by it, He will answer." The word "Allah" means "GOD" which is the preferred name to be called by and combined with titles. "The Supreme Name of God: Allah."*

Surah 114.1-3

>   *Say: I seek refuge in the Lord of mankind,*
>   *The King of mankind,*
>   *The God of mankind,*

There it is, there is a GOD of Heaven and Earth and all Creation, and there is a GOD of Mankind. Do you worship the GOD of Heaven and Earth, or the King of Mankind and the God of Mankind, are they not the same? Or are they different?

Correspondences between events in Jesus' and Krishna's life:

Author Kersey Graves (1813-1883), a Quaker from Indiana, compared Yeshua's and Krishna's life. He found what he believed were 346 elements in common within Christ and Hindu writings. That appears to be overwhelming evidence that incidents in Jesus' life copied from Krishna's. However, many of Graves' points of similarity are a real stretch.

He did report some fantastic coincidences:

- Yeshua and Krishna were called both a God and the Son of God.
- Both were sent from heaven to earth in the form of a man.
- Both were called Savior, and the second person of the Trinity.
- His adoptive human father was a carpenter.
- A spirit or ghost was their actual father.
- Krishna and Jesus were of royal descent.
- Both were visited at birth by wise men and shepherds, guided by a star.
- Angels in both cases issued a warning that the local dictator planned to kill the baby and had issued a decree for his assassination. The parents fled. Mary and Joseph stayed in Muturea; Krishna's parents stayed in Mathura.
- Both Yeshua and Krishna withdrew to the wilderness as adults and fasted.
- Both identified as "the seed of the woman bruising the serpent's head."
- Jesus was called "the lion of the tribe of Judah." Krishna was called "the lion of the tribe of Saki."
- Both claimed: "I am the Resurrection."
- Both referred to themselves having existed before their birth on earth.
- Both were "without sin."
- Both were god-men: being considered both human and divine.
- They were both considered omniscient, omnipotent, and omnipresent.
- Both performed many miracles, including the healing of disease. One of the first miracles that both performed was to make a leper whole. Each cured "all manner of diseases."
- Both cast out indwelling demons and raised the dead.
- Both selected disciples to spread his teachings.
- Both were meek and merciful. Both criticized for associating with sinners.
- Both encountered a Gentile woman at a well.
- Both celebrated a last supper. Both forgave enemies.
- Both descended into Hell and resurrected. Many people witnessed their ascensions into heaven.

> *Jesus states: Luke 9:10 "For the Son of Man has* **come to seek and to save that which was lost**. "

Hinduism is a monotheistic religion with belief systems that all heavenly bodies that are on the right hand or left hand of God are all respected as Avatars, Deltas, Divas, and GODS. Led to a great misunderstanding to anyone outside of Hinduism. Not that anyone in Hinduism cares what others think or respond to their beliefs, but it is a concern that is being used and voiced that Hinduism is a polytheistic religion. Rather than use and denouncing Hinduism on the Pulpit as having millions of Gods, it would be more of a Quest as a representative of Christianity or any other religion to understand why it is spelled out and misunderstood. It is not our Christian duties to use others and their beliefs as tools to create the sermon that is focused on criticism on others to make us sound convincing, we leave that to the Father of Lies, and criticism is just as Eve said it "The Serpent Beguiled me." Any Preacher who criticizes any other religious belief on the pulpit is guilty of following the leader and father of Lies and use context to "Beguile" their audience.

A clear statement to those who are Christians and know the word of God well. Being knowledgeable of the Word of God , we should follow, acknowledge and act upon what was written in our lives and not be critical of those of any other faith or belief systems (we should consider the above statement and in our heart acknowledge the lack or lost sheep statement) and work to understand and witness with compassion that those that you are trying to inform, teach or observe to for their ability to be spiritual in their own religious belief. We must use the knowledge of the word of God to convince slowly and others what the word meant and what it stands for, and the truth versus any cultural teachings, etc.

It all begins with you, take a look at yourself, an in-depth, more in-depth look and do a self-analysis. I am the vessel that GOD will acknowledge, use, see and hear? What are the characteristics needed for becoming a servant as he as admitted –Moses, Samuel, King David, Joseph, as "My servant."

We are sometimes our very own worst enemy only because of our very own stinking thinking. We find ourselves pondering in negative thoughts, negative words and even adverse actions. What are negative thoughts? We look and judge others, we blame the 'Devil' as soon as something goes wrong, and we criticize others and even ourselves, comparing your state to others. Self-criticism creates a complete turn of events, mind states and affects your environment, job, family, finances, and family. Using verbiage such as "I failed" or "I am a failure" "I am down," "I am not feeling well" "I am under the weather" "I hate this…or that," I am not good enough" "I can't …" "I don't think I deserve…" "I don't know…" I could add a hundred lines to this list, but at least these few will open up your mind.

Proverbs 29:24   *You are your own worst enemy if you take part in a crime. You will not be able, to tell the truth even when people threaten you.*

　　25   *Fear can be a trap, but if you trust in the Lord, you will be safe.*

　　26   *Many people want the friendship of a ruler, but the Lord is the only one who judges people fairly.*

Self-pity and pity-party are negative thoughts and can be a creative force towards a downward spiral for every aspect of life around you. You create your future because you have the creative power within you, it is a God-given gift and ability, and you need to re-think you, meditate upon you and ask the Divine supreme entity of this Universe to guide you towards a sound mind and a positive life.

Prejudice: *(bigotry, because of their sex, gender, beliefs, values, social class, age, disability, religion, sexuality, race/ethnicity, language, nationality, beauty, occupation, education, criminality, sports team affiliation or other personal characteristics).* The dislike of others due to ethnicity and skin color is a very negative attitude for everyone, especially when you religiosity and spirituality is your claim to fame, are a definite way to attract demonic influences and demonic sicknesses such as skin cancer, liver cancer, cancer of all nature, diabetes, high blood pressure. Prejudices, pride, and hate are the elements we need to eliminate in our thinking; we need to know where we came from, what is our heritage linked to our DNA or our changing DNA (for thought causes a minute change in the DNA order). People who are promoting prejudice and hatred and are fully aware that it is a sin and do know that this sin is more significant than murder. Pride, egotism and vanity referred to as Haughtiness is one of the most hated characteristics in any religious doctrine and is one of the abominations in the Bible. It is self-justification and selfish act, not only an inherent weakness of the mind and physical self but it also creates a chain reaction of instilling the same sin in the spirit of your children, which they will learn and carry practice in their lifetime. Therefore you are leading yourself and your lineage into an acquired sinful life that is an abomination to GOD. Even if you are not a believer in God or religion, you are a judgmental person with low esteem for the human race and bringing upon your lineage a curse that cannot be reversed, and for your awareness, you are subject to the same peace, love, joy, happiness as any other person. You are susceptible to the same sicknesses, illnesses, unfortunate circumstances, natures disaster such as Hurricanes, storms, floods, fire, volcanoes, avalanches, accidents, and everything that exists. A person with a heart full of prejudices against others does not make you different from any other person or persons; you are vulnerable to every blessing and disaster of any other person, someday another person may be there to save you in times of need. In the supermarket, there is white meat and dark meat, the better of the two is very expensive, very nutritional, the better meat, have more value, tastier, more in demand, better quality and healthier. Prejudice and its conditions bring you nothing, nothing of value, nothing of worth, nothing that matters. Sooner or later at about age 70 + we are all going to face the ultimate old-age dilemmas, and we will pass from one dimension to another, with a hope that we have created a better environment and programmed a better life for our children and grandchildren. Karma is the total of a person's actions in this present and past that will return in various ways in the future, and our lineage could face the harvest of the deeds we have engaged in the past.

Proverbs 6:16	*These **six things** doth the LORD hate: yea, **seven are an abomination** unto him:*
17	*A **proud** look, a **lying tongue**, and hands that **shed innocent blood**,*
18	*A heart that deviseth wicked imaginations, feet that be swift in running to mischief,*
19	*A **false witness** that **speaketh lies**, and he that **soweth discord** among brethren.*

As you can witness for the list of abominations in Proverbs 6, the tongue
and lying is the greatest abomination that is worst in the eyes of God. We see it on the news, in movies, in teachings and politics, in governments and in every public dominion daily.

Hinduism has multifaceted prejudices of caste, creed, ethnicity, etc. called the 'Varna system,' but was built on a hierarchy of Job roles, status and profession as well as Color (light skinned and Dark skinned). Krishna is the ninth incarnation of Lord Vishnu, and he was dark, dark to near blue. Thus God displays their messages typically in many ways to touch the heart.

Judaism same there If you are not a Jew then you are Gentile, they hated the Half-breed Jew-gentile Samarians, which was one of the first people Jesus witnessed to, and it was a woman at the well, who further seen to the entire city. Jesus came to and has focused on the elimination of this philosophy and doctrine, which still is a significant mindset of today.

Islam has a millet system and a Delphi Caliphate system of racism in regions, Segmentation and each country based on many characteristics. Islam is an ideology and not a race, but maybe striving to display Muslim as one people and may be defining it as a race, but not and are pressing towards avoiding racism as a characteristic exhibited in Islam towards all people are created equal, but righteousness is the benefit of a better life or person

These are great wars and fights of ancient and racism was their ignorance which we seem not to let go of even unto this day. Could it be that God is showering us with Natural disaster to know that we cannot fight against the powers and forces that he hath set upon this earth and that your thinking of superiority is worth less than a penny against the wiles of nature?

Sometimes Society also impounds people in that state, as it is the state of poverty that gets sustenance from the Government to maintain an impoverished society. Look and observe where are the inner cities and the impoverished areas within a town, state or nation. It is where there are feeble minded people who like "crabs in a barrel' pull each other down, rather than push each other up, so they can be pulled up. The inner city produces many that becomes a social disease (Poverty is a social disease) to society and the thinking is how do I make quick money; the thought of the quick money is a speedy way to imprison your life. Remember 'the Jewel' of man is 'his soul.' The 'soul' is what ties the body, mind, and spirit together to be 'a person' that God created. Without the soul, you become a 'Zombie' 'a walking dead,' a useless physical being that has no mind and no purpose.

According to Religion and scripture, "The Devil" does not want your body, he fights for your "soul," the soul is eternal, and between the fight of Good and Evil, the treasure, the booty, the bounty is the soul. Man is a living soul; unless he loses his soul, he becomes an empty vessel. The reason why the New Testament talks about Jesus sacrifice, and the sacrifice made for the security and redemption of humanity, to bring to them a path to Salvation, a way to save your soul and be connected to GOD and Divinity. He did not become a living sacrifice so that man can create a religion called "Christianity," he came to save mankind from extinction and to maintain them as true "living Soul" and to re-create the universal link and bond between GOD and Man and guard them against losing their soul to the Devil.

Every Religion teaches you to gain knowledge for enlightenment, how to achieve values in life for yourself and your people, but there is only one way to protect your soul. Jesus Christ and GOD,purposed, for he has to take on the full makeup of Man, fell the emotions, pain, love and joy, happiness and sadness and all other mental and physical feelings (for a spirit does not possess physical, psychological and emotional feelings as a living being does), thus the experiences that shows why God sometimes does not understand your grief, pain, or emotional states (he is a Spirit), therefore after millennium of prayers from Man , God finally took on the Human Body to fully understand all they feel, pain, love, joy, happiness, grief, sadness and all the physical, mental and emotional characteristics that a human body can experiences . He defeated the Devil as he understood what we feel and what we experience. He finally left his spirit for us to fill us with his power and source as 'The Holy Spirit' becomes a new addition to the human factor and Man now becomes four and five dimensions being and more, for on Earth is heaven and hell. There are many heavens; some scriptures define nine Heavens, some seven Heavens, Christianity talks about three heavens, where the third heaven divided into multiple heavens, which right here on Earth and we can see and experience it in various ways and even sight. Why are some people living the dream and I am not? Well, they are fortunate and inherited great wealth and peace love and joy, wealth and riches, success and prosperity, it is because someone in their lineage (and ancestry – grandparents, etc.) have prayed and committed to making sure that their generations are BLESSED and have made the sacrifice to be connected to GOD. You need to do the same for your lineage and generation to come for it is going to be more robust and harder as the time gets into a state of chaotic overwhelming of evil and demonic influences and population.

My mental states: are they clean, transparent and uncorrupt? Are there any sins in his life? Is there unforgiveness? Am I following the Commandments and instructions that GOD has given?

No man is perfect except Jesus, and GOD is aware of this, but you are a work in progress, and he will help you through. GOD will always support those who support themselves, even though it is written: "rely on GOD wholly."

A man is not bigger than how much he can pray or his prayer. Prayer is a humbling act that builds characteristic within and gives you the ability to unveil all the darkest thoughts and feelings (and also the greatest good and happy feelings) within unto an unseen spirit called GOD. Therefore it is therapeutic as well. Try praying in the broad sense, the more your faith in God increases and your belief in the existence of an all-powerful God; the more you will be able to develop a broad, robust spiritual connectivity to divinity, which eventually strengthens your mind and body. These projections influence your physical and spiritual dimensions, resulting in a definite attraction of the elements and circumstances. The entire bible, Quran, Bhagwat Gita, Vedas is full of prayers and hymns that are uttered by believers in a quest for the fulfillment of any needs, and also for the acknowledgment of worship, thanksgiving and extended love for God and his presence. Billions of people on this earth cannot be wrong in their belief system that there exist a supernatural spiritual divine supreme being or beings that have a concern and a role in the lives of people and all living beings. God did say I will send you a 'comforter,' 'a guide,' 'a counselor,' to keep you in all your ways. Fellowship with other people in a prayer mindset in one accord prays together it becomes an atmosphere of divine grace, where the spirit of God seems to be present and soothes the environment where the praying group focuses their minds in devotion and in concentrated, focused thoughts on that which is in their mind the controller of their spirit – God. The early church according to scripture and history achieved a lot of miracles and tremendous feats in their prayers, quite a lot of 'healing the sick'; making the lame walk, even deliver spiritual blows to their enemies and oppressors.

- **_Be Persistent:_** *The first key to answered prayer is persistence -- which means "to hold fast to," or hold onto tightly. God wants us to hold on tightly to His promises in prayer. Don't let disappointment cause you to let go of your faith.*
- **_Be Purposeful:_** *The Bible says one of the reasons we haven't received God's best is that we haven't asked Him (see James 4:2). But God wants us to share our hearts with Him. He wants children who are willing to dream His dreams.*
- **_Be Personal:_** *The most critical key to effective prayer is a personal relationship with our Heavenly Father. The man in the parable went to his friend when he needed help.*
- *Ask Believing*
- *Ask according to God's Will*
- *Must Be Sincere*
- *Must Be Humble*
- *Must Be Fervent*
- *Must Be Persistent*
- *Pray in Private*
- *Pray Being Obedient*
- *Pray Like God's Friend*

> **First key: Ask:** *Jesus said in Matthew 7:7, "Ask and it will be given to you" (emphasis added throughout). This is a fundamental starting point. However, it is one that too often misunderstood or not used. Jesus said in Matthew 7:7, "Ask and it will be given to you" (emphasis added throughout). This is a fundamental starting point. However, it is one that too often misunderstood or not used.*

- > **Second key: Have faith:** *Having faith—believing God will indeed hear and answer—is an essential key to receiving answers to our prayers. The apostle James explained in James 1:5-8, "If any of you lacks wisdom, let him ask of God. … But let him ask in faith, with no doubting, for he who doubts is like a wave of the sea driven and tossed by the wind. For let, not that man supposes that he will receive anything from the Lord; he is a double-minded man, unstable in all his ways."*

- > **Third key: Seek God's will:** *The apostle John wrote, "Now this is the confidence that we have in Him, that if we ask anything according to His will, He hears us. And if we know that He hears us, whatever we ask, we know that we have the petitions that we have asked of Him" (1 John 5:14-15).*

Know God's Will: to get answers to our prayers, what example did Jesus set that we should follow? John 5:30, last part. Are we also to understand God's will? Ephesians 5:17. How can we get to know His will?
2 Timothy 2:15.

Believe God: 1. According to Jesus Christ is it essential to believe God before we can receive what we ask of Him? Mark 11:24 *(Therefore I say unto you, what things soever ye desire when ye pray, believe that ye receive them, and ye shall have them.)*

Obey God: To get results from your prayers, you must not only know God's will and believe Him; you must also be willing to act on His Word.

- **Fear and Humility:** Too many have a confident attitude and think they can get along fine without God. They neither fear God nor respect His Word as the authority in their lives. If people with that mindset pray, does God respond? Let's understand.

- **Be Persistent:** Some people, if God doesn't answer right away, begin to lose faith and give up praying. They forget that although God promises to respond when we ask according to His will, He nowhere pledges to respond right away. God does not tell us exactly how or precisely when the answer will come.

Exodus 33:17 *(And the LORD said unto Moses, I will do this thing also that thou hast spoken: for thou hast found grace in my sight, and I know thee by name.) So the LORD said to Moses, "I will also do this thing that you have spoken; for you have found grace in my sight, and I know you by name."*

Deuteronomy 4:7 *(For what nation is there so great, who hath God so nigh unto them, as the LORD, our God, is in all things that we call upon him for?) "For what great nation is there that has God so near to it, as the LORD, our God, is to us, for whatever reason we may call upon Him?*

Deuteronomy 4:29-30 *"But from there you will seek the LORD your God, and you will find Him if you seek Him with all your heart and with all your soul. {30} "When you are in distress, and all these things come upon you in the latter days, when you turn to the LORD your God and obey His voice*

2 Chronicles 7:13-14 *"When I shut up heaven and there is no rain, or command the locusts to devour the land, or send pestilence among My people, {14} "if My people who are called by My name will humble themselves, and pray and seek My face, and turn from their wicked ways, then I will hear from heaven, and will forgive their sin and heal their land.*

Psalms 10:17-18 *LORD, you have heard the desire of the humble; you will prepare their heart; you will cause your ear to hear, {18} to do justice to the fatherless and the oppressed, that the man of the earth may oppress no more.*

Psalms 32:5-7	*I acknowledged my sin to you, and my iniquity I have not hidden. I said, "I will confess my transgressions to the LORD," And you forgave the iniquity of my sin.*
	Selah {6} for this cause everyone who is godly shall pray to You In a time when you may be found; surely in a flood of great waters, they shall not come near him. {7} you are my hiding place; you shall preserve me from trouble; you shall surround me with songs of deliverance. Selah
Psalms 34:14-19	*Depart from evil and do good; Seek peace and pursue it. {15} the eyes of the LORD are on the righteous, and His ears are open to their cry. {16} the face of the LORD is against those who do evil, to cut off the remembrance of them from the earth. {17} The righteous cry out, and the LORD hears and delivers them out of all their troubles. {18} The LORD is near to those who have a broken heart and saves such as have a contrite spirit. {19} many are the afflictions of the righteous, But the LORD delivers him out of them all.*
Psalms 37:3-9	*Trust in the LORD, and do good; dwell in the land, and feed on His faithfulness. {4} delight yourself also in the LORD, and He shall give you the desires of your heart. {5} commit your way to the LORD; Trust also in Him, And He shall bring it to pass. {6} He shall bring forth your righteousness as the light, and your justice as the noonday. {7} Rest in the LORD, and wait patiently for Him; Do not fret because of him who prospers in his way, Because of the man who brings wicked schemes to pass. {8} Cease from anger, and forsake wrath; do not fret; it only causes harm. {9} for evildoers shall be cut off; But those who wait on the LORD, they shall inherit the earth*
Psalms 50:14-15	*Offer to God thanksgiving, and pay your vows to the Most High. {15} call upon me in the day of trouble; I will deliver you, and you shall glorify me."*
Psalms 55:16 -18	*As for me, I will call upon God, and the LORD shall save me. {17} Evening and morning and at noon I will pray, and cry aloud, and He shall hear my voice. {18} He has redeemed my soul in peace from the battle that was against me, for there were many against me*
Psalms 69:29-33	*But I am poor and sorrowful; Let your salvation, O God, set me up on high. I will praise the name of God with a song and will magnify Him with thanksgiving. This also shall please the LORD better than an ox or bull, which has horns and hooves. The humble shall see this and be glad; and you who seek God, your hearts shall live. For the LORD hears the poor, and does not despise His prisoners.*
Psalms 91:14-16	*"Because he has set his love upon me. Therefore I will deliver him; I will set him on high because he has known my name. He shall call upon me, and I will answer him; I will be with him in trouble; I will deliver him and honor him. with long life, I will satisfy him and show him my salvation.*
Psalms 102:17	*He shall regard the prayer of the destitute, and shall not despise them prayer.*
Psalms 145:14	*The LORD upholds all who fall and rises up all who are bowed down*
Psalms 145:15	*the eyes of all look expectantly to You, And You give them their food in due season.*
Psalms 145:16	*you open your hand and satisfy the desire of every living thing.*
Psalms 145: 17	*The LORD is near to all who call upon Him, to all who call upon Him in Truth*
Psalms 145:19	*He will fulfill the desire of those who fear Him; He also will hear their cry and save them.*
Psalms 145:20	*The LORD preserves all who love Him, but all the wicked He will destroy*

Proverbs 15:8	*The sacrifice of the wicked is an abomination to the LORD, but the prayer of the upright is His delight.*
Proverbs 15:29	*The LORD is far from the wicked, But He hears the prayer of the righteous*
Isaiah 55:6-7	*Seek the LORD while He may be found, call upon Him while He is near.*
Isaiah 55:7	*Let the wicked forsake his way, and the unrighteous man his thoughts; Let him return to the LORD, And He will have mercy on him; And to our God, For He will abundantly pardon.*
Isaiah 58:6-9	*"Is this not the fact that I have chosen: To lose the bonds of wickedness, to undo the heavy burdens, to let the oppressed go free, and that you break every yoke?*
Isaiah 58:7	*is it not to share your bread with the hungry, and that you are bringing to your house the poor who are cast out; When you see the naked, that you cover him, And not hide yourself from your own flesh?*
Isaiah 58:8	*Then your light shall break forth like the morning, your healing shall spring forth speedily, and your righteousness shall go before you; the glory of the LORD shall be your rear guard.*
Isaiah 58:9	*Then you shall call, and the LORD will answer; you shall cry, and He will say, 'Here I am.' "If you take away the yoke from your midst, the pointing of the finger, and speaking wickedness,*
Jeremiah 29:11-13	*For I know the thoughts that I think toward you, says the LORD, thoughts of peace and not of evil, to give you a future and a hope. Then you will call upon me and go and pray to me, and I will listen to you, and you will seek me and find me when you search for me with all your heart.*
Jeremiah 33:2-3	*"Thus says the LORD who made it, the LORD who formed it to establish it (the LORD is His name):*
Jeremiah 33: 3	*'Call to me, and I will answer you, and show you great and mighty things, which you do not know.'*
Lamentations 3:21-26	*this I recall to my mind. Therefore I have hope.*
Lamentations 3:22	*Through the Lord's mercies we are not consumed because His compassions fail not.*
Lamentations 3:23	*they are new every morning; Great is your faithfulness.*
Lamentations 3:24	*"The LORD is my portion," says my soul, "Therefore I hope in Him!"*
Lamentations 3:25	*The LORD is good to those who wait for Him, to the soul who seeks Him.*
Lamentations 3:26	*it is good that one should hope and wait quietly for the salvation of the LORD.*
Matthew 6:6-15	*"But you, when you pray, go into your room, and when you have shut your door, pray to your Father who is in the secret place; and your Father who sees in secret will reward you openly.*
Matthew 6:7	*"And when you pray, do not use vain repetitions as the heathen do. For they think that they will be heard for their many words*
Matthew 6:8	*"Therefore do not be like them. For your Father knows the things, you have need of before you ask Him.*
Matthew 6:9	*"In this manner, therefore, pray: Our Father in heaven, hallowed be your name.*
Matthew 6:10	*your kingdom come. You will be done on earth as it is in heaven.*
Matthew 6:11	*give us this day our daily bread.*
Matthew 6:12	*and forgive us our debts, as we forgive our debtors.*
Matthew 6:13	*and do not lead us into temptation, but deliver us from the evil one. For yours are the kingdom and the power and the glory forever. Amen.*
Matthew 6:14	*"For if you forgive men their trespasses, you're heavenly Father will also forgive you.*
Matthew 6:15	*"But if you do not forgive men their trespasses, neither will your Father*

	forgive your trespasses
Matthew 7:7-11	"Ask, and it will be given to you; seek, and you will find; knock, and it will be opened to you
Matthew 7:8:	"For everyone who asks receives, and he who seeks finds, and to him who knocks it will be opened.
Matthew 7:9	"Or what man is there among you who, if his son asks for bread, will give him a stone?
Matthew 7:10	"Or if he asks for a fish, will he give him a serpent?
Matthew 7:11	"If you then, being evil, know how to give good gifts to your children, how much more will your Father who is in heaven give good things to those who ask Him!
Matthew 18:18-20	"Assuredly, I say to you, whatever you bind on earth will be bound in heaven, and whatever you loose on earth will be loosed in heaven.
Matthew 18:19 "	Again I say to you that if two of you agree on earth concerning anything that they ask, it will be done for them by My Father in heaven.
Matthew 18:20	"For where two or three are gathered together in my name, I am there in the midst of them."
Mark 11:24-26	"Therefore I say to you, whatever things you ask when you pray, believe that you receive them, and you will have them.
Mark 11:25	"And whenever you stand praying, if you have anything against anyone, forgive him that your Father in heaven may also forgive you your trespasses.
Mark 11:26	"But if you do not forgive, neither will your Father in heaven forgive your trespasses."
Luke 11:2-4	So He said to them, "When you pray, say: Our Father in heaven, hallowed be your name. Your kingdom comes. You will be done on earth as it is in heaven.
Luke 11:3	give us day by day our daily bread.
Luke 11:4	and forgive us our sins, for we also forgive everyone who is indebted to us. And do not lead us into temptation, but deliver us from the evil one."
Luke 11:10-13	"For everyone who asks receives, and he who seeks finds, and to him who knocks it will be opened.
Luke 11:11	"If a son asks for bread from any father among you, will he give him a stone? Or if he asks for a fish, will he give him a serpent instead of a fish?
Luke 11:12	"Or if he asks for an egg, will he offer him a scorpion?
Luke 11:13	"If you then, being evil, know how to give good gifts to your children, how much more will your heavenly Father give the Holy Spirit to those who ask Him!"
John 4:10	Jesus answered and said to her, "If you knew the gift of God, and who it is who says to you, 'Give Me a drink,' you would have asked Him, and He would have given you living water."
John 14:12-18	"Most assuredly, I say to you, he who believes in me, the works that I do he will do also, and greater works than these he will do because I go to My Father.
John 14:13	"And whatever you ask in my name, that I will do, that the Father may be glorified in the Son.
John 14:14	"If you ask anything in my name, I will do it.
John 14:15	"If you love me, keep my commandments.
John 14:16	"And I will pray the Father, and He will give you another Helper, that He may abide with you forever;
John 14:17	"the Spirit of truth, whom the world cannot receive because it neither sees

Him nor knows Him; but you know Him, for He dwells with you and will be in you.

John 14:*18*   "I will not leave you orphans; I will come to you.

John 15:5-14   "I am the vine, you are the branches. He who abides in me, and I in him, bears much fruit; for without me you can do nothing.

John 15:*6*   "If anyone does not abide in me, he is cast out as a branch and is withered; and they gather them and throw them into the fire, and they are burned.

John 15:*7*   "If you abide in me, and my words abide in you, you will ask what you desire, and it shall be done for you.

John 15:*8*   "By this My Father is glorified, that you bear much fruit; so you will be my disciples.

John 15:*9*   "As the Father loved Me, I also have loved you; abide in my love.

John 15:*10*   "If you keep my commandments, you will abide in my love, just as I have kept My Father's commandments and abide in His love.

John 15:*11*   "These things I have spoken to you, that my joy may remain in you, and that your joy may be full.

John 15:*12*   "This is my commandment, that you love one another as I have loved you.

John 15:*13*   "Greater love has no one than this than to lay down one's life for his friends.

John 15:*14*   "You are my friends if you do whatever I command you.

John 15:*16*   "You did not choose me, but I chose you and appointed you that you should go and bear fruit and that your fruit should remain, that whatever you ask the Father in My name He may give you.

Romans 10:11-13   For the Scripture says, "Whoever believes on Him will not be put to shame."

Romans 10:12   for there is no distinction between Jew and Greek, for the same Lord over all is rich to all who call upon Him.

Romans 10:13   for "whoever calls on the name of the LORD shall be saved."

Hebrews 4:14-16   Seeing then that we have a great High Priest who has passed through the heavens, Jesus the Son of God, let us hold fast our confession.

Hebrews 4:*15*   for we do not have a High Priest who cannot sympathize with our weaknesses, but was in all points tempted as we are, yet without sin.

Hebrews 4:*16*   Let us, therefore, come boldly to the throne of grace that we may obtain mercy and find grace to help in time of need.

Hebrews 11:6   But without faith, it is impossible to please Him, for he who comes to God must believe that He is and that He is a rewarder of those who diligently seek Him.

James 1:2-8   My brethren, count it all joy when you fall into various trials,

James 1:*3*   knowing that the testing of your faith produces patience.

James 1:*4*   But let patience have its perfect work, that you may be perfect and complete, lacking nothing.

James 1:*5*   if any of you lacks wisdom, let him ask of God, who gives to all liberally and without reproach, and it will be given to him.

James 1:*6*   but let him ask in faith, with no doubting, for he who doubts are like a wave of the sea driven and tossed by the wind.

James 1:*7*   For let not that man suppose that he will receive anything from the Lord;

James 1:*8*   he is a double-minded man, unstable in all his ways.

James 4: 6-10   But He gives more grace. Therefore He says: "God resists the proud, but gives grace to the humble."

James 4: 7   Therefore submit to God. Resist the devil, and he will flee from you.

James 4: 8   Draw near to God and He will draw near to you. Cleanse your hands, you sinners; and purify your hearts, you double-minded.

James 4: 9	*Lament and mourn and weep! Let your laughter be turned to mourning and your joy to gloom.*
James 4: 10	*Humble yourselves in the sight of the Lord, and He will lift you up.*
James 5:14-18	*Is anyone among you sick? Let him call for the elders of the church, and let them pray over him, anointing him with oil in the name of the Lord.*
James 5:15	*and the prayer of faith will save the sick, and the Lord will raise him up. And if he has committed sins, he will be forgiven.*
James 5:16	*confess your trespasses to one another, and pray for one another, that you may be healed. The effective, fervent prayer of a righteous man avails much.*
James 5:17	*Elijah was a man with a nature like ours, and he prayed earnestly that it would not rain, and it did not rain on the land for three years and six months.*
James 5:18	*and he prayed again, and the heaven gave rain, and the earth produced its fruit.*
1 John 3:21-23	*Beloved, if our heart does not condemn us, we have confidence toward God.*
1 John 3:22	*And whatever we ask we receive from Him because we keep His commandments and do those things that are pleasing in His sight.*
1 John 3:23	*and this is His commandment: that we should believe on the name of His Son Jesus Christ and love one another, as He gave us commandment.*
1 John 5:14	*Now this is the confidence that we have in Him, that if we ask anything According to His will, He hears us.*
1 John 3:1	*And if we know that He hears us, whatever we ask, we know that we have the petitions what we have asked of Him*

- Study the WORD of God: Let the Bible be your guidance
- Repentance and Forgiveness
- Seek the purpose of Man as per GOD's purpose
- Faith and Belief that GOD hears and will respond
- Let GOD be the one the Cleanse your Mind, Heart, Body
- Always Praise

Each time "**The angel of the LORD"** reaches out and accost, assist or communicates with the People, we know it is a message from GOD, and we do not mention the name of the Angel, but use the name of the LORD based on the circumstance and characteristic, or activity.

18 RELIGION II

The Supreme deity and Supreme GOD in Hinduism is Brahman, a cosmic and the highest universal principle of reality, the ultimate absolute soul in the Universe. Brahman as a metaphysical concept is the single binding unity within the diversity of all that exists in the universe, The Supreme Self. The oldest religion in the world is Hinduism, **Hinduism** (known to adherents as Sanatan Dharma, 'Eternal Order'). Although often viewed as a polytheistic faith, **Hinduism** is henotheistic. Some religions are secluded and dedicated to a small region of the world, and some religions are universal (for the whole world). Christianity and Islam are revelations for the Entire human race, whereas religions such a Judaism and Hinduism are dedicated to specific people and a specific region of the world. Judaism focused on a tiny country of Israel and the region of the Middle East, and a select race of people as written in scripture, by prophets and man as messages from God. Hinduism dedicated to the culture, people and around the country of India (originally Hindustan – a greater region than India).It is spreading and open to the world's population as teachings and scripture of the visitation and doctrines of GOD in an ancient age and is very much close to opening the knowledge of science and all the list of studies such as Psychology, Astronomy, Biology, Agriculture, Engineering, Archaeology, Architecture, Art and design, History, Business, Medicine, Philosophy and the list goes on. The scripture mainly "The Vedas" are four main books and multiple smaller books that were dispersed to a greater region of the INDO-Asia region and are slowly drifting to all other regions of the world. There was no specific drive to educate the rest of the world in this doctrine as specified in Islam and Christianity. Each region followed a specified section of the Vedas and created a denomination of the Hindu sect into a different religious denomination and an arm or limb or branch of Hinduism. Today's Judaism is taught in-depth to a select people and not exposed to the entire world as doctrine for everyone; it classifies people into two segments or division or race of 'Jews and Gentiles". If you are not a Jew, by lineage then you are a Gentile. Even Islam divides and segregates people into "Muslims and non-believers (non-Muslims). One main reason why the people of the world is getting more and more into conflicts resulting in hatred and unnecessary wars – leads to hard-core prejudices. We have in this world a division and segregation of humanity by race creating prejudices beyond comprehension and justification and then we have the separation and segregation of mankind by religious beliefs and abstract thinking that is linked to spirituality causing some to believe they are a special select by a Spirit – called GOD (In various names and language). Some are unsure of which spirit gives them the message, whether it is the spirit of Satan or the Spirit of God, whether it is a message or messages from God or the Devil. Many claims to communicate with God and have conversations with God, because filled with the Spirit of God and God is guiding them in their mind, thoughts, and actions. A question for the very Individual to answer…. For the proof of the actual communication, direction and action are only in the deliverance, none – no human can prove it as facts, but by faith and belief only. Yet there can be proof as per the great commission of Jesus Christ *"John 14:12: "Truly, truly, I say to you, he who believes in Me, the works that I do, he will also do; and greater works than these he will do; because I go to the Father."* The proof is that we can all perform many more miracles as Jesus ordained, and if you are healing the sick, opening blind eyes, make the lame walk, raise the dead, cast out demons and calm the storm, that's proof of the God in you. Moses, according to the bible and Koran was the only prophet who spoke to God's face to face and there are many incidents and doctrine where many other prophets encountered God and the Angels of the Lord. Mohamed was visited by the very same Angel of GOD (Gabriel) who appeared to Mary and Joseph delivering the message of Jesus' birth and his earthly existence. In every communication the message is spelled out by God as guidance, evidence and to understanding the difference between right and Wrong, how to live right, chained to the Adam and Eve free will decision to commit "wrong" or SIN leaving a trace within mankind's DNA and the will to commit sin and do wrong. Ancient Hindu scriptures defines multiple episodes of the Life of many incarnations of GOD as a living man on earth, and the primary purpose of the embodiment and reincarnation is to defeat evil, display and teach mankind the ways of God and how to live, worship, Karma and Dharma (actions, works, deeds, for salvation, a better life now and forever).

Sidebar:

God created humanity – Equal; He did not create one man with one more tailbone more than the other man, or one more eye that the other men or a different brain structure or architecture more than the other. Tying this to religion, a Muslim, Hindu, Christian or Jew has nothing more than any other man as created by God, so there should be no prejudice against any man where GOD's creation is concerned. Each may have a different belief system, faith and knowledge over the other in some areas. NONE on this earth today can prove the righteousness of his very own belief that IT is REALLY and TRULY from The God they believe in worship. Tthe reason is, GOD is not a Man and do not have or possess the ignorance of man to see each other different in whatever way or connection to the Divine. When God created Man from the Dust, the region's dust or clay, in other words, and common language "mud" "dirt" or "Dust", so we are all "mud-men, men of dust", there is no difference in a Jewish man being better than a Christian Mud/Dirt/Dustman or a Muslim mud/Dirt/dustman. Scientifically we are developed from "Stardust," which is the same as all particles of Stardust. The Hebrew word for dust in **Genesis 2:7 is aphar (Strong's #6083):** *clay, earth, mud, ashes, earth, ground, mortar, powder, rubbish. Mankind is God's workmanship, and if there are individuals that use their*

God-given knowledge and wisdom to define differences in any man, he is certainly using the words and nature of "The Devil" so maybe you should remove from your mind, from your diction and thoughts the issue of the difference in mankind that leads to prejudices, hate, racism, for your dust is definitely not better than any other dust and when your die, you dust will return to the earth as the dust from which you came. It does not return as "white dust," or "black dust" or "brown dust" or "yellow dust" and there are no special caucasian burial ground or black burial ground even not a White, Black, Brown, Yellow or Red heaven.

It is then clear that the God made Man with the same image with equal measure in every way the very IMAGE of God, and given the same 'breath of life through his nostrils. Therefore all men are equal, but some may have to be morphed due to nature, environment, and culture OR it could also have been the results of suffering or the evils in life and limitations of the connection to divine sustenance or moral corruption.

Our Human design is so sophisticated we are put together by the thousands of elements of the 'dust' put together with purposeful design in a complex organization glued together by the 'gluon' in our cells that holds our physical body together. These cells supplied with the right kind of energy and materials (food) or body processes it to maintain a perfect body, where the 'breath of life – the spirit of God' makes us a living being and ties together the Spirit, Mind, and body of a man.

It is not mentioned in what area God created man (assuming it is somewhere in the Middle East, the dirt is red-clay, Adamah (Biblical Hebrew : אדמה) is a word, translatable as ground or earth, Adam (אדם) literally means "red", etymological connection between Adam and adamah, adamah designating "red clay" or "red ground", The word adamah could be translated "red ground," and the name Adam, could be said to mean "red man" or "man from the red dirt."), but it did mention that he put in the Garden of Eden which between the four rivers, located in Iraq…. So then our citizenship should be "we are all Iraqis" Middle Eastern." So take into consideration this idea when you define any prejudicial differences of any man, for Adam had to be created from "The DUST – elements of the Earth" so as to survive in the atmosphere and earth as the other elements, and a lowliness, a humble substance, a natural substance so that you did not need a spacesuit to survive. The final tap on this subject is that you belong on earth and cannot travel to the heavens without God or his provision or you will disintegrate. The body becomes the host for "God's spirit" through the breath he instills in us, so we are Gods in a human body.

*On differentiation of Skin color, the theories point to Nature, climatic conditions, the source of sustenance, foods, and fusions within the DNA during the course of time and ages. There is also the theory of "The Devil" making his kind in his likeness." Genesis 6: 2-4 6 And it came to pass when men began to multiply on the face of the earth, and daughters were born unto them, 2. That the sons of God saw the daughters of men that they were fair, and they took them wives of all which they chose.3. And the Lord said, My spirit shall not always strive with man, for that he also is flesh: yet his days shall be a hundred and twenty years. Linked to **The Book Of Enoch**: Chapter 6 - 1 And it came to pass when the children of men had multiplied that in those days were born unto 2. them beautiful and comely daughters. And the angels, the children of the heaven, saw and lusted after them, and said to one another: 'Come; let us choose us wives from among the children of men 3. and beget us, children.' And Semjaza, who was their*

leader, said unto them: 'I fear ye will not 4 indeed agree to do this deed, and I alone shall have to pay the penalty of a great sin.' And they all answered him and said: 'Let us all swear an oath, and all bind ourselves by mutual imprecations 5. not to abandon this plan but to do this thing.' Then sware they all together and bound themselves 6. by mutual imprecations upon it. And they were in all two hundred; who descended in the days of Jared on the summit of Mount Hermon, and they called it Mount Hermon because they had sworn 7 and bound themselves by mutual imprecations upon it. And these are the names of their leaders: Samlazaz, their leader, Araklba, Rameel, Kokablel, Tamlel, Ramlel, Danel, Ezeqeel, Baraqijal, 8 Asael, Armaros, Batarel, Ananel, Zaq1el, Samsapeel, Satarel, Turel, Jomjael, Sariel. These are their chiefs of tens.4 There were giants in the earth in those days; and also after that, when the sons of God came in unto the daughters of men, and they bare children to them, the same became mighty men which were of old, men of renown.
This is the reason for such great wars of the Old Testament for God wanted to wipe out the contamination of the blood and bloodlines.

Christianity was founded by teachings and doctrines of Jesus Christ approximately around 33CE after Christ, by followers of Christ. **Christianity** originated in Roman-occupied Jerusalem, a predominantly but not entirely Jewish society, with traditional philosophies distinct from the Classical Greek thought which was dominant in the greater Roman Empire at the time. The **Christian Old Testament** overlaps with the Hebrew Bible and the **Greek** Septuagint; the Hebrew Bible known in **Judaism** as the Tanakh. The New Testament is a collection of writings by early **Christians**, believed to be mostly **Jewish** Disciples of **Christ**, written in first-century Koine **Greek**. Most facts came from The **Sumerian** language is one of the first known written words. The "proto-literate" period of **Sumerian** writing spans c. 3300 to 3000 BC. In this period, records are purely logographic, with no linguistic or phonological content. The oldest document of the proto-literate period is the Kish tablet. According to Medieval **Traditional** Jewish exegesis such as the Midrash (**Genesis Rabbah 38**), states that Adam spoke **Hebrew** because of the name he gives Eve which is "Isha" (**Genesis 2**:23). And "Chava" from (Genesis 3:20) which only makes sense when spoken in **Hebrew**.

As for **Buddhism**, it was founded by an Indian Prince Siddhartha Gautama in approximately 566BCE (Before Common Era), about 2500 years ago, The Tripitaka, Sutta-Nipata, Samyutta-Nikaya, Anguttara-Nikaya, and Dhammapada are the primary scripture of this religion. More than 370 million people are following Buddhism religion worldwide.

The oldest of the four main religions are **Hinduism**, has no beginning and this is having many important scriptures like Bhagwat Gita, Vedas, Puranas, Upanishads, Mahabharata, Ramayana, etc.

Islam founded 1400 years in Saudi Arabia by Mohamed, and the Quran is the primary scripture, literature, and doctrine.

Thus we wonder why there are so many religions. Do they all point to the same God? How do I know if I am praying, worshiping and focusing on the RIGHT God or which belief system? Or is God an Extraterrestrial being? **Religion** is between 200,000 and 10,000 years **old and even longer since the beginning of man.**

Man has limited intelligence and venturing to gain and expand his knowledge of everything. We do not know enough of our Earth, our body, our mind or how it operates and does what it does. The man has ZERO knowledge of the Universe or anything related to the universe, Scientists and Astronomers are all speculating and based on theory and visual images from telescope and space travel vehicles, etc. are the sum up of all scientific speculation of what the universe or anything out of the Atmosphere of earth defines.

So the man with his spiritual, religious experiences felt it is all from God as such document the experiences in either sound or written (by relating the experiences from generation to generation). "God is not primordial in the evolution of **religion.**" Creationism is the **religious** belief that the universe and life originated "from specific acts of divine **creation,**" as opposed to the scientific conclusion that they came about through natural processes.

It is a matter of your very own belief system and faith that will lead you to what-so-ever religion you feel drawn to, or be convinced by other parties or your very personal spiritual experience that assures you to pursue further into any specific religious faith. Many talks religion as a recruitment process to build a majority, but it is all about you and your salvation, your experience and your connection to GOD.

The One GOD in Hinduism:
The nature of the Hindu god: **Hindus** believe that there is one true **God**, the supreme spirit, called Brahman. Brahman has many forms, pervades the whole universe, and symbolized by the sacred syllable OM (or AUM).
The triumvirate is the Brahma and Vishnu Hindu gods. Brahma is the creator of the universe and Vishnu is the preserver; **Shiva** has the most important job out of all three of these; **Shiva** is the destroyer (this keeping of the balance of new and old). Brahma (nominative singular), **Brahman** (stem) (neuter gender) means the concept of the transcendent and immanent ultimate reality, Supreme Cosmic Spirit in Hinduism.

God (Brahman) is the one impersonal, ultimate, but unknowable, spiritual Reality, and is personalized Brahman as Brahma (Creator, with four heads symbolizing creative energy), Vishnu (Preserver, the god of stability and control), and Shiva (Destroyer, god of endings). Most Hindus worship two of Vishnu's ten mythical incarnations: most popular and incarnate as a man born on Earth -Krishna and Rama. On special occasions, Hindus may worship other gods, as well as family and individual deities or rather give reverence for specific purposes. Hindus claim that there are 330 million gods as this is related to the vision of John in heaven where he saw 10,000 x 10,000 x 000 x 000 (Revelations 5:11 - 1. *Then I looked, and I heard the voice of many angels around the throne, the living creatures, and the elders; and the number of them was ten thousand times ten thousand, and thousands of thousands).* **Thus any one of those angels that visits man or the earth is considered divine and From God and Part of God, as such is respected as a God from God. Hopefully, this will clear up some confusion on the Hindu Oneness and explains why they have so many gods. Re: the clarification of gods/Gods/GOD.**

In Hindu tradition, the diversity and plurality of the Gods exist yet points to One God in the various forms, a replication or incarnation in each era for a purpose and reason to save rescue humanity from Evil. There are many Gods many names and types of each God. Brahman is the Reality that transcends all personal names. Brahman is one; this one Reality is called Brahman, the Divine, or the Real—the infinite number of names and forms. The Rig Veda affirms, "Reality is One, and the doctrine and scripture defines all as one for they all originate and are created from one and put together they are all one reality, one divinity, and one entity

---

The Upanishads are considered sacred scriptures by the Hindus.
The following verses from the Upanishads refer to the Concept of God:
  i.   "*Ekam evadvitiyam*"
      "He is One only without a second."   [Chandogya Upanishad 6:2:1][1]
  ii. "*Na casya kascij janita na cadhipah.*"
      "Of Him there are neither parents nor lord."   [Svetasvatara Upanishad 6:9][2]
  iii. "*Na tasya pratima asti*"
      "There is no likeness of Him."   [Svetasvatara Upanishad 4:19][3]
  iv. The following verses from the Upanishad **allude to the inability of man to imagine** God in a particular form:
      "*Na samdrse tisthati rupam asya, na caksusa pasyati kas canainam.*"
      "His form is not to be seen; no one sees Him with the eye."

Similarly in the Bhagwat Gita: **God** has a form as the Supreme Person, Krishna, and is formless as the all-pervading effulgence, known as Brahman. Just as the sun globe is the source of the sunlight, Krishna is the source of the Brahman, as is confirmed in the **Gita** (14.27).
Gita is one of the most influential treatises in eastern philosophy. The Bhagavad-Gita is the eternal message of spiritual wisdom from ancient India. The word Gita **means** song

and the word. Bhagavad **means** God; often the Bhagavad-Gita is called the Song of God. Gita is one of the most influential treatises in eastern philosophy. The Bhagavad-Gita is the eternal message of spiritual wisdom from ancient India. The word Gita **means** song and the word. Bhagavad **means** God; often the Bhagavad-Gita is called the Song of God

Kalkhi – The return of God as the Tenth Reincarnation and avatar of Vishnu

https://en.wikipedia.org/wiki/Kalki
Kalki, also called Kalkin, is the tenth avatar of Hindu god Vishnu to end the Kali Yuga, one of the four periods in an endless cycle of existence (Krita) in Vaishnavism cosmology. He is described in the Puranas as the avatar who rejuvenates existence by ending the darkest and destructive period to remove adharma and ushering in the Satya Yuga while riding a white horse with a fiery sword. The description and details of Kalki are inconsistent among the Puranic texts. He is, for example, only an invisible force destroying evil and chaos in some texts, while an actual person who kills those who persecute others and portrayed as someone leading an army of Brahmin warriors in some. His mythology has been compared to the concepts of Messiah, Apocalypse, Frashokereti, and Maitreya in other religions.
Kalki is also found in Buddhist texts. In Tibetan Buddhism, the Kalachakra-Tantra describes 25 rulers, each named Kalki who rule from the heavenly Shambhala. The last Kalki of Shambhala destroys a barbarian Muslim army, after which Buddhism flourishes

Kalki is an avatara of Vishnu. Avatara means "descent" and refers to a descent of the divine into the material realm of human existence. The Garuda Purana lists ten avatars, with Kalki being the tenth. He is described as the avatar who appears at the end of the Kali Yuga. He ends the darkest, degenerating and chaotic stage of the Kali Yuga (period) to remove adharma and ushers in the Satya Yuga while riding a white horse with a fiery sword. He restarts a new cycle of time. He is described as a Brahmin warrior in the Puranas.
The Mahabharata with its lengthy revelations predicts the return of Vishnu as Kalki the Next Avatar of God (The next incarnation of God), and states that whenever the world is full of evil or overtaken by sin, God incarnates himself and comes down to earth to save humanity, restore and preserve mankind and release upon them more information and scriptures of life and the survival and the return to spirituality and worship and being what God created man to be

The same description in Revelations for the Return of Jesus Christ
https://simple.wikipedia.org/wiki/Kalki_Avatar_aur_Muhammad_Sahib#cite_note-3

> *Some writings claim Kalki to be Mohamed or rather Islam is claiming a Hindu Deity as the return of God in Islam.*
>
> *"Kalki Avatar aur Muhammad Sahib (Hindi: कल्कि अवतार और मुहम्मद साहिब) is a book written in 1969. It was written by Ved Prakash Upaddhay. [1] It was published by Saraswat Vedant Prakash Sanggha. It is written in Hindi.*
>
> *The book mainly attempts to argue that the Islamic prophet Muhammad was Kalki. Kalki is the last avatar of Vishnu according to Hindu scriptures and Puranas."*

The author is Hindu and a scholar of Sanskrit writing.

From the Bible -:
From the Old Testament: The One True GOD
God is Spirit, Life, and infinite, Immutable, Truth, Love, Eternal, Holy, Immortal, Invisible, Omnipresent, Omniscient, and Omnipotent.

Isaiah 44:6 -   *Thus saith the LORD the King of Israel, and his redeemer the LORD of hosts; I [am] the first, and I [am] the last; and beside me [there is] no God.*

1 Timothy 2:5   *For [there is] one God, and one mediator between God and men, the man Christ Jesus;*

Isaiah 43:11 -   *I, [even] I, [am] the LORD; and beside me [there is] no savior.*

1 Corinthians 8:6   *But to us [there is but] one God, the Father, of whom [are] all things, and we in him; and one Lord Jesus Christ, by whom [are] all things, and we by him*

James 2:19 -   *Thou believest that there is one God; thou doest well: the devils also believe, and tremble.*

Deuteronomy 6:4 *- Hear, O Israel: The LORD our God [is] one LORD:*

Isaiah 43:10 - *Ye [are] my witnesses saith the LORD, and my servant whom I have chosen: that ye may know and believe me, and understand that I [am] he: before me there was no God formed, neither shall there be after me*

John 10:30 -   *I and [my] Father are one*

Revelation 1:8 -   *I am Alpha and Omega, the beginning and the ending, saith the Lord, which is, and which was, and which is to come, the Almighty.*

Isaiah 42:8 -   *I [am] the LORD: that [is] my name: and my glory will I not give to another, neither my praise to graven images.*

Jude 1:25 -   *To the only wise God our Saviour, [be] glory and majesty, dominion and power, both now and ever. Amen.*

Mark 12:29 -   *And Jesus answered him, the first of all the commandments [is], Hear, O Israel; The Lord our God is one Lord:*

Deuteronomy 4:39 NKJV *"Know therefore this day, and consider it in your heart, that the*

LORD Himself is God in heaven above, and on the earth beneath there is no other."

Isaiah 45:5   "I am the LORD, and there is no other, there is no God beside me."

Malachi 2:10   "Have we, not all one Father? Has not one God created us?"

Deuteronomy 6:4, "Hear, O Israel: the Lord our God, the LORD is one! You shall love the LORD your God with all your heart, with all your soul, and with all your strength."

From the New Testament:

Matthew 4:10 "It is written, 'You shall worship the LORD your God, and Him only you shall serve.'"

Mark 12:32   "There is one God, and there is no other but He."

James 2:19   "You believe that there is one God; you do well."

Galatians 3:20 "Now a mediator does not mediate for one only, but God is one."

1 Timothy 2:5 "For there is one God, and one Mediator between God and men."

Deuteronomy 4:35, 39 — unto thee it was shewed, that thou mightest know that the LORD, he is God; there is none else beside him.

Deuteronomy 4: 39 Know therefore this day, and consider it in thine heart, that the LORD, he is God in heaven above, and upon the earth beneath: there is none else.

Deuteronomy 6:4 Hear, O Israel: The LORD our God is one LORD: [Note in Mark 12:28 34how Jesus and a Jewish scribe he encountered understood this text.]

Deuteronomy 32:39 See now that I, even I, am he, and there is no god with me: I kill, and I make alive; I wound, and I heal: neither is there any that can deliver out of my hand.

2 Samuel 7:22   Wherefore thou art great, O LORD God: for there is none like thee, neither is there any God beside thee, according to all that we have heard with our ears.

1 Kings 8:60   that all the people of the earth may know that the LORD is God and that there is none else.

Kings 5:15   And he returned to the man of God, he and all his company, and came, and stood before him: and he said, Behold, now I know that there is no God in all the earth, but in Israel: now therefore, I pray thee, take a blessing of thy servant.

Kings 19:15 And Hezekiah prayed before the LORD, and said, O LORD God of Israel, which dwellest between the cherubims, thou art the God, even thou alone, of all the kingdoms of the earth; thou hast made heaven and earth.

Nehemiah 9:6 Thou, even thou, art LORD alone; thou hast made heaven, the heaven of heavens, with all their host, the earth, and all things that are therein, the seas, and all that is therein, and thou preservest them all, and the host of heaven worshippeth thee.

Psalms 18:31 for who is God save the LORD? Or who is a rock save our God?

Psalms 86:10 for thou art great, and doest wondrous things: thou art God alone

Isaiah 37:16, O LORD of hosts, God of Israel, that dwellest between the cherubims, thou art the God, even thou alone, of all the kingdoms of the earth: thou hast made heaven and earth.

Isaiah 37: 20 Now, therefore, O LORD our God, save us from his hand, that all the kingdoms of the earth may know that thou art the LORD, even thou only.

Isaiah 43:10, 11 ye are my witnesses, saith the LORD, and my servant whom I have chosen: that ye may know and believe me, and understand that I am he: before me, there was no God formed , either shall there be after me. I, even I, am the LORD; and beside me, there is no savior. ["This is indeed the Christ, the Savior of the world." John 4:42]

Isaiah 44:6, 8 Thus saith the LORD the King of Israel, and his redeemer the LORD hosts; I am the first, and I am the last, and beside me, there is no God.

Isaiah 44: 8Fear ye not, neither are afraid: have not I told thee from that time, and have declared it? ye are even my witnesses. Is there a God beside me? yea, there is no God; I know not any.

Isaiah 45:21 Tell ye, and bring them near; yea, let them take counsel together: who hath declared this from ancient time? who hath told it from that time? Have not I the LORD? And there is no God else beside me; a just God and a Savior; there is none beside me.

Isaiah 46:9 for I am God, and there is none else; I am God, and there is none like me,

Hosea 13:4 yet I am the LORD thy God from the land of Egypt, and thou shalt know no god but me: for there is no savior beside me. ["Now we believe, not because of thy saying: for we have heard him ourselves, and know that this is indeed the Christ, the Savior of the world." John 4:42]

Joel 2:27 and ye shall know that I am in the midst of Israel and that I am the LORD your God, and none else: and my people shall never be ashamed.

Zechariah 14:9 And the LORD shall be king over all the earth: in that day shall there be one LORD, and his name one.

Mark 12:29-34 And Jesus answered him, The first of all the commandments is, Hear, O Israel; The Lord our God is one Lord: And thou shalt love the Lord thy God with all thy heart, and with all thy soul, and with all thy mind, and with all thy strength: this is the first commandment. And the second is like, namely this, Thou shalt love thy neighbor as thyself. There is none other commandment greater than these. And the scribe said unto him, Well, Master, thou hast said the truth: for there is one God; and there is none other but he: And to love him with all the heart, and with all the understanding, and with all the soul, and with all the strength, and to love his neighbor as himself, is more than all whole burnt offerings and sacrifices. And when Jesus saw that he answered discreetly, he said unto him, Thou art not far from the kingdom of God. And no man after that durst asks him any question.

John17:3 and this is life eternal, that they might know thee the only true God, and Jesus Christ, whom thou hast sent.

Romans 3:30 seeing it is one God, which shall justify the circumcision by faith, and uncircumcision through faith.

1 Corinthians 8:4-6 As concerning therefore the eating of those things that are offered in sacrifice unto idols, we know that an idol is nothing in the world and that there is none other God but one. For though there be that are called gods, whether in heaven or in earth, (as there be gods many, and lords many,) But to us there is but one God, the Father, of whom are all things, and we in him; and one Lord Jesus Christ, by whom are all things, and we by him.

Galatians 3:20 Now a mediator is not a mediator of one, but God is one.

Ephesians4:6 *One God and Father of all, who is above all, and through all, and in you all (the faithful in Christ Jesus - 1:1).*

1 Timothy 1:17 *now unto the King eternal, immortal, invisible, the only wise God, be honor and glory forever and ever. Amen.*

1 Timothy 2:5 *for there is one God, and one mediator between God and men, the man Christ Jesus;*

James2:19 *Thou believest that there is one God; thou doest well: the devils also believe and tremble.*

1 Corinthian 15: 58*"Therefore, my dear brothers, stand firm. Let nothing move you. Always give yourself fully to the work of the Lord, because you know that your labor in the Lord is not in vain." (vs. 58)*

Proverbs 3:5 *"Trust in the LORD with all thine heart, and lean not unto thine own understanding." In all thy ways acknowledge him, and he shall direct thy paths. 7 Be not wise in thine own eyes: fear the LORD, and depart from evil.*

He spoke frankly with the Samaritan woman, *"You Samaritans worship **what you do not know**; we worship **what we do know**, for salvation is **from the Jews (now to query "What is a JEW" or who are the Jews?)** ... The true worshipers will worship the Father in spirit and in truth for they are the kind of worshipers the Father seeks."* (John 4:21-23, NIV)

(1) Pray to GOD- The true GOD, The GOD of the Bible, the very real God that reveals himself to humanity in many ways. To all who seeks him.

1 Corinthians 8:4-6 - *we know that an idol is nothing in the world and that there is none other God but one.*

5 *For though there be that are called gods, whether in heaven or in the earth, (as there be gods many, and lords many,)*

6 *But to us, there is but one God, the Father, of whom are all things, and we in him; and one Lord Jesus Christ, by whom are all things, and we by him.*

Isaiah 45: 21-23 *Tell ye, and bring them near; yea, let them take counsel together: who hath declared this from ancient time? Who hath told it from that time? Have not I the LORD? And there is no God else beside me; a just God and a Saviour; there is none beside me.*

22 *Look unto me, and be ye saved, all the ends of the earth: for I am God, and there is none else.*

23 *I have sworn by myself, the word is gone out of my mouth in righteousness, and shall not return, that unto me every knee shall bow, every tongue shall swear.*

There are different views of GOD and the concepts of GOD from the diversity of Human interpretations. Seeing GOD oneness is dependent on your personal beliefs, and thus GOD becomes limited in Man's perspective of "man's Oneness of GOD" and not "GOD's perspective of GOD." God is infinite and not finite, and this is a grave mistake

MAN makes in their limitations of GOD as such the expectations are limited and not infinite and MAN limits GOD from Performing to above this limitation.

He is infinite, while everything He created is finite. "Finite" defined as "limited."

2 Corinthians 10:12 states, *but they measuring themselves by themselves, and comparing themselves among themselves, are not wise.*

Your life today is the way you have seen it (Prov. 23:7)

The limitation to GOD is very natural and can happen to anyone at any time, being unaware of you limiting GOD in your life. Some of the reasons related due to List below, and your experiences and your knowledge.

(1) Lack of Knowledge of GOD – the is and can be related to anyone new to the study of GOD and GOD's ability
(2) Fear – Fear of God, Fear of People, Failure, Rejection, Success, Financial failure, failure of losing Family and friends.
(3) Unbelief
(4) Disobedience
(5) Living in Sin
(6) Being Kept blinded by Satan
(7) Lack of Faith
(8) In Prayers
(9) Our Thoughts
(10) Not Listening and Not identifying the Voice of GOD
(11) Worshipping worldly things (Idolatry)
(12) Unforgiveness and thanklessness – Gratitude
(13) Insincerity

19 THE NAMES OF GOD

Knowing GOD and the knowledge of GOD are essential to humanity. Jesus helps us put the importance of the education of the Names of God in proper perspective, teaching us how we should begin our prayers in Matthew 6:9 KJV-note. By the *"name of God, we mean all those attributes through which He is revealed to us—His power, wisdom, holiness, justice, mercy, and truth.*

-They that know thy name will put their trust in thee. Psalm 9:10

-The people that do know their God shall be strong, and do exploits.

Man must have a personal relationship with GOD, and GOD demands that personal relationship to endow man with all that he has to offer. We vary in our dedication and devotion, and we receive blessings according to the depth, commitment, and relationship with GOD. God alone can read a man's mind and what's in his heart, but he requires us to speak out and verbalize our feelings as he has spoken everything into existence, including all creation. Therefore he is expecting a man, whom he created in his very own image to speak out praises, blessings, hymns, and conversations, such that the words travel into the realm and dimension created by GOD for the purpose.

Speaking and conversing with anyone requires recognition of the other person, thus a personal focus and attention when talking to someone, same is applicable when we pray, and we need to know GOD personally and know his name, acknowledge his name. We have been created with at least with a purpose to glorify God and give him all glory and worship. Names are associated with Characteristics as such GOD used many names when he is working through various circumstances and uses the title specific to the action he is about to perform, his dealings with humanity, the different aspect of himself focused on different relationships

Moses asked the Name of GOD – **Exodus 3:13** *"And Moses said unto God, Behold, when I come unto the children of Israel, and shall say unto them, The God of your fathers hath sent me unto you; and they shall say to me, what is his name? What shall I say unto them?"*

Exodus 14: - 4 And God said unto Moses, I AM THAT I AM: and he said, thus shalt thou say unto the children of Israel, I AM hath sent me unto you. What GOD was saying I am whatever you want me to be, I will be. If you want me to be a healer, I will be your healer. If you want me to be a helper, I will be a helper, etc. Man's greatest quest is to know GOD, to see God and to meet God. To be with God all the days of our lives, to worship, believe and have the greatest faith which works in sync with our psyche and our mind to morph our inner being, for GOD has given us a part of him, and he is there already. Just for us to discover and grow within, expand and enhance the spirit that he gave us.

Jacob asked the name of the Angel of the Lord

The name of God is El Elyon - Most High God (Sovereign over All) (*Elyon (Biblical Hebrew עליון; Masoretic ʿElyōn) is an epithet of the God of the Israelites in the Hebrew Bible. ʾĒl ʿElyōn is usually rendered in English as "God Most High," and similarly in the Septuagint as "Ο ΘΕΟΣ Ο ΥΨΙΣΤΟΣ" ("God the highest").)*

El Elyon - God Most High: *Then Melchizedek king of Salem brought out bread and wine. He was a priest of God Most High, and he blessed Abram, saying, "Blessed be Abram by God Most High, Creator of heaven and earth. And blessed be God Most High, who delivered your enemies into your hand." Then Abram gave him a tenth of everything (Genesis 14:18-20).*

> *Nebuchadnezzar then approached the opening of the blazing furnace and shouted, "Shadrach, Meshach, and Abednego, servants of the Most High God, come out! Come here!" So Shadrach, Meshach, and Abednego came out of the fire (Daniel 3:26).*

Use in the Bible: In the Old Testament, El Elyon occurs 28 times.
It occurs 19 times in Psalms. El Elyon first used in Gen 14:18.

> *Daniel 4:34 34" After this time had passed, I, Nebuchadnezzar, looked up to heaven. My sanity returned, and I praised and worshiped the Most High and honored the one who lives forever.*

The name of God is Adonai - My Lord, My Master   Genesis 15:2

The name of God is El Roi - God Who Sees   Genesis 16:13

The name of God is El Shaddai - God Almighty, God of Heaven Psalms 91:1

The name of God is Jehovah Ezer - The LORD our Helper   Hebrews 13:6

The name of God is Jehovah Jireh - LORD Will Provide   Genesis 22: 1-19

The name of God is El Olam the everlasting God   Genesis 21:33

The name of God is YHWH- Yahweh Jehovah will see you   Genesis 22:14

The name of God is Jehovah Roi - The Lord is My Shepherd   Genesis 16:13

The name of God is YWHW-m'kaddesh Jehovah who sanctifies Exodus 31:13

The name of God is Jehovah Sabaoth - LORD of hosts (of armies) Judges 4:13-15

The name of God is Jehovah Mekeddeshem - LORD Who Sanctifies Exodus 31: 12

The name of God is Jehovah Nissi -The LORD Our Banner   Exodus 17:11-13

The name of God is Jehovah Rapha/Rophe - LORD Who Heals   Exodus 3:14

The name of God is Jehovah Shalom - The LORD our Peace   Judges 6:24

The name of God is Jehovah Shammah - The LORD is there   Ezekiel 48:35

Where Jehovah means "Savior" or "is Salvation."

God has revealed himself to humanity in multiple ways and used names that represent the circumstances of his visit and related to the events that are at hand. Convincingly he announced himself to Paul of Tarsus by asking "Who art thou LORD?" **Acts 9:5** and The Lord responded by saying "I am Jesus." This statement shows and is the proof of Jesus being LORD and GOD, the name itself is a redemptive name as such the reason why we call upon God and Pronounce his name for we are seeking redemption for ourselves, the world, sins, evil and circumstances.

Elohim (El-Lo-Heem) – Hebrew word for "GOD." It is the Plural work for GOD and is the first name given of God in the Scriptures. Genesis1:1 "In the beginning, God (Elohim) created the heavens and the earth." Attention is drawn to the "EL" masculine aspect of the name and character of God. Elohim is mentioned 32 times in Genesis and additionally (God) over 2570+ times in other chapters of scripture. This name used depicts the characteristic of God as sovereign, and omnipotent, the great and ultimate power to create and govern. The name that God uses to reveal himself. God, Creator, Preserver, Keeper of His Covenant. The word God itself is translated from the Hebrew language to be "Elohim."

In Deuteronomy 10:17 " Jehovah your Elohim is Gods of god, and Lord of lords, the God or El which is great, mighty, and dreadful." The other word that "Elohim" derives from is "Alah," which means "to declare" or "to swear."

Jehovah: The Hebrew word translates to "LORD" uppercase, being the most used in the Old Testament (6823 times). A deeper meaning portrayed in *Genesis 28:13 " And, behold, the LORD stood above it, and said, I am the LORD God (**JEHOVAH ELOHIM**) of Abraham thy father, and the God of Isaac: the land whereon thou liest, to thee will I give it, and to thy seed;"*
The name derives from the Hebrew word Havah/Chavah – "to be" "to Live" "Being" defining the integration of life and being
"I Will Become What I Choose to Become." **(Exodus 3:14)** the explanation to Moses by GOD. "The Existing One."YHWH / YAHWEH / JEHOVAH: "LORD" **(Deuteronomy 6:4; Daniel 9:14)** – strictly speaking, the only proper name for God. Translated in English Bibles "LORD" (all capitals) to distinguish it from Adonai, "Lord." The revelation of the name is given to Moses "I Am who I Am" (Exodus 3:14). LORD -- holiness (Truth revealer), righteousness, redemption. JEHOVAH in caps represents LORD, where Adonai serves Lord, this significant text of uppercase (Capitals) and lower case defines the mighty and reality of more significant. Jehovah appeared about 6,823 times in the old testament and

is the name that God used in the older era, especially combined with Elohim as Jehovah-Elohim showing the authority and divinity of God the person and his character in some single revelations to man.

Jehovah verb "to be," thus "I am "present tense as he speaks to Moses is very clear "I am That I am" - I am what you want me to be. Therefore make your God mighty and high, as God gives himself names based on the Works to be done and based on his appearance by the characteristic of the circumstances.

Jehovah the God of revelation, The God of Righteousness and Holiness as he declares himself as the God that does not change.

> ***Exodus 34: 4***   *and he hewed two tables of stone like unto the first; and Moses rose up early in the morning, and went up unto mount Sinai, as the LORD (Jehovah) had commanded him, and took in his hand the two tables of stone.*
>
> ***Exodus 34: 5***   *And the LORD (Jehovah) descended in the cloud, and stood with him there, and proclaimed the name of the LORD (Jehovah).*
>
> ***Exodus 34: 6***   *And the LORD (Jehovah) passed by before him, and proclaimed, The LORD (Jehovah), The LORD(Jehovah) God, merciful and gracious, longsuffering, and abundant in goodness and truth,*
>
> ***Exodus 34: 7***   *Keeping mercy for thousands, forgiving iniquity and transgression and sin, and that will by no means clear the guilty; visiting the iniquity of the fathers upon the children, and upon the children's children, unto the third and to the fourth generation.*
>
> *Exodus 34: 8*   *And Moses made haste, and bowed his head toward the earth, and worshipped.*
>
> *Exodus 34: 9*   *And he said, If now I have found grace in thy sight, O Lord, let my Lord, I pray thee, go among us; for it is a stiff-necked people, and pardon our iniquity and our sin, and take us for thine inheritance.*

El-Shaddai: The Mighty God - El-Shaddai means God Almighty. "El" points to the power of God Himself, one who nourishes, supplies, and satisfies. God desires to bless man and provide in abundance all of man's needs. God is powerful enough to offer his people blessings. El Shaddai delivers everything we need to walk the path which God is taking us. Almighty God -- Our all-sufficient supply, Bestower of power, gifts, blessings, and the one who makes us fruitful. The name first appeared in **Genesis 17:1-2** and when Abram was ninety years old and nine, the LORD appeared to Abram, and said unto him, I am the Almighty God (El-Shaddai); walk before me and be thou perfect. 2: And I will make my covenant between me and thee, and will multiply thee exceedingly.

It is your faith that empowers you to place the power of God to work in your life. "Shad," "Shadayim "means "Breast" in relationship to "One, who nourishes, supplies, satisfies." "Dai" means "pours out," "heaps benefits" meaning that he provides and sustains and delivers blessings." "Shaddai" appears 41 times in the Old Testament, 29 times in JOB alone. Job's experiences due to the trials he endured on behalf of God, defines Job's faith in God, The all-sufficient sustainer, El Shaddai. God desires to bless man and provide in abundance all of man's needs.

El Shaddai means God Almighty, the all-powerful, the mighty God, with the ability and power to do anything and everything anytime, the expression and action of doing what is impossible at any time, for God are able, and with God anything and everything is possible. El Shaddai is the Name of God that delivers promises – The mighty promise deliverer and giver of gifts, sufficiency, and hope.

El-Shaddai spoke to Job

Job 40: 6 Then answered the LORD unto Job out of the whirlwind, and said,
Job 40: 7 Gird up thy loins now like a man: I will demand of thee, and declare thou unto me.
Job 40: 8 Wilt thou also disannul my judgment? wilt thou condemn me that thou mayest be righteous?
Job 40: 9 Hast thou an arm like God? or canst thou thunder with a voice like him?
Job 40: 10 Deck thyself now with majesty and Excellency, and array thyself with glory and beauty.
Job 40: 11 Cast abroad the rage of thy wrath: and behold every one that is proud, and abase him.
Job 40: 12 Look on every one that is proud, and bring him low, and tread down the wicked in their place.
Job 40: 13 Hide them in the dust together, and bind their faces in secret.
Job 40: 14 Then will I also confess unto thee that thine own right hand can save thee.
John 15:5 I am the vine, ye are the branches: He that abideth in me, and I in him, the same bringeth forth much fruit: for without me ye can do nothing

Adonai: A Plural word meaning "Lord, Lord, LORD" This is because GOD is called "Lord of Lords," The Lord who is GOD, In the Old, Testament Adonai occurs 434 times. There are heavy uses of Adonai in Isaiah (e.g., Adonai Jehovah). It occurs 200 times in Ezekiel alone and appears 11 times in Daniel Chapter 9. Adonai used in **Gen 15:2**. YHWH / YAHWEH / JEHOVAH: "LORD" **(Deuteronomy 6:4; Daniel 9:14)** – strictly speaking, the only proper name for God. Translated in English Bibles "LORD" (all capitals) to distinguish it from Adonai, "Lord." The revelation of the name given to Moses "I Am who I Am" (Exodus 3:14). Lord - Our

Sovereign God, Owner of all.

Jehovah-Jireh: THE LORD WHO PROVIDES
GENESIS 22, the name is literally, The Lord Who Sees, or The Lord Who Will See to It. The LORD will provide

Jehovah-Rapha: The Lord who Heals Exodus 15:25 And he cried unto the LORD; and the LORD showed him a tree, which when he had cast into the waters, the waters were made sweet: there he made for them a statute and an ordinance, and there he proved them, 26: And said, If thou wilt diligently hearken to the voice of the LORD thy God, and wilt do that which is right in his sight, and wilt give ear to his commandments and keep all his statutes, I will put none of these diseases upon thee, which I have brought upon the Egyptians: for I am the LORD that healeth thee. "God who sees," or by implication "God will provide." The name comes from the Bible where Abraham was about to sacrifice his only son, Isaac. God stopped him and provided a ram for the sacrifice. Abraham named the place, "Jehovah-Jireh." The LORD will provide - He will see our needs and meet them.

Jehovah-Rophe: Jehovah Heals - He will heal the bitter waters of this life

Jehovah-Nissi: THE LORD OUR BANNER- This name has to do with warfare. In this instance, the war involves God's very own. Our Father is willing to wage war on our behalf. In Exodus 17:15, Moses, recognizing that the Lord was Israel's banner under which they defeated the Amalekites, builds an altar named Jehovah-Nissi (the Lord our Banner). Jehovah Our Banner - We are brought together under Him, and He brings victory.

Jehovah-Shalom: The God of Peace. (Judges 21:25) In those days there was no king in Israel: every man did that which was right in his own eyes. Israel under oppression by the Midianites. They were forced to hide in caves. The Midianites took all their food, tools, and livestock. It was during this time of oppression that Israel cried out for deliverance. So God called Gideon to deliver them. By faith, Gideon erected an altar to Jehovah-shalom in expectation of victory and peace. (Judges 6:24) Then Gideon built an altar there unto the LORD, and called it Jehovah-shalom: unto this day it is yet in Ophrah of the Abiezrites. Peace expresses the deepest desire and need of the human heart. It represents the most significant measure of contentment and satisfaction in life

Jehovah-tsidkenu: *"THE LORD OUR RIGHTEOUSNESS" Righteousness is morally right or justifiable and also represents blamelessness, guiltless, holy, innocent, sinless.*

Jehovah-Rohi: The Lord is my Shepherd. Jehovah is Our Shepherd; we find the most tender, most intimate relationship between Jehovah and His people. The primary meaning of rohi is "to feed" or "lead to pasture," as a shepherd does his flock, (John 10:11) I am the good shepherd: the good shepherd giveth his life for the sheep.

Jehovah-Shammah: meaning "Jehovah is there" the name given by Ezekiel, Ezekiel 48:35, to a future holy city. Jehovah-Shammah is a name for God that is symbolic of Jerusalem. We find this name for God used in Ezekiel 48:35 (NLT): "The distance around the entire city will be 6 miles. And from that day the name of the city will be 'The Lord is there.'"

Jehovah-M'Kaddesh: Jehovah who sanctifies - He sets us apart unto Himself. We must know Jehovah-M'Kaddesh (the Lord who sanctifies us) before we can know Jehovah-shalom, for God only gives His peace to those who are righteous before Him.

Jehovah Sabaoth: 1 Samuel 1:3 used 285 times in the bible means the Almighty, Sovereign, and Self-Existent God over all the multitudes, whether an army, the sun, moon, and stars or creation itself, bringing divine power to the aid of His children. The LORD of Hosts rules the armies of heaven so they will obey His will. The Lord will allow His faithless people to be defeated. Lord of hosts is with us. We dare not budge an inch, for the Lord Himself holds us in our place, and there we will abide forever. Used together Jehovah Sabaoth means *The LORD of Armies* or *The LORD of Hosts*. The Lord reigns over a vast well ordered host in the heavenlies. Jehovah Sabaoth will fight all our battles as call upon him and voice our circumstances to him.

Jehovah-Sabaoth fights our battles for us.

Exodus 14:13-14 (NLT) 13 But Moses told the people, "Don't be afraid. Just stand still and watch the LORD rescue you today. The Egyptians you see today will never be seen again.

14 The LORD himself will fight for you. Just stay calm."

Joshua 5:13-15 (NLT) 13 When Joshua was near the town of Jericho; he looked up and saw a man standing in front of him with sword in hand. Joshua went up to him and demanded, "Are you friend or Foe?"

14 "Neither one," he replied. "I am the commander of the LORD's army." At this, Joshua fell with his face to the ground in reverence. "I am at your command," Joshua said. "What do you want your servant to do?"

15   The commander of the LORD's army replied, "Take off your sandals, for the place where you are standing is holy." And Joshua did as he was told.

Revelation 19:11-16 (NLT) 11   Then I saw heaven opened, and a white horse was standing there. Its rider was named Faithful and True, for he judges fairly and wages a righteous war.

12   His eyes were like flames of fire, and on his head were many crowns. A name was written on him that no one understood except himself.

13   He wore a robe dipped in blood, and his title was the Word of God.

14   The armies of heaven, dressed in the finest of pure white linen, followed him on white horses.

15   From his mouth came a sharp sword to strike down the nations. He will rule them with an iron rod. He will release the fierce wrath of God, the Almighty, like juice flowing from a winepress.

16   On his robe at his thigh was written this title: King of all kings and Lord of all lords.

Further references of the name Jehovah Sabaoth in the Old Testament: *1 Samuel 1:11; 1 Samuel 17:45; 2 Samuel 6:18; 2 Samuel 7:27; 1 Kings 19:14; 2 Kings 3:14; 1 Chronicles 11:9; Psalm 24:10; Psalm 48:8; Psalm 80:4; Psalm 80:19; Psalm 84:3; Isaiah 1:24; Isaiah 3:15; Isaiah 5:16; Isaiah 6:5; Isaiah 9:19; Isaiah 10:26; Isaiah 14:22; Jeremiah 9:15; Jeremiah 48:1; Hosea 12:5; Amos 3:13; Micah 4:4; Nahum 3:5; Hag 2:6; Zechariah 1:3; Malachi 1:6; Habakkuk 2:13; Zephaniah 2:9.*

כהת [8] Tav Hey Kaf Defusing Negative Energy	אכא [7] Aleph Kaf Aleph DNA of The Soul	ללה [6] Hey Lamed Lamed Dream State	מהש [5] Shin Hey Mem Healing	עלם [4] Mem Lamed Ayin Eliminating Negative Thoughts	סיט [3] Tet Yud Samech Miracle Making	ילי [2] Yud Lamed Yud Recapturing the Sparks	והו [1] Vav Hey Vav Time Travel
הקם [16] Mem Kuf Hey Dumping Depression	הרי [15] Yud Resh Hey Long Range Vision	מבה [14] Hey Bet Mem Farewell to Arms	יזל [13] Lamed Zayin Yud Heaven on Earth	ההע [12] Ayin Hey Hey Unconditional Love	לאו [11] Vav Aleph Lamed Banishing the Remnants of Evil	אלד [10] Daled Lamed Aleph Protection from Evil Eye	הזי [9] Yud Zayin Hey Angelic Influences
וחו [24] Vav Hey Chet Jealousy	מלה [23] Hey Lamed Mem Sharing the Flame	ייי [22] Yud Yud Yud Stop Fatal Attraction	נלך [21] Kaf Lamed Nun Eradicate Plague	פהל [20] Lamed Hey Pey Victory over Addictions	לוו [19] Vav Vav Lamed Dialing God	כלי [18] Yud Lamed Kaf Fertility	לאו [17] Vav Aleph Lamed Great Escape
ועד [32] Rash Shin Vav Memories	לכב [31] Bet Kaf Lamed Finish What You Start	אום [30] Mem Vav Aleph Building Bridges	ריי [29] Yud Yud Resh Removing Hatred	שאה [28] Hey Aleph Shin Soulmate	ירת [27] Tav Resh Yud Silent Partner	האא [26] Aleph Aleph Hey Order From Chaos	נתה [25] Hey Tav Nun Speak Your Mind
ייי [40] Zayin Yud Yud Speaking the Right Words	רהע [39] Ayin Hey Resh Diamond in the Rough	חעם [38] Mem Ayin Chet Circuitry	אני [37] Yud Nun Aleph The Big Picture	מנד [36] Daled Nun Mem Fear(Less)	כוק [35] Kuf Vav Kaf Sexual Energy	להח [34] Chet Hey Lamed Forget Thyself	יחו [33] Vav Chet Yud Revealing the Dark Side
מיה [48] Hey Yud Mem Unity	עולל [47] Lamed Shin Ayin Global Transformation	ערי [46] Yud Resh Ayin Absolute Certainty	סאל [45] Lamed Aleph Samech Power of Prosperity	ילה [44] Hey Lamed Yud Sweetening Judgment	וול [43] Lamed Vav Vav Defying Gravity	מיכ [42] Kaf Yud Mem Revealing the Concealed	ההה [41] Hey Hey Hey Self Esteem
פוי [56] Yud Vav Pey Dispelling Anger	מבה [55] Hey Bet mem Thought Into Action	נית [54] Tav Yud Nun Death of Death	ננא [53] Aleph Nun Nun No Agenda	עמם [52] Mem Mem Ayin Passion	הוש [51] Shin Chet Hey No Guilt	דני [50] Yud Nun Daled Enough is Never Enough	והו [49] Vav Hey Vav Happiness
מחי [64] Yud Chet Mem Casting Yourself in a Favorable Light	ענו [63] Vav Nun Ayin Appreciation	יהה [62] Hey Hey Yud Parent-Teacher, Not Preacher	ומב [61] Bet Mem Vav Water	מצר [60] Resh Zadik Mem Freedom	הרח [59] Chet Resh Hey Umbilical Cord	ייל [58] Lamed Yud Yud Letting Go	נמם [57] Mem Mem Nun Listening to Your Soul
מום [72] Mem Vav Mem Spiritual Cleansing	היי [71] Yud Yud Hey Prophecy & Parallel Universes	יבמ [70] Mem Bet Yud Design Beneath Disorder	ראה [69] Hey Aleph Resh Lost & Found	חבו [68] Vav Bet Chet Contacting Departed Souls	איע [67] Ayin Yud Aleph Great Expectations	מנק [66] Kuf Nun Mem Accountability	דמב [65] Bet Mem Daled Fear of God

http://www.thehealinggift.com/chart/

El Roi: The God who sees me. She [Hagar] gave this name to the LORD who spoke to her: "You are the God who sees me," for she said, "I have now seen the one who sees me." That is why the well was called Beer Lahai Roi [the "well of the Living One who sees me"]. — Genesis 16:13–14 (NIV)

Special Note: Hagar unable to bear the sight of seeing her son suffering and will die due to lack of water and food, She leaves him at a distance as she cannot bear to see him die, She sat down and began rocking back and forth in grief and prayer, crying out to God, lamenting and questioning her faith and belief that GOD who had named her son Ishmael is letting him die.

An unbearable circumstance for a mother or parent not to be able to help their children and helplessly calls out for divine help.

As the God of the Bible seeks after us to re-create an intimate relationship with man, he "draws near", "comes down" and finds after us which is the stories of the entire Bible of Man seeking God and his dependency to God and God seeking man to bring him back to being under the influence and ordinance of GOD. A Muslim theologian has said, "God reveals only his will, not himself. He remains forever hidden". God is here there and everywhere, and his presence and works are wherever you are and can be whatever you experience and can see, feel or hear.

The first commandment, *'You must not have any other God but me.'"* (Exodus 20:3) By taking this approach we set the Muslim at ease because this belief is the cornerstone of his faith. Most Muslims acknowledge that this commandment was the very first commandment (of 10) which Allah revealed through the prophet Moosa (Moses).
Moses gave to his father-in-law Jethro, a Midianite priest. We read that Moses told him,

Everything the LORD had done to Pharaoh and the Egyptians on behalf of Israel. He also said about all the hardships they had experienced along the way and how the LORD had rescued his people from all their troubles. Jethro was delighted when he heard about all the good things the LORD had done for Israel as he saved them from the hand of the Egyptians. "Praise be to the Lord," Jethro said, "for he has rescued you from the Egyptians and from Pharaoh ... I know now that God is greater than all other gods."(Exodus 18:8-11)

God miraculously saved them which amazed Nebuchadnezzar so much that he ordered everyone in his kingdom, *"I make this decree, 'If any people, whatever their race or nation or language speak a word against the God of Shadrack, Meshack and Abednego, they will be torn limb from limb... No other god can rescue like this.'"* (Daniel 3:29)
The LORD commanded the whole world to honor him using this specific title. It is written, *"There is no other God but me, a righteous God and Savior. There is none but me. Let the entire world look to me for salvation! For I am God; there is no other. I have sworn by my own name; ... Every knee will bend to me, and every tongue will confess allegiance to me."* (Isaiah 45:21-23)
  Moses (Musa) is mentioned more than any other individual in the Quran than anyone else; he was considered a prophet, messenger and a leader, sent by God to Pharaoh, Joseph was Yusuf, Aaron was Harun and the listing below. Therefore if Moses is the Prophet who met God YWHW and was given the authority and tasks and later the Commandments out of which the top 10 are the most critical, then he is the prophet over Judaism, Islam, and Christianity and worships the same God regardless of what name used in other Languages. Same goes for all the list of Bible characters in the list below, who praise the same GOD.

Eloah, Elohim, Elohai, El Shaddai, Tzevaot, Adonai, Ehyeh asher ehyeh, El Roi, Elyon, Elah

Elah (Aramaic: אֱלָה; pl. "elim") is the Aramaic word for God. The origin of the word is uncertain and it may be related to a root word, meaning "reverence". Elah is found in the Tanakh in the books of Ezra, Jeremiah (Jer 10:11, the only verse in the entire book written in Aramaic), and Daniel. Elah is used to describe both pagan gods and the Jews' God. The word 'Elah - ⬜ ⬜ *is also an Arabic word which means god. The name is etymologically related to Allah* ⬜ ⬜⬜ *used by Muslims.*

Elah Yisrael, God of Israel (Ezra 5:1)
Elah Yerushelem, God of Jerusalem (Ezra 7:19)
Elah Shemaya, God of Heaven (Ezra 7:23)
Elah-avahati, God of my fathers, (Daniel 2:23)
Elah Elahin, God of gods (Daniel 2:47)

The variation of Language and Pronunciation of the names of God based on region caused it all to sound as if there are different Gods, the God of the Jews, The God of the Arabs, The God of the Christians, but they are all ONE GOD. The word is thought to be derived by contraction from al-ilāh, which means "the god," and is related to El and Elah, the Hebrew and Aramaic words for God. You can dispute until the Rapture or for another million years, if it makes any logical sense, or worth the conflicting definitions, but it makes no difference in changing the TRUTH. The proof of the existence of God in the lives of anyone or any religious person, what are the deeds, the action, the ability, and the spiritual powers within that can be utilized to perform any of GOD's works externally. Can there be healings, and where are these healings taking place, are they happening in the Church, Synagogue, Temples or Mosques? Elijah called God's powers in the form of fire and consumed the offering and delivered 16 miracles and it is mentioned that it is the same Elijah in all the religions (Judaism, Islam, and Christianity), Elisha provided 32 miracles, according to Jesus teachings and anointing, we are ordained to replicate all the wonders done in the New Testament done in his times. The only proof of the real power of God expressed and displayed in the performance of saving his people, healing and providing for them as per their devotion and dedication to him.

The proof is in the Pudding, and the Karma and Dharma act of God and his People on Earth. Quoting Elijah to Ahab and Jezebel

1 Kings18: 21 *And Elijah came unto all the people, and said, how long halt ye between two opinions? if the LORD be God, follow him: but if Baal, then follows him. And the people answered him not a word.*

1 Kings18: 27 *And it came to pass at noon, that Elijah mocked them, and said, cry aloud: for he is a god; either he is talking, or he is pursuing, or he is in*

a journey, or peradventure he sleepeth, and must be awaked.

1 Kings18: 28   *And they cried aloud, and cut themselves after their manner with knives and lancets, till the blood gushed out upon them.*

1 Kings18: 29   *And it came to pass when midday was past, and they prophesied until the time of the offering of the evening sacrifice, that there was neither voice, nor any to answer, nor any that regarded.*

This dissimilarity has been since the hatred of Ishmael and Isaac and continues until this day, where the separation, enmity, and hatred are growing and becoming more substantial in numerical values and segregation of people by color, class, creed, country and belief system. Take away the GOD factor, and they are all left with two arms, two legs a body, two eyes, two ears, a nose, and an equal human form that is not different from the other. Except to prove where did the Red clay go and who has instilled in my hatred, animosity, ego and pride in us that is so strong and seems to be everlasting? Who did this if it is not God? Why am I thinking this way if it did not come from God? Why do I claim to be religious and a child of God when there is unbelievable hatred in my heart, mind, and soul, where did this come from? What are our similarities according to scriptural definitions and characteristics as a replica of divinity, which heavenly being are we the model of? Our way of life, our deeds, actions, Karma and Dharma reflects who we are and what the source that controls us is. The Same story about the same people at the same time mentioned in Three major religions about the same things, incidents and history and yet we cannot see eye-to-eye on shared understanding and understand that we are all looking at the same God. Praying to the same God, honoring the same prophets and disciples and following the same doctrine except for a minute Human twist where mankind's interpretations are different. Then we become radically bent on the negatives of the other person's belief system and pound it to the ground, instead of listening, understanding, knowing that these scriptures are messages from God for Mankind benefit and not humanity demise. If we worship the same God in the multiple ways and names and we follow the same doctrine, then who twists us in the meaning and deceives us into the changing and not understanding God's intentions and his master plan for humanity. We pray and believe in a God we cannot see, but with faith and believe we understand and feel his presence, and know that he is there and he is watching over us and is listening to our prayers, but we hold on to great animosity to brothers and sisters in other faith with such a human hatred that we feel that the persons that we are seeing, feeling, talking to and live among, work with, socialize and have fellowship with, play sports and are our environmental support are our enemies because of doctrines that crush, crumple, warp, mangle, distort, turn and swivel our minds away from GOD'S MAIN MESSAGE of "love",

"Love thy neighbor as thyself,"

"Turn the other cheek."

There will never be peace on earth, and we will never fulfill God's word, and promises in our lives if we continue in our world ways of harboring hate and hatred for the other Man and other people. The devil and Satan's will always twist your mind no matter how spiritual we are, no matter how much "tongue Talking' we do, no matter how much we pray and meditate, if we do not follow and understand those great commandments, we will never be approved.

1 John 4:1-21 *My beloved friends, <u>let us continue to love each other since love comes from God.</u> <u>Everyone who loves is born of God and experiences a relationship with God.</u>*

1 Corinthians 13:1-3 *If I speak in the tongues of men or of angels, but do not have love, I am only a resounding gong or a clanging cymbal. If I have the gift of prophecy and can fathom all mysteries and all knowledge, and if I have a faith that can move mountains, but do not have love, I am nothing. If I give all I possess to the poor and give over my body to hardship that I may boast, but do not have love, I gain nothing."*

Mark 12:29-31 *"The most important one," answered Jesus, "is this: 'Hear, O Israel: The Lord our God, the Lord is one. Love the Lord your God with all your heart and with all your soul and with all your mind and with all your strength.' The second is this: 'Love your neighbor as yourself. 'There is no commandment greater than these."*

1 John 4:1-21

1John 4:1 *Beloved, <u>believe not every spirit</u>, but <u>try the spirits whether they are of God:</u> <u>because many false prophets are gone out into the world</u>*

1John 4:2 *Hereby know ye the Spirit of God: Every spirit that confesseth that Jesus Christ is come in the flesh is of God:*

1John 4:3 *And every spirit that confesseth not that Jesus Christ is come in the flesh is not of God: and this is that spirit of antichrist, whereof ye have heard that it should come; and even now already is it in the world.*

1John 4:4 *Ye are of God, little children, and have overcome them: because greater is he that is in you than he that is in the world*

1John 4:5 *They are of the world: therefore speak they of the world, and the world heareth them.*

1John 4:6 *We are of God: he that knoweth God heareth us; he that is not of God heareth not us. Hereby know we the spirit of truth, and the spirit of error*

1John 4:7 *Beloved, let us love one another: for love is of God, and every one that loveth is born of God and knoweth God.*

1John 4:8 *He that loveth not knoweth not God; for God is love.*

1John 4:9 *In this was manifested the love of God toward us, because that God sent his only begotten Son into the world, that we might live through him*

1John 4:10 *Herein is love, not that we loved God, but that he loved us, and sent his Son to be the propitiation for our sins.*

1John 4:11 *Beloved, if God so loved us, we ought also to love one another.*

1John 4:12 *No man hath seen God at any time. If we love one another, God dwelleth in us,* *and his love is perfected in us.*

1John 4:13   *Hereby know we that we dwell in him, and he in us, because he hath given us of his Spirit.*

1John 4:14   *And we have seen and do testify that the Father sent the Son to be the Saviour of the world.*

1John 4:15   *Whosoever shall confess that Jesus is the Son of God, God dwelleth in him, and he in God.*

1John 4:16   *And we have known and believed the love that God hath to us. God is love, and he that dwelleth in love dwelleth in God, and God in him.*

1John 4:17   *Herein is our love made perfect, that we may have boldness in the day of judgment: because as he is, so are we in this world.*

1John 4:18   *There is no fear in love; but perfect love casteth out fear: because fear hath torment. He that feareth is not made perfect in love.*

1John 4:19   *We love him because he first loved us.*

1John 4:20   *If a man says, I love God, and hateth his brother, he is a liar: for he that loveth not his brother whom he hath seen, how can he love God whom he hath not seen?*

1John 4:21   *And this commandment have we from him, that he who loveth God love his brother also.*

Now that we are understanding God and his ways, how to get to God and know how to address and summon God, we need to know the similarities in the various religious books by the stories, history, and names all similar and a repeated in a much different manner

The Same story, the same people and the same incidents in the Bible, Torah and Koran. It is the same story told in a different context and interpretations.

Bible (English)	Qur'an (Arabic)
Aaron	Hārūn
Abel	Hābīl
Abraham	Ibrāhīm
Adam	Ādam
Eve	Hawwā
Amram	'Imrān
Cain	Qābīl
David	Dāwud
The Apostles	al-Hawariyyūn
Eber	Hūd
Elijah (Elias)	Ilyās
Elisha	al-Yasa'
Enoch	Idrīs
Ezekiel	Ḏū l-Kifl
Ezra	'Uzayr
Gabriel	Jibrīl
Gog and Magog	Ya'juj and Ma'juj
Goliath	Jālūṭṭ
Haman	Hāmān
Isaac	Isḥāq
Ishmael	Ismā'īl
Jacob	Ya'qūb
Jethro, Reuel, Hobab	Šu'ayb
Jesus	'Īsā
Joachim or Heli	Imraan
Job	'Ayyūb
John the Baptist	Yahyā
Jonah	Yūnus
Joseph	Yūsuf
Joseph's brothers	Yūsuf's brothers
Korah	Qārūn
Lot	Lūṭ
Lot's wife	Lūṭ's wife
Magog	Majuj
Mary	Maryam
Miriam	Mūsā's sister
Michael	Mīkāeel
Moses	Mūsā
Noah	Nūḥ
Pharaoh	Fir'awn
Potiphar	al-'Azīz
Potiphar's wife	al-'Azīz's wife; Zulaykha
Queen of Sheba	Queen of Saba'; Bilqīs
Samuel	Ṣamū'īl, Ṣamawāl but mentioned in the ahadithas Šam'ūn
Saul the King	Ṭālūt
Devil or Satan	Iblīs or Shaytān
Shem, Ham, and Japheth	Nūh's sons
Solomon	Sulaymān
Terah	Āzar
Zechariah	Zakariyyā
Zimr	al-Samiri

20 BREAKING BONDAGE AND CURSES

A Message delivered at the International Festival in New York

Gathering of Caribbean, European, American and Canadian

Praise the LORD Jesus Christ. Here at this International festival, I want to relate facts on cause and effect of bondage in these countries and about bondages through ancestry and governments. The Caribbean/West Indies, US, Canada Europe, and many other Nations still live under Ancestral Bondage:

- Australia & French Guiana were Prison Camps

- English Pilgrims were aboard the Mayflower in search of a place to practice religious freedom in 1620, in fear of persecution and imprisonment and were labeled Heretics. Help for them was Holland, forming a congregation in Leiden.

- Greece – Financial Bondage-/Debt Bondage= Modern day slavery related to Ancestral Sins

- **Some of the poorest countries in Caribbean/Central America/SA**: Haiti, Jamaica, Dominican Republic, Cuba, St Vincent +, St Lucia, Grenada, Dominica, Antigua and Barbuda, Guyana, Nicaragua, Honduras, Guatemala, El Salvador, Belize, Costa Rica, Panama, Bolivia, Paraguay, Ecuador, Columbia, Peru, Suriname, Venezuela, Uruguay.

- **Some of Poorest countries in Africa**: Congo, Somalia, Zimbabwe, Liberia, Niger, Malawi, Madagascar, Guinea, Burundi

- **Some of the Poorest countries in Asia**: North Korea, Afghanistan, Yemen, Nepal, Tajikistan, Bangladesh, Kyrgyzstan, Cambodia, Pakistan, Myanmar, Laos, Vietnam, Uzbekistan, Mongolia, India, Bhutan,

In the Caribbean, the United States of America, Europe, Asia, Middle East, etc., Our Ancestors were under the Bondage of Slavery in various forms. Most were deceived, forced and shackled against their will under the Spirit of Slavery and the Spirit of Bondage, by the Spanish, French, Dutch and British. This includes the Governments that were over them. In Guyana Hon. President Burnham legalized Obeah and Voodoo. This is an abomination to the nation of Guyana in every religion. To all you minister of religion whether you are Muslim, Christian, and Hindu or from any other faith, we must preach and deliver the message of breaking these bondages. Which of you condone with the practice of "Occult" The practice of "Obeah or Voodoo", if you do condone with it during the times of the previous Government that made it legal, then you are guilty by association and have put yourself under the bondages that the previous Government has legalized the practice of the occult. That Government has put the entire nation under occult bondage and has allowed many to practice the Occult and Satan's way.

The indenture system was created after the abolishment of slavery, to facilitate the lack and shortages in the labor force in the agriculture industry and plantations. The British, French, Dutch, Spanish, Portuguese they were all involved in the exploitation of the most populated, most impoverished countries. They know that the people are looking for opportunities to make a living, as such it was easy to convince these people to join in the journey across the sea to a new land for the betterment of their family and a better life. Many were forced to join the ships, many signed contracts, some were voluntarily, and many were "BEGUILED" by the Indians, British, French, and Dutch to make the journey. The British Plantation owners were the brainchild of the Indentured system. East Indian laborers were plentiful, and millions of East Indian Laborers were exported from India through the East India Company to and settled in the entire Caribbean, Fiji, Mauritius, Kenya, Uganda, South Africa, Formosa, Malacca, Philippines, New Zealand, Samoa, Madagascar, Solomon Islands, and Australia, etc

I agree with the strategy of giving people an open-door opportunity to start a new life in another place with the options of returning when the contract is over but followed by a life of hard labor, cruel treatment, physical, mental and spiritual abuse by the plantation owners. Living conditions were not as promised and the delivery of all the sacred word of honor violated, and the East Indians lived in inhumane conditions and inhumane work conditions with no choice of freedom or any other alternatives, they were under the bondage of the plantation owners and their staff,

You must pray and break off this evil that set upon the country and people and religion. This is the only country worldwide that has made this practice legal, and every one of you has been silent in opposing this new law that passed years ago. This LAW is still in existence, and this being said has put each of you in and under that law, making it an abomination to all religion. Witchcraft involves the manipulation and control of the minds of the people against their will (So yes you were all under that control ...such that the leadership can do what-ever they want). Witchcraft, Obeah and Voodoo is "One person or group of persons controlling or dominating the SOUL of another by a power other than the power of GOD or even self."

Here the Devil himself was in control, and I hope this identified by Today's leaders, priests, Pundits, and Maulanas and they make an effort to break, bound and cast out this spirit and its effect.

Our ancestor in the Caribbean, West Indies, USA, Canada, South America, and Europe also fell into bondages/Slavery through mental, spiritual, financial and social slavery. And/or maybe an implementer of such actions and sins, corruption, hatred, anger, bigotry, violence, murder, rape, Avarice, greed, Selfishness, and in association with those who commit these acts, and physical abuse on to others, that we may or may not be aware of, but have fallen under the generational sins they may have committed.

Bondage and Curses last for 400+ years and 7 Generations. We are not that far yet, and these countries have been in bondage for over 200 - 400 years. Their status has not been alleviated or elevated from being the Poor countries or third world countries yet. What is holding them back? Are they still under the financial control bondages of sovereign nations? Are they kept in that state because of the International Monetary Fund and banks? Have they not paid their share in blood sweat and tears? What would it take to bring them up to standards of a modern world? Are the people so full of ignorance and lack the wisdom to put their heads together to elevate their roots? Did God forget their existence or are they too far away from God.

2 Kings 21:6 - *And he made his son pass through the fire, **and observed times, and used enchantments, and dealt with famili**ar spirits and wizards: he wrought much wickedness in the sight of the LORD, to provoke [him] to anger.*

Hosea 4: 6 *My people are destroyed for lack of knowledge: because thou hast rejected knowledge, I will also reject thee, that thou shalt be no priest to me: seeing thou hast forgotten the law of thy God, I will also forget thy children.*

Proverbs 29:18 says: Where there is no vision, the people perish: but he that keepeth the law, happy is he.

Hosea 4:6 says: My people are destroyed for lack of knowledge: because thou hast rejected knowledge, I will also reject thee, that thou shalt be no priest to me: seeing thou hast forgotten the law of thy God, I will also forget thy children.

Willie Lynch- A plantation /Slave owner from the West Indies *wrote a document and have been summoned to the Virginia Colony by local slave owners to advise them on problems they have been having in managing their slaves and delivered a speech on the banks of the James River, Virginia in 1712. On his document "The Making of a Slave" a cultish act and scheme that will keep slaves in bondage for 400-1000 years. This document was shared with all Slave owners '" I have a foolproof method for controlling your black*

Slaves. "I shall assure you that distrust is stronger than trust and envy stronger than adulation, respect or admiration." "The Black slaves after receiving this indoctrination shall carry on and will become self refueling and self generating for hundreds of years, maybe Thousands." "It is necessary that your slaves trust and depend on us".

"If used intensely for one year, the slaves themselves will remain perpetually distrustful of each other."

I use fear, distrust, and envy for control purposes"" Destroying their dominant Male Mental Nature, driving Fear, insubordination and dependency to the max, and creating distrust and conflict among them- Which still exists today.

> *Nation of Islam leader Louis Farrakhan quoted the speech at the Million Man March in October 1995, making the speech better known in the process. He later cited Willie Lynch's scheme as an obstacle to unite African Americans in his open letter regarding the Millions More Movement in 2005.*
>
> *https://archive.org/stream/WillieLynchLetter1712/the_willi e_lynch_letter_the_making_of_a_slave_1712_djvu.txt*

Willie Lynch – A Plantation /Slave owner

The Willie

Lynch Letter: The Making Of A Slave!

This speech was delivered by Willie Lynch on the bank of the James River in the colony of Virginia in 1 712. Lynch was a British slave owner in the West Indies. He was invited to the colony of Virginia in 1712 to teach his methods to slave owners there. The term "lynching" is derived from his last name.

December 25, 1712

Gentlemen:

I greet you here on the bank of the James River in the year of our Lord one thousand seven hundred and twelve. First, I shall thank you, the gentlemen of the Colony of Virginia, for bringing me here. I am here to help you solve some of your problems with slaves. Your invitation reached me on my modest plantation in the West Indies, where I have experimented with some of the newest and still the oldest methods for control of slaves. Ancient Rome's would envy us if my program is

implemented. As our boat sailed south on the James River, named for our illustrious King, whose version of the Bible we cherish, I saw enough to know that your problem is not unique. While Rome used cords of wood as crosses for standing human bodies along its highways in great numbers, you are here using the tree and the rope on occasions. I caught the whiff of a dead slave hanging from a tree, a couple miles back. You are not only losing valuable stock by hangings, you are having uprisings, slaves are running away, your crops are sometimes left in the fields too long for maximum profit, You suffer occasional fires, your animals are killed.

Gentlemen, you know what your problems are; I do not need to elaborate. I am not here to enumerate your problems, I am here to introduce you to a method of solving them. In my bag here, I have a foolproof method for controlling your black slaves. I guarantee every one of you that if installed correctly it will control the slaves for at least 300 years [201 2]. My method is simple. Any member of your family or your overseer can use it. I have outlined a number of differences among the slaves and make the differences bigger. I use fear, distrust and envy for control.

These methods have worked on my modest plantation in the West Indies and it will work throughout the South. Take this simple little list of differences and think about them. On top of my list is "age" but it's there only because it starts with an "A." The second is "COLOR" or shade, there is intelligence, size, sex, size of plantations and status on plantations, attitude of owners, whether the slaves live in the valley, on a hill, East, West, North, South, have fine hair, course hair, or is tall or short. Now that you have a list of differences, I shall give you an outline of action, but before that, I shall assure you that distrust is stronger than trust and envy stronger than adulation, respect or admiration. The Black slaves after receiving this indoctrination shall carry on and will become self refueling and self generating for hundreds of years, maybe thousands. Don't forget you must pitch the old black Male vs. the young black Male, and the young black Male against the

old black male. You must use the dark skin slaves vs. the light skin slaves, and the light skin slaves vs. the dark skin slaves. You must use the female vs. the male. And the male vs. the female. You must also have you white servants and overseers distrust all Blacks. It is necessary that your slaves trust and depend on us. They must love, respect and trust only us. Gentlemen, these kits are your keys to control. Use them. Have your wives and children use them, never miss an opportunity. If used intensely for one year, the slaves themselves will remain perpetually distrustful of each other.

Thank you gentlemen

This is the actual letter

The Willie Lynch Letter: The Making Of A Slave!

This speech was delivered by Willie Lynch on the bank of the James River in the colony of Virginia in 1 712. Lynch was a

British slave owner in the West Indies. He was invited to the colony of Virginia in 1712 to teach his methods to slave

owners there. The term "lynching" is derived from his last name.

December 25, 1712

Gentlemen:

I greet you here on the bank of the James River in the year of our Lord one thousand seven hundred and twelve. First, I

shall thank you, the gentlemen of the Colony of Virginia, for bringing me here. I am here to help you solve some of your

problems with slaves. Your invitation reached me on my modest plantation in the West Indies, where I have experimented

with some of the newest and still the oldest methods for control of slaves. Ancient Rome's would envy us if my program is

implemented.

As our boat sailed south on the James River, named for our illustrious King, whose version of the Bible we cherish, I saw

enough to know that your problem is not unique. While Rome used cords of wood as crosses for standing human bodies

along its highways in great numbers, you are here using the tree and the rope on occasions. I caught the whiff of a dead

slave hanging from a tree, a couple miles back. You are not only losing valuable stock by hangings, you are having

uprisings, slaves are running away, your crops are sometimes left in the fields too long for maximum profit, You suffer

occasional fires, your animals are killed.

Gentlemen, you know what your problems are; I do not need to elaborate. I am not here to enumerate your problems, I am here to introduce you to a method of solving them. In my bag here, I have a foolproof method for controlling your black

slaves. I guarantee every one of you that if installed correctly it will control the slaves for at least 300 years [201 2]. My

method is simple. Any member of your family or your overseer can use it. I have outlined a number of differences among

the slaves and make the differences bigger. I use fear, distrust and envy for control.

These methods have worked on my modest plantation in the West Indies and it will work throughout the South. Take this

simple little list of differences and think about them. On top of my list is "age" but it's there only because it starts with an

"A." The second is "COLOR" or shade, there is intelligence, size, sex, size of plantations and status on plantations,

attitude of owners, whether the slaves live in the valley, on a hill, East, West, North, South, have fine hair, course hair, or

is tall or short. Now that you have a list of differences, I shall give you an outline of action, but before that, I shall assure

you that distrust is stronger than trust and envy stronger than adulation, respect or admiration. The Black slaves after

receiving this indoctrination shall carry on and will become self refueling and self generating for hundreds of years, maybe

thousands. Don't forget you must pitch the old black Male vs. the young black Male, and the young black Male against the

old black male. You must use the dark skin slaves vs. the light skin slaves, and the light skin slaves vs. the dark skin

slaves. You must use the female vs. the male. And the male vs. the female. You must also have you white servants and

overseers distrust all Blacks. It is necessary that your slaves trust and depend on us. They must love, respect and trust

only us. Gentlemen, these kits are your keys to control. Use them. Have your wives and children use them, never miss an

opportunity. If used intensely for one year, the slaves themselves will remain perpetually distrustful of each other.

Thank you gentlemen

Lets Make a Slave

It was the interest and business of slave holders to study human nature, and the slave nature in particular, with a view to

practical results. I and many of them attained astonishing proficiency in this direction. They had to deal not with earth,

wood and stone, but with men and by every regard they had for their own safety and prosperity they needed to know the

material on which they were to work. Conscious of the injustice and wrong they were every hour perpetuating and

knowing what they themselves would do. Were they the victims of such wrongs? They were constantly looking for the first

signs of the dreaded retribution. They watched, therefore with skilled and practiced eyes, and learned to read with great

accuracy, the state of mind and heart of the slave, through his sable face. Unusual sobriety, apparent abstractions,

sullenness and indifference indeed, any mood out of the common was afforded ground for suspicion and inquiry.

Let us make a slave. What do we need? First of all we need a black nigger man, a pregnant nigger woman and her baby

nigger boy. Second, we will use the same basic principle that we use in breaking a horse, combined with some more

sustaining factors. What we do with horses is that we break them from one form of life to another that is we reduce them

from their natural state in nature. Whereas nature provides them with the natural capacity to take care of their offspring,

we break that natural string of independence from them and thereby create a dependency status, so that we may be able

file://Y:\BPP_Books\temp\Fw It is never to late to get up off of your knees and fight for w... 8/20/2005

Page 2 of 4

to get from them useful production for our business and pleasure

Cardinal Principles for making a Negro

For fear that our future Generations may not understand the principles of breaking both of the beast together, the nigger

and the horse. We understand that short range planning economics results in periodic economic chaos; so that to avoid

turmoil in the economy, it requires us to have breath and depth in long range comprehensive planning, articulating both

skill sharp perceptions. We lay down the following principles for long range comprehensive economic planning. Both

horse and niggers is no good to the economy in the wild or natural state. Both must be broken and tied together for

orderly production. For orderly future, special and particular attention must be paid to the female and the youngest

offspring. Both must be crossbred to produce a variety and division of labor. Both must be taught to respond to a peculiar

new language. Psychological and physical instruction of containment must be created for both. We hold the six cardinal

principles as truth to be self evident, based upon the following the discourse concerning the economics of breaking and

tying the horse and the nigger together, all inclusive of the six principles laid down about. NOTE: Neither principle alone

will suffice for good economics. All principles must be employed for orderly good of the nation. Accordingly, both a wild

horse and a wild or nature nigger is dangerous even if captured, for they will have the tendency to seek their customary

freedom, and in doing so, might kill you in your sleep. You cannot rest. They sleep while you are awake, and are awake

while you are asleep. They are dangerous near the family house and it requires too much labor to watch them away from

the house. Above all, you cannot get them to work in this natural state. Hence both the horse and the nigger must be

broken; that is breaking them from one form of mental life to another. Keep the body take the mind! In other words break

the will to resist. Now the breaking process is the same for both the horse and the nigger, only slightly varying in degrees.

But as we said before, there is an art in long range economic planning. You must keep your eye and thoughts on the

Bruce K Deodat

female and the offspring of the horse and the nigger. A brief discourse in offspring development will shed light on the key

to sound economic principles. Pay little attention to the generation of original breaking, but concentrate on future

generations.

Therefore, if you break the female mother, she will break the offspring in its early years of development and when the

offspring is old enough to work, she will deliver it up to you, for her normal female protective tendencies will have been

lost in the original breaking process. For example take the case of the wild stud horse, a female horse and an already

infant horse and compare the breaking process with two captured nigger males in their natural state, a pregnant nigger

woman with her infant offspring. Take the stud horse, break him for limited containment.

Completely break the female horse until she becomes very gentle, whereas you or anybody can ride her in her comfort.

Breed the mare and the stud until you have the desired offspring. Then you can turn the stud to freedom until you need

him again. Train the female horse where by she will eat out of your hand, and she will in turn train the infant horse to eat

out of your hand also. When it comes to breaking the uncivilized nigger, use the same process, but vary the degree and

step up the pressure, so as to do a complete reversal of the mind. Take the meanest and most restless nigger, strip him of

his clothes in front of the remaining male niggers, the female, and the nigger infant, tar and feather him, tie each leg to a

different horse faced in opposite directions, set him a fire and beat both horses to pull him apart in front of the remaining

nigger. The next step is to take a bull whip and beat the remaining nigger male to the point of death, in front of the female

and the infant. Don't kill him, but put the fear of God in him, for he can be useful for future breeding.

The Breaking Process of the African Woman

Take the female and run a series of tests on her to see if she will submit to your desires willingly. Test her in every way,

because she is the most important factor for good economics. If she shows any sign of resistance in submitting completely to your will, do not hesitate to use the bull whip on her to extract that last bit of resistance out of her. Take care

not to kill her, for in doing so, you spoil good economic. When in complete submission, she will train her off springs in the

early years to submit to labor when the become of age. Understanding is the best thing. Therefore, we shall go deeper

into this area of the subject matter concerning what we have produced here in this breaking process of the female nigger.

We have reversed the relationship in her natural uncivilized state she would have a strong dependency on the uncivilized

nigger male, and she would have a limited protective tendency toward her independent male offspring and would raise

male off springs to be dependent like her. Nature had provided for this type of balance. We reversed nature by burning

and pulling a civilized nigger apart and bull whipping the other to the point of death, all in her presence. By her being left

alone, unprotected, with the male image destroyed, the ordeal caused her to move from her psychological dependent

state to a frozen independent state. In this frozen psychological state of independence, she will raise her male and female

offspring in reversed roles.

For fear of the young males life she will psychologically train him to be mentally weak and dependent, but physically

strong. Because she has become psychologically independent, she will train her female off springs to be psychological

independent. What have you got? You've got the nigger women out front and the nigger man behind and scared. This is a

perfect situation of sound sleep and economic. Before the breaking process, we had to be alertly on guard at all times.

file://Y:\BPP_Books\temp\Fw It is never to late to get up off of your knees and fight for w... 8/20/2005

Now we can sleep soundly, for out of frozen fear his woman stands guard for us. He cannot get past her early slave

molding process. He is a good tool, now ready to be tied to the horse at a tender age. By the time a nigger boy reaches

the age of sixteen, he is soundly broken in and ready for a long life of sound and efficient work and the reproduction of a

unit of good labor force. Continually through the breaking of uncivilized savage nigger, by throwing the nigger female

savage into a frozen psychological state of independence, by killing of the protective male image, and by creating a

submissive dependent mind of the nigger male slave, we have created an orbiting cycle that turns on its own axis forever,

unless a phenomenon occurs and re shifts the position of the male and female slaves. We show what we mean by

example. Take the case of the two economic slave units and examine them closely.

The Nigger Marriage

We breed two nigger males with two nigger females. Then we take the nigger males away from them and keep them

moving and working. Say one nigger female bears a nigger female and the other bears a nigger male. Both nigger

females being without influence of the nigger male image, frozen with an independent psychology, will raise their offspring

into reverse positions. The one with the female offspring will teach her to be like herself, independent and negotiable (we

negotiate with her, through her, by her, we negotiate her at will). The one with the nigger male offspring, she being frozen

with a subconscious fear for his life, will raise him to be mentally dependent and weak, but physically strong, in other

words, body over mind. Now in a few years when these two offspring's become fertile for early reproduction we will mate

and breed them and continue the cycle. That is good, sound, and long range comprehensive planning.

Warning: Possible Interloping Negatives

Earlier we talked about the non economic good of the horse and the nigger in their wild or natural state; we talked out the principle of breaking and tying them together for orderly production. Furthermore, we talked about paying particular

attention to the female savage and her offspring for orderly future planning, then more recently we stated that, by

reversing the positions of the male and female savages, we created an orbiting cycle that turns on its own axis forever

unless a phenomenon occurred and resift and positions of the male and female savages. Our experts warned us about

the possibility of this phenomenon occurring, for they say that the mind has a strong drive to correct and re-correct itself

over a period of time if I can touch some substantial original historical base, and they advised us that the best way to deal

with the phenomenon is to shave off the brute's mental history and create a multiplicity of phenomena of illusions, so that

each illusion will twirl in its own orbit, something similar to floating balls in a vacuum.

This creation of multiplicity of phenomena of illusions entails the principle of crossbreeding the nigger and the horse as we

stated above, the purpose of which is to create a diversified division of labor thereby creating different levels of labor and

different values of illusion at each connecting level of labor. The results of which is the severance of the points of original

beginnings for each sphere illusion. Since we feel that the subject matter may get more complicated as we proceed in

laying down our economic plan concerning the purpose, reason and effect of crossbreeding horses and nigger, we shall

lay down the following definition terms for future generations.

Orbiting cycle means a thing turning in a given path. Axis means upon which or around which a body turns. Phenomenon

means something beyond ordinary conception and inspires awe and wonder. Multiplicity means a great number. Sphere

means a globe. Cross breeding a horse means taking a horse and breeding it with an ass and you get a dumb backward

ass long headed mule that is not reproductive nor productive by itself.

Crossbreeding niggers mean taking so many drops of good white blood and putting them into as many nigger women as

possible, varying the drops by the various tone that you want, and then letting them breed with each other until another cycle of color appears as you desire. What this means is this; Put the niggers and the horse in a breeding pot, mix

some assess and some good white blood and what do you get? You got a multiplicity of colors of ass backward, unusual

niggers, running, tied to a backward ass long headed mule, the one productive of itself, the other sterile. (The one

constant, the other dying, we keep the nigger constant for we may replace the mules for another tool) both mule and

nigger tied to each other, neither knowing where the other came from and neither productive for itself, nor without each

other.

Control the Language

Crossbreeding completed, for further severance from their original beginning, we must completely annihilate the mother

tongue of both the new nigger and the new mule and institute a new language that involves the new life's work of both.

You know language is a peculiar institution. It leads to the heart of a people. The more a foreigner knows about the

language of another country the more he is able to move through all levels of that society. Therefore, if the foreigner is an

enemy of the country, to the extent that he knows the body of the language, to that extent is the country vulnerable to

attack or invasion of a foreign culture. For example, if you take a slave, if you teach him all about your language, he will

know all your secrets, and he is then no more a slave, for you can't fool him any longer. For example, if you told a slave

file://Y:\BPP_Books\temp\Fw It is never to late to get up off of your knees and fight for w... 8/20/2005

Page 4 of 4

that he must perform in getting out "our crops" and he knows the language well, he would know that "our crops" didn't

mean "our crops" and the slavery system would break down, for he would relate on the basis of what "our crops" really

meant. So you have to be careful in setting up the new language for the slaves would soon be in your house, talking to

you "man to man" and that is death to our economic system. In addition, the definitions of words or terms are only a

minute part of the process. Values are created and transported by communication through the body of the language. A

total society has many interconnected value system. All the values in the society have bridges of language to connect

them for orderly working in the society. But for these language bridges, these many value systems would sharply clash

and cause internal strife or civil war, the degree of the conflict being determined by the magnitude of the issues or relative

opposing strength in whatever form.

For example, if you put a slave in a hog pen and train him to live there and incorporate in him to value it as a way of life

completely, the biggest problem you would have out of him is that he would worry you about provisions to keep the hog

pen clean, or the same hog pen and make a slip and incorporate something in his language where by he comes to value

a house more than he does his hog pen, you got a problem. He will soon be in your house.

file://Y:\BPP_Books\temp\Fw It is never to late to get up off of your knees and fight for w... 8/20/2005

This letter by Willie Lynch, the refreshing of which is to draw attention to the people who were victims of the bondage of slavery, methods used to inject and twist minds and culture by psychological, subliminal and hypnotic means. Put them under subjection and creating division, conflicts against each other, not allow them to live in unison and a good relationship with the quest to inflict division "a divided house will fall" defining the letter as their a goal which is still in the hearts and minds of people and the outcome of what exists in our society today. It is time to open up your mind eye and look back, get a clear picture of what such tradition created by slave-owners can have a long-term effect on a society, open up your mind and envision solutions to the issue and problems that became instilled into the minds of a people, seek the answers to undoing this monstrosity and build a new mind frame in our today's society to look at your fellow man without hate or prejudice and see what needs to be remedied, what needs to change and what needs to be re-engineered into the mind to break the curve and twisting of the soul of our society towards betterment, mentally and psychologically which will influence our next generation and generations with vision and knowledge towards creation of a better future and taking advantages of the facilities and privileges that are available to us today . Which we are blinded to because we are "STILL SLAVES" "We are still in bondage" "We still lack the wisdom of who we are and what we are and our purpose on this earth and life." We are God's spirit walking around in a human body, but many have given way to the Devil to overtake the Spirit of Man and put that Spirit under subjection and leading us into a path of destruction with no way of turning around. Bringing to life this story is to enlighten all who were under the bondage of slavery salves and even those who were involved in being the Slave Masters. This is to inform all African American, American Indians, Latinos, Chinese American, Irish American, Italian American, and the many nations who participated in the development and building of the Nation of America and the United States, Europe, Caribbean, South America, and many other nations. It is primarily dedicated to the Plantation owners (mostly Caucasians – British Americans and Europeans who conquered and plundered many countries) who owned slaves and participated in the Willie Lynch methodology of putting people under the subjection of slavery and even to treat others with such cruelty and egoistic authoritarianism during those hard days. It is even unto today that these attitudes, attributes, and characteristic still exists in many human beings in many of these places. These tactics are mind control techniques that were used to not only controlling their subjects but put them through a suppressed state that they will never be able to get out of the little box mentality and mindset it was purposed to deliver. Even unto today, many people especially African Americans still live in that state of mind, as if they cannot see the means or ways or light at the end of the tunnel to bring them-self to elevate above certain limitations of life. They feel that they cannot achieve greatness, such as to be President, Governors, mayors, lawyers, Doctors; teachers get a higher education and get a government/ federal positions, Work in Banks, financial institutions, etc. The letter and its plans are plain straight EVIL and bring bondages to both slaves and slave Masters, slave owners and even those who were the field supervisors of the working force.

Many have broken through these barriers and have achieved reasonable success, get a higher education and job positions and status and must compliment the parental act and drives and parental desires to pray, break all these bondages and bless their family members with a blessing to get out of the dilemma. Many, having studied religion and scriptures found the truth in the establishment of slavery, bondage and curses in the old scriptures and worked dedicatedly using their God-given knowledge to break through and pray their family out if the misery injecting into the minds of their siblings with statements like "You are not going to live this kind of life; you are going to break the Glass ceiling and soar like an eagle and become someone of recognition, became of great status, become educated and achieve greatness in this world". We must give thanks to Christianity delivering a greater help to tune the attitudes and thinking of the Slavemasters to develop a Christian mind allowing Slaves to become Christians and listen to Sermons. Quite a large community remains within the mental state of the Willie Lynch influence and mental deformity that the rituals have injected and created. A special mention made to the siblings, and the grandchildren of plantation owners and Slave owners, this curse, this bondage, this sin, and occult practice is also upon you and your generations, which came from your great grandfathers and grandfathers. It is upon you and may not be visible in material values or environmental values, but exists in mind, will not go away until you break it off. Biblically this curse will roll on for about seven (7) generations and according to Willie Lynch paper and document will be there for 400 to 1000 years. I would suggest you get on board the bondage, curse-breaking train and get out of this spell, for as you can see the curses of "The behavior and attitudes of Plantation /Slave owners" are displayed in your household, your community, your city and in every part of the country and world. Do not feel you are an exclusion, you are more vulnerable and more volatile to these curses than the other ethnic nations, just because the others have endured and become morphed and hardened to the treatment, You are not, as such as soon as you face a Little of the same treatment your Grandfathers put upon others, you crack, your break, you lose your mind, becomes psychopathic, suicidal, drug addicts due to depression and negative cognitive unsettling spirits, not knowing where and what is the issue that they cannot get out of poverty and an impoverished state of mind.

We must understand that these attitudes, treatment and consistent bombardment of suffering, as well as aggression, causes a phenomenon that affects the chemical and biological changes in our system, both mentally and physically and alters our DNA, becoming fused by mental and biological trauma over a long period. In the older days, the results were division, the division between whites and people of color, including the thought of inferiority and superiority. Today it has given birth to division between Whites and whites, Blacks and Blacks, Asian and Asian, whites and Blacks, Whites and Asians, division by tribal recognition, division by environmental and social status, race, class, creed, political affiliations, church denominations, and people are using every means to be divided and to measure each other into superiority and inferiority. Can you imagine what will be the state of our children minds shortly or next generations even their behavior in later days? These experiments caused weakness in society, deficiency in the physical human being, where the man within the man weakened, and on the other hand the man in the man becomes stronger and more aggressive, being in a state of mental subconsciousness of fight or flight, leading to anger, violence, aggressive behaviors, and uncontrollable negative characteristics consistently.

> The Greatest 'Plea', whether you are Black, White, Yellow, Red, Green, Brown, Multinational, Latino, Asian, Indian or from all other nationality or ethnicity, you must understand how these mental, physical and spiritual phenomena can affect our welfare, our culture, our mindset, our jobs, our monies and everything about us because it becomes a mind frame that was internalized for ages, as such it is displayed and externalized with barriers and limitations that comes from the Mind within.

This concept that was delivered and practiced by the Slave owners, not only affected slaves and the slave community but was also concerned the Plantation owners, their families, children, and grandchildren as well as their entire community. The psychological changes that developed among whites, Indians, slaves and all other races in the neighborhood went unnoticed to many in the form of curses and bondages that has been subliminally injected into the individual's mind and passed down from generations to generations through culture, social and environmental practices:

(1) Many forms of bondage
(2) Releases spirits of division, murder, racism, abuse, and curses
(3) Psychological changes include the development of a criminal mindset
(4) Harbors and manifestation of hate releasing a spirit that goes with it
(5) A spirit of division and divisiveness
(6) A negative spirit of superiority and measured inferiority
(7) A weakness and insecurity of being alone and loneliness

(8) A racist subjective mind - The Eurocentrism of Hegel's philosophy, where their culture and social environment lessen the recognition of a human being, subjected labeled as inferior

(9) RACISM is a spirit, it is a Demon, and it comes directly from SATAN, who was Lucifer, the fairest (whitest), most beautiful, most decorated Angel, who became to most powerful Devil, and it brings about grave sickness as per biblical Mariam – Leprosy, which is today's Cancer.

The subject of Racism: One-person states "if you were blind, you would never know how to be a racist, or what racism means."

Another person stated "If you choose to close your eyes and speak to the other person, then you will understand we are not people of Color, for the flesh is real dirt, dust that we are created from" and when we die, we become dust again.

Another said "Therefore the color of you- A mud Man (*because we came created from the dust of the earth*), is brighter or darker than the other person " MUD MAN" "Your Mud is better."

"ADAM made from dirt that was Red in color, in the Middle-East and given the "Breath of Life from God," "Eve was made from the Rib (flesh) of ADAM, therefore was also RED," where did the White and Black Dirt come from? Is it from the Center of the Earth or is it from cross-breeding? Therefore you ask yourself, where are my flesh from? Before questioning the Flesh or color of another man, you may very well have the mind of the devil to create division on the earth by the color of skin.

Learn about other people, their culture, foods, festivals, medicine and herbal remedies, Today's western world is exploring and exploiting the Asian, Eastern religions and doctrines as they are finding unfathomable information that can help them heal their minds and bodies.

Question to ask yourself: "As a Racist, am I immune from Cancer, Diabetes, High Blood Pressure, Liver and Heart failure, etc., does it make me a better or greater person than the person of another color? Am I a child of God and the other person not a child of God? Or am I the creation of the Devil and the other person's the Sons of God? Why do I feel this hatred and animosity? Is it something that is being subliminally injected into my mind by social media, TV, Politics, and Environment or is it because it has been in my DNA for hundreds or thousands of years, or is it a demonic spirit?"

Ephesians 6: 12 For we wrestle not against flesh and blood, but against principalities, against powers, against the rulers of the darkness of this world, against spiritual wickedness in high places.

We wrestle against powers and principalities and spiritual wickedness in high places, are you in a high place? Or are you a minion that the devil threw merely a small dart and made you a 'holy devil' that you look at the other man and hate him because of the color of his skin? Are there any other differences that you can compare? *In Mark's gospel, Simon was the first man to receive salvation through the Blood of Jesus because he was the Man who helped Jesus carried the Cross, which was full of Jesus' blood*

Luke 16:22	*and it came to pass, that the beggar died, and was carried by the angels into Abraham's bosom: the rich man also died and was buried;*
Luke 16:23	*and in hell he lift up his eyes, being in torments, and seeth Abraham afar off, and Lazarus in his bosom.*
Luke 16:24	*And he cried and said, Father Abraham, have mercy on me, and send Lazarus, that he may dip the tip of his finger in water, and cool my tongue; for I am tormented in this flame.*
Luke 16:25	*but Abraham said, Son, remember that thou in thy lifetime receivedst thy good things, and likewise Lazarus evil things: but now he is comforted, and thou art tormented.*
Galatians 3:28	*"There is neither Jew nor Greek, neither slave nor free, male nor female, for you are all one in Christ Jesus." For as the body is one, and hath many members, and all the members of that one body, being many, are one body: so also is Christ.*

1 Corinthians 12: 13 For by one Spirit are we all baptized into one body, whether we be Jews or Gentiles, whether we be bond or free; and have been all made to drink into one Spirit.

Reference: **(RACISM AND RATIONALITY IN HEGEL.S PHILOSOPHY OF SUBJECTIVE SPIRIT)** *Darrel Moellendorf*

http://www.fb03.uni-frankfurt.de/58976054/Racism-and-Rationality-in-Hegel_s-Philosophy-of-Subjective-Spirit.pdf

The lecture notes recorded in 1825 by two of Hegel's students, Kehler and Griesheim, indicate that Hegel made the following rather contradictory statement:
No color has any superiority, it being merely a matter of being accustomed To it, although one can speak of the objective superiority of the Caucasian race as against that of the Negro. Caucasians, Georgians, etc. are descended from the Turks, and the finest types are to be found among these people. The finest color is that in which what is internal is most Visible, the color which is determined from within outwards in an animal manner . It is the condition of the interior, the animal and spiritual Interior, making itself more visible which is the objective superiority of The white skin color."

"They [Blacks] cannot be said to be uneducable, for not only have they Occasionally received Christianity with the greatest thankfulness and Spoke movingly of the freedom they have gained from it after prolonged Spiritual servitude, but in Haiti, they have even formed a state on Christian principles."

*(10)*Racism has wounded people all around the world – the core of it affects our minds and bodies in various psychosomatic illnesses: Cancer, High Blood

Pressure, Liver disorder, Diabetes, heart disease, etc. It is stated that nations cannot and will not be healed until they get rid of racism or nullify the

practices of racism, putting an end to all forms of racism. This is worst than idolatry and satanic worship. In the Bible, God inflicts Miriam with leprosy because of her outburst of racism towards Moses, because Moses wife Zipporah was a Cushite woman (an Ethiopian woman)

https://www.biblegateway.com/resources/all-women-bible/Zipporah

Numbers 12: 1 *Miriam and Aaron began to talk against Moses because of his Cushite wife, for he had married a Cushite.* ² *"Has the* LORD *spoken only through Moses?" they asked. "Hasn't he also spoken through us?" And the* LORD *heard this. (Now Moses was a very humble man, more humble than anyone else on the face of the earth.)*

⁴ *At once the* LORD *said to Moses, Aaron, and Miriam, "Come out to the tent of meeting, all three of you." So the three of them went out.* ⁵ *Then the* LORD *came down in a pillar of cloud; he stood at the entrance to the tent and summoned Aaron and Miriam. When the two of them stepped forward,* ⁶ *he said, "Listen to my words:*

"When there is a prophet among you,
  I, the LORD, **reveal myself to them in visions,**
  I speak to them in dreams.
⁷ **But this is not true of my servant Moses;**
  he is faithful in all my house.
⁸ **With him I speak face to face,**
  clearly and not in riddles;
  he sees the form of the LORD.
Why then were you not afraid
  to speak against my servant Moses?"

⁹ *The anger of the* LORD *burned against them, and he left them.*

¹⁰ *When the cloud lifted from above the tent, Miriam's skin was leprous[it became as white as snow. Aaron turned toward her and saw that she had a defiling skin disease,* ¹¹ *and he said to Moses, "Please, my lord, I ask you not to hold against us the sin we have so foolishly committed.* ¹² *Do not let her be like a stillborn infant coming from its mother's womb with its flesh half eaten away."*

(11) *John A. Powell, a professor at Berkeley and social justice advocate, in his very insightful book "Racing to Justice." "Racialization or ethni-ci-zation is the process of ascribing ethnic or racial identities to a group that did not identify itself as such. [1] Racialization and ethni-ci-zation are often born out of the desire for domination or division. Often the racialized and ethnicized group gradually identifies with and even embraces the ascribed identity." These processes have been common across the history of colonialism, nationalism, and racial and ethnic hierarchies* Racism and discrimination cause Stress, Depression, Common cold, hypertension, cardiovascular diseases, Cancer in an increased above normal state and a whole list of sicknesses and will get you nowhere in life, except for more hatred in your heart (Causing a possible heart-failure)

If you are not a believer of Christianity, or Hinduism, or Islam, then pick up a Buddhist book or the Talmud, The Tanak, it will give knowledge and enlightenment – "my people suffer because of Lack of Knowledge" the greatest commandment is "love thy neighbor as thyself." Here is a list

- Christianity, New Testament.

- Islam, the Holy Quran.

- Hinduism has many holy books, but most popular is Shreemad Bhagavad Gita, Upanishads and Veda.

- Buddhism, Tripitakas.

- Sikhism, Guru Granth Sahib.

- Judaism has religious books. The Torah, Talmud and the Midrash

- Baha'ism, Kitáb-i-Aqdas.

- Confucianism, four texts as containing the central ideas of Confucian thought: two chapters from the Book of Rites, namely, the Great Learning, the Doctrine of the Mean; the Analects, and Mencius.

- Jainism, the Agamas.

- Shintoism, Kojiki.

Prayers against Racism:

Lord God of The heavens and Earth, you have created us all in your image, one imageof yourself in spirit and we all have the same equivalence of your spirit, mercy, and grace, We p ray that you remove the blindness and scales from my eyes as you have done to Paul the Apostle, by blinding him first so that after removing the scales he can possess the spiritual vision and not any other vision, touch our hearts and soften these hardened hearts, remove any animosities that we may possess within and cast aside our prejudices, touch my lips of clay that I may deliver them kind words and good sound, remove bigotry and racism from our hearts and give us the vision to see that we are all one people under God on one Earth that you have created for us and give us the unction to remove the racism that existed since the beginning of time, For we are neither Jew nor gentile, neither black nor white, nor red , yellow, brown or green in the color of our skin, but we are sons of God as was created to be. Bring peace and resolution to our tensions of division and divisiveness and let us have the eyes, ears, mouth, and vision to see that God has created every man equal in his image, for his purpose and there is none that is greater or lesser in the eyes of God. I pray you to release these feelings and mindsets of inequality from within us

For in Hebrew 4:12 it is clear "For the word of God is quick, and powerful, and sharper than any two-edged sword, piercing even to the dividing asunder of soul and spirit, and of the joints and marrow, and is a discerner of the thoughts and intents of the heart. Neither is there any creature that is not manifest in his sight, but all things are naked and opened unto the eyes of him with whom we have to do."

For in Ephesians 6:12 "For we wrestle NOT against flesh and blood, but against principalities, against powers, against rulers of the darkness of this world, against spiritual wickedness in high places, "and we know that the rulers of darkness are evil spirits and demon under Satan whose purpose is to create divisiveness. Let not my heart be contaminated and let not my spirit be corrupt and let not my body become the vessel for Satan and his demons in displaying and demonstrating and acting in bigotry and racism. For it is written n Proverbs 11:9 "The hypocrite with his mouth destroys his neighbor, but through knowledge, the righteous will be delivered." AMEN

Read and gain some knowledge of spirituality and life teachings according to the Sages, Prophets, Rabbis, Pastors, Priests, Gurus and learn, your eyes will be open, and you will eventually find the door to the right channel and whatever religion fits to your curriculum and later be justified what is the latest true teachings and doctrine of God, but do not be the dumbest person or remain the dumbest person in town with no knowledge of life on earth. No one comes to God unless God pulls them into his kingdom and God will send out a messenger or deliver some way to connect with you. Therefore if you are reading this book assures that this is God's way of connecting with you and channeling direction to you. Religious life is a tough one, it is not easy and will not always be a bed of roses or the Green Pastures in Psalms 23, It a tough road to follow and a tough life to live, but it has its benefits, and it is not always about this short phase of life. The Purpose of living, the road to redemption, and the manual of living life abundantly, only because you will always be under rather than over and will still are in submission rather than in control. I know many who are too great a person to read the Bible or gain the knowledge of any other religious books. Some are too self-centered, ashamed, and too macho to talk to a friend or to talk to God (pray)

John Chapter 10

1   Verily, verily, I say unto you, He that entereth not by the door into the sheepfold, but climbed up some other way, the same is a thief and a robber.

2   But he that entereth in by the door is the shepherd of the sheep.

3   To him the porter openeth; and the sheep hear his voice: and he calleth his own sheep by name, and leadeth them out.

4   And when he putteth forth his own sheep, he goeth before them, and the sheep follow him: for they know his voice.

5   And a stranger will they not follow but will flee from him: for they know not the voice of strangers.

6   This parable spake Jesus unto them: but they understood not what things they were which he spake unto them.

7   Then said Jesus unto them again, Verily, verily, I say unto you, I am the door of the sheep.

8   All that ever came before me are thieves and robbers: but the sheep did not hear them.

9   I am the door: by me, if any man enters in, he shall be saved and shall go in and out, and find pasture.

10   **The thief cometh not, but for to steal, and to kill, and to destroy: I come that they might have life and that they might have it more abundantly**

21 ABUNDANT LIFE

"Abundant life" refers to **life** in its abounding fullness of joy and strength for mind, body, and soul. **"Abundant life"** signifies a contrast to feelings of lack, emptiness, and dissatisfaction, and such feelings may motivate a person to seek for the **meaning** of **life** and a change in their **life**.

John 10:10	*The thief comes only to steal and kill and destroy; I came that they may have life, and have it abundantly.*
Psalms 16:11	*You will make known to me the path of life; In Your presence is fullness of joy; In Your right hand there are pleasures forever.*
Galatians 2:20	*"I have been crucified with Christ; and it is no longer I who live, but Christ lives in me; and the life which I now live in the flesh I live by faith in the Son of God, who loved me and gave Himself up for me.*
John 1:12	*But as many as received Him, to them He gave the right to become children of God, even to those who believe in His name,*
James 1:17	*Every good thing given and every perfect gift is from above, coming down from the Father of lights, with whom there is no variation or shifting shadow.*
Matthew 4:4	*But He answered and said, "It is written, 'MAN SHALL NOT LIVE ON BREAD ALONE, BUT ON EVERY WORD THAT PROCEEDS OUT OF THE MOUTH OF GOD.'"*
Psalm 31:19	*how great is Your goodness, Which You have stored up for those who fear You, Which You have wrought for those who take refuge in You, Before the sons of men!*
2 Corinthians 5:17	*Therefore if anyone is in Christ, he is a new creature; the old things passed away; behold, new things have come.*
Corinthians 2:9:	"No eye has seen, no ear has heard, no mind has conceived what God has prepared for those who love him." The apostle Paul tells us that God is able to do exceedingly abundantly above all that we ask or think, and He does it by His power, a power that is at work within us if we belong to Him
ASK GOD for what you want:	Matthew 7:7 Ask, and it shall be given you; seek, and ye shall find; knock, and it shall be opened unto you:

How can we live an abundant life?

- Have an abundance of sound mental ability. ...
- Be grateful for what you have. ...
- Smile. ...
- Start your day's right. ...
- Prepare yourself for opportunities. ...
- Make the most out of every opportunity. ...
- Build friendships along the way. ...
- Build upon what you've built.
- Love – give love and love will come back
-

This word "abundant" in Greek is *perisson*, meaning "exceedingly, very highly, beyond measure, more, superfluous, a quantity so abundant as to be considerably more than what one would expect or anticipate."

We fight and create conflict over politics, religion, and various forms of prejudice and become judgmental and not focus on the main issue at hand. This is the deceiver, and he has us in his palms so that you don't dash your foot against a stone. YEAH. He uses our Religiosity and twists the Doctrine, altering the meanings, and injecting these characteristics and attributes in our minds. Do not use your religion to create division, anger, hatred, and animosity for your fellow man. If each religion can follow the basics of their ten commandments, the world would be a better place.

If your conflict with religion **is so great and cumbersome in that it contaminates your spirit and takes away your peacefulness, you need to prove its existence is more important, more powerful that other religions, you need to utilize that power to heal sicknesses, cast out demons, change circumstances from Bad to good and pray to elevate your country, family and people. Not let it cause you mental turbulence and destruction of family and friends. Prayer not only changes people, situations and even the course of history, but also those who pray!**
Destruction is associated with demonic activities

God incarnates himself many times to **save humanity and teach them LOVE and SALVATION**- how to get reconnected to GOD. The last incarnation did more than teach; He came **to "Save those that are Lost,"** He **healed** all kinds of sicknesses, **Raised the Dead**, **cast out demons,** etc. and sacrificed himself for Mankind. And this can be replicated. Now if you can use your religion and your religiosity to accomplish those acts, it would be a great and wonderful achievement. See "you can fool some of the people some of the time, and you can fool all the people some of the time, but you cannot fool all the people all the time, and when it comes to GOD, you cannot fool HIM for even one second" *Richard Ing- Waging spiritual warfare*

I recognized the incredible possibilities of national transformation—not by patterns we would recommend to God, but by the power, we could release through prayer to God. Here are the guidelines we began to learn for worship at this dimension:

> ***Hosea 4:6*** *My people are destroyed for lack of knowledge:*
>
> ***Proverbs 29:18*** *Where there is no vision, the people perish:*

But GOD said in

> **"2 Ch 7:14** *If my people, which are **called** by **my** name, shall humble themselves, and pray, and seek **my** face, and turn from their wicked ways; then will I hear from heaven, and will forgive their sin, and will heal their land."*
>
> **1Tim 2: 1-3** *I exhort therefore, that, first of all, supplications, prayers, intercessions, and giving of thanks, be made for all men; 2. For kings, and for all that are in authority; that we may lead a quiet and peaceable life in all godliness and honesty. Or this is good and acceptable in the sight of God our Savior;*

22 FIRST – BREAK GENERATIONAL CURSES

I am going to Pray and lead you through breaking **the Generational Curses**, **Pray for the countries** and the people and this gathering as well. Please put away your Pride, Ego, attitudes, religiosity and humble yourself and join me. Every Pastor, Every Pundit, Every Moulana, every Magi, Cleric, etc. should formulate their prayer and pray against these bondages if you do not have one written in your doctrine use this English Text that is Witten

Breaking generational curses – (the internet also has a lot of similar prayers to fit your specific needs)

Heavenly Father, in Jesus Name I confess all sins and iniquities committed by me, my parents, and all my ancestors that have introduced curses and bondages into my family generation and family line. I rebuke, Break and lose myself and my family line and all my generations from my sins and all sins committed by me, my family members and any other persons within my family, my ancestors, and bloodline. I break the power of every spoken curse pronounced to us, and I take back the grounds that were yielded to the devil and put under the evil influence. I reclaim all blessings that were stolen or taken away and claim blessings instead.

I now renounce, break all curses and evil words and sever all links of iniquity and generational curses I may have inherited from my parents, grandparents and all other ancestors and break all unholy soul ties formed between myself all different generations and ancestors.

Father, I pray and ask that all known or unknown generational bondage and curses, going backward throughout time, be made null and void through the Power of the Shed Blood of the Lord Jesus Christ. I give you all thanks, In Jesus' name, Amen.

In the name of Jesus Christ of Nazareth, I lose myself from any bondages passed down to me from my ancestors, and I command any evil spirits that dwell in these circumstances and have taken advantage of these cords of iniquity, generational curses, and unholy soul ties to leave now in Jesus name!

Almighty God, in the name of Jesus

I give thanks for the United States of America that has given me from an immigrant status, citizenship, a home, Education and the American Dream, and I bless the government and leaders and those in authority. I give thanks for the Countries of Guyana, (Ghana, Jamaica, Columbia, Puerto Rico, Greece, and Italy) (Name your country or countries)

I pray and ask of you, In the name of Jesus and by his power and authority and his blood. To bind every spiritual Principalities and power of the air and all demonic forces that are over these countries Mentioned, command them to cease in their operations, and cast them out from these countries and take back the power they control. Break every bondage, curses, hex, and evil that works in darkness, break every Generational curse that has been upon the country and its people, break all Voodoo and occult bondage and rebuke and bind all these spirits from operating.

LORD, Break every bondage and curse of Low self-esteem, Negative or pessimistic thinking, guilt, anger, doubt and unbelief, fear, grief and disappointment, unforgiveness, occult involvement, illicit sexual behavior, rejection and shame, generational influence,

Bless these nations, release the blessings from above upon these lands, deliver wisdom, knowledge, power, and authority, success and prosperity and make it right to the ideas of freedom and justice and brotherhood for all.

Guard them against war, from fire, wind, and storm, guard us against corruption, fear, confusion.

Give our Leaders vision and courage, power and ability, wisdom as they ponder decisions affecting peace and the future of these countries and the world

Make these vast lands, and elevate the status of the people, with knowledge, wealth, success, spirituality and understanding of you and let them know your will that they may fulfill the destiny ordained for them and us in the Salvation of the nations and restoring of all things in Christ. Bless them with Peace, love, and harmony, bless them with success and prosperity, bless them with wisdom and knowledge, bless them with financial wealth and bless them with a favor that they become a financial resource for helping thousands and millions and a blessing to you.

Rebuke all sicknesses from their bodies and mind of the people and bless them with good health and a sound mind. Bless them *with recognition and authority in the city and the country, at their Jobs and in their homes and environment. Bless them that*

They come to know you and give those visions, insights, direction, and guidance toward a higher calling and a better abundant life.

And Finally we bind all corruption in the country, and in the Government, rebuke and bind all operations of Satan and his emissaries in operating in the Government and the country in the areas of Alcoholism, Drug Addiction, Murder and criminal activities, Thefts and Bribery, All power drunkenness, Every abuse of power and money, All deceit and trickery, All selfishness and egotism, all ignorance and lack of common sense and knowledge. We bind and rebuke the stubborn spirit of the people and the spirit of Fear and anxiety, the spirit of passivity and weakness and those who use religiosity to create conflict, hatred, and division, and we pray as ask the Lord God of Heaven and Earth to put a curse upon it as specified.

We pray LORD that you take control of every aspect of spirituality and governance of the country and its people and sine your light upon them, remove everything that is not of you and fill them with everything from you

Breaking curses and bondages are not only physical; it is the highest spiritual battle of our mental states. The devil whispers into our minds the evil contents and temptations for us to get into a sinful state and commit sin in the various forms. It is a tremendous psychological battle and as defined in many doctrines from all the diverse religion is a battle not physical but spiritual.

Satan, I confessed my past involvement into your evil works. I repent for all my sins and command you and all your evil demons and spirits to leave me, leave my family, leave my environment, leave my job and my finances alone, in the name of the Lord Jesus Christ and by his power, might, and authority. I rebuke, renounce and break all vows and agreements I may have made by my own words and by any words that have been spoken over my family and me. I am now under the authority of the Lord Jesus, and His blood has covered me and washed me of all my sins. I am free from any hold, bondage, hex or curse you have had over our lives and command you, in the name of Jesus to leave me now, never to return or interfere in our undertaking and our businesses and life. In Jesus Name AMEN.

Lord God in Jesus name, I break all oath, chants, any pact, spells, and curses, any evil spells or agreements I have had or undertaken knowingly or unknowingly, even by the association of friends and family. All negative powers are broken and return to its source in Jesus Name. I break and cancel all Generational curses, agreements, bondages that came from my ancestors, my grandparents or my parents or anyone in my bloodline all the way back to Adam, in Jesus name, and I claim the blessings and authority of Lord Jesus Christ in my life and my family's lives.

Jihad. The literal **meaning of Jihad** is struggle or effort, and it **means** much more than holy war. Muslims use the word **Jihad** to describe three different kinds of conflict: A believer's internal struggle to live out the Muslim faith as well as possible. ... Holy war: the battle to defend Islam and Islamic beliefs and culture created or documented in scripture. Its a battle within the mind and "If there is no peace within, there is no peace on the outside, If there is no peace within the mind of a Muslim, he is overtaken by the whisperer (Shaitan who whispers in the minds of men and creates turmoil within and leads to turbulence , confusion, unrest and chaos in the minds of men leading into temptations , resulting in sin, hatred, anger etc What Jihad is not, it is not a declaration of war against other religions (The Koran reference the Jews and Christians as " people of the Book" "The Bible") who should be respected and protected for the are all from one root Abraham and the Abrahamic lineage. Which also related to all other religions for there is not a physical war against the flesh, but against principalities and powers of the air: There are interpretations, and there are interpretations. The old languages are not always in alignment with the modern day meaning and understandings, and that goes for all doctrine. These misinterpretations can be a misconception and a purpose that is not aligned with the modern-day man's arguments, because of the missing vowels and the short/compressed syllables that was written in a poetic form. The man has tried to interpret the language as carefully as possible. GOD is HOLY, and if GOD is holy, then God will not allow unholy actions on any of his believers.

It is arguable that in old scriptures such as OLD testament, Vedas, Koran, etc. there are wars and gross killings, murder and slaughter of nations and people, Genocides that occur from generation to generation, from Era to era, but we need to examine those writings closely and more in-depth to understand why? Purpose and reasoning for these commands and actions of people and their interpretations of God's word. I will leave that for future arguments or discussion. In these modern times as Man's law becomes the cultural patterns to follow, we must adhere to the new ways and such like the New Testament and the real message of God which is "LOVE" "Compassion" "Humility" "Charity" "Longsuffering" and "Fear of God."

Jinns are spirits created by God out of the fire and are dark spirits that inhabit dark places on the earth. They are lower than Angels and even human beings, but they can serve as 'a whisperer' into the minds of living people. The following powerful Islamic prayers confirm the existence of the devil and the fear it drives in the hearts of men

Chapter 114 – Surah An-Nas (Mankind)
Bismillahir-Rahmanir-Raheem
Qul 'A'udhu Bi-Rabbin-Nas
Malikin-Nas
Ilahin-Nas
Min-Sharril-Waswasil-Khan-Nas
Al-Ladhi Yuwas-wisu Fee Sudurin-Nas
Mina Al-Jinnati Wan-Nas "

"Say: I seek refuge with (Allah) the lord of mankind, The King of mankind, The Allah (God) of mankind, From the evil of the whisperer (devil l who whispers evil in the hearts of men), who withdraws (from his whispering in one's heart after one remembers Allah), Who whispers in the breasts of mankind, Of jinn's and men."

Chapter 113 – Surah Al-Falaq (Dawn)

" Bismillahir-Rahmanir-Raheem
Qul 'A'udhu Bi-Rabbil-Falaq
Min Sharri Ma Khalaq
Wa Min Sharri Ghasiqin 'Idha Waqab
Wa Min Sharri-Naffathati Fil-'Uqadi
Wa Min Sharri Hasidin 'Idha Hasad "

Say : I seek refuge with (Allah) the Lord of the daybreak, From the evil of what He has created; And from the evil of the darkening (night) as it comes with its darkness; (or the moon as it sets or goes away). And from the evil of the witchcraft when they blow in the knots, and from the evil of the envier when he envies. "

Chapter 109 – Surah Al-Kafiroun (The Unbeliever)
" Bismillahir-Rahmanir-Raheem
Qul ya ayyuhal-Kafiroun
La 'a-budu ma ta'-bu-doun
Wa la antum 'abidouna ma 'a-bud
Wa la ana 'abidum-ma 'abadttum
Wa la antum 'abiduna ma 'a-bud
Lakum deenukum wa li-ya deen "

"Say O Al-Kafiroun (disbelievers in Allah , in His Oneness , in His Angels , in His Books , in His Messengers , in the Day of Resurrection , and in Al-Qadar , etc.)! I worship not that which you worship, nor will you worship that which I worship. And I shall not worship that which you are worshipping. Nor will you worship that which I worship. To you be your religion and to me my religion (Islamic Monotheism). "

Definition: You must believe in Allah (GOD) otherwise you are a non-believer. Islam believes in GOD and has defined a doctrine for everyone to believe in GOD. The Arabic word for God is "ALLAH" therefore, there is no confusion that we do not believe in GOD. Every sect of humanity lives according to their culture in the region they are from as such there are laws created by Man for another man to live by and maintain standards. Christians have their own, so does the Hindus, Buddhist, Jews, Chinese, etc.

They all believe in GOD, but the definition is different based on their culture and the interpretations of their doctrine, whether, by the name of Jehovah, Jesus, Allah, Vishnu, Krishna, Brahma, Buddha, they all believe in God and are therefore in ordinance with GOD.

Ephesians 6: 10- 18 in the Bible explains: (NIV) The Armor of God

10   *Finally, be strong in the Lord and in his mighty power.*

11   *Put on the full armor of God, so that you can take your stand against the devil's schemes.*

12   *For our struggle is not against flesh and blood, but against the rulers, against the authorities, against the powers of this dark world and against the spiritual forces of evil in the heavenly realms.*

13   *Therefore put on the full armor of God, so that when the day of evil comes, you may be able to stand your ground, and after you have done everything, to stand.*

14   *Stand firm then, with the belt of truth buckled around your waist, with the breastplate of righteousness in place, 15 and with your feet fitted with the readiness that comes from the gospel of peace.*

16   *In addition to all this, take up the shield of faith, with which you can extinguish all the flaming arrows of the evil one.*

17   *Take the helmet of salvation and the sword of the Spirit, which is the word of God.*

18   *And pray in the Spirit on all occasions with all kinds of prayers and requests. With this in mind, be alert and always keep on praying for all the Lord's people.*

**The Bhagavad-Gita Translated by Dr. Ramananda Prasad
Courtesy of the International Gita Society
http://reluctant-messenger.com/bhagavad-gita.htm**

The message of Gita came to humanity because of Arjuna's unwillingness to do his duty as a warrior, because fighting involved destruction and killing. Nonviolence or Ahimsa is one of the most fundamental tenets of Hinduism. All lives, human or non-human, are sacred. This immortal discourse between the Supreme Lord, Krishna, and His devotee-friend, Arjuna, occurs not in a temple, a secluded forest, or on a mountain top but on a battlefield on the eve of a war and is recorded in the great epic, Mahaabhaarata. In Gita Lord Krishna advises Arjuna to get up and fight. This may create a misunderstanding of the principles of Ahimsa if the background of the war of Mahaabhaarata is not kept in mind. Therefore, a brief historical description is in order. ....

The big war of Mahaabhaarata was thus inevitable. The Paandavs were unwilling participants. They had only two choices: Fight for their right as a matter of duty or run away from war and accept defeat in the name of peace and nonviolence. Arjuna, one of the five Paandava brothers, faced the dilemma in the battlefield whether to fight or run away from war for the sake of peace.

Arjuna's dilemma is, in reality, the universal dilemma. Every human being faces dilemmas, big and small, in their everyday life when performing their duties. Arjuna's dilemma was the biggest of all. He had to make a choice between fighting the war and killing his most revered guru, very dear friends, close relatives, and many innocent warriors or running away from the battlefield for the sake of preserving the peace and nonviolence.

The main objective of the Gita is to help people ¾ struggling in the darkness of ignorance ¾ cross the ocean of transmigration and reach the spiritual shore of liberation while living and working in the society. The central teaching of the Gita is the attainment of freedom or happiness from the bondage of life by doing one's duty. Always remember the glory and greatness of the creator and do your duty efficiently without being attached to or affected by the results even if that duty may at times demand

The most powerful of the prayers in Hinduism are the MahaMrityunjaya Mantra, suggested as the great death-conquering mantra from the Rig Veda 7:59.12

Om Trayambakam Yajamahe, Sugandhim Pushti Vardhanam, Urvarukmiv Bandhanat, Mrityurmokshaya Mamratat.

Trayambakam : *One who has three eyes. Lord Shiva is the only one who has it.*
Yajamahe: *One who is prayed or worshiped.*
Sugandhim: *Good Smell.*
Pushti: *Prosperous, Fulfilled.*
Vardhanam: *One who makes happy, prosperous, gives peace of mind and takes care of you.*
Urvarukmiv: *Like it or no one else.*
Bandhanat: *Associated or bonding.*
Mrityur- *From Death.*
Mokshaya: *Free us or send us heaven.*
Ma: *Not Amritat: Immortal.*

The Gayathri Mantra: *A universal prayer which is in the Vedas – Rig Veda 3:62.10, a sacred chant that is dedicated to God in the form of adoration, meditation, and Prayer. The Brahman and universal divine energy, the vital spiritual energy, the essence of our life existence, removal of mal-effects and suffering, the bringer of happiness, clearer of our minds and spiritual balance. It is one of the oldest and has great mystical vibrations since these are all mantras that function and infused by the sound of the Sanskrit words and sound. It is seen as the opening and awakening of the mind and connects to the soul.*

Om Bhur Bhuvaḥ Swaḥ, Tat-savitur Vareñyaṃ, Bhargo Devasya Dhīmahi, Dhiyo Yonaḥ Prachodayāt

Meaning: We meditate on that most adored Supreme Lord, the creator, whose effulgence (divine light) illumines all realms (physical, mental and spiritual). May this divine light illumine our intellect?

Analysis: Word meaning: Om: The primeval sound; Bhur: the physical body/physical realm; Bhuvah: the life force/the mental realm Suvah: the soul/spiritual realm; Tat: That (God); Savitur: the Sun, Creator (source of all life); Vareñyam: adore; Bhargo: effulgence (divine light); Devasya: supreme Lord; Dhīmahi: meditate; Dhiyo: the intellect; Yo: May this light; Nah: our; Prachodayāt: illumine/inspire.

Hindu and Buddhist teachings state that there are seven realms, spheres or dimensions, which are planes of existence, each one is a higher level of spirituality, more advanced than the previous and if we can reach the seventh, we are connected to the Supreme Being-God

The pronunciation and the tone are very important and specific; it needs to be accurately sung or chanted out, which could sometimes be a negative if chanted incorrectly. It would be better to read the meaning of the Prayers and experience the same effect

In the Bhagwat Gita, LORD Krishna explained to Arjuna the King, to observe? Demons are all over and they are invisible, as he was teaching Arjuna and gave him the vision to see beyond the physical dimension and physical realm to see within the enemy that they were all possessed with demons and rakshasa (demons) most of these demons were demons of greed, lust, envy, pride, gluttony, and sloth, just as mentioned in the scriptures, this was written over 5000 years before Jesus.

If we do not adhere to the new revelations of GOD, We will venture to destroy humanity and will be the destroyer of Countries and eventually the world. Some nations believe there is another EARTH that they can migrate to at this time. If one country destroys another country and millions of people because of doctrines of Old that causes separation and segregation, none from any and all religions will survive, though some are welcoming to this type of occult thinking, that DEATH is a glorified state and that GOD will redeem you after death and glorify you in heaven, you are plain straight foolish, selfish, conceited and do not adhere to the commandments of God, therefore you are "beguiled" by the devil himself

Jesus stated that the second greatest commandment of all is "LOVE THY NEIGHBOR AS THYSELF."

Matthew 22:36-40 New International Versions (NIV)

36 "Teacher, which is the greatest commandment in the Law?"

37   Jesus replied: "'Love the Lord your God with all your heart and with all your soul and with your entire mind.'

38   This is the first and greatest commandment.

39   And the second is like it: 'Love your neighbor as yourself.'

40   All the Law and the Prophets hang on these two commandments."

What is the commandment of Jesus Christ?
The New Commandment is a term used in Christianity to describe Jesus's commandment to "love one another" which, according to the Bible, was given as part of the final instructions to his disciples after the Last Supper had ended, and after Judas Iscariot had departed in John 13:30.

---

23 THE COMMANDMENTS

What is the order of the Ten Commandments?

- **I am the LORD thy God.**

- **No other gods before me.**

- **No graven images or likenesses.**

- **Not take the LORD's name in vain.**

- **Remember the sabbath day.**

- **Honour thy father and thy mother.**

- **Thou shalt not kill.**

- **Thou shalt not commit adultery.**

  The Talmud notes that the Hebrew numerical value (gematria) of the word "Torah" is 611,

  And combining Moses' **611 commandments** with the first two of the **Ten Commandments**

24 FOOLISHNESS OF MAN

What is a fool? A Person who lacks judgment or prudence, one who requires the ordinary powers or ability of understanding; a person who behaves in a silly way without thinking; a foolish or stupid person; **"*A person who has been tricked or deceived into appearing or acting for amusement.*"** Foolishness is the result of a person who acts senselessly, ill-considerate, unwisely or consistently being the fool. In Scriptural meaning, foolishness is misusing the intelligence God has given him. A fool uses his reasoning skills to make wrong decisions. Solomon the wisest of men according to the bible states that a foolish person is a selfish, self-centered, arrogant person controlled by their very own emotions, unable to accept correction and advice from any other person and refuses to accept responsibility for any decision or consequences of decisions made, but blames others, including God. The Bible paints some graphic pictures of a fool, and their follies, Solomon in Proverbs defines the fool like the fool beyond a fool, and the scriptures are harsh with intent for the wise to be cautious of the fool, and the foolishness of man can be dangerous to themselves as well as others around them. A simple example could be if you hang around a drug dealer, you will eventually become one or become a victim of drugs and a drug addict, in this case, who is the fool? *(Proverbs 27:22 **Though thou shouldest bray a fool in a mortar among wheat with a pestle**, yet will not his foolishness depart from him – the meaning of "Bray" is to grind or pound to powder,). It is one of the most difficult tasks to turn a fool around into a wise person and have them change for their foolish ways, due to the characters they may possess, only by faith and prayer, consistent witnessing and teaching that their mind can be subliminally changed and converted to a new way of thinking, maybe through Neuro-linguistic Programming you will be successful, But the Bible clearly teaches to be cautious of a fool. Furthermore, do not let anyone call you a 'fool' for the words of people can become an anchor in your mind.*

In a Google search for Foolishness of Man brings up a whole plethora of biblical quotations, references and sermons of the 'Foolishness of man', which depicts the importance of the subject and how it is related to Man and spirituality and the lessons on the subject for learning purposes of repeated incidents in history and the days went by.

It is only a fool who would make the same mistake over and over without learning from the last mistake *(Proverbs 26:11 As a dog returneth to his vomit, so a fool returneth to his folly; 2 Peter 2:22 But it is happened unto them according to the true proverb, The dog is turned to his own vomit again; and the sow that was washed to her wallowing in the mire.).*

In Islam: Chapter 2 :13 Surat L-baqarah : And when it is said unto them: believe as the people believe, they say: shall we believe as the foolish believe? are not they indeed the foolish? But they know not.

Chapter 2:130:　　　And who forsaketh the religion of Abraham saves him who befooleth himself? Verily We chose him in the world, and lo! in the Hereafter he is among the righteous.

Bhagwat Gita: 9:12 These bewildered fools of futile desires, futile endeavors, futile

knowledge, and futile understanding; certainly assume the nature of the atheistic and the demoniacs.

9:11　　　Fools deride me in my divine human form, unable to comprehend my supreme nature as the Ultimate Controller of all living entities

The Bible has the best definitions, we will utilize scriptures from the Bible to define the foolishness of man, and this includes using it for sharing the wisdom to the lost generations and the generations of today, who are walking away and separating themselves from scripture, spirituality and religion – THIS is considered to be foolish and the greater of the foolishness where the young millennial generations are getting lost , is put upon the shoulders of the Elders, Parents, Pastors and ministers, Pundits and priests, Imams, Islamic clerics as it is the responsibility of the Elder of this generation to find a way and the means to draw the younger generation into religious beliefs and spirituality. It may bring about long drawn arguments and debate about not being the responsibilities of the elders or pastors, ministers, imams, priests, gurus, pundits, etc.... It is not a battle that you will win or will ever win. We the generations of today are failing the young generations by our actions, deeds and being the role models for the young people as they are watching and seeing, listening and hearing as we the elders of this present day is allowing the messages to slip through our fingers and letting the darkness invade our minds as we enhance our greed, avarice, and quest for power and moving the Church and religiosity from the church to the parliament buildings and Government agencies as of old where the Church was the Government, today the Government controls the Church and politics across the world has the most significant influence on the Church, and the leaders are becoming as defined above, allowing themselves to become puppets of politicians and leaders in high places.

John 8:44 (NIV) You belong to your father, the devil, and you want to carry out your father's desires. He was a murderer from the beginning, not holding to the truth, for there is no truth in him. When he lies, he speaks his native language, for he is a liar and the father of lies.

Jesus said in Matthew 18:11 For the Son of man is come to save that which was lost.

Luke 19:10 For the Son of man is come to seek and to save that which was lost. For in James 4:17 Therefore to him that knoweth to do good, and doeth it not, to him it is a sin.

(These are the saints who know the scriptures and are knowledgeable in the word, yet choose to acknowledge and honor the sins of many who are in power rather than doing the good that the scripture commands, acknowledging the sinful nature and lies as the anointing of God and have brought upon themselves (just as the Pharisees and Sadducees have done in crucifying Christ) the tarnishing of their Christian Character and the authenticity of their Christian lives.

https://www.biblegateway.com/passage/?search=1+Timothy+3&version=ESV

1 Timothy 3: **Qualifications for Overseers**

1   *The saying is trustworthy: If anyone aspires to the office of overseer, he desires a noble task.*

2   *Therefore an overseer must be above reproach, the husband of one wife, sober-minded, self-controlled, respectable, hospitable, able to teach,*

3   *not a drunkard, not violent but gentle, not quarrelsome, not a lover of money.*

4   *He must manage his own household well, with all dignity keeping his children submissive,*

5   *for if someone does not know how to manage his own household, how will he care for God's church?*

6   *He must not be a recent convert, or he may become puffed up with conceit and fall into the condemnation of the devil.*

7   *Moreover, he must be well thought of by outsiders, so that he may not fall into disgrace, into a snare of the devil.*

Qualifications for Deacons

8   *Deacons likewise must be dignified, not double-tongued, [c] not addicted to much wine, not greedy for dishonest gain.*

9   *They must hold the mystery of the faith with a clear conscience.*

10   *And let them also be tested first; then let them serve as deacons if they prove themselves blameless.*

11   *Their wives likewise must be dignified, not slanderers, but sober-minded, faithful in all things.*

12   *Let deacons each be the husband of one wife, managing their children and their own households well.*

13   *For those who serve well as deacons gain a good standing for themselves and also great confidence in the faith that is in Christ Jesus.*

Parents: *Proverbs 22:6 Train up a child in the way he should go; even when he is old, he will not depart from it.*
This also applies to all other religion and all similar organization that has any quest to manage people and followers of a faith.

The most basic type of foolishness is denying God's existence or saying "no" to God **(Psalm 14:1).** The Bible associate's folly with a quick temper **(Proverbs 14:16–17),** perverse speech **(Proverbs 19:1),** and disobedience to parents (Proverbs 15:5). We are born with innate foolishness, but discipline will help train us in wisdom **(Proverbs 22:15).**

*Proverbs 19:3 says that foolishness is counterproductive: "A person's own folly leads to their ruin." Jesus in **Mark 7:24** uses a word which means "senselessness" and is translated "foolishness." In that context, Jesus describes what comes out of the heart of man and defiles him. Foolishness is one of the evidence that man has a defiled, sinful nature.*

*Proverbs 24:9 says, "The schemes of folly are a sin." Foolishness, then, is really the breaking of God's law, for sin is lawlessness **(1 John 4:4).***

To the fool, God's way is foolishness. *"The message of the cross is foolishness to those who are perishing."* **(1 Corinthians 1:18; verse 23).** The gospel seems to be foolishness to the unsaved because it doesn't make sense to them. The fool is completely out of phase with God's wisdom. The gospel goes against the unbeliever's native intelligence and reason, yet *"God was pleased through the foolishness of what was preached to save those who believe"* **(1 Corinthians 1:21).**

The believer in Christ receives the very nature of God **(2 Peter 1:4),** which includes the mind of **Christ (1 Corinthians 2:16).** By relying on the Holy Spirit's indwelling power, the believer can reject foolishness. His thoughts can please the Lord, and he can make decisions that glorify God as he enriches his life and the lives of those around him **(Philippians 4:8–9; Ephesians 5:18—6:4).**

When it comes to our eternal destiny, one is either a fool to reject the gospel of Christ and God, or one is wise, saying he believes in Christ and commits his life to Him (see **Matthew 7:24–27).** The believer discovers that the gospel—what he thought was foolishness—is, in reality, the wisdom of God providing his eternal salvation.

Jeremiah 10:14   *every man is stupid, devoid of knowledge; every goldsmith is put to shame by his idols; for his molten images are deceitful, and there isno breath in them*

Jeremiah 51:17	*all mankind is stupid, devoid of knowledge; every goldsmith is put to shame by his idols, for his <u>molten images are deceitful, and there is no</u> breath in them.*
1 Corinthians 1:20	*Where is <u>the wise man? Where is the scribe? Where</u> is the debater of this age? Has not God made foolish <u>the wisdom of the world?</u>*
<u>***Jeremiah 10:21***</u>	*for the shepherds have become stupid and have not sought the LORD; Therefore they have not prospered, and all their flock is scattered.*
2 Timothy 3:9	*But they will not make further progress; for their folly will be obvious to all, just as Jannes's and Jambres's folly was also.*
Jeremiah 10:8	*But they <u>are altogether stupid and foolish in their discipline</u> of delusion--their idol is wood!*
Jeremiah 4:22	*"For My people are foolish, they know Me not; They are stupid children and have no understanding They are shrewd to do evil, but to do good they do not know."*
Hosea 7:11	*so Ephraim <u>has become like a silly dove, without sense;</u> they call to Egypt, they go to Assyria.*
Job 4:21	*'Is not their tent-cord plucked up within them? They die, yet without wisdom.'*
Job 12:24	*"He deprives of intelligence the chiefs of the earth's people and makes them wander in a pathless waste.*
Job 17:4	*"For you have kept their heart from understanding. Therefore You will not exalt them.*
Galatians 3:1	*You foolish Galatians, who had bewitched you, before whose eyes Jesus Christ was publicly portrayed as crucified?*
1 Corinthians 3:20	*and again, "THE LORD KNOWS THE REASONINGS of the wise, THAT THEY ARE USELESS."*
1 Corinthians 1:27	*but God has chosen the foolish things of the world to shame the wise, and God has chosen the weak things of the world to shame the things which are strong,*

25 THE PURPOSE OF MAN'S LIFE ON EARTH

The purpose of man's life on earth is a question which many have pondered about for thousands of years but the answer to which has often become elusive. We do not ask this question anymore because we seem to have given up on the possibility that a solution found. We have also relied on science to give us the answer but with its one-sided way of looking at things it does not seem promising that a solution can ever be found or confirmed.

Our error lies in our wrong concept about a man and our earth and the whole of Creation in general. We have a crazy idea about everything, and our religious beliefs have only compounded matters by not being able to offer any logical explanation, relying instead on blind faith which is entirely at odds which what God wants for His creatures.

Over thousands of years then we have come to look at one side only. We think that man is the physical body because science has told us so and religion has not been able to offer any credible counter-argument, we just assume that our physical existence is the only one there is that when we die the disintegration of our physical bodies becomes dust and we cease to exist. In short in our worldview, there do not seem to be any purpose to it all.

The purpose of life according to our prevailing belief is to live as best we can and accumulate material wealth, get married and have children and if possible, have as many earthly honors as possible and be successful in these then our purpose has been achieved. We are regarded as actualized human beings, successful human beings and so on.

According to our belief, we live only once, and as such we should materially make the best out of it. The reality of our lives, however, is often different and testifies to the fact that this worldview is wrong. What is the purpose of being born, growing up, and going to school, getting a job, getting married and accumulating material wealth only to leave all these things behind again when we die?

It is inconceivable to imagine that the great God would create us just for this purpose. The great Creator is far too perfect and comprehensive in his to believe that He has created human beings only for the purpose for which we have generally accepted as the case today.

What we have accepted as the way of our lives today is our creation. We have devised this way and purpose of lives for ourselves. The goal for which we were created was lost to us due to the thousands of years where we failed to listen to all the messengers and messages sent to us by God.

"I have created the jinn and humankind only for My worship." (Quran 51:56)

Say (O Muhammad): He is God [Who is] One, God, the Eternal Refuge. He neither begets nor is born, nor is there to Him any equivalent. [Quran, 112] (Definition in Islam we believe in One GOD as well. Therefore GOD is one, and it does not matter whether you are Muslim, Hindu, Buddhist or Christian

26 PURPOSE OF MAN

The Bible makes it abundantly clear that God created man and that he created man for His glory. Therefore, the ultimate goal of man, according to the Bible, is just to glorify God. Man is a unique creation; no life form has surpassed human life and human intelligence. Weaker in many areas, still the strongest in consciousness, knowledge, and spirituality, a uniqueness being created by God in the very image of God and that image is the Spirit of God for God is a spirit. Man being created in and with the image of God has the ability that God gave to him to be like God, to perform feats and acts like God. Even though many scholars are going to argue this point, God did create man and gave him dominion over the earth and all other living beings, thus he is purposefully created to perform Godlike duties upon the planet. The man can enhance his physical and spiritual being, connecting to God in many ways and be able to communicate with God in a fellowship of conversation, activities, duties, following instructions and teachings from God to be more like God. The spirit of Jesus Christ in the latter times is a confirmation that God does have a higher purpose for man and will never leave man to become obsolete or exterminated from the Earth. We are to make however sure we are in sync with God to ensure that our longevity, our nature and our surviving and fulfill the purpose of God.

Genesis 1: 26 *Then God said, "Let us make mankind in our image, in our likeness, so that they may **rule** over the fish in the sea and the birds in the sky, over the livestock and all the wild animals, and over all the creatures that move along the ground."*

27 *So God created mankind in his own image,*
in the image of God he created them; male and female he created them.

28 *And God blessed them, and God said unto them, Be **fruitful,** and **multiply**, and **replenish the earth**, **and subdue it**: and **have dominion** over the fish of the sea, and over the fowl of the air, and over every living thing that moveth upon the earth.*

30 *And God Said, "I give you every seed-bearing plant on the face of the whole earth and every tree that has fruit with seed in it. They will be yours for food. 30 And to all the beasts of the earth and all the birds in the sky and all the creatures that move along the ground—everything that has the breath of life in it—I give every green plant for food." And it was so.*

Ecclesiastes 12:13 *the end of the matter; all has been heard. Fear God and keep his commandments, for this is the whole duty of man.*

1 Corinthians 10:	*So, whether you eat or drink, or whatever you do, do all to the glory of God.*
Genesis 1:26	*Then God said, "Let us make man in our image, after our likeness. And let them have dominion over the fish of the sea and over the birds of the heavens and over the livestock and over all the earth and over every creeping thing that creeps on the earth."*
Romans 12:1	*I appeal to you, therefore, brothers, by the mercies of God, to present your bodies as a living sacrifice, holy and acceptable to God, which is your spiritual worship.*
Revelation 4:9-11	*And whenever the living creatures give glory and honor and thanks to him who is seated on the throne, who lives forever and ever, the twenty-four elders fall down before him who is seated on the throne and worship him who lives forever and ever. They cast their crowns before the throne, saying, "Worthy are you, our Lord and God, to receive glory and honor and power, for you created all things, and by your will, they existed and were created."*
Proverbs 19:21	*Many are the plans in the mind of a man, but it is the purpose of the Lord that will stand.*
Genesis 1:28	*And God blessed them. And God said to them, "Be fruitful and multiply and fill the earth and subdue it and have dominion over the fish of the sea and over the birds of the heavens and over every living thing that moves on the earth."*
Psalm 138:8	*The Lord will fulfill his purpose for me; your steadfast love, O Lord, endures forever. Do not forsake the work of your hands.*
1 Peter 4:11	*Whoever speaks, as one who speaks oracles of God; whoever serves, as one who serves by the strength that God supplies—in order that in everything God may be glorified through Jesus Christ. To him belong glory and dominion forever and ever. Amen.*
Ephesians 1:11-12	*In him we have obtained an inheritance, having been predestined according to the purpose of him who works all things according to the counsel of his will, so that we who were the first to hope in Christ might be to the praise of his glory.*
Romans 7:18	*For I know that nothing good dwells in me, that is, in my flesh. For I have the desire to do what is right, but not the ability to carry it out.*
John 17:17-20	*sanctify them in the truth; your word is the truth. As you sent me into the world, so I have sent them into the world. And for their sake, I consecrate myself, that they also may be sanctified in truth. "I do not ask for these only, but also for those who will believe in me through their word,*
John 4:24	*God is a spirit, and those who worship him must worship in spirit and truth."*
Psalm 150:6	*let everything that has breath praise the Lord! Praise the Lord!*
Mark 16:16	*whoever believes and is baptized will be saved, but whoever does not believe will be condemned.*
Psalm 128:1-6	***A Song of Ascents. Blessed is everyone who fears the Lord, who walks in his ways! You shall eat the fruit of the*** *labor of your hands; you shall be blessed, and it shall be well with you. Your wife will be like a fruitful vine within your house; your children will be like olive shoots around your table. Behold, thus shall the man be blessed who fears the Lord. The Lord blesses you from Zion! May you see the prosperity of Jerusalem all the days of your life!*
Colossians 2:	*For in him the whole fullness of deity dwells bodily,*
Philippians 3:10-11	*That I may know him and the power of his resurrection, and may share his sufferings, becoming like him in his death, that by any means possible I may attain the resurrection from the dead.*

Ephesians 6:12	*for we do not wrestle against flesh and blood, but against the rulers, against the authorities, against the cosmic powers over this present darkness, against the spiritual forces of evil in the heavenly places.*
Romans 8:30	*and those whom he predestined he also called, and those whom he called he also justified, and those whom he justified he also glorified.*
Romans 8:28	*and we know that for those who love God all things work together for good, for those who are called according to his purpose.*
John 17:3	*and this is an eternal life that they know you the only true God, and Jesus Christ whom you have sent.*
Matthew 11:29	*Take my yoke upon you, and learn from me, for I am gentle and lowly in heart, and you will find rest for your souls.*
Micah 6:8	*He has told you, O man, what is good; and what does the Lord require of you but to do justice, and to love kindness, and to walk humbly with your God?*
Jeremiah 29:11	*for I know the plans I have for you, declares the Lord, plans for welfare and not for evil, to give you a future and a hope.*
Isaiah 55:11	*so shall my word be that goes out from my mouth; it shall not return to me empty, but it shall accomplish that which I purpose, and shall succeed in the thing for which I sent it.*
Isaiah 43:21	*the people whom I formed for myself that they might declare my praise.*
Ecclesiastes 3:1-3	*For everything there is a season, and a time for every matter under heaven: a time to be born, and a time to die; a time to plant, and a time to pluck up what is planted; a time to kill, and a time to heal; a time to break down, and a time to build up;*
Genesis 1:27	*So God created man in his own image, in the image of God he created him; male and female he created them.*
1 John 5:12	*whoever has the Son has life; whoever does not have the Son of God does not have life.*
Philippians 1:6	*And I am sure of this, that he who began a good work in you will bring it to completion at the day of Jesus Christ.*
Genesis 2:1-25	*Thus the heavens and the earth were finished, and all the host of them. And on the seventh day, God finished his work that he had done, and he rested on the seventh day from all his work that he had done. So God blessed the seventh day and made it holy because on its God rested from all his work that he had done in creation. These are the generations of the heavens and the earth when they were created, in the day that the Lord God made the earth and the heavens. When no bush of the field was yet in the land, and no small plant of the field had yet sprung up—for the Lord God had not caused it to rain on the land, and there was no man to work the ground,*
Hebrews 9:27	*And just as it is appointed for man to die once, and after that comes judgment,*
1 Thessalonians 5:23	*Now may the God of peace himself sanctify you completely, and may your whole spirit and soul and body be kept blameless at the coming of our Lord Jesus Christ.*
Genesis 3:16	*To the woman he said, "I will surely multiply your pain in childbearing; in pain, you shall bring forth children. Your desire shall be for your husband, and he shall rule over you."*
Titus 2:11-14	*For the grace of God has appeared, bringing salvation for all people, training us to renounce ungodliness and worldly passions, and to live self-controlled, upright, and godly lives in the present age, waiting for our blessed hope, the appearing of the glory of our great God and Savior Jesus Christ, who gave*

himself for us to redeem us from all lawlessness and to purify for himself a people for his own possession who are zealous for good works.

1 Corinthians 15:45   Thus it is written, "The first man Adam became a living being"; the last Adam became a life-giving spirit.

Proverbs 1:7   The fear of the Lord is the beginning of knowledge; fools despise wisdom and instruction.

1 Kings 5:5   And so I intend to build a house for the name of the Lord my God, as the Lord said to David my father, 'Your son, whom I will set on your throne in your place, shall build the house for my name.'

Genesis 2:18   Then the Lord God said, "It is not good that the man should be alone; I will make him a helper fit for him."

Micah 7:8   Rejoice not over me, O my enemy; when I fall, I shall rise; when I sit in darkness, the Lord will be a light to me.

Genesis 2:24   Therefore a man shall leave his father and his mother and hold fast to his wife, and they shall become one flesh.

27 GODS PLAN FOR MAN

God's Plan is for all of humanity, not a part, not only Christians and Jews; It is geared for Hindus, Muslims, Buddhist and all other religious sects including the Atheist Regardless of which church we belong to or grown up in, regardless of the custom or, environment and the culture and practice there is a common denominator. God has a general plan of salvation for every human being on earth. This does not apply to Christians and Jews only; it is for everyone. Many people believe God specifically selects them and others who are non-Christians are left to be the feast of the devil. The truth is Christians are the ones that the Devil targets the most, and this is due to the fact that Christians have gained quite a lot of knowledge of God and the truth, and revelations towards salvation, they follow the principles instructions and commandments, but weaken themselves by pride and ego that releases the characteristics of the devil into their psyche which opens up a doorway for the Prince of the air to sail through, take possession of their spirit, mind and physical bodies in a quiet undetectable manner slowly chomping away at their faith in God, their belief in the word and themselves and creating doubt of everything they once believed .

There is One God and to define in better terms one God's family, for God is not a singular word but a plural word, but invested his spirit in One Human Man, by inseminating a virgin woman and creating a Human Body for him to manifest for a short period. What was the purpose? Why would God look upon humanity on earth and put a plan together so that he will come to earth as a Man himself to redeem man from the very curse of mankind *(Psalm 8:4-6 What is a man, that thou art mindful of him? And the son of man, that thou visitest him? 5. For thou hast made him a little lower than the angels, and hast crowned him with glory and honour.6. Thou madest him to have dominion over the works of thy hands; thou hast put all things under his feet:)* God came to redeem mankind many times before, but always come as a spirit in a human form, but could not redeem man due to the makeup of man. God had to return as a man with the physical, mental and spiritual make-up of mankind, experience the emotions, the pains, the joy, the mind and thought process, the intimate connections of relationship with men, women, children, feel, see, hear, touch, taste, and experience all that the human man experiences, to understand and comprehend man properly. He had to be born of the flesh, with blood running through his veins, keeping the body, mind, spirit and soul free from evil and any outside interference of the Devil, so as to fully reclaim mankind and deliver the proper salvation through the purity of the blood and a sacrifice thereof, because it was the blood that got contaminated, and Blood is the life force of man.

It stated that Life is in the Blood and life force is sustained by the blood which is the living water controlled by the spirit.

Leviticus 17: 11 - *For the life of the flesh* is *in the blood: and I have given it to you upon the altar to make an atonement for your souls: for it is the blood that maketh an atonement for the soul.*

12 *Therefore I said unto the children of Israel, no soul of you shall eat the blood; neither shall any stranger that sojourneth among you eat blood.*

Everyone knows that we must have enough blood flowing around our body or else our bodily functions deteriorate and we die. Blood is fundamental to the role of every cell of every component in our bodies. Blood actively maintains life by providing a vital role for all cells, tissues, and organs, and thus the presence of the whole body. Life, that mysterious something that science has never yet been able to define or fathom, is said by God to be in the blood of the flesh so that there can be no life without the blood.

Leviticus 17:11 *"For the life of the flesh is in the blood: and I have given it to you upon the altar to make atonement for your souls: for it is the blood that maketh atonement for the soul."*

Leviticus 17:14 *"For it is the life of all flesh; the blood of it is for the life hereof."*

Leviticus 7:26, 27 *"Moreover ye shall eat no manner of blood, whether it be of fowl or of beast, in any of your dwellings. Whatsoever soul it be that eateth any manner of blood, even that soul shall be cut off from his people."*

We are saved by the Blood of Jesus and so dependent on that course of salvation. The sacrifice of this divine blood was a method of God trying to redeem his creation which after creating his physical form, had to input the life driving living water of blood to sustain it and giving it a divine spirit to hold up that massive earthly compound of human dust and flesh

The church of Jesus Christ is called His body and we "are members of His body." As such all members are related by the blood of Christ as long as you are adopted as an heir of Jesus and baptized in his name, being baptized In the name of the Father, Son, and Holy Ghost. We are initially related through Adam, by flesh and blood and we all became contaminated by the sin and fall of the same, since Adam's sin which was a result of physical death and the loss of the Divine nature and spiritually connectivity to God, this flaw was passed down through our DNA and genetics for generations and generations.

Acts 17:26 *"And hath made of one blood all nations of men for to dwell on all the face of the earth."*

Genesis *2:7 "And [God] breathed into his nostrils the breath of life; and man became a living soul."*

It is not physically possible to re-wind and connects this genetic flaw in every man woman and child of the world because the bent damaged DNA is far beyond repair, and the only way is to do Noah's flood and wipe the entire earth's living beings off and start over again. God did swear to himself that he will not repeat Noah's event.

Isaiah 54: 6   *For the <u>LORD hath called thee as a woman forsaken</u> and grieved in spirit, and a wife of youth, when thou wast refused, saith thy God.*

Isaiah 54:7   *For a small moment have I forsaken thee; but with great mercies will I gather thee.*

Isaiah 54:8   *In a little wrath I hid my face from thee for a moment; but with everlasting kindness will I have mercy on thee, saith the LORD thy Redeemer.*

Isaiah 54:9   *For this is as the waters of Noah unto me: for as I have sworn that the waters of Noah should no more go over the earth; so have I sworn that I would not be wroth with thee, nor rebuke thee.*

Isaiah 54:10   *For the mountains shall depart, and the hills be removed; but my kindness shall not depart from thee, neither shall the covenant of my peace be removed, saith the LORD that hath mercy on thee.*

Genesis 9:4   *Your blood is the source of all of life for your flesh "But flesh with the life thereof, which is the blood thereof, shall ye (Children of Israel) not eat."*

The dependency of true salvation, we must rely on the perfect divine sinless blood of Jesus to give us the salvation and redeems us from the sinful nature and contaminated blood within our body and allow our mind to become renewed – a new man mentally and spiritually which will influence the body to carve itself and reform its spiritual DNA as a possibility.

The very nature of the flesh was wretched and miserable. The blood was contaminated and until we identify and associate ourselves to the "law of the Spirit of life in Christ Jesus." (Romans 8:2). The sin offering of the Son of God was uncontaminated, sinless, and perfect blood applied to man's sinful condition

"For the law of the Spirit of life in Christ Jesus hath made me free from the law of sin and death. That the righteousness of the law might be fulfilled in us, who

walk not after the flesh but after the Spirit. For to be carnally minded is death, but to be spiritually minded is life and peace. But ye are not in the flesh, but in the Spirit, if so be that the Spirit of God dwells in you. Now if any man have not the Spirit of Christ, he is none of his. But if the Spirit of him that raised up Jesus from the dead dwell in you, he that raised up Christ from the dead shall also quicken your mortal bodies by his Spirit that dwelleth in you." (Romans 8:2, 4, 6, 9, 11).

Now about the Blood, let us visit the salvation –

John 4: 3	*He left Judaea and departed again into Galilee.*
John 4: 4.	*And he must need to go through Samaria.*
John 4: 5.	*Then cometh he to a city of Samaria, which is called Sychar, near to the parcel of cob gave to his son Joseph.*
John 4: 6.	*Now Jacob's well was there. Jesus therefore, being wearied with his journey, sat thus on the well: and it was about the sixth hour.*
John 4: 7.	*There cometh a woman of Samaria to draw water: Jesus saith unto her, Give me to drink.*
John 4: 8.	*(For his disciples were gone away unto the city to buy meat.)*
John 4: 9.	*Then saith the woman of Samaria unto him, **How is it that thou, being a Jew, askest drink of me, which am a woman of Samaria? For the Jews have no dealings with the Samaritans**.*
John 4: 10.	*Jesus answered and said unto her, If thou knewest the gift of God, and who it is that saith to thee, Give me to drink; thou wouldest have asked of him, and he would have given thee living water.*
John 4: 11.	*The woman saith unto him, Sir, thou hast nothing to draw with, and the well is deep: from whence then hast thou that living water?*
John 4: 12.	***Art thou greater than our father Jacob, which gave us the well, and drank thereof himself, and his children, and his cattle**?*
John 4: 13.	*Jesus answered and said unto her, Whosoever drinketh of this water shall thirst again:*
John 4: 14.	*But whosoever drinketh of the water that I shall give him shall never thirst, but the water that I shall give him shall be **in him a well of water springing up into everlasting life**.*
John 4: 15.	*The woman saith unto him, Sir, give me this water, that I thirst not, neither come hither to draw.*
John 4: 16.	*Jesus saith unto her, Go, call thy husband, and come hither.*
John 4: 17.	*Thewoman answered and said, I have no husband. Jesus said unto her, Thouhast well said, I have no husband:*
John 4: 18	*For thou hast had five husbands; and he whom thou now hast is not thy husband: in that saidst thou truly.*
John 4: 19	*The woman saith unto him, Sir, I perceive that thou art a prophet.*
John 4: 20	*Our fathers worshipped in this mountain; and ye say, that in Jerusalem is the place where men ought to worship.*

John 4: 21	Jesus saith unto her, Woman, believe me, the hour cometh when ye shall neither in this mountain nor yet at Jerusalem, worship the Father.
John 4: 22	Ye worship ye know not what: we know what we worship: for salvation is of the Jews.
John 4: 23	But the hour cometh, and now is when the true worshippers shall worship the Father in spirit and in truth: for the Father seeketh such to worship him.
John 4: 24	God is a Spirit: and they that worship him must worship him in spirit and in truth.
John 4: 25	The woman saith unto him, I know that Messias cometh, which is called Christ: when he is come, he will tell us all things.
John 4: 26	Jesus saith unto her, **_I that speak unto thee am he._**
	Here Jesus witnessed to a Samaritan woman and gave her the secrets of salvation as well as identified himself to her that "yes I am greater than your forefathers and I am the GOD that they (forefathers) talked about "I am HE"John 4: 27 And upon this came his disciples, and marveled that he talked with the woman: yet no man said, What seekest thou? or, Why talkest thou with her?
John 4: 2	The woman then left her waterpot, and went her way into the city, and saith to the men,
John 4: 29	Come, see a man, which told me all things that ever I did: **_is not this the Christ_**?
John 4: 30	Then they went out of the city, and came unto him.

For salvation is of the Jews. —This Verse troubled critics who seek to construct the Gospel out of their judgments of what it should be and for its meaning and representation. It is part of the original text, and we must accept the Gospel as belonging to the Hebrews, and this touch of Jewish theology is in entire harmony with it. Therefore we must be thankful that the Messiah is from a Hebrew lineage. All that rejects will not be saved. The contrast between the Samaritan and the Jewish worship lay in its history, its state at that time, and its rejection of the fuller teaching of the prophetical books of the Old Testament. "In every way, the Jews had many advantages, but chiefly that unto them were committed the oracles of God." Little as they knew the treasure they possessed, and are the guardians of spiritual truth for the world, and in a sense deeper than they could fathom, "salvation is of the Jews." Jesus also opens the doors to the Gentiles as well, as he had delivered salvation to the Samaritan woman (not even named), therefore salvation is no longer kept under cover and hidden but is made available to everyone, Jew, Gentiles, Greeks, Romans, Samarians, Chinese, Indians, and all the rest of the world, which may have created a feeling of losing dominion and losing possession of the heavenly treasures, which at one time was solely for one nation and one people to be the doorway towards salvation and connection to God. The door is open wide, and the curtains were torn in half, and all the Gentile world can go directly to God through the spirit and be saved.

They willingly believed and knew he was "The Christ" "Anointed son of God" "The Messiah" for they ALL came to meet him.

*Jesus demonstrating that God's Masterplan is for everyone, his first start was with the Samarians of the Town of which is called Sychar and proved His way of life and His **will** as to how we humans should live.*

John 4:22   *"Ye worship ye know not what: we know what we worship: for salvation is of the Jews."*

So what do we know about the salvation of the Jews, what are their customs and practice, what are their doctrine that they maintained, respected and put into laws. It does not matter for Jesus came and made amends, correction, abolished many and deliver a new clarification of the methods and his most important message was "Love, love, love everyone as yourself" follow me, my path, my example, my way, my life and look at my life as the pattern to govern yours.

GOD has ordained many with the great commission of reaching out to unsaved people and deliver the message "the Gospels "according to him, the Great Commission is to reach all people. Jesus stated that he is come to seek and save those that are lost, which means that whom-so-ever he delivered the gospel to or those who have received the message are in the category of the knowledgeable and will have to spend the time and effort to enhance their knowledge and follow the teachings, live their lives as an example that Jesus has set forth and been the light of the world.

"I have come to save that which is Lost

"Light of the world."

"Salt of the world."

Most church-going Christians are in the school of learning and are endorsed in Bible studies to gain the entire knowledge of the Gospel to follow the path of Jesus and deliver the message "To the entire world without prejudice."

Matthew 28:19   *Go ye therefore, and teach all nations, baptizing them in the name of the Father, and of the Son, and of the Holy Ghost: 20: Teaching them to observe all things whatsoever I have commanded you: and, lo, I am with you alway, even unto the end of the world. Amen*

Mark 16:15   *And he said unto them, go ye into all the world, and preach the gospel to every creature. 16 He that believeth and baptized shall be* *saved, but he that believeth not shall be damned*

Jesus set the example in his teaching from the age of 12, when he stayed back in the synagogue and engaged in teaching the Doctors of the law and the Spiritual Leaders, making a great reference to the Scripture from the Book and giving definitive lessons that they were amazed at his knowledge , but at the same time wanted to NOT acknowledge his ability and skill and refer to his parents – as they were of no recognition and referred to his earthly lineage of Joseph and Mary of **Nazareth.**

We must understand that Jesus was full of the spirit and wisdom and as he grew, he became more and more knowledgeable and wise through the Spirit of God

He further spends the rest of his days teaching and displaying great feats and examples of what he was teaching, which includes much healing in every area, all kind of sicknesses, mental, spiritual, moral, physical and demonic. He displayed that all could be healed and has commission his disciples with great authority and power to follow his example and COMMANDED them to do so in his name. For the problematic circumstances, he educated them that it not only takes knowledge of the scripture but spiritual ability through Prayer and Fasting.

He Stressed that Prayer, Fasting, Meditation and honoring the word of GOD is more important in survival and deliverance, including performing all the miracles that he has accomplished, a cross-section of healing that displays all areas of sickness within a human being, showing that all kind of diseases be cured through Faith and Belief and Change of heart towards becoming a new man in the Gospels. The endowment of power involves worthy sacrifice, dedication, and devotion to learning and practicing as well as living a good Christian life.

Jesus on many occasions drifted off into the wee hours of the night to Pray and meditates, especially in the Nautical hour, which is stated as the most auspicious time when the heavens are open.

The free will given to man at creation is a factor that every man must utilize with humility, submission, and obedience to the commandments of the LAWS of GOD to become holy to walk in the sacred shadows of God's Spirit.

Philippians 4:6 *be careful for nothing, but in everything by prayer and supplication with thanksgiving let your request be made unto God. 7. And the peace of God, which passed all understanding, shall keep your hearts and minds through Christ Jesus. Scripture is the foundation to prayer; it is already spelt out in the Bible and can be interpreted in multiple ways and applied in many circumstances and life situations.*

Ephesians 6:18 *"Praying always with all prayer and supplication in the spirit and* *watching thereunto with all perseverance and supplication for all saints."*

Psalms 119:15   *I will meditate on your precepts and fix my eyes on your ways*

A cleansing of the mind, a change of the mind and a clean heart are compulsory for a Christian as is given by the law and commandments, for Jesus spoke of the greatest commandment is "love, Love, love thy neighbor as thyself."

The entire **Psalms 119** deals with prayer, meditation, focus on change as well as reference what GOD has done and examples set for us to follow.

Jesus demands us to pick up our cross and follow him, to change our focus and avoid all the distractions of this world, such as the reason Peter and his friends had to leave their fishing trade and materials left behind and follow. The example of moving anything that will distract you from the real spiritual focus on God and the mission at hand.

People form their very own rules and regulations to make it fits into their very own curriculum by creating their laws and regulations to design their religious ways and bring with them the "convenience" to worship and be a Christian the way they feel. It leads to heresy, and the occult for it is written

The children of God if not kept in guidance steadily have adopted many Pagan worship and customs, practicing them bit by bit until it became embedded into religious practices, or rather re-embedded into their spiritual practice. Many Celebrations and feasts and holidays are part of the cultural tradition integrated into today's modern religious practices inherited from pagan religions.

Jesus warned the religious leaders that the day would come when all will reject the commandments and the Religious LAWS so that they can keep up with tradition **(Mark 7:9)**

Jesus fellowship includes socializing in dinner, supper and breaking of bread where they all together and in one accord in prayer. The three years ministry of Jesus was compressed into teaching his disciples the entire gospel and whilst doing so performed abundant healing as part of his teachings and demonstration 'Here I am a Man just like you and have given you the same authority and power, deliver the knowledge of this great truth and how to perform these miraculous healings... give unto you. Not to keep and rejoice over this new-found knowledge to do duties as servants of GOD to be Servants of MEN all for the ultimate goal of saving the lost and bringing salvation to the entire earth'.

John 4: 22   *He further defined that Salvation will come through the Jews and are of the Jews. "The Oracles of God was given to the Jews" Roman 3: 1-2*

Romans 2: 28-29 - *Not outward but inward and in the spirit*

Gal 6: 15-16 *"All Christians are spiritual Jews" and are bound by the spiritual laws and to keep the spiritual laws. The true people of God are not physic but spiritual. Therefore the word "Jew" and the "Land of Israel" are both spiritual words referring to spiritual people and a spiritual place.*

Ephesians 1: 9-1
Ephesians 1: 9 Having made known unto us the mystery of his will, according to his good pleasure which he hath purposed in himself:
Ephesians 1:10 That in the dispensation of the fullness of times he might gather together in one all things in Christ, both which are in heaven, and which are on earth; even in him:
Ephesians 1: 11 In whom also we have obtained an inheritance, being predestinated according to the purpose of him who worketh all things after the counsel of his own will:

28 NAUTICAL HOUR

The prayer time Jesus uses is early in the morning when everyone was asleep and according to.

Hebrews 6:12 *That ye be not slothful, but followers of them who through faith and patience inherit the promises.*

Philippians 3:14 *"Hope "keeps the Christian from or becoming bored. Like an athlete, train hard and run well, remembering the reward lies ahead*

Matthew 20:1 *For the kingdom of heaven is like unto a man that is an householder, which went out early in the morning to hire laborers into his vineyard.*

2. *And when he had agreed with the laborers for a penny a day, he sent them into his vineyard.*

3 *And he went out about the third hour, and saw others standing idle in the marketplace,*

4 *And said unto them; Go ye also into the vineyard, and whatsoever is right I will give you. And they went their way.*

5 *Again he went out about the sixth and ninth hour and did likewise.*

6 *And about the eleventh hour he went out, and found others standing idle, and saith unto them, why stand ye here all the day idle?*

7 *They say unto him because no man hath hired us. He saith unto them, go ye also into the vineyard; and whatsoever is right, that shall ye receive.*

8 *So when even was come, the lord of the vineyard saith unto his steward, Call the laborers, and give them their hire, beginning from the last unto the first.*

9 *And when they came that were hired about the eleventh hour, they received every man a penny.*

10 *But when the first came, they supposed that they should have received more; and they likewise received every man a penny.*

11 *And when they had received it, they murmured against the Goodman of the house,*

12 *Saying, these last have wrought but one hour and thou hast made them equal unto us, which have borne the burden and heat of the day.*

13 *But he answered one of them, and said, Friend, I do thee no wrong: didst, not thou agree with me for a penny?*

14 *Take that thine is, and go thy way: I will give unto this last, even as unto thee.*

15 *Is it not lawful for me to do what I will with mine own? Is thine eye evil, because I am good?*

16 *So the last shall be first, and the first last: for many be called, but few chosen.*

Jesus further clarified the membership rules of the Kingdom of heaven – entrances are by God's grace alone. In a parable, God is the householder, and believers are laborers.

Proverbs 6: 9-11 *How long wilt thou sleep, O sluggard? When wilt thou arise out of thy sleep?*

10 *Yet a little sleep, a little slumber, a little folding of the hands to sleep:*

11 *So shall thy poverty come as one that travelleth, and thy want as an armed man?*

19:15, *Slothfulness casteth into a deep sleep; and an idle soul shall suffer hunger.*

20: 13 *Love not sleep, lest thou come to poverty; open thine eyes, and thou shalt be satisfied with bread.*

1Timothy 4: 1-2 . **Now the spirit speaks expressively, that in the latter times some shall depart from the faith, giving heed to seducing spirits, and doctrines of the devils; speaking lies in hypocrisy; their conscience seared with a hot iron.**

II Timothy 3: 1-7 *This know also, that in the last days perilous times shall come.*

2 *For men shall be lovers of their own selves, covetous, boasters, proud, blasphemers, disobedient to parents, unthankful, unholy,*

3 *Without natural affection, trucebreakers, false accusers, incontinent, fierce, despisers of those that are good,*

4 *Traitors, heady, high-minded, lovers of pleasures more than lovers of God;*

5 *Having a form of godliness, but denying the power thereof: from such turn away.*

6 *For of this sort are they which creep into houses, and lead captive silly women laden with sins, led away with divers' lusts,*

7 *Ever learning, and never able to come to the knowledge of the truth.*

The Hebrews rejected Jesus because he broke all their laws and his doctrine did not fit their commandments. The Ishmaelite (true blood brothers of the Jews), considered him a Prophet and accepted his words, acknowledge the "people of the Book", but maintained an animosity because of Esau, and Ishmael and the rejection from Abraham and the doubt of who is really God's choice and The Jews were ordained to go out into the world and teach everyone "the Gospels Of Jesus Christ" but made a choice not to do so, for it violates their doctrine in multiple contents, and kept their Secrets to themselves (now opened up to studies) . So back to Buddhism -- where most of what Jesus said and taught was taught thousand years ago by Gautama Siddhartha.
 The problems with this World in one context about two blood brothers who cannot live like family and spreads that hatred across the world, because of their own selfish reasons, used whatever method to beat their doctrine into the heads of people who have no knowledge of these doctrines and history so that they can amass a crowd of believer, their actions tells their story, as such their Karma and dharma is genuinely not in sync with God.
We must understand that God curses the earth because of "ONE MAN's Disobedience" what will God do for the many Nations and many people disobedience, this ..... our present issues and problems we face in this world today and is becoming the world's biggest problem and becoming larger than life itself. To think that it all began with One Man (Abraham), two women (Sarah and Hagar), two children (Ishmael and Isaac) hatred, animosity, jealousy, claim to fame, the claim of a promise from God, and their generations are paying the price of their differences and indifference.

The Baha'i faith tried to morph the two into a love triangle, the Hindu religion indulgence in a game of thrones, Christianity is the doorway to even the playing field and merge the human connectivity to the brothers and their lineage, if Christianity really decipher the scriptures and apply the commandments of God upon it followers and follow the great commission wholeheartedly. This means there must be no biases, no hatred, no digging up the old anthill and dig up the peace pipes and let these people of tarnished mentality and blind eyes open up and see the vision as it is meant to be, for in the bible God did Change his mind many times God does not Change, But he does change his mind:

*Jeremiah 26:3 3 If so, be they will hearken, and turn every man from his evil way, that I may **repent me of the evil**, which I purpose to do unto them because of the evil of their doings.*

*Genesis 6: 6-7 6 And it **repented the Lord** that he had made man on the earth, and it grieved him at his heart.*
7   And the Lord said, I will destroy man whom I have created from the

face of the earth; both man, and beast, and the creeping thing, and the fowls of the air; for it repenteth me that I have made them. ("The LORD was grieved that He had made man on the earth, and His heart was filled with pain.")

Isaiah 38:1   *In those days was Hezekiah sick unto death. And Isaiah the prophet the son of Amoz came unto him, and said unto him, thus saith the Lord, set thine house in order: for thou shalt die, and not live.*

2   *Then Hezekiah turned his face toward the wall and prayed unto the Lord,*

3   *And said, Remember now, O Lord, I beseech thee, how I have walked before thee in truth and with a perfect heart, and have done that which is good in thy sight. And Hezekiah wept sore.*

4   **Then came the word of the Lord to Isaiah, saying,**

5   **Go, and say to Hezekiah,** *Thus saith the Lord, the God of David thy father, I have heard thy prayer, I have seen thy tears: behold, I will add unto thy days fifteen years.*

Additionally, Abraham, Moses, Jonah, David they all negotiated with God and came to a compromise, where God changed his mind conditionally

Based on Doctrines of Old we don't need a spaceship to travel physically across. Our bodies are physically required to survive on Earth and cannot survive on other planets in the present form. Vedic literature talks about the Soul and Spirit within the body that it Trans-mutate electronically and reassembles into beings as it travels in Spirit and Soul through wormholes and Black holes.

Biblical GOD had to use the elements of the earth to create a body that can be sustained on the earth's atmosphere that hosts the Spirit and Soul of a being (Breath of life through his nostrils and man became a living being- This is where GOD injected the spirit and soul into Man's Earth body)

It is a Weird chatter of words, but it is a bit more complicated than this little definition. SO It all goes back to the Karmic cycle of the Human soul. We are definitely a hybrid clone of some being.

29 ROAD TO SALVATION

Proclaim the Truth:

> *John 8:32 – And ye shall know the truth, and the truth shall make you free.*

Jesus himself is the truth that makes us free. He is the source of the fact, the perfect standard of what is right. He frees us from the consequences of sin, from self-deception, and from deception by Satan. He shows clearly the way to eternal life with God. Thus Jesus does not give us the right to do whatever we want, but freedom to follow God. As we seek the face of God and to serve him, Jesus perfect truth frees us to be all that God meant us to be

Jesus explained that with his coming, the kingdom of God inaugurated. When he ascended into heaven, God's Kingdom would remain in the hearts of all believers through the presence of the Holy Spirit. But the Kingdom of God will not be fully

Work to spread God's Kingdom across the world realize until Jesus Christ comes again to judge all people and remove all evil from the world. Until that time believers are to

Act 1:3	*To whom also he shewed himself alive after his passion by many infallible proofs, being seen of them forty days, and speaking of the things pertaining to the kingdom of God:*
Acts 2:1-4	*And when the day of Pentecost was fully come, they were all with one accord in one place.*
2.	*And suddenly there came a sound from heaven as of a rushing mighty wind, and it filled all the house where they were sitting.*
3.	*And there appeared unto them cloven tongues like as of fire, and it sat upon each of them.*
4.	*And they were all filled with the Holy Ghost and began to speak with other tongues, as the Spirit gave them utterance.*

Pentecost was held 50 days after Passover. Pentecost was also known as the *feast of weeks,* and the Feast of Harvest. It was one of the three major annual feasts, a festival of thanksgiving for the harvested crops. Jesus crucified at Passover time, and he ascended 40 days after his resurrection. The Holy Spirit came 50 days after his resurrection, ten days after his ascension. Jews of many nations gathered in Jerusalem for this Festival. It results in a worldwide harvest of new believers – thus these first converts called Christians (followers of Christ).

The fulfillment of John the Baptist's words about the Holy Spirit's baptizing with fire and of the Prophet Joel's words about the outpouring of the Holy Spirit. Why tongues of fire? Tongues symbolize speech and the communication of the Gospel. "Cloven Tongues" means the fire separated and rested on each of them. Fire signifies God's purifying presence, which burns away the undesirable elements of our lives and sets our hearts aflame to ignite the lives of others. On Mount Sinai, fire came down on one place; at Pentecost, fire came down on many believers, symbolizing that God's presence is now available to all who believes. God confirmed the validity After Peter's powerful, Spirit-filled message, the people were deeply moved and asked. "What shall we do?" The basic question we must ask, it is not enough to be sorry for our sins – we must let God forgive them, and then we must live like forgiven people. If you want to follow Christ, you must "repent, and be baptized." To repent means to turn away from sin, changing the direction of your life from selfishness and rebellion against God's Laws. At the same time, you must turn to Christ, depending on him for forgiveness, mercy, guidance, and purpose. We cannot save ourselves – only God can keep us. Baptism shows the identification with Christ and with the community of believers. It is a condition of discipleship and a sign of faith.

Act 2: 36-39

36   *Therefore let all the house of Israel know assuredly, that God hath made the same Jesus, whom ye   have crucified, both Lord and Christ.*

37   *Now when they heard this, they were pricked in their heart, and said unto Peter and to the rest of the apostles, Men, and brethren, what shall we do?*

38   *Now when they heard this, they were pricked in their heart, and said unto Peter and to the rest of the apostles, Men, and brethren,*

what shall we do?

39   *For the promise is unto you, and to your children, and to all that are afar off, even as many as the LORD our God shall call.*

Acts 10: 44-48

44   *While Peter yet spake these words, the Holy Ghost fell on all them which heard the word.*

45   *And they of the circumcision which believed were astonished, as many as came with Peter, because that on the Gentiles also was poured out the gift of the Holy Ghost.*

46   *For they heard them speak with tongues, and magnify God. Then answered Peter,*

47   *Can any man forbid water, that these should not be baptized, which have received the Holy Ghost as well as we?*

48   *And he commanded them to be baptized in the name of the Lord. Then prayed they him to tarry certain days.*

Cornelius was wealthy, a Gentile, and a military man. Peter was a Jewish fisherman turner preacher, both very different in many ways and characteristic, status, thinking and belief system, but God's plan included both of them. In Cornelius's house that day, a new chapter in Christian history was written as a Jewish Christian Leader and a gentile Christian convert each discovered something significant about each other. Cornelius needed Peter to hear the Gospel and know that Gentiles included in God's plan.

Acts 19: 1-6

1 *And it came to pass, that, while Apollos was at Corinth, Paul having passed through the upper coasts came to Ephesus: and finding certain disciples,*

2 *He said unto them, have ye received the Holy Ghost since ye believed? And they said unto him; We have not so much as heard whether there be any Holy Ghost.*

3 *And he said unto them, Unto what then were ye baptized? And they said, Unto John's baptism.*

4 *Then said Paul, John verily baptized with the baptism of repentance, saying unto the people, that they should believe on him which should come after him, that is, on Christ Jesus*

5 *When they heard this, they were baptized in the name of the Lord Jesus.*

*6 And when Paul had laid his hands upon them, the Holy Ghost came on
them; and they spake with tongues, and prophesied.*

Ephesus was the capital and leading business center of the Roman province of
Asia (present-day Turkey). A hub of sea and land transportation, it ranked with
Antioch of Syria and Alexandria in Egypt as one great city of the Mediterranean
Sea. Paul stayed in Ephesus for over two years. This is where he spent time
writing these epistles.

John's baptism was a sign of repentance from sin only, not a sign of a new life in
Christ. Ephesians believers needed further instruction on the message and
ministry of Jesus Christ. They believed in Jesus as the Messiah but did not
understand the significance of his death and resurrection or the work of the
Holy Spirit. Therefore becoming a Christian involves turning away from sin
(repentance) and turning to Christ (faith). These "Believers" were incomplete.
God was confirming to these believers, who did not initially know about the
Holy Spirit, that they were a part of the church. The Holy Spirit's filling endorsed
them as believers

When Paul laid hands on these disciples, they received the Holy Spirit, just as
the disciples did at Pentecost, and there were outward, visible signs of the Holy
Spirit's presence. The Holy Spirit came upon the Gentiles and non-Jews.

*Acts 22: 16   And now why tarriest thou? Arise, and be baptized, and
wash away thy sins, calling on the name of the Lord.*

To be born again one must

(1)Repent
(2) Be baptized in the Name of Jesus Christ
(3) Receive the Holy Ghost with the initial evidence of speaking in tongues
(4) Live life as commanded by Christ
(5) Live life full of the Holy Spirit

30 BAPTISM

Baptism is an important and essential act in the Christian life; it is the acceptance of Christianity and Jesus Christ as the son of God and the savior of Humanity. It is a ritual that legalizes the contract or covenant with God and an agreement to live the life of a disciple before God and to change ways from old to a new way of life. The remission of sin and a drowning of the old man (or person) as you are immersed under water, a washing away of all old ways, forgiven and forgotten sins as the covenant with God as another chance to serve God and as a new person you rise above out of the water is a renewing of the person into a new man. An Affirmation in our desire to follow Jesus, his teachings and be a compliment and replica of Jesus and the life he had commanded.

> Romans 6: 3-4 "Or do you not know that as many of us as were baptized into Christ Jesus were baptized into His death? Therefore we were buried with Him through baptism into death, that just as Christ was raised from the dead by the glory of the Father, even so, we also should walk in newness of life."

In the Days of Noah, the waters of the flood put an end to this evil in the Old Testament; baptism represents an end to living a self-centered life of doing my own will and beginning a new life of doing the will of God in the New Testament.

John's baptism, signifying repentance, is not the same as Christian baptism, as seen in Acts 18:24–26 and 19:1–7. Christian baptism has a more profound significance.

Apollos heard only with John the Baptist said about Jesus (Luke 3:1 to 18), so his message was not the complete story. John focused on repentance from sin, the first step. But the whole message is to repent from sin then believe in Christ. Apollo's did not know about Jesus's life, crucifixion and resurrection, nor did he know about the coming of the Holy Spirit.

John's baptism was a sign of repentance from sin only, not a significant new life right. Like upon us these Ephesians believers needed to further instruction on the message and ministry of Jesus Christ stop they believed in Jesus as the Messiah, but they did not understand the significance of his death and resurrection or the work of the Holy Spirit. Becoming a published involves turning from sin which is repentance and turning to Christ in the. These believers were incomplete. The book of acts is about believers receive the Holy Spirit in a variety of ways. Usually, the Holy Spirit filled a person as soon as he or she professed faith. Pentecost was to a formal outpouring of the Holy Spirit to the church. The other outpourings are the book of acts where God's way of in 19 new believers to the church. The Mark of the true church is not merely right Doctrine, but great action, to the evidence the Holy Spirit's work. When Paul laid hands on these disciples, they received the Holy Spirit, just as the disciples did in the cost, and their work outboard, visible signs of the Holy Spirit's presence, as the Holy Spirit came upon Gentiles

> *First Corinthians 12:13 says, "We were all baptized by one Spirit so as to form one body—whether Jews or Gentiles, slave or free—and we were all given the one Spirit to drink." Baptism by water is a "reenactment" of the baptism by the Spirit. "I confess faith in Christ; Jesus has cleansed my soul from sin, and I now have a new life of Sanctification."*

The church is composed of many types of people from a variety of backgrounds with a multitude of gifts and. It is easy for these differences to divide people, as was the case in Corinth. Despite the differences, old believers have one thing in common – St. in price. On this essential through the church finds unity. One Holy Spirit baptizes all believers into one body of believers, which is the church. We don't lose our identities, but we have an overriding oneness in Christ. When a person becomes a Christian, the Holy Spirit takes up residence, and he or she is born into God's family.

Luke 3:16 "John answered, saying unto them all, I indeed baptize you with water; but one mightier than I cometh, the latchet of whose shoes I am not worthy to unloose: he shall baptize you with the Holy Ghost and with fire:"

John baptism with water symbolizes the washing away of sins. It coordinated with his message of repentance and reformation. Jesus is a baptism with fire equips one with the power to do God's will and began on the day of Pentecost when the Holy Spirit came upon the believers in the form of tongues of fire and empowering them to proclaim Jesus resurrection in many languages. The baptism with fire or so symbolizes the work of the Holy Spirit in bringing God's judgment on those who refuse to repent.

Matthew 3:13-17 "Then cometh Jesus from Galilee to Jordan unto John, to be baptized of him. But John forbad him, saying, I have need to be baptized of thee, and comest thou to me? And Jesus answering said unto him, Suffer it to be so now: for thus it becometh us to fulfill all righteousness. Then he suffered him. And Jesus, when he was baptized, went up straightway out of the water: and, lo, the heavens were opened unto him, and he saw the Spirit of God descending like a dove, and lighting upon him: And lo a voice from heaven, saying, This is my beloved Son, in whom I am well pleased."

Mark 1:9-11 *"And it came to pass in those days, that Jesus came from Nazareth of Galilee, and was baptized of John in Jordan. And straightway coming up out of the water, he saw the heavens opened, and the Spirit like a dove descending upon him: And there came a voice from heaven, saying, thou art my beloved Son, in whom I am well pleased."*

If John's baptism was for repentance from sin, why was Jesus baptized? While even the most significant prophets (Isaiah, Jeremiah, and Ezekiel) had to confess their sinfulness and need for repentance, Jesus didn't need to admit sin – he was sinless. Jesus didn't need forgiveness, and was baptized for the following reasons (1) to begin his mission to bring the message of salvation to all people (2) to show support for John's ministry, (3) identify with our humanity and sin, (4) to give us an example to follow John's baptism was different from Christian baptism in the church because Paul and John's followers baptized again. Jesus grew up in Nazareth, where he had lived since he was a young boy. Nazareth was a small town in Galilee, located about halfway between the Sea of Galilee and the Mediterranean Sea. The city was despised and avoided by many Jews because it was a host for Roman troops in the region. Devout Jews hated the Romans for making them pay taxes and for showing no respect to God.

The spirit descended Dove light upon Jesus, and a voice from heaven proclaimed the father's approval of Jesus as his divine son. The fact that Jesus is God's divine son is the foundation for all we read about Jesus the gospel. Here we see all three members of the trinity – God the father, God the son, God the Spirit in a physical man

John 1:29-33 *"The next day John seeth Jesus coming unto him, and saith, Behold the Lamb of God, which taketh away the sin of the world. This is he of whom I said After me cometh a man which is preferred before me: for he was before me. And I knew him not: but that he should be made manifest to Israel, therefore am I come baptizing with water. And John bare record, saying, I saw the Spirit descending from heaven like a dove, and it abode upon him. And I knew him not: but he that sent me to baptize with water, the same said unto me, Upon whom thou shalt see the Spirit descending, and remaining on him, the same is he which baptizeth with the Holy Ghost."*

Luke 3:21, 22 *"Now when all the people were baptized, it came to pass, that Jesus also being baptized, and praying, the heaven was opened, And the Holy Ghost descended in a bodily shape like a dove upon him, and a voice came from heaven, which said, Thou art my beloved Son; in thee I am well pleased."*

Every morning the Lamb was sacrificed in the temple for sins of the people. Isaiah prophesied that the Messiah, God's servant, would be led to slaughter like a lamb. To pay the penalty for sin, in life had to be given – God chose to provide the sacrifice self. The sins of the world removed when Jesus died as a perfect second. This way our sins are you the sin of the world mean everyone's sin, the sin of each. Jesus paid the price for your sin by his death. You can receive forgiveness by confessing your sins to him and asking for his forgiveness. Although John the Baptist was a well-known preacher and attracted large crowds, he was content Jesus take the higher place. True humility, the basis for greatness reaching, teaching or other works we do for Christ. When you are content to do with the once you do that Jesus Christ is honored for it, God will do great things to you. John the Baptist's baptism by water was preparatory, because it was for repentance and symbolizes the washing away of sins Jesus by contrast, would baptize with the Holy Spirit. He would send the Holy Spirit upon all believers and empowering them to live and teach the message of salvation and began after Jesus had risen from the dead and ascended into heaven.

Acts 2:38 - Then Peter said unto them, Repent, and be baptized every one of you in the name of Jesus Christ for the remission of sins, and ye shall receive the gift of the Holy Ghost, And Peter said to them if you want to follow Christ's, you must repent and be baptized. To repent means to turn from sin, changing the direction of your life from selfishness and rebellion against God's laws to obeying the commandments and God's laws. At the same time, you must turn to Christ, depending on him for forgiveness, mercy, guidance, and the purpose. We cannot save ourselves – only God can save us stop baptism shows identification with Christ and with the community of believers. It is a condition of discipleship and a sign of the Holy Spirit

John 3:5 *Jesus answered, Verily, verily, I say unto thee, except a man be born of water and [of] the Spirit, he cannot enter into the kingdom of God.*

Acts 22:16 *And now why tarriest thou? Arise, and be baptized, and wash away thy sins, calling on the name of the Lord.*

Mark 16:16 *He that believeth and is baptized shall be saved; but he that believeth not shall be damned.*

1 Peter 3:21 *The like figure whereunto [even] baptism doth also now save us (not the putting away of the filth of the flesh, but the answer of a good conscience toward God,) by the resurrection of Jesus Christ:*

Romans 6:4 *Therefore we are buried with him by baptism into death: that like as Christ was raised up from the dead by the glory of the Father, even so, we also should walk in newness of life.*

Matthew 28:19 *Go ye therefore, and teach all nations, baptizing them in the name of the Father, and of the Son, and of the Holy Ghost:*

Colossians 2:12-13 *Buried with him in baptism, wherein also ye are risen with [him] through the faith of the operation of God, who hath raised him from the dead.*

Ephesians 4:5 *One Lord, one faith, one baptism,*

Acts 2:41 *Then they that gladly received his word were baptized: and the same day there were added [unto them] about three thousand souls.*

Romans 6:3-4 *Know ye not, that so many of us as were baptized into Jesus Christ were baptized into his death?*

Galatians 3:27 *For as many of you as have been baptized into Christ have put on Christ.*

Matthew 3:16 *And Jesus, when he was baptized, went up straightway out of the water: and, lo, the heavens were opened unto him, and he saw the Spirit of God descending like a dove, and lighting upon him:*

Matthew 3:11 *I indeed baptize you with water unto repentance: but he that cometh after me is mightier than I, whose shoes I am not worthy to bear: he shall baptize you with the Holy Ghost, and [with] fire:*

Acts 8:38 *And he commanded the chariot to stand still: and they went down both into the water, both Philip and the eunuch; and he baptized him.*

Colossians 2:12 *Buried with him in baptism, wherein also ye are risen with [him] through the faith of the operation of God, who hath raised him from the dead.*

Romans 6:3 *Know ye not, that so many of us as were baptized into Jesus Christ were baptized into his death?*

31 EFFECTIVE BONDAGE BREAKING PRAYER

Jesus gave the perfect example of how to pray and address GOD with our needs. These are the essentials in life that will keep us guided and in a straight way in being focused on God, His glory and what he has in store for us.

Jesus teaches his disciples here that God is our **father** in Heaven and we should make sure we address him as our father with respect, calling on him

Hallowed means Holy, we are acknowledging the holiness and purity of GOD and acknowledging this holiness as we strive to achieve the same through his guidance. The **kingdom of God** is perfect, pure and holy AND WE CALL UPON God to replicate the same here on Earth.

The **daily bread** of man is to find satisfaction and fulfillment spiritually, mentally, physically and morally. We seek GOD guidance and provision to fulfill our basic needs which meets his accomplishment for man.

Trespasses include debts, sins, shame, Guilt, etc., So GOD, please forgive us for all our trespasses and forgive all those who do the same to us, for if you do not forgive, you will not receive forgiveness and God will not forgive us.

Keep us far for places, actions, and intents, our mind, body, and spirit in the right frame, the right mindset and let us be in the right place so not to be led or tempted to do anything that is against your will or evil and deliver us from all those situations. The Kingdom of all belongs to GOD, all power and all Glory belongs to GOD, forever

Having learned the purpose of prayer and how to execute effectively, there is a great need to break away all bondages, obstacles, and ANYTHING THAT IS AN OBSTRUCTION IN YOUR NORMAL LIFE that will lead you to a Christ-like lifestyle.

People of all walks of life suffer from the many folds of bondage. Some of these include:

Low Self-esteem

Negative thinking and action

Guilt old and new

Anger especially to close associates

Fear

Doubt and unbelief

Unforgiveness

Occult Involvement

Addictive behavior

Illicit Sexual activity

Aftermath of abuse

Rejection and shame

Generational curses and setbacks

Most of these are designed by Satan to keep you in bondage, and it is perfectly designed that you will not believe that you are under the influence of Satan's spell.

GOD Appearances to Man

God is invisible, a spirit and cannot be seen, but does appear on occasions to man for purposes of convincing man that he does exist and delivering messages to very specific and chosen few. These appearances are called "Theophanies," where God shows himself in human forms or any preferred form of his desire.

- In the beginning, after the creation of Adam and Eve, God steps down into the Garden of Eden and have fellowship with Adam and Eve.

- God appeared to Abraham in the form of three men

Genesis 18:2-32

    2.   *And he lifts his eyes and looked, and, lo, three men stood by him: and when he saw them, he ran to meet them from the tent door, and bowed himself toward the ground,*

3 .   And said, My LORD, if now I have found favor in thy sight, pass not away, I
        pray thee, from thy servant:

4.   Let a little water, I pray you, be fetched, and wash your feet, and rest
        yourselves under the tree:

5.   And I will fetch a morsel of bread, and comfort ye your hearts; after that ye
        shall pass on: for therefore are ye come to your servant. And they said, so do,
        as thou hast said.

6.   And Abraham hastened into the tent unto Sarah, and said, Make ready quickly
        three measures of fine meal, knead it, and make cakes upon the hearth.

7.   And Abraham ran unto the herd, and fetched a calf tender and good, and gave
        it unto a young man, and he hasted to dress it.

8.   And he took butter, and milk, and the calf which he had dressed, and set it
        before them, and he stood by them under the tree, and they did eat.

9.   And they said unto him, Where is Sarah thy wife? And he said, Behold, in the
        tent.

10.   And he said, I will certainly return unto thee according to the time of life; and,
        lo, Sarah thy wife shall have a son. And Sarah heard it in the tent door, which
        was behind him.

11.   Now Abraham and Sarah were old and well stricken in age, and it ceased to
        be with Sarah after the manner of women.

12.   Therefore Sarah laughed within herself, saying, After I am waxed old shall I
        have pleasure, my lord being old also?

13.   And the LORD said unto Abraham; Wherefore did Sarah laugh, saying, Shall I
        of a surety bear a child, which am old?

14.   Is anything too hard for the LORD? At the time appointed I will return unto
        thee, according to the time of life, and Sarah shall have a son.

15.   Then Sarah denied, saying, I laughed not; for she was afraid. And he said, Nay;
        but thou didst laugh.

16.   And the men rose up from thence, and looked toward Sodom: and Abraham
        went with them to bring them on the way.

17.   And the LORD said, Shall I hide from Abraham that thing which I do;

18.   Seeing that Abraham shall surely become a great and mighty nation, and all
        the nations of the earth shall be blessed in him?

19.   For I know him, that he will command his children and his household after
        him, and they shall keep the way of the LORD, to do justice and judgment; that
        the LORD may bring upon Abraham that which he hath spoken of him.

20.   And the LORD said, Because the cry of Sodom and Gomorrah is great, and
        because their sin is very grievous;

21.   I will go down now, and see whether they have done altogether according to
        the cry of it, which is come unto me; and if not, I will know.

22.   And the men turned their faces from thence and went toward Sodom: but
        Abraham stood yet before the LORD

23.   And Abraham drew near, and said, Wilt thou also destroy the righteous with
        the wicked?

24.   Peradventure there be fifty righteous within the city: wilt thou also destroy

and not spare the place for the fifty righteous that are therein?

25. That be far from thee to do after this manner, to slay the righteous with the wicked: and that the righteous should be as the wicked, that be far from thee: Shall not the Judge of all the earth do, right?

26. And the LORD said, If I find in Sodom fifty righteous within the city, then I will spare all the place for their sakes.

27. And Abraham answered and said, behold now, I have taken upon me to speak unto the LORD, which am but dust and ashes:

28. Peradventure there shall lack five of the fifty righteous: wilt thou destroy all the city for lack of five? And he said, If I find there forty and five, I will not destroy it.

29. And he spake unto him yet again, and said, Peradventure there shall be forty found there. And he said I will not do it for forty's sake.

30. And he said unto him, oh let not the LORD be angry, and I will speak: Peradventure there shall thirty be found there. And he said I will not do it if I find thirty there.

31. And he said, behold now, I have taken upon me to speak unto the LORD: Peradventure there shall be twenty found there. And he said I will not destroy it for twenty's sake.

32. And he said, oh let not the LORD be angry, and I will speak yet but this once: Peradventure ten shall be found there. And he said I will not destroy it for ten's sake.

- Three heavenly beings (angels) that assume the bodies of human beings to be seen by Abraham and can communicate in Human Language with him Abraham being a devout man, identified them as strangers and invited them into his tent for food and room

- Abraham personal encounter with God, for God, has respected Abraham as a friend and delivered salvation to him, his family and anyone associated with him.

Exodus 14:13-22

13. And Moses said unto the people, Fear ye not, stand still, and see the salvation of the LORD, which he will show to you today: for the Egyptians whom ye have seen today, ye shall see them again no more forever.

14. The LORD shall fight for you, and ye shall hold your peace.

15. And the LORD said unto Moses, Wherefore criest thou unto me? Speak unto the children of Israel that they go forward:

16. But lift thou up thy rod, and stretch out thine hand over the sea, and divide it: and the children of Israel shall go on dry ground through the midst of the sea.

17. And I behold, I will harden the hearts of the Egyptians, and they shall follow

them: and I will get me honor upon Pharaoh, and upon all his host, upon his chariots, and upon his horsemen.

18. And the Egyptians shall know that I am the LORD, when I have gotten me honor upon Pharaoh, upon his chariots, and upon his horsemen.

19. And the Angel of God, which went before the camp of Israel, removed and went behind them; and the pillar of the cloud went from before their face, and stood behind them:

20. And it came between the camp of the Egyptians and the camp of Israel, and it was a cloud and darkness to them, but it gave light by night to these: so that the one came not near the other all the night.

21. And Moses stretched out his hand over the sea, and the LORD caused the sea to go back by a strong east wind all that night and made the sea dry land, and the waters were divided.

22. And the children of Israel went into the midst of the sea upon the dry ground: and the waters were a wall unto them on their right hand, and on their left.

Exodus 15:25 And he cried unto the LORD; and the LORD showed him a tree, which when he had cast into the waters, the waters were made sweet: there he made for them a statute and an ordinance, and there he proved them,

Exodus 32:7-14

7. And the LORD said unto Moses, Go, get thee down; for thy people, which thou broughtest out of the land of Egypt, have corrupted themselves:

8. They have turned aside quickly out of the way which I commanded them: they have made them a molten calf, and have worshipped it, and have sacrificed thereunto, and said these be thy gods, O Israel, which have brought thee up out of the land of Egypt.

9. And the LORD said unto Moses; I have seen this people, and, behold, it is a stiff-necked people:

10. Now, therefore, let me alone, that my wrath may wax hot against them, and that I may consume them: and I will make of thee a great nation.

11. And Moses besought the LORD his God, and said, LORD, why doth thy wrath wax hot against thy people, which thou hast brought forth out of the land of Egypt with great power, and with a mighty hand?

12. Wherefore should the Egyptians speak, and say, for mischief did he bring them out, to slay them in the mountains, and to consume them from the face of the earth? Turn from thy fierce wrath, and repent of this evil against thy people.

13. Remember Abraham, Isaac, and Israel, thy servants, to whom thou swarest by thine own self, and saidst unto them, I will multiply your seed as the stars of heaven, and all this land that I have spoken of will I give unto your seed, and they shall inherit it forever.

14. And the LORD repented of the evil which he thought to do unto his people.

1 Kings 18: 20-40 So Ahab sent unto all the children of Israel and gathered the *prophets together unto Mount Carmel.*

21.   *And Elijah came unto all the people, and said, how long halt ye between two opinions? If the LORD be God, follow him: but if Baal, then follow him. And the people answered him not a word.*

22.   *Then said Elijah unto the people, I, even I only, remain a prophet of the LORD; but Baal's prophets are four hundred and fifty men.*

23.   *Let them, therefore, give us two bullocks, and let them choose one bullock for themselves, and cut it in pieces, and lay it on wood, and put no fire under and I will dress the other bullock, and lay it on wood, and put no fire under:*

24.   *And call ye on the name of your gods, and I will call on the name of the LORD: and the God that answereth by fire let him be God. And all the people answered and said it is well spoken.*

25.   *And Elijah said unto the prophets of Baal, choose you one bullock for yourselves, and dress it first; for ye are many, and call on the name of your gods, but put no fire under.*

26.   *And they took the bullock which was given them, and they dressed it, and called on the name of Baal from morning even until noon, saying, O Baal, hear us. But there was no voice, nor any that answered. And they leaped upon the altar which was made.*

27.   *And it came to pass at noon, that Elijah mocked them, and said, cry aloud: for he is a god; either he is talking, or he is pursuing, or he is in a journey, or peradventure he sleepeth, and must be awaked.*

28.   *And they cried aloud, and cut themselves after their manner with knives and lancets, till the blood gushed out upon them.*

29.   *And it came to pass when midday was past, and they prophesied until the time of the offering of the evening sacrifice, that there was neither voice, nor any to answer, nor any that regarded.*

30.   *And Elijah said unto all the people, come near unto me. And all the people came near unto him. And he repaired the altar of the LORD that was broken down.*

31.   *And Elijah took twelve stones, according to the number of the tribes of the sons of Jacob, unto whom the word of the LORD came, saying, Israel shall be thy name:*

32.   *And with the stones he built an altar in the name of the LORD: and he made a trench about the altar, as great as would contain two measures of seed.*

33.   *And he put the wood in order, and cut the bullock in pieces, and laid him on the wood, and said, Fill four barrels with water, and pour it on the burnt sacrifice, and on the wood.*

34.   *And he said, Do it the second time. And they did it the second time. And he said, Do it the third time. And they did it the third time.*

35.   *And the water ran round about the altar, and he filled the trench also with water.*

36.   *And it came to pass at the time of the offering of the evening sacrifice, that Elijah the prophet came near, and said, LORD God of Abraham, Isaac, and of Israel, let it be known this day that thou art God in Israel, and that I am thy servant, and that I have done all these things at thy word.*

37.   *Hear me, O LORD, hear me, that this people may know that thou art the LORD*

God, and that thou hast turned their heart back again.

38. *Then the fire of the LORD fell and consumed the burnt sacrifice, and the wood, and the stones, and the dust, and licked up the water that was in the trench*

39. *And when all the people saw it, they fell on their faces: and they said, The LORD, he is the God; the LORD, he is the God.*

40. *And Elijah said unto them, Take the prophets of Baal; let not one of them escape. And they took them: and Elijah brought them down to the brook Kishon, and slew them there.*

Daniel 6: 4-24

4. *Then the presidents and princes sought to find occasion against Daniel concerning the kingdom, but they could find none occasion nor fault; forasmuch as he was faithful, neither was there any error or fault found in him.*

5. *Then said these men, we shall not find any occasion against this Daniel, except we find it against him concerning the law of his God.*

6. *Then these presidents and princes assembled together to the king, and said thus unto him, King Darius, live forever.*

7. *All the presidents of the kingdom, the governors, and the princes, the counselors, and the captains, have consulted together to establish a royal statute, and to make a firm decree, that whosoever shall ask a petition of any God or man for thirty days, save of thee, O king, he shall be cast into the den of lions.*

8. *Now, O king, establish the decree and sign the writing, that it be not changed, according to the law of the Medes and Persians, which altereth not.*

9. *Wherefore king Darius signed the writing and the decree.*

10. *Now when Daniel knew that the writing was signed, he went into his house; and his windows being open in his chamber toward Jerusalem, he kneeled upon his knees three times a day, and prayed, and gave thanks before his God, as he did aforetime.*

11. *Then these men assembled and found Daniel praying and making supplication before his God.*

12. *Then they came near, and spake before the king concerning the king's decree; Hast thou not signed a decree, that every man that shall ask a petition of any God or man within thirty days, save of thee, O king, shall be cast into the den of lions? The king answered and said, The thing is true, according to the law of the Medes and Persians, which altereth not.*

13. *Then answered they and said before the king, That Daniel, which is of the children of the captivity of Judah, regardeth not thee, O king, nor the decree that thou hast signed, but maketh his petition three times a day.*

14. *Then the king, when he heard these words, was sore displeased with himself, and set his heart on Daniel to deliver him: and he labored till the going down of the sun to deliver him.*

15. *Then these men assembled unto the king, and said unto the king, Know, O king, that the law of the Medes and Persians is, That no decree nor statute which the king establisheth may be changed.*

16. *Then the king commanded, and they brought Daniel and cast him into the den of lions. Now the king spake and said unto Daniel, Thy God whom thou servest continually, he will deliver thee.*

17.   And a stone was brought, and laid upon the mouth of the den; and the king sealed it with his own signet, and with the signet of his lords; that the purpose might not be changed concerning Daniel.

18.   Then the king went to his palace, and passed the night fasting: neither were instruments of musick brought before him: and his sleep went from him.

19.   Then the king arose very early in the morning and went in haste unto the den of lions.

20.   And when he came to the den, he cried with a lamentable voice unto Daniel: and the king spake and said to Daniel, O Daniel, servant of the living God, is thy God, whom thou servest continually, able to deliver thee from the lions?

21.   Then said Daniel unto the king, O king, live forever.

22.   My God hath sent his angel, and hath shut the lions' mouths that they have not hurt me: forasmuch as before him innocency was found in me; and also before thee, O king, have I done no hurt.

23.   Then was the king exceedingly glad for him, and commanded that they should take Daniel up out of the den. So Daniel was taken up out of the den, and no manner of hurt was found upon him because he believed in his God.

24.   And the king commanded, and they brought those men which had accused Daniel, and they cast them into the den of lions, them, their children, and their wives; and the lions had the mastery of them, and brake all their bones in pieces, or ever they came at the bottom of the den.

Daniel 9:

1.   In the first year of Darius the son of Ahasuerus, of the seed of the Medes, which was made king over the realm of the Chaldeans;

2.   In the first year of his reign I Daniel understood by books the number of the years, whereof the word of the LORD came to Jeremiah the prophet, that he would accomplish seventy years in the desolations of Jerusalem.3.   And I set my face unto the Lord God, to seek by prayer and supplications, with fasting, and sackcloth, and ashes

4.   And I prayed unto the LORD my God, and made my confession, and said, O Lord, the great and dreadful God, keeping the covenant and mercy to them that love him, and to them that keep his commandments;

5.   We have sinned, and have committed iniquity, and have done wickedly, and have rebelled, even by departing from thy precepts and from thy judgments:

6.   Neither have we hearkened unto thy servants the prophets, which spake in thy name to our kings, our princes, and our fathers, and to all the people of the land.

7.   O LORD, righteousness belongeth unto thee, but unto us confusion of faces, as at this day; to the men of Judah, and to the inhabitants of Jerusalem, and unto all Israel, that are near, and that are far off, through all the countries whither thou hast driven them, because of their trespass that they have trespassed against thee.

8.   O Lord, to us belongeth confusion of face, to our kings, to our princes, and to our fathers, because we have sinned against thee.

9.   To the Lord our God belong mercies and forgiveness, though we have rebelled against him;

10.   Neither have we obeyed the voice of the LORD our God, to walk in his laws, which he set before us by his servants the prophets.

11.   Yea, all Israel have transgressed thy law, even by departing, that they might not obey thy voice; therefore the curse is poured upon us, and the oath that is written in the law of Moses the servant of God because we have sinned against him.

12.   And he hath confirmed his words, which he spake against us, and against our judges that judged us, by bringing upon us a great evil: for under the whole heaven hath not been done as hath been done upon Jerusalem.

13. As it is written in the law of Moses, all this evil is come upon us: yet made we, not our prayer before the LORD our God, that we might turn from our iniquities, and understand thy truth.

14. Therefore hath the LORD watched upon the evil and brought it upon us: for the LORD our God is righteous in all his works which he doeth: for we obeyed not his voice.

15. And now, O Lord our God, that hast brought thy people forth out of the land of Egypt with a mighty hand, and hast gotten thee renown, as at this day; we have sinned, we have done wickedly.

16. O LORD, according to all thy righteousness, I beseech thee, let thine anger and thy fury be turned away from thy city Jerusalem, thy holy mountain: because for our sins, and for the iniquities of our fathers, Jerusalem and thy people are become a reproach to all that are about us.

17. Now, therefore, O our God, hear the prayer of thy servant, and his supplications, and cause thy face to shine upon thy sanctuary that is desolate, for the Lord's sake.

18. O my God, incline thine ear, and hear; open thine eyes, and behold our desolations, and the city which is called by thy name: for we do not present our supplications before thee for our righteousnesses, but for thy great mercies.

19. O Lord, hear; O Lord, forgive; O Lord, hearken and do; defer not, for thine own sake, O my God: for thy city and thy people are called by thy name.

20. And whiles I was speaking, and praying, and confessing my sin and the sin of my people Israel, and presenting my supplication before the LORD my God for the holy mountain of my God;

21. Yea, whiles I was speaking in prayer, even the man Gabriel, whom I had seen in the vision at the beginning, being caused to fly swiftly, touched me about the time of the evening oblation.

22. And he informed me, and talked with me, and said, O Daniel, I am now come forth to give thee skill and understanding.

23. At the beginning of thy supplications, the commandment came forth, and I am come to shew thee; for thou art greatly beloved: therefore understand the matter, and consider the vision.

24. Seventy weeks are determined upon thy people and upon thy holy city, to finish the transgression, and to make an end of sins, and to make reconciliation for iniquity, and to bring in everlasting righteousness, and to seal up the vision and prophecy, and to anoint the most Holy.

25. Know therefore and understand, that from the going forth of the commandment to restore and to build Jerusalem unto the Messiah the Prince shall be seven weeks, and threescore and two weeks: the street shall be built again, and the wall, even in troublous times.

26. And after threescore and two weeks shall Messiah be cut off, but not for himself: and the people of the prince that shall come shall destroy the city and the sanctuary, and the end thereof shall be with a flood, and unto the end of the war desolations are determined.

27. And he shall confirm the covenant with many for one week: and in the midst of the week he shall cause the sacrifice and the oblation to cease, and for the overspreading of abominations, he shall make it desolate, even until the consummation and that determined shall be poured upon the desolate.

Acts 12: 5-10

5. Peter, therefore, was kept in prison: but prayer was made without ceasing of

6. the church unto God for   him.
And when Herod would have brought him forth, the same night Peter was sleeping between two soldiers, bound with two chains: and the keepers before the door kept the prison.
7. And, behold, the angel of the Lord came upon him, and a light shined in the prison: and he smote Peter on the side, and raised him up, saying, Arise up quickly. And his chains fell off from his hands.
8. And the angel said unto him, Gird thyself, and bind on thy sandals. And so he did. And he saith unto him, Cast thy garment about thee and follow me.
9. And he went out, and followed him, and wist not that it was true which was done by the angel, but thought he saw a vision.
10. When they were past the first and the second ward, they came unto the iron gate that leadeth unto the city; which opened to them of his own accord: and they went out, and passed on through one street, and forthwith the angel departed from him.

In the Bible, Prayers were much focused, significant and for a specific purpose. There is a reason, a want, a need to ASK GOD and make a request, most of these prayers were answered by God who delivered a life-changing experience for everyone, including those who prayed and those who were inclusive and interceded in prayer.

Faith and belief system are inborn in every human being as long as you acknowledge the inner psyche that leads us to the intimate talk and the confidence in our conscious and subconscious minds which in faith is related to a supreme entity within and without, inside the body and mind and in existence in the world. This is the experience, because we are not able to experience external to the world, but can only ready, study and learn from science and theology, scriptures and religious texts that there exists a universe controlled, monitored and managed by a supreme being, which we call "GOD."

So how can we benefit from that Supreme Being we call GOD? People from all over the world acknowledge that there exists GOD and we call GOD by various language and various names in our native language. Today's religion created biases based on the names they know God by and creates animosities and segregation, anger and strive over the very same being they call GOD. Their belief system was escalated to OWN their GOD to such an extent as to create wars and commit the most heinous crimes over what they cannot see and only can experience in the spirit.

What are our benefits from GOD; we need to become impersonal through spirituality and experience the presence of GOD internally before he can show up externally.

To find answers, we must first ask and find solutions to the following:

- Why do we suffer?
- How can we cope with life's anxieties, calamities, and traumas?
- How can we make our family's lives happier?
- What happens to us when we die?
- Will, we are able to experience Death and explain it?
- Can we meet with our families and loved ones after death?
- How can we be sure that GOD will fulfill all that we ask? And will he meet his promises to the People and to us?

32 ANGELS

- Origin of Angels

- Angels are heavenly beings

- Angels are Created beings

- Angels are Intelligent, having free will and are holy

Angels are numerous in revelations states there were 10,000 x 10,000, 10,000, and x 10,000 all-powerful, swift and traveled greater and faster than the speed of light in our human concept of momentum. They are in the order of a hierarchy of army with positions and ranks, duties and roles. They are also ministering angels and have a ministry in heaven and on earth. Satan (Lucifer is also an angel who kicked out of Heaven with 1/3 of the other angels under his authority.

Seven angels or archangels are given to the seven days of the week: Michael, Gabriel, Raphael, Uriel, Selaphiel, Raguel or Jegudiel, and Barachiel.

Angelic Council, an Orthodox icon of the seven archangels, left to right: Jegudiel, Gabriel, Selaphiel, Michael, Uriel, Raphael, and Barachiel. Beneath the mandorla of Christ-Immanuel (God is with us) are representations of Cherubim (blue) and Seraphim (red).

The Origin of Angels, Angels are heavenly beings, created by God and are very intelligent. The do have free-will and are holy, powerful, numerous in numbers as stated above, they are very swift, defying gravity and the speed of sound and light, having ranks and positions, they are also ministering angels in heaven and on earth. They are spirits and are immaterial and incorporeal, invisible and can manifest in any living body that possesses very individual personalities.

Hebrews 1:14. Angels are ministering angels sent to bear witness to those who are available for Salvation.

Hebrews 1:7   Angels are spirits, immaterial and incorporeal, they are invisible but can appear in manifestations to be seen, they are generally messengers of GOD and functions thus most of the time. Being created beings, they have a definite beginning unlike the description and nature of the creator- GOD; They are immortally described in (Collassians1:16) with various ranks

Angels depicted and described in existence in all religions; they are supernatural, benevolent celestial beings and are messengers and mediators for God between heaven and humanity. They are there to protect, minister, teach, and carry out commands of God and tasks given by the heavenly.

Angels do possess a superior intelligence over all forms of life in this world. They are not omniscient and are holy, morally perfect and detest evil, humble and obedient to the will of God. Mighty beings, greater than human beings, in biblical times, one Angel were responsible for killing 185,000 Assyrians in Isaiah 37:36 and one Angel will bind Satan. One Angel was responsible for destroying 70,000 through pestilence in II Samuel 24:15. In *Revelations 5:11 that there are ten thousand times ten thousand, and thousands of thousands*, but do not procreate, not given in marriage and are of neutral gender though most listed as masculine. They listed in ranks in an Angelic Heavenly order of hierarchy, namely in the order of Thrones, dominions, principalities, and powers. The order from highest are Cherubim's, Seraphim's, Archangels, Angels,

with the help of God, Jesus created the six archangels to form the seven Spirits of God. (Rev 4:5)

The six archangels gave birth to the 24 Elders of Heaven. (Rev 4:4)

The 24 Elders gave birth to the 12 tribes of Heaven, which grew to uncountable numbers. Human beings can not command them, but do stand guard as protector and guides to human beings as instructed by God in answer to prayers.

33 PRAYERS IN THE BIBLE

Each for a specific purpose and applies to specific circumstances

The Lord's Prayer (How to pray – a Template)

(Matthew 6:5-15)

5   *And when thou prayest, thou shalt not be as the hypocrites are: for they love to pray standing in the synagogues and in the corners of the streets, that they may be seen of men. Verily I say unto you; They have their reward.*

6   *But thou, when thou prayest, enter into thy closet, and when thou hast shut thy door, pray to thy Father which is in secret; and thy Father which seeth in secret shall reward thee openly.*

7   *But when ye pray, use not vain repetitions, as the heathen do: for they think that they shall be heard for their much speaking.*

8   *Be not ye, therefore, like unto them: for your, Father knoweth what things ye have need of before ye ask him.*

9   *After this manner, therefore, pray ye: Our Father which art in heaven, Hallowed be thy name.*

10   *Thy kingdom come. Thy will be done in earth, as it is in heaven.*

11   *Give us this day our daily bread.*

12   *And forgive us our debts, as we forgive our debtors.*

13   *And lead us not into temptation, but deliver us from evil: For thine is the kingdom and the power, and the glory, forever. Amen.*

14   *For if ye forgive men their trespasses, your heavenly Father will also forgive you:*

15   *But if ye forgive not men their trespasses, neither will your Father forgive your trespasses.*

Moses' Prayer for Israel in the Wilderness *(Exodus 32:9-14)*

Moses was on Mt Sinai for 40 days and nights receiving the covenant from God and discussing the future of Israel, including the Ten Commandments that were inscribed on the Stone tables by the Finger of God. The Israelite rebelled against Aaron and requested they build an image of a new God and gathered together their jewelry and built a golden calf, which they worshipped and claim the image being their God that actually brought them out of Egypt, which then led to blasphemy. God 's reaction, enraged with anger and stated to Moses

9   *And the LORD said unto Moses; I have seen this person, and, behold, it is a stiff-necked people:*

10   *Now, therefore, let me alone, that my wrath may wax hot against them, and that I may consume them: and I will make of thee a great nation."*

Moses response in defense to the Israelite was a very challenging one to God

and tried to make justification and intercede for them.

11   *And Moses besought the LORD his God, and said, LORD, why doth thy wrath wax hot against thy people, which thou hast brought forth out of the land of Egypt with great power, and with a mighty hand?*

12   *Wherefore should the Egyptians speak, and say, for mischief did he bring them out, to slay them in the mountains, and to consume them from the face of the earth? Turn from thy fierce wrath, and repent of this evil against thy people.*

13   *Remember Abraham, Isaac, and Israel, thy servants, to whom thou swarest by thine own self, and saidst unto them, I will multiply your seed as the stars of heaven, and all this land that I have spoken of will I give unto your seed, and they shall inherit it forever.*

14   **And the LORD repented of the evil which he thought to do unto his people.**

Drawing attention to verse 14, where the LORD repented for what he was thinking. This is a dangerous situation for GOD is a spirit and cannot relate to Human thoughts and Feelings as a Human. Thus God came in the Form of Jesus a Human Being to experience the human factor of feelings, emotions, sensitivities, experiences as a human being. The little reaction from God could be a devastating effect on the entire population and could be their very destruction. Moses used quite a bit of convincing prayer communication to turn the mind/emotion of God around so as not to respond to the anger he had against the Israelite

David's Prayer for Pardon and Confession of Sin *(Psalm 51)*

David had committed adultery with Bathsheba, got her pregnant, baby died, David sent Bathsheba Uriah to the battlefield and had gotten him killed in the front lines. In 2 Samuel 12, Nathan received word from God to deliver a message and convict David, giving him details in a parable.

A parable that Nathan told David concerning David's sin and his response
Nathan's Parable and David's Confession 2 Samuel 12

2 Samuel 12:1   *Then the Lord sent Nathan to David. And he came to him and said to him: "There were two men in one city, one rich and the other poor.*

2 Samuel 12:2   *The rich man had exceedingly many flocks and herds.*

2 Samuel 12:3   *But the poor man had nothing, except one little ewe lamb which he had bought and nourished; and it grew up together with him and with his children. It ate of his own food and drank from his own cup and lay in his bosom, and it was like a daughter to him.*

2 Samuel 12:5   *So David's anger was greatly aroused against the man, and he said to Nathan, "As the Lord lives, the man who has done this shall surely die!*

2 Samuel 12:6   *And he shall restore fourfold for the lamb, because he did this thing and*

because he had no pity."

2 Samuel 12:7   Then Nathan said to David, "You are the man! Thus says the Lord God of Israel: 'I anointed you king over Israel, and I delivered you from the hand of Saul.

2 Samuel 12:8   I gave you your master's house and your master's wives into your keeping and gave you the house of Israel and Judah. And if that had been too little, I also would have given you much more!

2 Samuel 12:9   Why have you despised the commandment of the Lord, to do evil in His sight? You have killed Uriah the Hittite with the sword; you have taken his wife to be your wife, and have killed him with the sword of the people of Ammon.

2 Samuel 12:10   Now, therefore, the sword shall never depart from your house, because you have despised Me, and have taken the wife of Uriah the Hittite to be your wife.'

2 Samuel 12:11   Thus says the Lord: 'Behold, I will raise up adversity against you from your own house; and I will take your wives before your eyes and give them to your neighbor, and he shall lie with your wives in the sight of this sun.

2 Samuel 12:12   For you did it secretly, but I will do this thing before all Israel, before the sun.'"

2 Samuel 12:13 So David said to Nathan, "I have sinned against the Lord."

And Nathan said to David, "The Lord also has put away your sin; you shall not die.

2 Samuel 12:14   However, because by this deed you have given great occasion to the enemies of the Lord to blaspheme, the child also who is born to you shall surely die."

2 Samuel 12:15 Then Nathan departed to his house.

Psalms 51

*Psa 51:**1** Have mercy upon me, O God, according to thy lovingkindness: according unto the multitude of thy tender mercies blot out my transgressions.*

*Psa 51:**2** Wash me thoroughly from mine iniquity, and cleanse me from my sin.*

*Psa 51:**3** For I acknowledge my transgressions: and my sin is ever before me.*

*Psa 51:**4** Against thee, thee only, have I sinned, and done this evil in thy sight: that thou mightest be justified*

*Psa51:**5**] Behold, I was shapen in iniquity; and in sin did my mother conceive me.*

*Psa 51:**6** Behold, thou desirest truth in the inward parts: and in the hidden part thou shalt make me to know wisdom.*

*Psa 51:**7** Purge me with hyssop, and I shall be clean: wash me, and I shall be whiter than snow.*

*Psa 51:**8** Make me to hear joy and gladness; that the bones which thou hast broken may rejoice.*

*Psa 51:**9** Hide thy face from my sins, and blot out all mine iniquities.*

*Psa 51:**10** Create in me a clean heart, O God; and renew a right spirit within me*

*Psa 51:**11** Cast me not away from thy presence; and take not thy holy spirit from me.*

*Psa 51:**12** Restore unto me the joy of thy salvation; and uphold me with thy free spirit.*

*Psa 51:**13** Then will I teach transgressors thy ways, and sinners shall be converted unto thee.*

*Psa 51:**14** Deliver me from bloodguiltiness, O God, thou God of my salvation: and my tongue shall sing aloud of thy righteousness.*

*Psa 51:**15** O Lord, open thou my lips; and my mouth shall shew forth thy praise.*

*Psa 51:**16** For thou desirest not sacrifice; else would I give it: thou delightest not in burnt offering.*

*Psa 51:**17** The sacrifices of God are a broken spirit: a broken and a contrite heart, O God, thou* *wilt not despise.*

*Psa 51:**18** Do good in thy good pleasure unto Zion: build thou the walls of Jerusalem.*

*Psa 51:**19**Then shalt thou be pleased with the sacrifices of righteousness, with burnt offering and whole burnt offering: then shall they offer bullocks upon thine altar.*

Hezekiah's Petitions for Deliverance and Healing *(2 Kings 19:14-19; 20:1-7)*

2Kings19:14 *And Hezekiah received the letter of the hand of the messengers, and read it: and Hezekiah went up into the house of the LORD, and spread it before the LORD.*

2Kings19:15 *And Hezekiah prayed before the LORD, and said, O LORD God of Israel, which dwellest between the cherubims, thou art the God, even thou alone, of all the kingdoms of the earth: thou hast made heaven and earth*

2Kings19:16 *LORD, bow down thine ear, and hear: open, LORD, thine eyes, and see: and hear the words of Sennacherib, which hath sent him to reproach the living God.*

2Kings19:17 *Of a truth, LORD, the kings of Assyria have destroyed the nations and their lands,*

2Kings19:18 *And have cast their gods into the fire: for they were no gods, but the work of men's hands, wood, and stone: therefore they have destroyed them.*

2Kings19:19 *Now, therefore, O LORD our God, I beseech thee, save thou us out of his hand, that all the kingdoms of the earth may know that thou art the LORD God, even thou only.*

2 Kings 20:1 *In those days was Hezekiah sick unto death. And the prophet Isaiah the son of Amoz came to him, and said unto him, In those days was Hezekiah sick unto death. And the prophet Isaiah the son of Amoz came to him, and said unto him, Thus saith the*

2 Kings 20:2 *Then he turned his face to the wall, and prayed unto the LORD, saying,*

2 Kings 20:3 *I beseech thee, O LORD, remember now how I have walked before thee in truth and with a perfect heart, and have done that which is good in thy sight. And Hezekiah wept sore.*

2 Kings 20:4 *And it came to pass, afore Isaiah was gone out into the middle court, that the word of the LORD came to him, saying,*

2 Kings 20:5 *Turn again, and tell Hezekiah the captain of my people, Thus saith the LORD, the God of David thy father, I have heard thy prayer, I have seen thy tears: behold, I will heal thee: on the third day thou shalt go up unto the house of the LORD.*

2 Kings 20:6 *And I will add unto thy days fifteen years, and I will deliver thee and this city out of the hand of the king of Assyria, and I will defend this city for mine own sake, and for my servant David's sake.*

2 Kings 20:7 *And Isaiah said, Take a lump of figs. And they took and laid it on the boil, and he recovered.*

David's Psalm of Surrender *(Psalm 139)*

1   *O LORD, thou hast searched me, and known me.*

2   *Thou knowest my downsitting and mine uprising; thou understandest my thought afar off*

3   Thou compassest my path and my lying down, and art acquainted with all my ways.

4   For there is not a word in my tongue, but, lo, O LORD, thou knowest it altogether.

5   Thou hast beset me behind and before and laid thine hand upon me.

6   Such knowledge is too wonderful for me; it is high, I cannot attain unto it.

7   Whither shall I go from thy spirit? Or whither shall I flee from thy presence?

8   If I ascend up into heaven, thou art there: if I make my bed in hell, behold, thou art there.

9   If I take the wings of the morning and dwell in the uttermost parts of the sea;

10   Even there shall thy hand lead me, and thy right hand shall hold me.

11   If I say, surely the darkness shall cover me; even the night shall be light about me.

12   Yea, the darkness hideth not from thee; but the night shineth as the day: the darkness and the light are both alike to thee.

13   For thou hast possessed my reins: thou hast covered me in my mother's womb.

14   I will praise thee; for I am fearfully and wonderfully made: marvelous are thy works; and that my soul knoweth right well.

15   My substance was not hid from thee, when I was made in secret, and curiously wrought in the lowest parts of the earth.

16   Thine eyes did see my substance, yet being unperfect; and in thy book all my members were written, which in continuance were fashioned, when as yet there was none of them.

17   How precious also are thy thoughts unto me, O God! How great is the sum of them!

18   If I should count them, they are more in number than the sand: when I awake, I am still with thee.

19   Surely thou wilt slay the wicked, O God: depart from me, therefore, ye bloody men.

20   For they speak against thee wickedly, and thine enemies take thy name in vain.

21   Do not I hate them, O LORD that hates thee? And am not I grieved with those that rise up against thee?

22   I hate them with perfect hatred: I count them mine enemies.

23   Search me, O God, and know my heart: try me, and know my thoughts:

24   And see if there be any wicked way in me, and lead me in the way everlasting.

Nehemiah's Prayer for Success (Nehemiah 1:1-2:9)

1   The words of Nehemiah, the son of Hachaliah. And it came to pass in the month Chisleu, in the twentieth year, as I was in Shushan the palace,

2   That Hanani, one of my brethren, came, he and certain men of Judah; and I asked them was that had escaped, which were left of the captivity, and concerning Jerusalem.

9   But if ye turn unto me, and keep my commandments, and do them; though there were of you cast out unto the uttermost part of the heaven, yet will I gather them from thence, and will bring them unto the place that I have chosen to set my name there.

Acts 7:55,59

55   But he, being full of the Holy Ghost, looked up stedfastly into heaven, and saw the glory of God, **standing** on the right hand of God,

59   And they stoned Stephen, calling upon God, and saying, Lord Jesus, receive my spirit.

Jesus' Prayer of Submission at Gethsemane (Luke 22:39-46)

39   And he came out, and went, as he was wont, to the mount of Olives; and his disciples also followed him.

40   And when he was at the place, he said unto them, Pray that ye enter not into temptation.

41   *And he was withdrawn from them about a stone's cast, and kneeled down, and prayed,*

42   *Saying, Father, if thou be willing, remove this cup from me: nevertheless not my will, but thine, be done.*

43   *And there appeared an angel unto him from heaven, strengthening him.*

44   *And being in an agony, he prayed more earnestly: and his sweat was as it were great drops of blood falling down to the ground.*

45   *And when he rose up from prayer and was come to his disciples, he found them sleeping for sorrow,*

46   *And said unto them, Why sleep ye? rise and pray, lest ye enter into temptation.*

Ephesians 3:14-20 (The Message)

14   *For this, cause I bow my knees unto the Father of our Lord Jesus Christ,*

15   *Of whom the whole family in heaven and earth is named,*

16   *That he would grant you, according to the riches of his glory, to be strengthened with might by his Spirit in the inner man;*

17   *That Christ may dwell in your hearts by faith; that ye, being rooted and grounded in love,*

18   *May be able to comprehend with all saints what is the breadth, and length, and depth, and height;*

19   *And to know the love of Christ, which passeth knowledge, that ye might be filled with the fullness of God.*

20   *Now unto him, that is able to do exceeding abundantly above all that we ask or think, according to the power that worketh in us,*

21   *Unto him be glory in the church by Christ Jesus throughout all ages, world without end. Amen.*

Ephesians 1:15-23

15   *Wherefore I also, after I heard of your faith in the Lord Jesus, and love unto all the saints,*

16   *ease not to give thanks for you, making mention of you in my prayers;*

17   *That the God of our Lord Jesus Christ, the Father of glory, may give unto you the spirit of wisdom and revelation in the knowledge of him:*

18   *The eyes of your understanding being enlightened; that ye may know what is the hope of his calling, and what the riches of the glory of his inheritance in the saints,*

19   *And what is the exceeding greatness of his power to us-ward who believe, according to the working of his mighty power,*

20   *Which he wrought in Christ when he raised him from the dead and set him at his own right hand in the heavenly places,*

21   *Far above all principality, and power, and might, and dominion, and every name that is named, not only in this world but also in that which is to come:*

22   *And hath put all things under his feet, and gave him to be the head over all things to the church,*

23   *Which is his body, the fulness of him that filleth all in all?*

Abraham - Great Negotiator (Abraham negotiated with God on sparing Sodom and Gomorrah)

20   *And the LORD said, Because the cry of Sodom and Gomorrah is great, and because their sin is very grievous;*

21   *I will go down now, and see whether they have done altogether according to the cry of it, which is come unto me; and if not, I will know.*

22   *And the men turned their faces from thence and went toward Sodom: but Abraham stood yet before the LORD*

23   *And Abraham drew near, and said, Wilt thou also destroy the righteous with the wicked?*

24   *Peradventure there be fifty righteous within the city: wilt thou also destroy and not spare the place for the fifty righteous that are therein?*

25   *That be far from thee to do after this manner, to slay the righteous with the wicked: and that the righteous should be as the wicked, that be far from thee: Shall not the Judge of all the earth do right?*

26   *And the LORD said, If I find in Sodom fifty righteous within the city, then I will spare all the place for their sakes.*

27   *And Abraham answered and said, Behold now, I have taken upon me to speak unto the Lord, which am but dust and ashes:*

28   *Peradventure there shall lack five of the fifty righteous: wilt thou destroy all the city for lack of five? And he said, If I find there forty and five, I will not destroy it.*

29   *And he spake unto him yet again, and said, Peradventure there shall be forty found there. And he said I will not do it for forty's sake.*

30   *And he said unto him, Oh let not the Lord be angry, and I will speak: Peradventure there shall thirty be found there. And he said I will not do it if I find thirty there.*

31   *And he said, Behold now, I have taken upon me to speak unto the Lord: Peradventure there shall be twenty found there. And he said I will not destroy it for twenty's sake.*

32   *And he said, Oh let not the Lord be angry, and I will speak yet but this once: Peradventure ten shall be found there. And he said I will not destroy it for ten's sake.*

33   *And the LORD went his way, as soon as he had left communing with Abraham: and Abraham returned unto his place.*

Jacob - Wrestling with God

9   *And Jacob said, O God of my father Abraham, and God of my father Isaac, the LORD which saidst unto me, Return unto thy country, and to thy kindred, and I will deal well with thee:*

10   *I am not worthy of the least of all the mercies, and of all the truth, which thou hast shewed unto thy servant; for with my staff I passed over this Jordan, and now I am*

become two bands

11   *Deliver me, I pray thee, from the hand of my brother, from the hand of Esau: for I fear him, lest he will come and smite me, and the mother with the children.*

12   *And thou saidst, I will surely do thee good, and make thy seed as the sand of the sea, which cannot be numbered for multitude.*

13   *And he lodged there that same night; and took of that which came to his hand a present for Esau, his brother;*

14   *Two hundred she goats, and twenty he goats, two hundred ewes, and twenty rams,*

15   *Thirty milch camels with their colts, forty kine, and ten bulls, twenty she asses, and ten foals.*

16   *And he delivered them into the hand of his servants, every drove by themselves; and said unto his servants, Pass over before me, and put a space betwixt drove and drove.*

17   *And he commanded the foremost, saying, When Esau my brother meeteth thee, and asketh thee, saying, Whose art thou? and whither goest thou? and whose are these before thee?*

18   *Then thou shalt say, They be thy servant Jacob's; it is a present sent unto my lord Esau: and, behold, also he is behind us.*

19   *And so commanded he the second, and the third, and all that followed the droves, saying, On this manner shall ye speak unto Esau when ye find him.*

20   *And say ye moreover, Behold, thy servant Jacob is behind us. For he said, I will appease him with the present that goeth before me, and afterward I will see his face; peradventure he will accept of me.*

21   *So went the present over before him: and himself lodged that night in the company.*

22   *And he rose up that night, and took his two wives, and his two womenservants, and his eleven sons, and passed over the ford Jabbok.*

23   *And he took them, and sent them over the brook, and sent over that he had.*

24   *And Jacob was left alone, and there wrestled a man with him until the breaking of the day.*

25   *And when he saw that he prevailed not against him, he touched the hollow of his thigh; and the hollow of Jacob's thigh was out of joint, as he wrestled with him.*

26   *And he said, Let me go, for the day breaketh. And he said I will not let thee go, except thou bless me.*

27   *And he said unto him, What is thy name? And he said, Jacob.*

28   *And he said, Thy name shall be called no more Jacob, but Israel: for as a prince hast thou power with God and with men, and hast prevailed.*

29   *And Jacob asked him, and said, Tell me, I pray thee, thy name. And he said, Wherefore is it that thou dost ask after my name? And he blessed him there.*

30   *And Jacob called the name of the place Peniel: for I have seen God face to face, and my life is preserved.*

31   *And as he passed over Penuel, the sun rose upon him, and he halted upon his thigh.*

32   *Therefore the children of Israel eat not of the sinew which shrank, which is upon the hollow of the thigh, unto this day: because he touched the hollow of Jacob's thigh in the sinew that shrank.*

Hannah's Prayer with a Price

1 Samuel 1: 8 *Then said Elkanah her husband to her, Hannah, why weepest thou? and why eatest thou not? and why is thy heart grieved? am not I better to thee than ten sons?*

9 *So Hannah rose up after they had eaten in Shiloh, and after they had drunk. Now Eli the priest sat upon a seat by a post of the temple of the LORD.*

10 *And she was in bitterness of soul, and prayed unto the LORD, and wept sore.*

11 *And she vowed a vow, and said, O LORD of hosts, if thou wilt indeed look on the affliction of thine handmaid, and remember me, and not forget thine handmaid, but wilt give unto thine handmaid a man child, then I will give him unto the LORD all the days of his life, and there shall no razor come upon his head.*

12 *And it came to pass, as she continued praying before the LORD, that Eli marked her mouth.*

13 *Now Hannah, she spake in her heart; only her lips moved, but her voice was not heard: therefore Eli thought she had been drunken.*

14 *And Eli said unto her, How long wilt thou be drunken? put away thy wine from thee.*

15 *And Hannah answered and said, No, my lord, I am a woman of a sorrowful spirit: I have drunk neither wine nor strong drink, but have poured out my soul before the LORD.*

16 *Count not thine handmaid for a daughter of Belial: for out of the abundance of my complaint and grief have I spoken hitherto.*

17 *Then Eli answered and said, Go in peace: and the God of Israel grant thee thy petition that thou hast asked of him.*

18 *And she said, Let thine handmaid find grace in thy sight. So the woman went her way and did eat, and her countenance was no more sad.*

19 *And they rose up in the morning early, and worshipped before the LORD, and returned, and came to their house to Ramah: and Elkanah knew Hannah, his wife, and the LORD remembered her*

Hannah's Prayer of Praise

Then Hannah prayed: 1 Samuel 2:1-11

1 Samuel 2:1   *My heart rejoices in the Lord!*
The Lord has made me strong.
Now I have an answer for my enemies;
I rejoice because you rescued me.
1 Samuel 2:2 No one is holy like the Lord!
There is no one besides you;
there is no Rock like our God.

1 Samuel 2:3   *"Stop acting so proud and haughty!*
Don't speak with such arrogance!

For the Lord is a God who knows what you have done;
he will judge your actions.

1 Samuel 2:4 The bow of the mighty is now broken,
and those who stumbled are now strong.

1 Samuel 2:5 Those who were well fed are now starving,
and those who were starving are now full.
The childless woman now has seven children,
and the woman with many children wastes away.

1 Samuel 2:6 The Lord gives both death and life;
he brings some down to the grave but raises others up.

1 Samuel 2:7 The Lord makes some poor and others rich;
he brings some down and lifts others up.

1 Samuel 2:8 He lifts the poor from the dust
and the needy from the garbage dump.
He sets them among princes,
placing them in seats of honor.
For all the earth is the Lord's,
and he has set the world in order.

1 Samuel 2:9 "He will protect his faithful ones,
but the wicked will disappear in darkness.
No one will succeed by strength alone.

1 Samuel 2:10 Those who fight against the Lord will be shattered.
He thunders against them from heaven;
the Lord judges throughout the earth.
He gives power to his king;
he increases the strength of his anointed one."

Solomon's Prayer for Wisdom

1 Kings 9:1 "O God of my ancestors and Lord of mercy, who have made all things by your word,

2 and by your wisdom have formed humankind To have dominion over the creatures you have made,

3 and rule the world in holiness and righteousness, and pronounce judgment in uprightness of soul,

4 give me the wisdom that sits by your throne and do not reject me from among your servants.

5 For I am your servant the son of your serving girl, a man who is weak and short-lived, with little understanding of judgment and laws;

6 for even one who is perfect among human beings
will be regarded as nothing without the wisdom that comes from you.

7   *You have chosen me to be king of your people*
and to be judge over your sons and daughters.

8   *You have given command to build a temple on your holy mountain,*
and an altar in the city of your habitation, a copy of the holy tent that you
prepared from the beginning.

9   *With you is wisdom, she who knows your works and was present when you*
made the world; she understands what is pleasing in your sight and what
is right according to your commandments.

10   *Send her forth from the holy heavens, and from the throne of your glory*
send her, that she may labor at my side, and that I may learn what is
pleasing to you.

11   *For she knows and understands all things, and she will guide me wisely in*
my actions and guard me with her glory.

12   *Then my works will be acceptable, and I shall judge your people justly, and*
shall be worthy of the throne of my father.

13   *For who can learn the counsel of God? Or who can discern what the Lord*
wills?

14   *For the reasoning of mortals is worthless, and our designs are likely to fail;*

15   *for a perishable body weighs down the soul, and this earthy tent burdens*
the thoughtful mind.

16   *We can hardly guess at what is on earth, and what is at hand we find with*
labor; but who has traced out what is in the heavens?

17   *Who has learned your counsel, unless you have given wisdom and sent*
your holy spirit from on high?

18   *And thus the paths of those on earth were set right, and people were*
taught what pleases you, and were saved by wisdom."

Acts 4:23-31 New International Version (NIV)

The Believers Pray

23   *On their release, Peter and John went back to their own people and reported all that the chief priests and the elders had said to them. 24 When they heard this, they raised their voices together in prayer to God. "Sovereign Lord," they said, "you made the heavens and the earth and the sea, and everything in them. 25 You spoke by the Holy Spirit through the mouth of your servant, our father David: "'why do the nations rage and the people's plot in vain?*

26   *The kings of the earth rise up, and the rulers band together against the Lord and against his anointed one.*

27   *Indeed Herod and Pontius Pilate met together with the Gentiles and the people of Israel in this city to conspire against your holy servant Jesus, whom you anointed. 28 They did what your power and will had decided beforehand should happen. 29 Now, Lord, consider their threats and enable your servants to speak your word with great boldness. 30 Stretch out your hand to heal and perform signs and wonders through the name of your holy servant Jesus."*

31   *After they prayed, the place where they were meeting was shaken. And they were all filled with the Holy Spirit and spoke the word of God boldly.*

Jonah's Prayer: Out of the Depths

Jonah 2: 1 *Then Jonah prayed unto the Lord his God out of the fish's belly,*

2 *And said, I cried by reason of mine affliction unto the Lord, and he heard me; out of the belly of hell cried I, and thou heardest my voice.*

3 *For thou hadst cast me into the deep, in the midst of the seas; and the floods compassed me about: all thy billows and thy waves passed over me.*

4 *Then I said, I am cast out of thy sight, yet I will look again toward thy holy temple.*

5 *The waters compassed me about, even to the soul: the depth closed me round about; the weeds were wrapped about my head.*

6 *I went down to the bottoms of the mountains; the earth with her bars was : yet hast thou brought up my life from corruption, O Lord my God.*

7 *When my soul fainted within me I remembered the Lord: and my prayer came in unto thee, into thine holy temple.*

8 *They that observe lying vanities forsake their own mercy.*

9 *But I will sacrifice unto thee with the voice of thanksgiving; I will pay that I have vowed. Salvation is of the Lord.*

10 *And the Lord spake unto the fish, and it vomited out Jonah upon the dry land.*

David's Prayer of Repentance for cleansing and pardon

Psalms51:1 *to the Chief Musician. A Psalm of David; when Nathan the prophet came unto him after he had gone into Bathsheba. Have mercy upon me, O God, according to thy lovingkindness: According to the multitude of thy tender mercies blot out my transgressions.*

51:2 *Wash me thoroughly from mine iniquity, And cleanse me from my sin.*

51:3 *For I know my transgressions, And my sin is ever before me.*

51:4 *Against thee, thee only, have I sinned, And done that which is evil in thy sight; That thou mayest be justified when thou speakest And be clear when thou judgest.*

51:5 *Behold, I was brought forth in iniquity; And in sin did my mother conceive me.*

51:6 *Behold, thou desirest truth in the inward parts; And in the hidden part thou wilt make me to know wisdom.*

51:7 *Purify me with hyssop, and I shall be clean: Wash me, and I shall be whiter than snow.*

51:8 *Make me to hear joy and gladness, That the bones which thou hast broken may rejoice.*

51:9 *Hide thy face from my sins, And blot out all mine iniquities.*

51:10 *Create in me a clean heart, O God; And renew a right spirit within me.*

51:11 *Cast me not away from thy presence; And take not thy holy spirit from me.*

51:12 *Restore unto me the joy of thy salvation; And uphold me with a willing spirit.*

51:13 *Then will I teach transgressors thy ways, And sinners shall be converted unto thee.*

51:14 *Deliver me from bloodguiltiness, O God, thou God of my salvation; And my tongue shall sing aloud of thy righteousness.*

51:15 *O Lord, open thou my lips; And my mouth shall show forth thy praise.*

51:16 *For thou delightest not in sacrifice; Else would I give it: Thou hast no pleasure in burnt-offering.*

51:17   *The sacrifices of God are a broken spirit: A broken and contrite heart, O God, thou wilt not despise.*

51:18   *Do good in thy good pleasure unto Zion: Build thou the walls of Jerusalem.*

51:19   *Then will thou delight in the sacrifices of righteousness, In burnt-offering and in the whole burnt-offering: Then will they offer bullocks upon thine altar.*

Job's Confession

1   *Then Job answered the LORD, and said,*

2   *I know that thou canst do everything and that no thought can be withholden from thee.*

3   *Who is he that hideth counsel without knowledge? therefore have I uttered that I understood not; things too wonderful for me, which I knew not.*

4   *Hear, I beseech thee, and I will speak: I will demand of thee, and declare thou unto me.*

5   *I have heard of thee by the hearing of the ear: but now mine eye seeth thee.*

6   *Wherefore I abhor myself and repent in dust and ashes.*

7   *And it was so, that after the LORD had spoken these words unto Job, the LORD said to Eliphaz the Temanite, My wrath is kindled against thee, and against thy two friends: for ye have not spoken of me the thing that is right, as my servant Job hath.*

8   *Therefore take unto you now seven bullocks and seven rams, and go to my servant Job, and offer up for yourselves a burnt offering; and my servant Job shall pray for you: for him will I accept: lest I deal with you after your folly, in that ye have not spoken of me the thing which is right, like my servant Job.*

9   *So Eliphaz the Temanite and Bildad the Shuhite and Zophar the Naamathite went, according as the LORD commanded them: the LORD also accepted Job.*

10   *And the LORD turned the captivity of Job when he prayed for his friends: also the LORD gave Job twice as much as he had before.*

11   *Then came there unto him all his brethren, and all his sisters, and all they that had been of his acquaintance before, and did eat bread with him in his house: and they bemoaned him, and comforted him over all the evil that the LORD had brought upon him: every man also gave him a piece of money, and every one an earring of gold.*

12   *So the LORD blessed the latter end of Job more than his beginning: for he had fourteen thousand sheep, and six thousand camels, and a thousand yoke of oxen, and a thousand she asses.*

13   *He had also seven sons and three daughters.*

14   *And he called the name of the first, Jemima; and the name of the second, Kezia; and the name of the third, Keren-happuch.*

15   *And in all the land were no women found so fair as the daughters of Job: and their father gave them inheritance among their brethren.*

16   *After this lived Job an hundred and forty years, and saw his sons, and his sons'generations.*

17   *So Job died, being old and full of days.*

Jesus' Prayer for Unity John 17

1. *These words spake Jesus, and lifted up his eyes to heaven, and said, Father, the hour is come; glorify thy Son, that thy Son also may glorify thee:*

2. *As thou hast given him power over all flesh, that he should give eternal life to as many as thou hast given him.*

3. *And this is life eternal, that they might know thee the only true God, and Jesus Christ, whom thou hast sent.*

4. *I have glorified thee on the earth: I have finished the work which thou gavest me to do.*

5. *And now, O Father, glorify thou me with thine own self with the glory which I had with thee before the world was.*

6. *I have manifested thy name unto the men which thou gavest me out of the world: thine they were, and thou gavest them me; and they have kept thy word.*

7. *Now they have known that all things whatsoever thou hast given me are of thee.*

8. *For I have given unto them the words which thou gavest me; and they have received them, and have known surely that I came out from thee, and they have believed that thou didst send me.*

9. *I pray for them: I pray not for the world, but for them which thou hast given me; for they are thine.*

10. *And all mine are thine, and thine are mine; and I am glorified in them.*

11. *And now I am no more in the world, but these are in the world, and I come to thee. Holy Father, keep through thine own name those whom thou hast given me, that they may be one, as we are.*

12. *While I was with them in the world, I kept them in thy name: those that thou gavest me I have kept, and none of them is lost, but the son of perdition; that the scripture might be fulfilled.*

13. *And now come I to thee; and these things I speak in the world, that they might have my joy fulfilled in themselves.*

14. *I have given them thy word; and the world hath hated them, because they are not of even as I am not of the world.*

15. *I pray not that thou shouldest take them out of the world, but that thou shouldest keep them from the evil.*

16. *They are not of the world, even as I am not of the world.*

17. *.Sanctify them through thy truth: thy word is truth.*

18. *.As thou hast sent me into the world, even so have I also sent them into the world.*

19. *for them I sanctify myself, that they also might be sanctified through the truth.*

20. *Neither pray I for these alone, but for them also which shall believe on me through their word;*

21. *That they all may be one; as thou, Father, art in me, and I in thee, that they also may be one in us: that the world may believe that thou hast sent me.*

22. *And the glory which thou gavest me I have given them; that they may be one, even as we are one:*

23. *I in them, and thou in me, that they may be made perfect in one; and that the world may know that thou hast sent me, and hast loved them, as thou hast loved me.*

24. *.Father, I will that they also, whom thou hast given me, be with me where I am; that*

they may behold my glory, which thou hast given me: for thou lovedst me before the foundation of the world.

25. *O righteous Father, the world hath not known thee: but I have known thee, and these have known that thou hast sent me.*

26. *And I have declared unto them thy name, and will declare it: that the love wherewith thou hast loved me may be in them, and I in them.*

Old Testament

Abraham's Intercession for Sodom & Gomorrah Genesis 18:23-33

23. *And Abraham drew near, and said, Wilt thou also destroy the righteous with the wicked?*

24. *Peradventure there be fifty righteous within the city: wilt thou also destroy and not spare the place for the fifty righteous that are therein?*

25. *That be far from thee to do after this manner, to slay the righteous with the wicked: and that the righteous should be as the wicked that be far from thee: Shall not the Judge of all the earth do right?*

26. *And the LORD said, If I find in Sodom fifty righteous within the city, then I will spare all the place for their sakes.*

27. *and Abraham answered and said, Behold now, I have taken upon me to speak unto the LORD, which am but dust and ashes:*

28. *Peradventure there shall lack five of the fifty righteous: wilt thou destroy all the city for lack of five? And he said, If I find there forty and five, I will not destroy it.*

29. *and he spake unto him yet again, and said, Peradventure there shall be forty found there. And he said I will not do it for forty's sake.*

30. *And he said unto him, Oh let not the LORD be angry, and I will speak: Peradventure there shall thirty be found there. And he said I will not do it if I find thirty there.*

31 *, Behold now, I have taken upon me to speak unto the LORD: Peradventure there shall be twenty found there. And he said I will not destroy it for twenty's sake.*

32 *And he said, Oh let not the LORD be angry, and I will speak yet but this once: Peradventure ten shall be found there. And he said I will not destroy it for ten's sake.*

33 *And the LORD went his way, as soon as he had left communing with Abraham: and Abraham returned unto his place.*

Daniel's Prayer Daniel 9:4-19

4 *And I prayed unto the LORD my God, and made my confession, and said, O Lord, the great and dreadful God, keeping the covenant and mercy to them that love him, and to them that keep his commandments;*

5 *We have sinned, and have committed iniquity, and have done wickedly, and have rebelled, even by departing from thy precepts and from thy judgments:*

6 *Neither have we hearkened unto thy servants the prophets, which spake in thy name to our kings, our princes, and our fathers, and to all the people of the*

land.

7   *O LORD, righteousness belongeth unto thee, but unto us confusion of faces, as at this day; to the men of Judah, and to the inhabitants of Jerusalem, and unto all Israel, that are near, and that are far off, through all the countries whither thou hast driven them, because of their trespass that they have trespassed against thee.*

8   *O Lord, to us belongeth confusion of face, to our kings, to our princes, and to our fathers,*

9   *To the Lord our God belong mercies and forgiveness, though we have rebelled against him;*

10   *Neither have we obeyed the voice of the LORD our God, to walk in his laws, which he set before us by his servants the prophets.*

11   *Yea, all Israel have transgressed thy law, even by departing, that they might not obey thy voice; therefore the curse is poured upon us, and the oath that is written in the law of Moses the servant of God because we have sinned against him.*

12   *And he hath confirmed his words, which he spake against us, and against our judges that judged us, by bringing upon us a great evil: for under the whole heaven hath not been done as hath been done upon Jerusalem.*

13   *As it is written in the law of Moses, all this evil is come upon us: yet made we not prayer before the LORD our God, that we might turn from our iniquities, and understand thy truth.*

14   *Therefore hath the LORD watched upon the evil and brought it upon us: for the LORD our God is righteous in all his works which he doeth: for we obeyed not his voice.*

15   *And now, O Lord our God, that hast brought thy people forth out of the land of Egypt with a mighty hand, and hast gotten thee renown, as at this day; we have sinned, we have done wickedly.*

16   *O LORD, according to all thy righteousness, I beseech thee, let thine anger and thy fury be turned away from thy city Jerusalem, thy holy mountain: because for our sins, and for the iniquities of our fathers, Jerusalem and thy people are become a reproach to all that are about us.*

17   *Now, therefore, O our God, hear the prayer of thy servant, and his supplications, and cause thy face to shine upon thy sanctuary that is desolate, for the Lord's sake.*

18   *O my God, incline thine ear, and hear; open thine eyes, and behold our desolations, and the city which is called by thy name: for we do not present our supplications before thee for our righteousnesses, but for thy great mercies.*

19   *O Lord, hear; O Lord, forgive; O Lord, hearken and do; defer not, for thine own sake, O my God: for thy city and thy people are called by thy name.*

David's Prayer for Protection Psalm 3

3   *But thou, O LORD, art a shield for me; my glory, and the lifter up of mine head.*

4   *I cried unto the LORD with my voice, and he heard me out of his holy hill. Selah.*

5   *I laid me down and slept; I awaked; for the LORD sustained me.*

6   *I will not be afraid of ten thousand of people, that have set themselves against*

me round about.

7   *Arise, O LORD; save me, O my God: for thou hast smitten all mine enemies upon the cheek bone; thou hast broken the teeth of the ungodly.*

8   *Salvation belongeth unto the LORD: thy blessing is upon thy people. Selah.*

David's Prayer for Favor Psalm 4
David's Prayer for Guidance Psalm 5

1   *Give ear to my words, O LORD, consider my meditation.*

2   *Hearken unto the voice of my cry, my King, and my God: for unto thee will I pray.*

3   *My voice shalt thou hear in the morning, O LORD; in the morning will I direct my prayer unto thee, and will look up.*

4   *For thou art, not a God that hath pleasure in wickedness: neither shall evil dwell with thee.*

5   *The foolish shall not stand in thy sight: thou hatest all workers of iniquity.*

6   *Thou shalt destroy them that speak leasing: the LORD will abhor the bloody and deceitful man.*

7.   *me, I will come into thy house in the multitude of thy mercy: and in thy fear will I worship toward thy holy temple.*

8   *Lead me, O LORD, in thy righteousness because of mine enemies; make thy way straight before my face.*

9   *For there is no faithfulness in their mouth; their inward part is very wickedness; their throat is an open sepulcher; they flatter with their tongue.*

10   *Destroy thou them, O God; let them fall by their own counsels; cast them out in the multitude of their transgressions; for they have rebelled against thee.*

11   *But let all those that put their trust in thee rejoice: let them ever shout for joy, because thou defendest them: let them also that love thy name be joyful in thee.*

12   *For thou, LORD, wilt bless the righteous; with favor wilt thou compass him as with a shield.*

David's Prayer for Mercy Psalm 6

1   *O LORD, rebuke me not in thine anger, neither chasten me in thy hot displeasure.*

2   *Have mercy upon me, O LORD; for I am weak: O LORD, heal me; for my bones are vexed.*

3   *My soul is also sore vexed: but thou, O LORD, how long?*

4   *LORD, deliver my soul: oh save me for thy mercies' sake.*

5   *For in death there is no remembrance of thee: in the grave who shall give thee thanks?*

6   *I am weary with my groaning; all the night make I my bed to swim; I water my couch with my tears.*

7   *Mine eye is consumed because of grief; it waxeth old because of all mine enemies.*

8   *Depart from me, all ye workers of iniquity; for the LORD hath heard the voice of*

my weeping.

9   *The LORD hath heard my supplication; the LORD will receive my prayer.*

10   *Let all mine enemies be ashamed and sore vexed: let them return and be ashamed suddenly.*

David's Prayer from Persecution Psalm 7

1   *O LORD my God, in thee do I put my trust: save me from all them that persecute me, and deliver me:*

2   *Lest he tear my soul like a lion, rending it in pieces, while there is none to deliver.*

3   *O LORD my God, If I have done this; if there be iniquity in my hands;*

4   *If I have rewarded evil unto him that was at peace with me; (yea, I have delivered him that without cause is mine enemy :)*

5   *Let the enemy persecute my soul, and take it; yea, let him tread down my life upon the earth, and lay mine honor in the dust. Selah.*

6   *Arise, O LORD, in thine anger, lift up thyself because of the rage of mine enemies: and awake for me to the judgment that thou hast commanded.*

7   *So shall the congregation of the people compass thee about for their sakes, turn thou on high?*

8   *The LORD shall judge the people: judge me, O LORD, according to my righteousness, and according to mine integrity that is in me.*

9   *Oh let the wickedness of the wicked come to an end; but establish the just: for the righteous God trieth the hearts and reins.*

10   *My defense is of God, which saveth the upright in heart.*

11   *God judgeth the righteous, and God is angry with the wicked every day.*

12   *If he turn not, he will whet his sword; he hath bent his bow and made it ready.*

13   *He hath also prepared for him the instruments of death; he ordaineth his arrowsagainst the persecutors.*

14   *Behold, he travaileth with iniquity, and hath conceived mischief, and brought forthfalsehood.*

15   *He made a pit, and digged it, and is fallen into the ditch which he made.*

16   *His mischief shall return upon his own head, and his violent dealing shall come down ate.*

17   *I will praise the LORD according to his righteousness: and will sing praise to the name of the LORD most high.*

David's Prayer for God's Help Psalm 13

1   *How long wilt thou forget me, O LORD? Forever? How long wilt thou hide thy face from me?*

2   *How long shall I take counsel in my soul, having sorrow in my heart daily? How long shall mine enemy be exalted over me?*

3   *Consider and hear me, O LORD my God: lighten mine eyes, lest I sleep the sleep of death;*

4   *Lest mine enemy say, I have prevailed against him; and those that trouble me rejoice when I am moved.*

5   *But I have trusted in thy mercy; my heart shall rejoice in thy salvation.*

6   I will sing unto the LORD because he hath dealt bountifully with me.

David's Prayer Psalm 23

1   The LORD is my shepherd; I shall not want.

2   He maketh me to lie down in green pastures: he leadeth me beside the still waters.

3   He restoreth my soul: he leadeth me in the paths of righteousness for his name's sake.

4   Yea, though I walk through the valley of the shadow of death, I will fear no evil: for thou art with me; thy rod and thy staff they comfort me.

5   Thou preparest a table before me in the presence of mine enemies: thou anointest my head with oil; my cup runneth over.

6   Surely goodness and mercy shall follow me all the days of my life: and I will dwell in the house of the LORD forever.

David's Prayer for Trust Psalm 25

1   Unto thee, O LORD, do I lift up my soul?

2   O my God, I trust in thee: let me not be ashamed, let not mine enemies triumph over me.

3   Yea, let none that wait on thee be ashamed: let them be ashamed which transgress without cause.

4   Shew me thy ways, O LORD; teach me thy paths.

5   Lead me in thy truth, and teach me: for thou art the God of my salvation; on thee do I wait all the day.

6   Remember, O LORD, thy tender mercies and thy loving kindnesses; for they have been ever of old.

7   Remember not the sins of my youth, nor my transgressions: according to thy mercy remember thou me for thy goodness' sake, O LORD.

8   Good and upright is the LORD: therefore will he teach sinners in the way.

9   The meek will he guide in judgment: and the meek will he teach his way.

10   All the paths of the LORD are mercy and truth unto such as keep his covenant and his testimonies.

11   For thy name's sake, O LORD, pardon mine iniquity; for it is great.

12   What man is he that feareth the LORD? Him shall he teach in the way that he shall choose.

13   His soul shall dwell at ease, and his seed shall inherit the earth.

14   The secret of the LORD is with them that fear him, and he will shew them his covenant.

15   Mine eyes are ever toward the LORD; for he shall pluck my feet out of the net.

16   Turn thee unto me, and have mercy upon me; for I am desolate and afflicted.

17   The troubles of my heart are enlarged: O bring thou me out of my distresses.

18   Look upon mine affliction and my pain, and forgive all my sins.

19   Consider mine enemies; for they are many, and they hate me with cruel hatred.

20   O keep my soul, and deliver me: let me not be ashamed; for I put my trust in thee.

21   Let integrity and uprightness preserve me; for I wait on thee.

22   Redeem Israel, O God, out of all his troubles.

David's Prayer & Fasting Psalm 35 Against enemies

1   Plead my cause, O LORD, with them that strive with me: fight against them that

fight against me.

2   *Take hold of shield and buckler, and stand up for mine help.*

3   *Draw out also the spear, and stop the way against them that persecute me: say unto my soul, I am thy salvation.*

4   *Let them be confounded and put to shame that seek after my soul: let them be turned back and brought to confusion that devise my hurt.*

5   *Let them be as chaff before the wind: and let the Angel of the LORD chase them.*

6   *Let their way be dark and slippery: and let the Angel of the LORD persecute them.*

7   *For without cause have they hid for me their net in a pit, which without cause they have digged for my soul.*

8   *Let destruction come upon him at unawares; and let his net that he hath hid catch himself: into that very destruction let him fall.*

9   *And my soul shall be joyful in the LORD: it shall rejoice in his salvation.*

10   *All my bones shall say, LORD, who is like unto thee, which deliverest the poor from him that is too strong for him, yea, the poor and the needy from him that spoileth him?*

11   *False witnesses did rise up; they laid to my charge things that I knew not.*

12   *They rewarded me evil for good to the spoiling of my soul.*

13   *But as for me, when they were sick, my clothing was sackcloth: I humbled my soul with fasting, and my prayer returned into mine own bosom.*

14   *I behaved myself as though he had been my friend or brother: I bowed down heavily, as one that mourneth for his mother.*

15   *But in mine adversity they rejoiced, and gathered themselves together: yea, the abjects gathered themselves together against me, and I knew it not; they did tear me, and ceased not:*

16   *With hypocritical mockers in feasts, they gnashed upon me with their teeth.*

17   *Lord, how long wilt thou look on? Rescue my soul from their destructions, my darling from the lions.*

18   *I will give thee thanks in the great congregation: I will praise thee among much people.*

19   *Let not them that are mine enemies wrongfully rejoice over me: neither let them wink with the eye that hate me without a cause.*

20   *For they speak not peace: but they devise deceitful matters against them that are quiet in the land.*

21   *Yea, they opened their mouth wide against me, and said, aha, aha, our eye hath seen it.*

22   *This thou hast seen, O LORD: keep not silence: O Lord, be not far from me.*

23   *Stir up thyself, and awake to my judgment, even unto my cause, my God and my Lord.*

24   *Judge me, O LORD my God, according to thy righteousness; and let them not rejoice over me.*

25   *Let them not say in their hearts, Ah, so would we have it: let them not say, We have swallowed him up.*

26   *Let them be ashamed and brought to confusion together that rejoice at mine hurt: let them be clothed with shame and dishonor that magnify themselves against me.*

27   *Let them shout for joy, and be glad, that favor my righteous cause: yea, let them say continually, Let the LORD be magnified, which hath pleasure in the prosperity of his servant.*

28   *And my tongue shall speak of thy righteousness and of thy praise all the day long.*

David's Prayer for Forgiveness Psalm 51

1   *Have mercy upon me, O God, according to thy lovingkindness: according unto the multitude of thy tender mercies blot out my transgressions.*

2   *Wash me thoroughly from mine iniquity, and cleanse me from my sin.*

3   *For I acknowledge my transgressions: and my sin is ever before me.*

4   *Against thee, thee only, have I sinned, and done this evil in thy sight: that thou lightest be justified when thou speakest and be clear when thou judgest.*

5   *Behold, I was shapen in iniquity; and in sin did my mother conceive me.*

6   *Behold, thou desirest truth in the inward parts: and in the hidden part thou shalt make me to know wisdom.*

7   *Purge me with hyssop, and I shall be clean: wash me, and I shall be whiter than snow.*

8   *Make me to hear joy and gladness; that the bones which thou hast broken may rejoice.*

9   *Hide thy face from my sins, and blot out all mine iniquities.*

10   *Create in me a clean heart, O God; and renew a right spirit within me.*

11   *Cast me not away from thy presence, and take not thy holy spirit from me.*

12   *Restore unto me the joy of thy salvation, and uphold me with thy free spirit.*

13   *Then will I teach transgressors thy ways; and sinners shall be converted unto thee.*

14   *Deliver me from bloodguiltiness, O God, thou God of my salvation: and my tongue shall sing aloud of thy righteousness.*

15   *O Lord, open thou my lips; and my mouth shall shew forth thy praise.*

16   *For thou desirest not sacrifice; else would I give it: thou delightest not in burnt offering.*

17   *The sacrifices of God are a broken spirit: a broken and a contrite heart, O God, thou wilt not despise.*

18   *Do good in thy good pleasure unto Zion: build thou the walls of Jerusalem.*

19   *Then shalt thou be pleased with the sacrifices of righteousness, with burnt offering and whole burnt offering: then shall they offer bullocks upon thine altar.*

Elijah's Prayer for the Widow's Son 1 Kings 17:20-22

20   *And he cried unto the LORD, and said, O LORD my God, hast thou also brought evil upon the widow with whom I sojourn, by slaying her son?*

21   *And he stretched himself upon the child three times, and cried unto the LORD, and said, O LORD my God, I pray thee, let this child's soul come into him again*

22   *And the LORD heard the voice of Elijah, and the soul of the child came into him again, and he revived*

Elijah's Prayer at Mt. Carmel 1 Kings 18:36-39

36   *And it came to pass at the time of the offering of the evening sacrifice, that Elijah the prophet came near, and said, LORD God of Abraham, Isaac, and of Israel, let it be known this day that thou art God in Israel, and that I am thy servant, and that I have*

done all these things at thy word.

37   *Hear me, O LORD, hear me, that this people may know that thou art the LORD God, and that thou hast turned their heart back again.*

38   *Then the fire of the LORD fell and consumed the burnt sacrifice, and the trench.*

39   *And when all the people saw it, they fell on their faces: and they said, The LORD, he is the God; the LORD, he is the God.*

Elisha's Prayer 2 Kings 6:15-18

15   *And when the servant of the man of God was risen early, and gone forth, behold, an host compassed the city both with horses and chariots. And his servant said unto him, Alas, my master! how shall we do?*

16   *And he answered, Fear not: for they that be with us are more than they that be with them.*

17   *And Elisha prayed, and said, LORD, I pray thee, open his eyes, that he may see. And the LORD opened the eyes of the young man; and he saw: and, behold, the mountain was full of horses and chariots of fire round about Elisha.*

18   *And when they came down to him, Elisha prayed unto the LORD, and said, Smite this people, I pray thee, with blindness. And he smote them with blindness according to the word of Elisha.*

Esther and the Nation of Israel Prayer & Fasting Esther 4 & 5

1   *When Mordecai perceived all that was done, Mordecai rent his clothes, and put on sackcloth with ashes, and went out into the midst of the city, and cried with a loud and a bitter cry;*

2   *And came even before the king's gate: for none might enter into the king's gate clothed with sackcloth.*

3   *And in every province, whithersoever the king's commandment and his decree came, there was great mourning among the Jews, and fasting, and weeping, and wailing; and many lay in sackcloth and ashes.*

4   *So Esther's maids and her chamberlains came and told it her. Then was the queen exceedingly grieved, and she sent raiment to clothe Mordecai,and to take away his sackcloth from him: but he received it not.*

5   *Then called Esther for Hatach, one of the king's chamberlains, whom he had appointed to attend upon her, and gave him a commandment to Mordecai, to know what it was, and why it was.*

6   *So Hatach went forth to Mordecai unto the street of the city, which was before the king's gate.*

7   *And Mordecai told him of all that had happened unto him, and of the sum of the money that Haman had promised to pay to the king's treasuries for the Jews, to destroy them.*

8   *Also he gave him the copy of the writing of the decree that was given at Shushan to destroy them, to shew it unto Esther, and to declare it unto her, and to charge her that she should go in unto the king, to make supplication unto him, and to make request before him for her people.*

9   *And Hatach came and told Esther the words of Mordecai.*

10   *Again Esther spake unto Hatach, and gave him commandment unto Mordecai;*

11   *All the king's servants, and the people of the king's provinces, do know, that*

whosoever, whether man or women, shall come unto the king into the inner court, who is not called, there is one law of his to put him to death, except such to whom the king shall hold out the golden scepter, that he may live: but I have not been called to come in unto the king these thirty days.

12   And they told to Mordecai Esther's words.

13   Then Mordecai commanded to answer Esther, Think not with thyself that thou shalt escape in the king's house, more than all the Jews.

14   For if thou altogether holdest thy peace at this time, then shall there enlargement and deliverance arise to the Jews from another place; but thou and thy father's house shall be destroyed: and who knoweth whether thou art come to the kingdom for such a time as this?

15   Then Esther bade them return Mordecai this answer,

16   Go, gather together all the Jews that are present in Shushan, and fast ye for me, and neither eat nor drink three days, night or day: I also and my maidens will fast likewise; and so will I go in unto the king, which is not according to the law: and if I perish, I perish.

17   So Mordecai went his way and did according to all that Esther had commanded him.

Esther 5

1   Now it came to pass on the third day, that Esther put on her royal apparel, and stood in the inner court of the king's house, over against the king's house: and the king sat upon his royal throne in the royal house, over against the gate of the house.

2   And it was so, when the king saw Esther the queen standing in the court, that she obtained favor in his sight: and the king held out to Esther the golden scepter that was in his hand. So Esther drew near and touched the top of the scepter.

3   Then said the king unto her, What wilt thou, queen Esther? and what is thy request? it shall be even given thee to the half of the kingdom.

4   And Esther answered, If it seem good unto the king, let the king and Haman come this day unto the banquet that I have prepared for him.

5   Then the king said, Cause Haman to make haste, that he may do as Esther hath said. So the king and Haman came to the banquet that Esther had prepared.

6   And the king said unto Esther at the banquet of wine, What is thy petition? and it shall be granted thee: and what is thy request? even to the half of the kingdom, it shall be performed.

7   Then answered Esther, and said, My petition and my request is;

8   If I have found favor in the sight of the king, and if it please the king to grant my petition, and to perform my request, let the king and Haman come to the banquet that I shall prepare for them, and I will do tomorrow as the king hath said.

9   Then went Haman forth that day joyful and with a glad heart: but when Haman saw Mordecai in the king's gate, that he stood not up, nor moved for him, he was full of indignation against Mordecai.

10   Nevertheless, Haman refrained himself: and when he came home, he sent and called for his friends, and Zeresh, his wife.

11   And Haman told them of the glory of his riches, and the multitude of his children, and all the things wherein the king had promoted him, and how he

had advanced him above the princes and servants of the king.

12 *Haman said moreover, Yea, Esther the queen did let no man come in with the king unto the banquet that she had prepared but myself; and tomorrow am I invited unto her also with the king.*

13 *Yet all this availeth me nothing, so long as I see Mordecai the Jew sitting at the king's gate.*

14 *Then said Zeresh his wife and all his friends unto him, Let a gallows be made of fifty cubits high, and to morrow speak thou unto the king that Mordecai may be hanged thereon: then go thou in merrily with the king unto the banquet. And the thing pleased Haman, and he caused the gallows to be made.*

Ezra Prayer & Fasting 8:21-23

20 *Also of the Nethinims, whom David and the princes had appointed for the service of the Levites, two hundred and twenty Nethinims: all of them were expressed by name.*

21 *Then I proclaimed a fast there, at the river of Ahava, that we might afflict ourselves before our God, to seek of him a right way for us, and for our little ones, and for all our substance.*

22 *For I was ashamed to require of the king a band of soldiers and horsemen to help us against the enemy in the way: because we had spoken unto the king, saying, The hand of our God is upon all them for good that seek him, but his power and his wrath is against all them that forsake him.*

23 *So we fasted and besought our God for this: and he was entreated of us.*

Hannah's Prayer for a Child 1 Samuel 1:10-12

10 *And she was in bitterness of soul, and prayed unto the LORD, and wept sore.*

11 *And she vowed a vow, and said, O LORD of hosts, if thou wilt indeed look on the affliction of thine handmaid, and remember me, and not forget thine handmaid, but wilt give unto thine handmaid a man child, then I will give him unto the LORD all the days of his life, and there shall no razor come upon his head.*

12 *And it came to pass, as she continued praying before the LORD, that Eli marked her mouth.*

Hannah's Prayer of Thanksgiving 1 Samuel 2:1-10

1 *And Hannah prayed, and said; My heart rejoiceth in the LORD, mine horn is exalted in the LORD: my mouth is enlarged over mine enemies; because I rejoice in thy salvation.*

2 *There is none holy as the LORD: for there is none beside thee: neither is there any rock like our God.*

3 *exceeding proudly; let not arrogancy come out of your mouth: for the LORD is a God of knowledge, and by him, actions are weighed.*

4 *The bows of the mighty men are broken, and they that stumbled are girded with strength.*

5 *They that were full have hired out themselves for bread; and they that were hungry*

ceased: so that the barren hath born seven; and she that hath many children is waxed feeble.

6   The LORD killeth, and maketh alive: he bringeth down to the grave and bringeth up.

7   The LORD maketh poor, and maketh rich: he bringeth low, and lifteth up.

8   He raiseth up the poor out of the dust, and lifteth up the beggar from the dunghill, to set them among princes, and to make them inherit the throne of glory: for the pillars of the earth are the LORD's, and he hath set the world upon them

9   He will keep the feet of his saints, and the wicked shall be silent in darkness; for by strength shall no man prevail.

10   The adversaries of the LORD shall be broken to pieces; out of heaven shall he thunder upon them: the LORD shall judge the ends of the earth, and he shall give strength unto his king, and exalt the horn of his anointed.

Hezekiah 2 Kings 20

2 Kings 20: 1   In those days was Hezekiah sick unto death. And the prophet Isaiah the son of Amoz came to him, and said unto him, Thus saith the LORD, Set thine house in order; for thou shalt die, and not live.

2   Then he turned his face to the wall, and prayed unto the LORD, saying,

3   I beseech thee, O LORD, remember now how I have walked before thee in truth and with a perfect heart, and have done that which is good in thy sight. And Hezekiah wept sore.

4   And it came to pass, afore Isaiah was gone out into the middle court, that the word of the LORD came to him, saying,

5   Turn again, and tell Hezekiah the captain of my people, Thus saith the LORD, the God of David thy father, I have heard thy prayer, I have seen thy tears: behold, I will heal thee: on the third day thou shalt go up unto the house of the LORD.

6   And I will add unto thy days fifteen years, and I will deliver thee and this city out of the hand of the king of Assyria, and I will defend this city for mine own sake, and for my servant David's sake.

7   And Isaiah said, Take a lump of figs. And they took and laid it on the boil, and he recovered.

8   And Hezekiah said unto Isaiah, What shall be the sign that the LORD will heal me, and that I shall go up into the house of the LORD the third day?

9   And Isaiah said, This sign shalt thou have of the LORD, that the LORD will do the thing that he hath spoken: shall the shadow go forward ten degrees, or go back ten degrees?

10   And Hezekiah answered, It is a light thing for the shadow to go down ten degrees: nay, but let the shadow return backward ten degrees.

11   And Isaiah the prophet cried unto the LORD: and he brought the shadow ten degrees backward, by which it had gone down in the dial of Ahaz.

12   At that time Berodachbaladan, the son of Baladan, king of Babylon, sent

letters and a present unto Hezekiah: for he had heard that Hezekiah had been sick.

13   *And Hezekiah hearkened unto them, and showed them all the house of his precious things, the silver, and the gold, and the spices, and the precious ointment, and all the house of his armor, and all that was found in his treasures: there was nothing in his house, nor in all his dominion, that Hezekiah showed them not.*

14   *Then came Isaiah the prophet unto king Hezekiah, and said unto him, What said these men? and from whence came they unto thee? And Hezekiah said, They are come from a far country, even from Babylon.*

15   *And he said, What have they seen in thine house? And Hezekiah answered, All the things that are in mine house have they seen: there is nothing among my treasures that I have not showed them.*

16   *And Isaiah said unto Hezekiah, Hear the word of the LORD.*

17   *Behold, the days come, that all that is in thine house, and that which thy fathers have laid up in store unto this day, shall be carried into Babylon: nothing shall be left, saith the LORD.*

18   *And of thy sons that shall issue from thee, which thou shalt beget, shall they take away; and they shall be eunuchs in the palace of the king of Babylon.*

19   *Then said Hezekiah unto Isaiah, Good is the word of the LORD which thou hast spoken. And he said, Is it not good if peace and truth be in my days?*

20   *And the rest of the acts of Hezekiah, and all his might, and how he made a pool, and a conduit, and brought water into the city, are they not written in the book of the chronicles of the kings of Judah?*

21   *And Hezekiah slept with his fathers: and Manasseh, his son, reigned in his stead.*

Jacob's Deliverance From Essau Genesis 32:9-12

9   *And Jacob said, O God of my father Abraham, and God of my father Isaac, the LORD which saidst unto me, Return unto thy country, and to thy kindred, and I will deal well with thee:*

10   *I am not worthy of the least of all the mercies, and of all the truth, which thou hast showed unto thy servant; for with my staff I passed over this Jordan, and now I am become, two bands.*

11   *Deliver me, I pray thee, from the hand of my brother, from the hand of Esau: for I fear him, lest he will come and smite me, and the mother with the children.*

12   *And thou saidst, I will surely do thee good, and make thy seed as the sand of the sea, which cannot be numbered for multitude.*

Jacob At Peniel Genesis 32:24-30

24   *And Jacob was left alone, and there wrestled a man with him until the breaking of the day.*

25   *And when he saw that he prevailed not against him, he touched the hollow of his thigh; and the hollow of Jacob's thigh was out of joint, as he wrestled with him.*

26   *And he said, Let me go, for the day breaketh. And he said I will not let thee go, except thou bless me.*

27   And he said unto him, What is thy name? And he said, Jacob.

28   And he said, Thy name shall be called no more Jacob, but Israel: for as a prince hast thou power with God and with men, and hast prevailed.

29   And Jacob asked him, and said, Tell me, I pray thee, thy name. And he said, Wherefore is it that thou dost ask after my name? And he blessed him there.

30   And Jacob called the name of the place Peniel: for I have seen God face to face and my life is preserved.

Jehoshaphat for Deliverance 2 Chronicles 20

1   Chronicles 20:

1   It came to pass after this also, that the children of Moab, and the children of Ammon, and with them other beside the Ammonites, came against Jehoshaphat to battle.

2   Then there came some that told Jehoshaphat, saying, There cometh a great multitude against thee from beyond the sea on this side Syria; and, behold, they be in Hazazontamar, which is Engedi.

3   And Jehoshaphat feared, and set himself to seek the LORD, and proclaimed a fast throughout all Judah

4   And Judah gathered themselves together, to ask help of the LORD: even out of all the cities of Judah they came to seek the LORD.

5   And Jehoshaphat stood in the congregation of Judah and Jerusalem, in the house of the LORD, before the new court,

6   And said, O LORD God of our fathers, art not thou God in heaven? and rulest not thou over all the kingdoms of the heathen? And in thine hand is there not power and might, so that none is able to withstand thee?

7   Art, not thou our God, who didst drive out the inhabitants of this land before thy people Israel, and gavest it to the seed of Abraham, thy friend forever?
And they dwelt therein, and have built thee a sanctuary therein for thy name, saying,

9   If, when evil cometh upon us, as the sword, judgment, or pestilence, or famine, we stand before this house, and in thy presence, (for thy name is in this house,) and cry unto thee in our affliction, then thou wilt hear and help.

10   And now, behold, the children of Ammon and Moab and mount Seir, whom thou wouldest not let Israel invade when they came out of the land of Egypt, but they turned from them and destroyed them not;

11   Behold, I say, how they reward us, to come to cast us out of thy possession, which thou hast given us to inherit.

12   O our God, wilt thou not judge them? for we have no might against this great company that cometh against us; neither know we what to do: but our eyes are upon thee.

13   And all Judah stood before the LORD, with their little ones, their wives, and their children.

14   Then upon Jahaziel the son of Zechariah, the son of Benaiah, the son of Jeiel, the son of Mattaniah, a Levite of the sons of Asaph, came the Spirit of the LORD in the midst of the congregation;

15   And he said, Hearken ye, all Judah, and ye inhabitants of Jerusalem, and thou

king Jehoshaphat, Thus saith the LORD unto you, Be not afraid nor dismayed by reason of this great multitude; for the battle is not yours, but God's.

16   *Tomorrow go ye down against them: behold, they come up by the cliff of Ziz; and ye shall find them at the end of the brook, before the wilderness of Jeruel.*

17   *Ye shall not need to fight in this battle: set yourselves, stand ye still, and see the salvation of the LORD with you, O Judah and Jerusalem: fear not, nor be dismayed; tomorrow go out against them: for the LORD will be with you.*

18   *And Jehoshaphat bowed his head with his face to the ground: and all Judah and the inhabitants of Jerusalem fell before the LORD, worshipping the LORD.*

19   *And the Levites, of the children of the Kohathites, and of the children of the Korhites, stood up to praise the LORD God of Israel with a loud voice on high.*

20   *And they rose early in the morning, and went forth into the wilderness of Tekoa: and as they went forth, Jehoshaphat stood and said, Hear me, O Judah, and ye inhabitants of Jerusalem; Believe in the LORD your God, so shall ye be established; believe his prophets, so shall ye prosper.*

21   *And when he had consulted with the people, he appointed singers unto the LORD, and that should praise the beauty of holiness, as they went out before the army, and to say, Praise the LORD; for his mercy endureth forever.*

22   *And when they began to sing and to praise, the LORD set ambushments against the children of Ammon, Moab, and mount Seir, which were come against Judah; and they were smitten.*

23   *For the children of Ammon and Moab stood up against the inhabitants of mount Seir, utterly to slay and destroy them: and when they had made an end of the inhabitants of Seir, every one helped to destroy another.*

24   *And when Judah came toward the watch tower in the wilderness, they looked unto the multitude, and, behold, they were dead bodies fallen to the earth, and none escaped.*

25   *And when Jehoshaphat and his people came to take away the spoil of them, they found among them in abundance both riches with the dead bodies, and precious jewels, which they stripped off for themselves, more than they could carry away: and they were three days in gathering of the spoil, it was so much.*

26   *And on the fourth day they assembled themselves in the valley of Berachah; for there they blessed the LORD: therefore the name of the same place was called, The valley of Berachah, unto this day*

27   *Then they returned, every man of Judah and Jerusalem, and Jehoshaphat in the forefront of them, to go again to Jerusalem with joy; for the LORD had made them to rejoice over their enemies.*

28   *And they came to Jerusalem with psalteries and harps and trumpets unto the house of the LORD.*

29   *And the fear of God was on all the kingdoms of those countries when they had heard that the LORD fought against the enemies of Israel.*

30   *So the realm of Jehoshaphat was quiet: for his God gave him rest round about.*

31   *And Jehoshaphat reigned over Judah: he was thirty and five years old when he began to reign, and he reigned twenty and five years in Jerusalem. And his mother's name was Azubah, the daughter of Shilhi*

32   And he walked in the way of Asa, his father, and departed not from it, doing that which was right in the sight of the LORD.

33   Howbeit the high places were not taken away: for as yet the people had not prepared their hearts unto the God of their fathers.

34   Now the rest of the acts of Jehoshaphat, first and last, behold, they are written in the book of Jehu, the son of Hanani, who is mentioned in the book of the kings of Israel.

35   And after this did Jehoshaphat king of Judah join himself with Ahaziah king of Israel, who did very wickedly:

36   And he joined himself with him to make ships to go to Tarshish: and they made the ships in Eziongaber.

37   Then Eliezer the son of Dodavah of Mareshah prophesied against Jehoshaphat, saying, because thou hast joined thyself with Ahaziah, the LORD hath broken thy works. And the ships were broken, that they were not able to go to Tarshish.

Jonah 2:2-9

Jonah 2:1 Then Jonah prayed unto the LORD his God out of the fish's belly,

2   And said, I cried by reason of mine affliction unto the LORD, and he heard me; out of the belly of hell cried I, and thou heardest my voice.

3   For thou hadst cast me into the deep, in the midst of the seas; and the floods compassed me about: all thy billows and thy waves passed over me.

4   Then I said, I am cast out of thy sight, yet I will look again toward thy holy temple.

5   The waters compassed me about, even to the soul: the depth closed me round about; the weeds were wrapped about my head.

6   I went down to the bottoms of the mountains; the earth with her bars was about me forever: yet hast thou brought up my life from corruption, O LORD my God.

7   When my soul fainted within me I remembered the LORD: and my prayer came in unto thee, into thine holy temple.

8   They that observe lying vanities forsake their own mercy.

9   But I will sacrifice unto thee with the voice of thanksgiving; I will pay that I have vowed. Salvation is of the LORD.

10   And the LORD spake unto the fish, and it vomited out Jonah upon the dry land.

Moses Intercession for His People Exodus 32:11-13 32:31-32

11   And Moses besought the LORD his God, and said, LORD, why doth thy wrath wax hot against thy people, which thou hast brought forth out of the land of Egypt with great power, and with a mighty hand?

12   Wherefore should the Egyptians speak, and say, for mischief did he bring them out, to slay them in the mountains, and to consume them from the face of the earth? Turn from thy fierce wrath, and repent of this evil against thy people.

13   Remember Abraham, Isaac, and Israel, thy servants, to whom thou swarest by thine own self, and saidst unto them, I will multiply your seed as the stars of heaven, and all this land that I have spoken of will I give unto your seed, and they shall inherit it forever.

31   And Moses returned unto the LORD, and said, oh, this people have sinned a great sin, and have

made them gods of gold.

32 *Yet now, if thou wilt forgive their sin--; and if not, blot me, I pray thee, out of thy book which thou hast written.*

33 *And the LORD said unto Moses, Whosoever hath sinned against me, him will I blot out of my book.*

Moses Intercession for Miriam Numbers 12:13

14 *And the LORD said unto Moses, if her father had but spit in her face, should she not be ashamed seven days? Let her be shut out from the camp seven days, and after that let her be received in again.*

15 *And Miriam was shut out from the camp seven days: and the people journeyed not till Miriam was brought in again.*

Moses and the Lord Exodus 33:12-13, 33:15, 16

12 *And Moses said unto the LORD, See, thou sayest unto me, Bring up this people: and thou hast not let me know whom thou wilt send with me. Yet thou hast said, I know thee by name, and thou hast also found grace in my sight.*

13 *Now, therefore, I pray thee, if I have found grace in thy sight, show me now thy way that I may know thee, that I may find grace in thy sight: and consider that this nation is thy people.*

14 *And he said, my presence shall go with thee, and I will give thee rest.*

15 *And he said unto him; If thy presence go not with me, carry us not up hence.*

16 *For wherein shall it be known here that I and thy people have found grace in thy sight? is it not in that thou goest with us? So shall we be separated, I and thy people, from all the people that are upon the face of the earth?*

17 *And the LORD said unto Moses; I will do this thing also that thou hast spoken: for thou hast found grace in my sight, and I know thee by name.*

18 *And he said, I beseech thee, show me thy glory.*

19 *And he said, I will make all my goodness pass before thee, and I will proclaim the name of the LORD before thee; and will be gracious to whom I will be gracious, and will show mercy on whom I will show mercy.*

Moses' 40 Day Prayer Deuteronomy 9:18-20; 9:25-29

18 *And I fell down before the LORD, as at the first, forty days and forty nights: I did neither eat bread nor drink water, because of all your sins which ye sinned, in doing wickedly in the sight of the LORD, to provoke him to anger.*

19 *For I was afraid of the anger, and hot displeasure, wherewith the LORD was wroth against you to destroy you. But the LORD hearkened unto me at that time also.*

20 *And the LORD was very angry with Aaron to have destroyed him: and I prayed for Aaron also the same time.*

21 *And I took your sin, the calf which ye had made, and burnt it with fire, and stamped it, and ground it very small, even until it was as small as dust: and I cast the dust thereof into the brook that descended out of the mount.*

22 *And at Taberah, and at Massah, and at Kibrothhattaavah, ye provoked the LORD to wrath.*

23 *Likewise when the LORD sent you from Kadeshbarnea, saying, Go up and possess the land which I have given you; then ye rebelled against the*

commandment of the LORD your God and ye believed him not, nor hearkened to his voice.

24   *Ye have been rebellious against the LORD from the day that I knew you.*

25   *Thus I fell down before the LORD forty days and forty nights, as I fell down at the first; because the LORD had said he would destroy you.*

26   *I prayed therefore unto the LORD, and said, O Lord GOD, destroy not thy people and thine inheritance, which thou hast redeemed through thy greatness, which thou hast brought forth out of Egypt with a mighty hand.*

27   *Remember thy servants, Abraham, Isaac, and Jacob; look not unto the stubbornness of this people, nor to their wickedness, nor to their sin:*

28   *Lest the land whence thou broughtest us out say, Because the LORD was not able to bring them into the land which he promised them, and because he hated them, he hath brought them out to slay them in the wilderness.*

29   *Yet they are thy people and thine inheritance, which thou broughtest out by thy mighty power and by thy stretched-out arm.*

Nehemiah's Prayer & Fasting Nehemiah 1:3-11

3   *And they said unto me, the remnants that are left of the captivity there in the province are in great affliction and reproach: the wall of Jerusalem also is broken down, and the gates thereof are burned with fire.*

4   *And it came to pass, when I heard these words, that I sat down and wept, and mourned certain days, and fasted, and prayed before the God of heaven,*

5   *And said, I beseech thee, O LORD God of heaven, the great and terrible God that keepeth covenant and mercy for them that love him and observe his commandments:*

6   *Let thine ear now be attentive, and thine eyes open, that thou mayest hear the prayer of thy servant, which I pray before thee now, day and night, for the children of Israel thy servants, and confess the sins of the children of Israel, which we have sinned against thee: both I and my father's house have sinned.*

7   *We have dealt very corruptly against thee, and have not kept the commandments, nor the statutes, nor the judgments, which thou commandedst thy servant Moses.*

8   *Remember, I beseech thee, the word that thou commandedst thy servant, Moses, saying, If ye transgress, I will scatter you abroad among the nations:*

9   *But if ye turn unto me, and keep my commandments, and do them; though there were of you cast out unto the uttermost part of the heaven, yet will I gather them from thence, and will bring them unto the place that I have chosen to set my name there.*

10   *Now, these are thy servants and thy people, whom thou hast redeemed by thy great power, and by thy strong hand.*

11   *O LORD, I beseech thee, let now thine ear be attentive to the prayer of thy servant, and to the prayer of thy servants, who desire to fear thy name: and prosper, I pray thee, thy servant this day, and grant him mercy in the sight of this man. For I was the king's cupbearer.*

Samson Judges 16:28

28   *And Samson called unto the LORD, and said, O Lord God, remember me, I pray thee, and strengthen me, I pray thee, only this once, O God, that I may be at once avenged of the Philistines for my two eyes.*

29   *And Samson took hold of the two middle pillars upon which the house stood, and on which it was borne up, of the one with his right hand, and of the other with his left.*

30   *And Samson said, Let me die with the Philistines. And he bowed himself with all his might, and the house fell upon the lords, and upon all the people that were therein. So the dead which he slew at his death were more than they which he slew in his life.*

31   *Then his brethren and all the house of his father came down, and took him, and brought him up, and buried him between Zorah and Eshtaol in the buryingplace of Manoah, his father. And he judged Israel twenty years.*

Nehemiah and Israel Prayer & Fasting Nehemiah 9:1

1   *Now in the twenty and fourth day of this month, the children of Israel were assembled with fasting, and with sackclothes, and earth upon them.*

2   *And the seed of Israel separated themselves from all strangers, and stood and confessed their sins and the iniquities of their fathers.*

3   *And they stood up in their place, and read in the book of the law of the LORD their God one-fourth part of the day, and another fourth part they confessed and worshipped the LORD their God.*

4   *Then stood up upon the stairs, of the Levites, Jeshua, and Bani, Kadmiel, Shebaniah, Bunni, Sherebiah, Bani, and Chenani, and cried with a loud voice unto the LORD their God.*

5   *Then the Levites, Jeshua, and Kadmiel, Bani, Hashabniah, Sherebiah, Hodijah, Shebaniah, and Pethahiah, said, Stand up and bless the LORD your God for ever and ever: and blessed be thy glorious name, which is exalted above all blessing and praise.*

6   *Thou, even thou, art LORD alone; thou hast made heaven, the heaven of heavens, with all their host, the earth, and all things that are therein the seas, and all that is therein, and thou preservest them all; and the host of heaven worshippeth thee.*

7   *Thou art the LORD the God, who didst choose Abram, and broughtest him forth out of Ur of the Chaldees, and gavest him the name of Abraham;*

8   *And foundest his heart faithful before thee, and madest a covenant with him to give the land of the Canaanites, the Hittites, the Amorites, and the Perizzites, and the Jebusites, and the Girgashites, to give it, I say, to his seed, and hast performed thy words; for thou art righteous:*

9 And didst see the affliction of our fathers in Egypt, and heardest their cry by the Red sea;

10 And shewedst signs and wonders upon Pharaoh, and on all his servants, and on all the people of his land: for thou knewest that they dealt proudly against them. So didst thou get thee a name, as it is this day.

11 And thou didst divide the sea before them so that they went through the midst of the sea on the dry land; and their persecutors thou threwest into the deeps, as a stone into the mighty waters.

Nehemiah 9: 12-38

12 Moreover, thou leddest them in the day by a cloudy pillar; and in the night by a pillar of fire, to give them light in the way wherein they should go.

13 Thou camest down also upon mount Sinai, and spakest with them from heaven, and gavest them right judgments, and true laws, good statutes, and commandments:

14 And madest known unto them thy holy sabbath, and commandedst them precepts, statutes, and laws, by the hand of Moses, thy servant:

15 And gavest them bread from heaven for their hunger, and broughtest forth water for them out of the rock for their thirst, and promisedst them that they should go in to possess the land which thou hadst sworn to give them.

16 But they and our fathers dealt proudly, and hardened their necks, and hearkened not to thy commandments,

17 And refused to obey, neither were mindful of thy wonders that thou didst among them; but hardened their necks, and in their rebellion appointed a captain to return to their bondage: but thou art a God ready to pardon, gracious and merciful, slow to anger, and of great kindness, and forsookest them not.

18 Yea, when they had made them a molten calf, and said, This is thy God that brought thee up out of Egypt, and had wrought great provocations;

19 Yet thou in thy manifold mercies forsookest them not in the wilderness: the pillar of the cloud departed not from them by day, to lead them in the way; neither the pillar of fire by night, to shew them light, and the way wherein they should go.

20 Thou gavest also thy good spirit to instruct them, and withheldest not thy manna from their mouth, and gavest them water for their thirst.

21 Yea, forty years didst thou sustain them in the wilderness so that they lacked nothing; their clothes waxed not old, and their feet swelled not.

22 Moreover, thou gavest them kingdoms and nations, and didst divide them into corners: so they possessed the land of Sihon, and the land of the king of Heshbon, and the land of Og king of Bashan.

23 Their children also multipliedst thou as the stars of heaven and broughtest them into the land, concerning which thou hadst promised to their fathers, that they should go in to possess it.

24 So the children went in and possessed the land, and thou subduedst before them the inhabitants of the land, the Canaanites, and gavest them into their hands, with their kings, and the people of the land, that they might do with them as they would.

25 And they took strong cities, and a fat land, and possessed houses full of all goods, wells digged, vineyards, and oliveyards, and fruit trees in abundance: so they did eat, and were filled, and became fat, and delighted themselves in thy great goodness.

26 Nevertheless, they were disobedient, and rebelled against thee, and cast thy law behind

their backs, and slew thy prophets which testified against them to turn them to thee, and they wrought great provocations.

27 *Therefore thou deliveredst them into the hand of their enemies, who vexed them: and in the time of their trouble, when they cried unto thee, thou heardest them from heaven; and according to thy manifold mercies, thou gavest them saviors, who saved them out of the hand of their enemies.*

28 *But after they had rest, they did evil again before thee: therefore leftest thou them in the land of their enemies, so that they had the dominion over them: yet when they returned and cried unto thee, thou heardest them from heaven; and many times didst thou deliver them according to thy mercies;*

29 *And testifiedst against them, that thou mightest bring them again unto thy law: yet they dealt proudly, and hearkened not unto thy commandments, but sinned against thy judgments, (which if a man do, he shall live in them;) and withdrew the shoulder, and hardened their neck, and would not hear.*

30 *Yet many years didst thou forbear them, and testifiedst against them by thy spirit in thy prophets: yet would they not give ear: therefore gavest thou them into the hand of the people of the lands.*

31 *Nevertheless for thy great mercies' sake thou didst not utterly consume them, nor forsake them; for thou art a gracious and merciful God.*

32 *Now, therefore, our God, the great, the mighty, and the terrible God, who keepest covenant and mercy, let not all the trouble seem little before thee, that hath come upon us, on our kings, on our princes, and on our priests, and on our prophets, and on our fathers, and on all thy people, since the time of the kings of Assyria unto this day.*

33 *Howbeit thou art just in all that is brought upon us; for thou hast done right, but we have done wickedly:*

34 *Neither have our kings, our princes, our priests, nor our fathers, kept thy law, nor hearkened unto thy commandments and thy testimonies, wherewith thou didst testify against them.*

35 *For they have not served thee in their kingdom, and in thy great goodness that thou gavest them, and in the large and fat land which thou gavest before them, neither turned they from their wicked works.*

36 *Behold, we are servants this day, and for the land that thou gavest unto our fathers to eat the fruit thereof and the good thereof, behold, we are servants in it:*

37 *And it yieldeth much increase unto the kings whom thou hast set over us because of our sins: also they have dominion over our bodies, and over our cattle, at their pleasure, and we are in great distress.*

38 *And because of all this we make a sure covenant, and write it; and our princes, Levites, and priests, seal unto it.*

Solomon's Prayer for Wisdom 1 Kings 3:6-9

6 *And Solomon said, Thou hast showed unto thy servant David my father great mercy, according as he walked before thee in truth, and in righteousness, and in uprightness of heart with thee; and thou hast kept for him this great kindness, that thou hast given him a son to sit on his throne, as it is this day.*

7 *And now, O LORD my God, thou hast made thy servant king instead of David, my father: and I am but a little child: I know not how to go out or come in.*

8 *And thy servant is in the midst of thy people which thou hast chosen, a great people,*

that cannot be numbered nor counted for multitude.

9   *Give therefore thy servant an understanding heart to judge thy people, that I may discern between good and bad: for who is able to judge this thy so great a people?*

Solomon's Prayer to Dedicate the Temple 1 Kings 8:23-61

23   *And he said, LORD God of Israel, there is no God like thee, in heaven above, or on earth beneath, who keepest covenant and mercy with thy servants that walk before thee with all their heart:*

24   *Who hast kept with thy servant David, my father that thou promisedst him: thou spakest also with thy mouth, and hast fulfilled it with thine hand, as it is this day.*

25   *Therefore now, LORD God of Israel, keep with thy servant David my father that thou promisedst him, saying, There shall not fail thee a man in my sight to sit on the throne of Israel; so that thy children take heed to their way, that they walk before me as thou hast walked before me.*

26   *O God of Israel, let thy word, I pray thee, be verified, which thou spakest unto thy servant David, my father.*

27   *But will God indeed dwell on the earth? behold, the heaven and heaven of heavens cannot contain thee; how much less this house that I have built?*

28   *Yet have thou respect unto the prayer of thy servant, and to his supplication, O LORD my God, to hearken unto the cry and to the prayer, which thy servant prayeth before thee today:*

29   *That thine eyes may be open toward this house night and day, even toward the place of which thou hast said, My name shall be there: that thou mayest hearken unto the prayer which thy servant shall make toward this place.*

30   *And hearken thou to the supplication of thy servant, and of thy people Israel, when they shall pray toward this place: and hear thou in heaven thy dwelling place: and when thou hearest, forgive.*

31   *If any man trespass against his neighbor and an oath be laid upon him to cause him to swear, and the oath come before thine altar in this house:*

32   *Then hear thou in heaven, and do, and judge thy servants, condemning the wicked, to bring his way upon his head; and justifying the righteous, to give him according to his righteousness.*

33   *When thy people Israel be smitten down before the enemy, because they have sinned against thee, and shall turn again to thee, and confess thy name, and pray, and make supplication unto thee in this house:*

34   *Then hear thou in heaven, and forgive the sin of thy people Israel, and bring them again unto the land which thou gavest unto their fathers.*

35   *When heaven is shut up, and there is no rain, because they have sinned against thee; if they pray toward this place, and confess thy name, and turn from their sin, when thou afflictest them:*

36   *Then hear thou in heaven, and forgive the sin of thy servants, and of thy people Israel, that thou teach them the good way wherein they should walk, and give rain upon thy land, which thou hast given to thy people for an inheritance.*

37   *If there be in the land famine, if there be pestilence, blasting, mildew, locust, or if there be caterpillar; if their enemy besiege them in the land of their cities; whatsoever plague, whatsoever sickness there be;*

38   *What prayer and supplication soever be made by any man, or by all thy people Israel, which shall know every man the plague of his own heart, and spread forth his hands toward this house:*

39   *Then hear thou in heaven thy dwelling place, and forgive, and do, and give to every man*

according to his ways, whose heart thou knowest; (for thou, even thou only, knowest the hearts of all the children of men;)

40   *That they may fear thee all the days that they live in the land which thou gavest unto our fathers.*

41   *Moreover, concerning a stranger, that is not of thy people Israel, but cometh out of a far country for thy name's sake;*

42   *(For they shall hear of thy great name, and of thy strong hand, and of thy stretched out arm;) when he shall come and pray toward this house;*

43   *Hear thou in heaven thy dwelling place, and do according to all that the stranger calleth to thee for: that all people of the earth may know thy name, to fear thee, as do thy people Israel; and that they may know that this house, which I have built, is called by thy name.*

44   *If thy people go out to battle against their enemy, whithersoever thou shalt send them, and shall pray unto the LORD toward the city which thou hast chosen, and toward the house that I have built for thy name:*

45   *Then hear thou in heaven their prayer and their supplication, and maintain their cause.*

46   *If they sin against thee, (for there is no man that sinneth not,) and thou be angry with them and deliver them to the enemy, so that they carry them away captives unto the land of the enemy, far or near;*

47   *Yet if they shall bethink themselves in the land whither they were carried captives, and repent, and make supplication unto thee in the land of them that carried them captives, saying, We have sinned, and have done perversely, we have committed wickedness;*

48   *And so return unto thee with all their heart, and with all their soul, in the land of their enemies, which led them away captive, and pray unto thee toward their land, which thou gavest unto their fathers, the city which thou hast chosen, and the house which I have built for thy name:*

49   *Then hear thou their prayer and their supplication in heaven thy dwelling place, and maintain their cause,*

50   *And forgive thy people that have sinned against thee, and all their transgressions wherein they have transgressed against thee, and give them compassion before them who carried them captive, that they may have compassion on them:*

51   *For they be thy people, and thine inheritance, which thou broughtest forth out of Egypt, from the midst of the furnace of iron:*

52   *That thine eyes may be open unto the supplication of thy servant, and unto the supplication of thy people Israel, to hearken unto them in all that they call for unto thee.*

53   *For thou didst separate them from among all the people of the earth, to be thine inheritance, as thou spakest by the hand of Moses thy servant, when thou broughtest our fathers out of Egypt, O LORD God.*

54   *And it was so, that when Solomon had made an end of praying all this prayer and supplication unto the LORD, he arose from before the altar of the LORD, from kneeling on his knees with his hands spread up to heaven.*

55   *And he stood, and blessed all the congregation of Israel with a loud voice, saying,*

56   *Blessed be the LORD, that hath given rest unto his people Israel, according to all that he promised: there hath not failed one word of all his good promise, which he promised by the hand of Moses, his servant.*

57   *The LORD our God be with us, as he was with our fathers: let him not leave us, nor forsake us:*

58   *That he may incline our hearts unto him, to walk in all his ways, and to keep his commandments, and his statutes, and his judgments, which he commanded our fathers.*

59   *And let these my words, wherewith I have made supplication before the LORD, be nigh unto the LORD our God day and night, that he maintain the cause of his servant, and the*

cause of his people Israel at all times, as the matter shall require:

60   *That all the people of the earth may know that the LORD is God and that there is none else.*

61   *Let your heart, therefore, be perfect with the LORD our God, to walk in his statutes, and to keep his commandments, as at this day.*

34 NEW TESTAMENT PRAYERS

Jesus Temptation & Fasting Matthew 4:1-11

Then was Jesus led up of the spirit into the wilderness to be tempted of the devil. This temptation shows that Jesus was human, and it gave Jesus the opportunity to reaffirm God's plan for his ministry. It also provides us with an example to follow when tempted. Jesus temptation was a remarkable demonstration of his sinlessness. He would face temptation and would not give in. This time of testing showed that Jesus was the son of God, able to overcome Satan and his temptations. Satan's temptations focused on three crucial areas: (1) physical needs and desires, (2) possessions and power, (3) pride all of which are the characteristics of Satan and just a few methods he uses to get into the head and mind of any and everyone who succumbs to his temptations. Jesus referenced the Old Testament words of the scriptures. Once again confirms the word of God is an excellent weapon against the attacks of Satan and also confirms that the scriptures of the Old Testament are also the word of God.

Temptations: Jesus fasted for 40 Days as such he was hungry and he could have done a miracle to fortify his hunger, and Satan knew the means of creating this mindset due to this physical needs, pressed Jesus to "do His will" and be disobedient like Adam in the Garden of Eden

The temple was the tallest building in the area and the central place of worship for the Jews and a symbol of the future, and Satan showed Jesus from the top of the mountain the entire world and its kingdoms as a visual temptation for power. Jesus is displaying the power of the Word of God against evil, Satan and temptations.

Matthew 4

1: Then was Jesus led up of the spirit into the wilderness to be tempted of the devil.

2: And when he had fasted forty days and forty nights, he was afterward an hungred.

3 :And when the tempter came to him, he said, If thou be the Son of God, command that these stones be made bread.

4: But he answered and said, It is written, Man shall not live by bread alone, but by

5: Then the devil taketh him up into the holy city, and setteth him on a pinnacle of the temple,

6: And saith unto him, If thou be the Son of God, cast thyself down: for it is written, He shall give his angels charge concerning thee: and in their hands they shall bear thee up, lest at any time thou dash thy foot against a stone.

7: Jesus said unto him, It is written again, Thou shalt not tempt the Lord thy God.

8: Again, the devil taketh him up into an exceeding high mountain, and sheweth him all the kingdoms of the world, and the glory of them;

9: And saith unto him, All these things will I give thee, if thou wilt fall down and worship me.

10: Then saith Jesus unto him, Get thee hence, Satan: for it is written, Thou shalt worship the Lord thy God, and him only shalt thou serve.

11: Then the devil leaveth him, and, behold, angels came and ministered unto him.

Jesus teaches on Praying

Jesus had already prepared his disciples and provided them with the knowledge and weapons of spiritual warfare, teaching them prayer is personal and not for bragging and displaying your holiness demeanor in public, plus not to pray as though you are reciting a chant or mantra saying the same thing over and over.

NLT: "some people think that repeating the same words over and over – like a magic incantation – will ensure that God will hear them. It is not wrong to come to God with the same requests – Jesus encourages persistent prayer. But he condemns the shallow repetition of words not offered with a sincere heart. We can never pray too much if our prayers are honest and sincere. Before you start to pray, make sure you mean what you say."

"Jesus is not implying that God leads us into temptation. He is simply asking for deliverance from Satan and his deceit. All Christians struggle with temptation. Sometimes it is so subtle that we don't even realize what is happening to us. God has promised that he won't let us be tempted beyond our endurance (1 Corinthian 10:13). Ask God to help you recognize temptation and to be strong to overcome it and choose God's way."

Matthew 6:5-9

5   *And when thou prayest, thou shalt not be as the hypocrites are: for they love to pray to stand in the synagogues and in the corners of the streets, that they may be seen of men. Verily I say unto you; They have their reward.*

6   *But thou, when thou prayest, enter into thy closet, and when thou hast shut thy door, pray to thy Father which is in secret; and thy Father which seeth in secret shall reward thee openly.*

7   *But when ye pray, use not vain repetitions, as the heathen do: for they think that they shall be heard for their much speaking.*

8   *Be not ye, therefore, like unto them: for your, Father knoweth what things ye have need of before ye ask him.*

9   *After this manner, therefore, pray ye: Our Father which art in heaven, Hallowed be thy name.*

10   *Thy kingdom come, Thy will be done in earth, as it is in heaven.*

11   *Give us this day our daily bread.*

12   *And forgive us our debts, as we forgive our debtors.*

13   *And lead us not into temptation, but deliver us from evil: For thine is the kingdom and the power, and the glory, forever. Amen.*

The prayer is self-explanatory as God is showing us the methods and the verbiage that can be used on our daily prayer

as a guide to our prayers and needs. Here is a framework on God, Worship, thanking

Forgiveness and obedience and not a display of arrogance and claiming to have moral standards or beliefs to which

You really and truly do not conform to and being pretentious.

Jesus Prayer for Lazarus John 11:41-42

Jesus used this circumstance of Lazarus death to display the "Glory of God" and it was done to convince the many that had gathered that he is the son of God and God will answer the request and prayer of his son. Jesus had already performed miracles of bringing people back to life (1) Jaures's daughter in Matthew 9:18-26, (2) The Widow's son in Luke 7:11-15. Many of the Jewish religious leaders were in disbelief, denial and doubtful of Jesus and his abilities to perform miracles and the lack of evidence as a protection of their selfish interest. This opposition to their belief that Jesus was the Messiah and God in the flesh, a living man on earth and the representation of divinity itself, having heard of all the miracles already performed, but not in their presence, especially after feeding 5000 and "the bread of life" teachings. Jesus deliberately delays His journey to Bethany until Lazarus dies. When He finally arrives near the home of the two sisters He loves, Lazarus has already been buried for four days, bringing proof of the glory of God in the presence of the religious bodies.

John 11:41

41   *Then they took away the stone from the place where the dead was laid. And Jesus lifted up his eyes, and said, Father, I thank thee that thou hast heard me.*

42   *And I knew that thou hearest me always: but because of the people which stand by I said it, that they may believe that thou hast sent me.*

43   *And when he thus had spoken, he cried with a loud voice, Lazarus, come forth.*

44   *And he that was dead came forth, bound hand and foot with graveclothes: and his face was bound about with a napkin. Jesus saith unto them, Lose him and let him go.*

Key to this prayer is the shout after praying, "A prayer and a shout."

Jesus prayer. Jesus prays for himself (Students *application bible –New Living Translation*)

"Father the time has come, Glorify your son and so he can give back glory to you. For you have given him authority over everyone in all of the earth. He gives eternal life – to know you the only true God, and Jesus Christ, the one you sent to earth. I brought glory to you here by doing everything you told me to do. And now, Father, bring me into your glory we share before the world began. I have mentioned these men about you. They were in the world, but then you gave them to me. They were always yours, and you gave them to me, and they have kept your word. Now they know that everything I have is a gift from you, for I have passed on to them the words you gave me; and they accepted them and knew that I come from you, and they believe you sent me.

My prayer is not for the world, but for those you have given to me, because they belong to you. And all of them, since they are mine, belongs to you; and you have given them back to me, so they are my glory! Now I am departing the world; I am leaving them behind and coming to you. Holy Father, keep them and care for them – all those you have given me – so that they will be united just as we are. During my time here, I have kept them safe. I guarded them so that no one was lost, except the one headed for destruction, as the scripture foretold. And now I am coming to you. I have told them many things while I was with them so they will be filled with my joy. I have given them your word. And the world hates them because they do not belong to the world, just as I do not. I am not asking you to take them out of the world, but to keep them safe from the evil one. They are not part of this world any more than I am. Make them pure and holy by teaching them your words of truth. As you sent me into the world. I am sending them into the world. And I give myself entirely to you so they also might be entirely yours.

I am praying not only for these disciples but also for all who will ever believe in because of their testimony. My prayer for all of them is that they will be one, just as you and I are one, Father – that just as you are one in me and I am in you, so they will be in us, and the world will believe you sent me."

The world is a significant battleground where the forces under Satan's power and Those under God's authority are at war. Satan and his emissaries are motivated by bitter hatred for Christ and his disciples and worshippers. Here Jesus prays for his disciples and all who are following him, praying that God would keep his chosen believers safe from Satan's power, making them pure and holy, uniting them under the truth. Jesus teaches that eternal life achieved by knowing God through him, knowing the father through the son, building a personal relationship with God through Jesus Christ. Jesus mission is almost over, and he is asking God to restore him to his original place of honor and authority. This unity he is asking the disciples to be united in harmony and love as the Father, Son, and Holy Spirit are united. Jesus teaching is focused on joy and wants everyone to enjoy and be joyful through him as the source. When we are living close and under his teachings, following his instructions we will experience the immeasurable joy and God care and attention will be drawn to us, delivering victory over all circumstances. Understand that this world is under sin orchestrated by Satan and sin is in abundance because of Satan's agenda. Christians are sanctified, cleansed and made holy through the word of God, believing and following, applying ourselves to a relationship with Jesus.

Jesus in Gethsemane

Matthew 26:39   *And he went a little farther, and fell on his face, and prayed, saying, O my Father, if it be possible, let this cup pass from me: nevertheless not as I will, but as thou Wilt*

Matthew 2642:   *He went away again the second time, and prayed, saying, O my Father, if this cup may not pass away from me, except I drink it, thy will be done.*

Jesus High Priestly Prayer John 17   A special prayer for the disciples

John 17: 1-26

1   *These words spake Jesus, and lifted up his eyes to heaven, and said, Father, the hour is come; glorify thy Son, that thy Son also may glorify thee:*

2   *As thou hast given him power over all flesh, that he should give eternal life to as many as thou hast given him.*

3   *And this is life eternal, that they might know thee the only true God, and Jesus Christ, whom thou hast sent.*

4   *I have glorified thee on the earth: I have finished the work which thou gavest me to do.*

5   *And now, O Father, glorify thou me with thine own self with the glory which I had with thee before the world was.*

6   *I have manifested thy name unto the men which thou gavest me out of the world: thine they were, and thou gavest them me, and they have kept thy word.*

7   Now they have known that all things whatsoever thou hast given me are of thee.

8   For I have given unto them the words which thou gavest me; and they have received them, and have known surely that I came out from thee, and they have believed that thou didst send me.

9   I pray for them: I pray not for the world, but for them which thou hast given me; for they are thine.

10   And all mine are thine, and thine are mine, and I am glorified in them.

11   And now I am no more in the world, but these are in the world, and I come to thee. Holy Father, keep through thine own name those whom thou hast given me, that they may be one, as we are.

12   While I was with them in the world, I kept them in thy name: those that thou gavest me I have kept, and none of them is lost, but the son of perdition; that the scripture might be fulfilled.

13   And now come I to thee; and these things I speak in the world, that they might have my joy fulfilled in themselves.

14   I have given them thy word; and the world hath hated them, because they are not of the world, even as I am not of the world.

15   I pray not that thou shouldest take them out of the world, but that thou shouldest keep them from the evil.

16   They are not of the world, even as I am not of the world.

17   Sanctify them through thy truth: thy word is truth.

18   As thou hast sent me into the world, even so, have I also sent them into the world.

19   And for their sakes, I sanctify myself, that they also might be sanctified through the truth.

20   Neither pray I for these alone, but for them also which shall believe on me through their word;

21   That they all may be one; as thou, Father, art in me, and I in thee, that they also may be one in us: that the world may believe that thou hast sent me.

22   And the glory which thou gavest me I have given them; that they may be one, even as we are one:

23   I in them, and thou in me, that they may be made perfect in one; and that the world may know that thou hast sent me, and hast loved them, as thou hast loved me.

24   Father, I will that they also, whom thou hast given me, be with me where I am; that they may behold my glory, which thou hast given me: for thou lovedst me before the foundation of the world.

25   O, righteous Father, the world hath not known thee: but I have known thee, and these have known that thou hast sent me.

26   And I have declared unto them thy name and will declare it: that the love wherewith thou hast loved me may be in them, and I in them.

Jesus at the Cross
Luke 23:34, 46   Matthew 27:46

> 34   *Then said Jesus, Father, forgive them; for they know not what they do. And they parted his raiment and cast lots.*

Paul for the Corinthians 2 Corinthians 13:7 –

> 7   *Now I pray to God that ye do no evil; not that we should appear approved, but that ye should do that which is honest, though we be as reprobates.*

Paul for the Philippians
Philippians 1:9-11

> 9   *And this I pray, that your love may abound yet more and more in knowledge and in all judgment;*
> 10   *That ye may approve things that are excellent; that ye may be sincere and without offense till the day of Christ.*
> 11   *Being filled with the fruits of righteousness, which are by Jesus Christ, unto the glory and praise of God.*

Paul For the Ephesians
Ephesians 3:14-21

> 14   *For this, cause I bow my knees unto the Father of our Lord Jesus Christ,*
> 15   *Of whom the whole family in heaven and earth is named,*
> 16   *That he would grant you, according to the riches of his glory, to be strengthened with might by his Spirit in the inner man;*
> 17   *That Christ may dwell in your hearts by faith; that ye, being rooted and grounded in love,*
> 18   *May be able to comprehend with all saints what is the breadth, and length, and depth, and height;*
> 19   *And to know the love of Christ, which passeth knowledge, that ye might be filled with all the fullness of God.*
> 20   *Now unto him, that is able to do exceeding abundantly above all that we ask or think, according to the power that worketh in us,*
> 21   *Unto him be glory in the church by Christ Jesus throughout all ages, world without end. Amen.*

Paul for the Colossians   Colossians 1:9-17

> 9.   *For this cause we also, since the day we heard it, do not cease to pray for you, and to desire that ye might be filled with the knowledge of his will in all wisdom and spiritual understanding;*
> 10   *That ye might walk worthy of the Lord unto all pleasing, being fruitful in every good work, and increasing in the knowledge of God;*
> 11   *Strengthened with all might, according to his glorious power, unto all patience and longsuffering with joyfulness;*
> 12   *Giving thanks unto the Father, which hath made us meet to be partakers of*

the inheritance of the saints in light:

13 *Who hath delivered us from the power of darkness, and hath translated us into the kingdom of his dear Son:*

14 *n whom we have redemption through his blood, even the forgiveness of sins:*

15 *Who is the image of the invisible God, the firstborn of every creature?*

16 *For by him were all things created, that are in heaven, and that are in earth, visible and invisible, whether they be thrones, or dominions, or principalities, or powers: all things were created by him, and for him:*

17 *And he is before all things, and by him, all things consist.*

35 WHAT ARE THE OPTIONS

We live in a World
- Full of war
- Hatred
- Misery
- Sickness
- Suffering
- Famine and Starvation
- Poverty
- Disease
- Unusual death
- Crime
- Unusual negative incidents around Humanity
- Natural disaster
- Physical and Social Environmental factors that affect humanity negatively
- Heat waves
- Freezing temperatures and Ice storms

These change every human being and forces them to adapt with a fight or flight attributes, culturing them into becoming stronger, more durable and able to resist and withstand the natural disasters that they face in their lives. They adapt to the adverse conditions and circumstances in life.

We live in a world full of hate and anger, many songwriter and musicians wrote and recorded songs of this hate and violence, trying to make a change for the betterment of the next generation. The prisons are full of inmates who overexpressed themselves verbally and physically and have stepped over the boundaries of the law, committed crimes of hate and overcome by anger which took effect on their action. The hurt and pain they caused are irreparable and brought about painful memories, traumas and unbearable physical and emotional pains to many. Some have remorse, and some do not, and their personal lives destroyed because of the overwhelming negative emotion thrusting their flesh in action. Today's generation bowed their heads to look at their phones and electronic devices and know not the formidable simplicity are relationship developed by verbal communication, most communication is electronic in the form of text and social media and the connection involved with the emotional touch of voice face to face is lost, and emotions are becoming numb.

A lesson and message from GOD are "to Love," which is the greatest commandment "love thy neighbor as thyself." God created man for fellowship, to live and love and be good fellows to one another, and gave that commandment for them to follow and hath given them the ability to choose love and abundant life which is the product of love.

This Love is to live and love in the various faction of love is resonating with the spirit of GOD, adapting and expanding while growing in the mind by the act of Love.

"Love and the display of Love is the key to end worlds suffering and injustice.

People have boxed GOD to be a tiny little being that fits into their curriculum as such GOD has become littler and littler, smaller and smaller than the man himself. His faith and belief and concept of GOD are limited and lower than their jobs and their managers at work.

We need to change if wanting to live life abundantly as ordained and allowed by GOD, for GOD is the creator of all things, and he is also the sustainer of life and the giver of life and elements of the unimaginable. We need to personalize GOD as part of ourselves, the spirit that lives within us and the maker of all circumstances in our life. If we allow GOD to be GOD, then and only then can we prosper and live life as God ordained it to be, abundantly.

James 4: 8 Draw closer to GOD and he will draw closer to you, cleanse your hands, ye sinners; and purify your hearts; ye double minded

James warned the believers not only to hear the truth but also to put it into action, put faith with faith that works and put works into action.

James gives five suggestions

    (1) *Submit to God*

    (2) *Resist the devil*

    (3) *Cleanse your hands and purify your hearts. Lead a pure life*

    (4) *Let there be tears, sorrow and sincere grief for your sins, repent and replace it with God's purity*

    (5) *Humble yourself before God, and he will lift you up*

1 John 4:16   God is love

Numbers 23:19   God's promise of a Paradise on earth

36 SPIRITUAL WARFARE

Ephesians 6:12: For we wrestle not against flesh and blood, but against principalities, against powers, against the rulers of the darkness of this world, against spiritual wickedness in high places

Ephesians 6: 10 -18

*Ephesians 6: **10*** *Finally, my brethren, be strong in the Lord, and in the power of his might.*

*Ephesians 6: **11*** *Put on the whole armor of God that ye may be able to stand against the wiles of the devil.*

*Ephesians 6: **12*** *For we wrestle not against flesh and blood, but against principalities, against powers, against the rulers of the darkness of this world, against spiritual wickedness in high places.*

*Ephesians 6: **13*** *Wherefore take unto you the whole armor of God, that ye may be able to withstand in the evil day, and having done all, to stand.*

*Ephesians 6: **14*** *Stand therefore, having your loins girt about with truth, and having on the breastplate of righteousness;*

*Ephesians 6: **15*** *And your feet shod with the preparation of the gospel of peace;*

*Ephesians 6: **16*** *Above all, taking the shield of faith, wherewith ye shall be able to quench all the fiery darts of the wicked.*

*Ephesians 6: **17*** *And take the helmet of salvation, and the sword of the Spirit, which is the word of God:*

*Ephesians 6: **18*** *Praying always with all prayer and supplication in the Spirit, and watching thereunto with all perseverance and supplication for all saints;*

Luke 10:19 *Behold, I give unto you power to tread on serpents and scorpions, and over all the power of the enemy: and nothing shall by any means hurt you.*

Luke 4: 18-19 *The Spirit of the Lord is upon me, because he hath anointed me to preach the gospel to the poor; he hath sent me to heal the brokenhearted, to preach deliverance to the captives, and recovering of sight to the blind, to set at liberty them that are bruised, 19. To preach the acceptable year of the Lord.*

Isaiah 61: Chapter 61

1. *The Spirit of the Lord GOD is upon me; because the LORD hath anointed me to preach good tidings unto the meek; he hath sent me to bind up the brokenhearted, to proclaim liberty to the captives, and the opening of the prison to them that are bound;*
2. *To proclaim the acceptable year of the LORD, and the day of vengeance of our God; to comfort all that mourn;*
3. *To appoint unto them that mourn in Zion, to give unto them beauty for ashes, the oil of joy for mourning, the garment of praise for the spirit of heaviness; that they might be called trees of righteousness, the planting of the LORD, that he might be glorified.*
4. *And they shall build the old wastes, they shall raise up the former desolations, and they shall repair the waste cities, the desolations of many generations.*
5. *And strangers shall stand and feed your flocks, and the sons of the alien shall be your plowmen and your vinedressers.*
6. *But ye shall be named the Priests of the LORD: men shall call you the Ministers of our God: ye shall eat the riches of the Gentiles, and in their glory shall ye boast yourselves.*
7. *For your shame, ye shall have double, and for confusion, they shall rejoice in their portion: therefore in their land, they shall possess the double: everlasting joy shall be unto them.*
8. *For I the LORD love judgment, I hate robbery for burnt offering; and I will direct their work in truth, and I will make an everlasting covenant with them.*
9. *And their seed shall be known among the Gentiles, and their offspring among the people: all that see them shall acknowledge them, that they are the seed which the LORD hath blessed.*
10. *I will greatly rejoice in the LORD; my soul shall be joyful in my God; for he hath clothed me with the garments of salvation, he hath covered me with the robe of righteousness, as a bridegroom decketh himself with ornaments, and as a bride adorneth herself with her jewels.*
11. *For as the earth bringeth forth her bud, and as the garden causeth the things that are sown in it to spring forth; so the Lord GOD will cause righteousness and praise to spring forth before all the nations.*

The mind is the main battleground, the battle for health in our bodies, fight for our finances and sustenance and maintenance. The mind is the battleground where Satan attacks and drives his evilness into the thoughts and perceptions of everyone. Satan's weapon and his method of creating a war against the creation of God as the battle against each other and defeats us. We are becoming the vessels of the Heavenly warfare, for the Fallen Angels and Demons have brought the war to earth because God created man as his next beloved apart from the Angels. This is why he taught us to pray "Thy will be done on Earth as it is in Heaven" for multiple reasons, we will emulate or replicate what is going on in heaven or what is done in heaven upon the earth. A prayer that the Earth is presently not being managed or run the way it is handled, it should be as things are happening in Heaven, But as we read on through scripture, we are finding that heaven is also having problems, brotherly Angels are getting contaminated with thoughts and egoistic attitudes of power quest to be more than they should be and we are also running amuck in Heaven and it is not in tiny pockets, we are reading that one-third of the Angels kicked out of Heaven. So where is the order and where do the orderly's, a battle ensue where one brotherly Angel wanted to become the head of the household and started a war, a war that is killing other heavenly beings.

The story of a family and two brothers one on one side the other on the opposite sides, this has been replicated in the bible multiple times with Cain and Abel, Isaac and Ishmael, Esau and Jacob, Jacob's son's and Joseph, David's sons, Sampson, and the list is endless.

Cain and Abel: A role of jealousy and envy, this is characteristic that lies in every one of us, and can be displayed whenever we are overtaken with jealousy, resentment, inferiority or pushed to wanting more of what the others have. We are to honor each other regardless of what life brings or whatever the circumstances may be, it always, always leads to disaster and a down spiral

Esau and Jacob: Twins, but not identical, conspiracy, favoritism, and covetousness is the spirit behind this story, even involved mother deceitfulness against her husband in allowing her motives to be carried out. We are to work together as a family to bring about the ordination of what our duties and roles in society, family and our generations to come.

Joseph and his brothers: the sins of the father are passed down to the sons; the very nature of Jacob's crime against his brother Esau is repeating itself in the lives of his sons. The brothers know that their younger brother is a dreamer and one of the favorites of their father behaved just like Cain and Jacob, in trying to cheat the little brother of his blessings and shatter his dreams, which they did not realize were visions and dreams from God. Joseph himself was a bit of a teaser and taunter, consistently stating that all, including his father and mother, would bow down to him.

The Prodigal son: One is well behaved and following his family and father's tradition, culture and occupation, taking care of the home and the family, the other is rebellious, irresponsible and having a different vision for his life, a mere reference to the Pharisees and displaying that sometimes we over think and get beyond what we are ordained to be, yet the father is forgiving and always have the love in his heart.

It is not uncommon for sibling rivalry to exist in any home, it is a characteristic of free will and the feelings of jealousy, envy, avarice, covetousness, greed, lack of restraint, lack of discernment of the spirit and possible satanic influences. We are given these stories and lessons in the Bible as a teaching methodology of bringing awareness to this of attributes we should be careful not to adopt or partake or make it a part of our nature.

> 1 Corinthians 10:3-5 -   *For though we walk in the flesh, we do not war after the flesh:4 (For the weapons of our warfare are not carnal, but mighty through God to the pulling down of strong holds;) 5 Casting down imaginations and every high thing that exalteth itself against the knowledge of God, and bringing into captivity every thought to the obedience of Christ*

Breaking generational curses

Heavenly Father I confess any sins and iniquities of my parents, and any of my ancestors. I renounce, break and cancel and sever all links and connections of evil and generational curses I have inherited from parents, grandparents or any of my ancestors. I cut all unholy ties between myself and my generations before and all other ancestors.

In the name of Jesus, I now lose myself and my future generations from any bondage that has come down or passed on from ancient times and my ancestors and I command any evil spirits which have affected us through any iniquity, generational curses, and unholy ties to leave me now in the name of Jesus!

BREAKING GENERATIONAL CURSES:

"In the name of the Lord Jesus Christ, and by the power and authority of the word and Jesus Christ loose myself free from all generational sins, weaknesses, and curses, including any links to our unhealthy DNA connectivity and inheritance that are unholy and possess any negative spiritual connection or sicknesses. I break all unhealthy, unholy ties between myself, my parents, my grandparents, my blood relatives I have had with others in the past all the way back to the beginning of time even unto the times of Adam and EVE in the name of Jesus Christ. I am now free, free from any of these unhealthy, unholy ties through the blood of the lamb and the power and authority Jesus Christ."

Breaking generational curses

Heavenly Father, in Jesus Name I confess the sins and iniquities of myself, my parents, and ancestors that have introduces curses and bondages into my family line. I rebuke, Break and free myself and my family line from any of these curses and inequities of my ancestors. I break the power of all spoken curses; take back the grounds that I yielded to the devil. I now claim blessings instead. In the name of Jesus

I pray and ask of you, In the name of Jesus and by his power, by his might and by his authority and through his blood, To bind every spiritual Principalities and power of the air and all demonic forces that are over my home, my city, my country and all other countries of the world. I command these demons, spirits, and devils to cease in their operations, and cast them out from these countries and take back the power they control. Break every bondage, curses, hex, and evil that works in darkness, Break every Generational curse that has been upon the country and its people, Break all Voodoo and occult bondage and rebuke and bind all these spirits from operating.
Remove the blindness and scales from their eyes and let them see and experience your presence,
Rebuke all sicknesses from my body and mind and bless me with good health and a sound mind. Bless me with recognition and authority in the city and the country, at my Job and in my homes and environment. Bless me that I will come to know you and give me visions, insights, direction, and guidance toward a higher calling and a better abundant life

37 TESTIMONIALS

Being from Hindu Brahmin ancestral background and a born-again Apostolic Pentecostal Christian, engaging in ministry and working towards evangelism in the Caribbean, South America and possibly the continent of Africa and Indo-Asia

Ancestry and heritage are from Northern India, Brahmins, and a Vedic Aryan culture. Father was a very educated man in the Hindu Scriptures and language of Sanskrit, literate in reading and interpreting the Sanskrit written scriptures.

Being called and driven by GOD and religion and having studied Hinduism intensely with the thought that this will help fellow countrymen and people, bringing them out of the Lack of knowledge of GOD, and breaking the bondages and their struggles

Ancestors are from the **priestly tribe (like the Levites), and their roles in society are the Priests, Intellects, and educators. Lineage grew up studying the doctrines of Hinduism** or should be studying the Vedic scriptures.

There are hundreds of denominations in Hinduism, being from a Vedic culture which is the religion of the Indo-Aryans of northern India. It is a historical predecessor of modern **Hinduism**, Aryan-Indians worships GOD in purity, no images, no meat and fish, no Blood sacrifices, no Idols or Images, etc

Baptism in Hinduism (called Janeu- sort of a Bar Mitzvah) at the age of 10; this is where the journey to manhood begins and to undertake the role and a priest or educator assigned to a Guru (teacher).

Read the Bible and studied Islam (read a transliterated version of the Quran) and at that time did condemn the religions because of various scripture that I disagreed with, learning about Abraham and Lot and all the sacrifices of the Old Testament and the wrath of God. I felt that this is not a divine religion. Read the Quran and did the same especially with specific parts that demean women, and marriages that are of a very tender age. Both the Bible and the Quran talks about killing, and all those who are too are then the focus on spiritual divinity and spiritual enlightenment.

Choices of study were Psycho-analysis and Hypnotherapy for the purpose of operating a school and training program in the Caribbean, the West Indies, Guyana, South America, Asia, Africa, Indo-Asia to help people in their sicknesses related to psychosomatic illnesses, Depression, Pains and the multitudes of environmental and social stress related sickness through Clinical Hypnotherapy. This is a way of helping people in third world countries where there is a limited number of medical facilities, hospitals, pharmacies and a limited number of Doctors and no healthcare. People are dependent on the land for herbal medicines, the knowledge of the older folks and knowledge that was passed down from generation to generation, and the limitation of books and ancient medicinal cures. Medicinal Drugs and medical attention were costly, and most cannot afford. People live with their symptoms, deformities, and what-ever-ailment they suffered. The goal was to remedy their mind and use the various mind-therapies to remove the pain and suffering and let them at least enjoy life and be happy while still being a victim of sickness.

Furthermore... the superpower of the worldplundered these countries in the earlier days; resources sucked out from these countries, the life force and resources , people used and abused and put under bondage by these super-powers and left to dry. They did not put back much into these countries to build infrastructure or facilities to cater for the population. The image that comes to mind is "Vampirism". Great Britain, Spain, Portugal, Netherland, France, Italy and some others sucked the life blood and juice of these countries and left them under a rut, using the pretext of colonization to fulfill their greed and avarice, and express their authority and supremacy to look down upon the local people and those that were put under bondage as savages and non-human being. The Portuguese started the Slave trade and the British feasted on the idealogy and created a system to deliver labor force across the world. Today Karma is taking its toll and doing its duties.

Moving to Florida was a significant change that God orchestrated in my life, from Wall Street Financial District and New York hustles to Tampa bay retirement homestead slow paced life, from six-figure salaries to ZERO.
Stripped of everything and was at the verge of losing my mind, my sanity, and family, unemployed and starving for a job for sustenance. The most significant impact on my life and in the course of looking for work, was witnessed to by a friend who further enlightened me in the scripture and the truth of the bible.

Romans 8: 28   *And we know that all things work together for good to them That love God, to them who are the called according to his purpose.*

29   *For whom he did foreknow, he also did predestinate to be conformed to the image of his Son, that he might be the firstborn among many brethren.*

30   *Moreover whom he did predestinate, them he also called: and whom he called, them he also justified: and whom he justified, them he also glorified.*

31   *What shall we then say to these things? If God be for us, who can be against us?*

GOD was severely dealing with me, seeking a Hindu temple for worship but none existed in my area at that time. Finally went to a charismatic church in Plant city and baptized in the name of the father, son and Holy Ghost.

The renewing began, and the enlightenment was getting stronger, convictions and reflections of all the visions and dreams GOD started to resurface. Slowly realized that GOD had a significant part in life and was being prepared for some works. Still stuck in the knowledge of Hindu philosophy and it was tough to let go. Mind was in an analytical stage, and I looked at every lesson deeply, in a critical mode to find the truth. Filled with the Holy Ghost and Baptized again (now for the third time) in the Name of Jesus

Greatest quest and desire to know and learn more about GOD, and questioned GOD in everything

> ISAIAH 45:11 **thus saith the LORD, the Holy One of Israel, and his Maker, Ask me of things to come concerning my sons, and concerning the work of my hands command ye me.**

In a vision and dream, I realized it was GOD in an invisible form.

It was a very vivid, long and multiple visions.

My Question "GOD Why ME?

The Answer from GOD "Why Not you? Do you know who you are?"

And I confoundedly responded, "No! Please tell me and show me."

The LORD: "You are the answer to your mother's prayer, a gift from me as the answer to her prayers."

The Lord revealed to me in a dream and vision, my mother, praying the "Hannah's prayer and asked for SONS."

Being the first son of my mother after three daughters, my mother endured quite a lot of insults by many relatives and people for not bearing a son (Even in times of old everyone wants a Son, it is meaningful and a blessing, for the ancient Hindu religion, Judaism, Christianity , Islam, a son is essential). She was advised by many to perform much occult and weird worship to receive the blessing of bearing a son. My mother was of an Aryan Brahmin background and do not believe in any occult or cultural practices, but was invited to church by my Uncle T (who was a minister/ teacher in a church) and prayed Hannah's prayer.

> 1 Samuel 1:10-11 "And she was in bitterness of soul, and prayed to the Lord and wept in anguish. Then she made a vow and said, 'O Lord of hosts, if You will indeed look on the affliction of Your maidservant and remember me, and not forget Your maidservant, but will give Your maidservant a male child, then I will give him to the Lord all the days of his life, and no razor shall come upon his head"

> I Samuel 1:17 The Priest –"Go in peace, and the God of Israel grant your petition which you have asked of Him."

Soon I would be born, and three more sons were born to my mother
Unfortunately, my mother never revealed the fullness of this story as such in my quest, the details revealed to me in a vision and a dream which I did confirm with my Father and other members of the family.

My life filled with **much near death experiences,** and **I always escaped death and danger one way or the other (miraculously and unexplainable).**

I soon realized that I am guided, protected and always pulled or pushed to study scriptures….Hinduism, Islam, Judaism, Buddhism, Christianity, Shaktism, Jainism, Shaivism, Confucianism philosophy even the New Age philosophy, reasoning is that you need to know the culture and philosophy of all whom you are venturing to meet and bear witness of God

After this long, vivid vision, I was convicted in my spiritual path and finally succumb to being a convert... For I know what my callings are and What God wants me to be and to do, for he was my guide and will be my guide.

> ***ISAIAH 61: 1***   *It was revealed to me and the day of vengeance of our God; to comfort all that mourn; 3; To appoint unto them that mourn in Zion, to give unto them beauty for ashes, the oil of joy for mourning, the garment of praise for the spirit of heaviness; that they might be called trees of righteousness, the planting of the LORD, that he might be glorified.4; And they shall build the old wastes, they shall raise up the former desolations, and they shall repair the waste cities, the desolations of many generations.*

> ***The most intriguing Question in the Bible:***
> *Exodus 4: 24- And it came to pass by the way in the inn, that the LORD met him, and sought to kill him.*
> How can this be possible, GOD commissioned Moses, Moses argued with God, and God made all the changes to work with Moses, Now that he is going …. By the way at the Inn, GOD wanted to kill Moses?

A more in-depth study revealed that Moses was disobedient, his son was not circumcised and that same moment, his wife Zipporah was also not under the Hebrew covenant, because she is the Princess, daughter of Jethro, a Midianite HIGH Priest.

So GOD just commissioned you to perform great tasks and the next moment …..Because of disobedience (Man's first sin), GOD will take the appropriate action

YEP…This is serious business. I am just about ready, and all I need is the essential tool of all…. The Living WORD OF GOD I finally realized and learned that the truth is right here in God's word through Jesus Christ and was even described in Bhagwat Gita and the Hindu Scriptures in the exact description as in Revelations.

Visualize My philosophy: The value of life is not your position, assets, money and your friends; it is to look beyond and utilize all your assets, knowledge and powers within for the purpose to better the world and uplift those who can't help themselves. All that we possess, and can acquire, is always in the open hand. With faith and belief, you can do it anywhere, anytime, anyhow. And all physical values and wealth can be gone or achieved in a flash. It is to take your friends and family, brothers and sisters in faith towards a higher calling and save & secure their soul (inner soul), which is the treasure and jewel of life itself. Not the physical body or the spirit, but the salvation of the soul and get connected GOD and his word & wisdom, his anointing, and powers and receive the enlightenment to do his works as per his requirements in your life.

Sorry you cannot Bling God, you can't see bling Nature, and you can't buy bling Health, you can protect and enhance it. But with GOD, (the Omnipresent, omnipotent & Omniscient, the true living God) all things are possible.

The difference with other religions of the East/West/North/South is that People strive through penance and physical/Spiritual sacrifices to reach enlightenment (Moksha and Nirvana) to experience the presence of GOD, BUT Jesus came to reach out and seek ALL Mankind, holy and unholy with Love and compassion through repentance and forgiveness.

Finally, it is necessary to understand how your body works, how it is related to the functionality and integration of your mind, thus you have to know how your mind operates. In turn, is all linked to the spiritual concepts of the Body/Mind operations and the synchronization of the entire Body/Mind/Spirit and its connectivity to the Universe and divinity, creation and what controls creation. How the sun, moon, and start are influencing your well being, how the weather patterns have favorable or adverse reactions to your nature.

Understanding the physical components of your body is critical to maintaining good health, but it cannot be sole operations, is influenced by the way you think, your action and deeds, your mental state and your concepts of happiness, peace love joy and how you meddle with other forms of life especially Human interaction. The scriptures are teachings and doctrines that reference every aspect of life and are examples historically of every situation that has already occurred and are teachings on what historically took place and how it was dealt with, the instructions of how to handle many situations in life and what are your responses and how to respond to various circumstances.

The book is not specifically dedicated to Christianity, or any other specific religion, but utilized the Christian bible and doctrines as a teaching tool. It is the only doctrine that depicts and relates the miraculous and the control of the supernatural the mode of thinking is to renew your mind, removing all stinking thinking and inject the clean, pure thoughts that will help you mentally, physically and morally through spirituality. The doctrines teach how to become one with the Universe and utilize the nature of God to be the tool to force us to fear divinity and work in unison with the deity for the better good of self.

The focus is to bring humanity back to spirituality, regardless of what religious society you are a part or membership thereof. Changing mind and hearts from any non-religious mentality back to spirituality, and understand the nature of the man and his connection to divinity. You need to spend time understanding the "you," your physical body, how it works, your mind, your spirit and what makes the body function. What makes the three dimension of this one man tick and live and how and why we need God and spirituality in our lives to make us perfect human beings, functional human beings as a representation of the divine God and why we are in this world, what is our purpose and how we can be purposeful and follow the path that was written for mankind to follow.

Dark depressive thoughts and negative thinking is a mode of induction into the mind the dark influences of evil, injecting emotional instability and chaos, boisterous mind frames compared to storms and turbulence in the atmosphere that is a reflection of your inner minds and inner self. This kind of thinking and dark thought induction into the mind causes us to go into the violent reaction and influences our body to react negatively causing turbulence into the calmness and seamless flow of body, mind and spirit harmony. These are the physio-psychological actions that caused unrest and results in psychosomatic illnesses that further into physical diseases and sicknesses. Negative self-talk and anger, rude attitudes, negative thoughts, reactions to others do a great deal of harm to our mind, which in turn deliver negative response to the body and forms a cyclic action that grows and grows and reiterates itself into a cyclic body, mind and spirit flow, throwing us into a dark abyss of confusion and chaos. Self-talk forms our emotions and creates powerful feelings that are either positive or negative depending on the type of self-talk. A great deal of Fear, anger, worry, violent mindset comes out of negative self –talk, therefore it is written that you need to renew your mind – you must understand that the mind is the gift from GOD and is the God-particle that was blown into the nostrils of man to be, act and be as God is or wants you to be. Therefore Man (You) are Gods of your own, but will have to develop that mind, cleans ourselves, think pure, act appropriately and consider that our bodies are the home of the God-particle, the mind, and spirit that was given to us by God. You are not of any lower form of animal; you are built in a sophisticated way with a purpose to be like the being of the universe – that Supreme Being called GOD.

Romans: 12: 1   *I appeal to you, therefore, my brothers, by the mercies of God to present your bodies as a living sacrifice, holy and acceptable to God, which is your spiritual worship.*

Romans 12:2 -   *Do not be conformed to this world, but be transformed by the renewal of your mind, that by testing you may discern what is the will of God, what is*

	good and acceptable and perfect.
Ephesians 4:2	*and to be renewed in the spirit of your minds*
2Corinthians 4:16	*So we do not lose heart. Though our outer self is wasting away, our inner self is being renewed day by day*
Romans 7:18 -25	*For I know that nothing good dwells in me, that is, in my flesh. For I have the desire to do what is right, but not the ability to carry it out. For I do not do the good I want, but the evil I do not want is what I keep doing. Now if I do what I do not want, it is no longer I who do it, but sin that dwells within me. So I find it to be that when I want to do right, evil lies close at hand. For I delight in the law of God, in my inner being*

The direction is to move towards, as we create an internal mind of peace and happiness, and a brilliant, clean, pure approach to good living and life, we sow goodness within, and our demeanor becomes more positive, intelligent, clarity of the futures and harmony with the environment and community, you build a resistance to the darkness and life becomes pleasurable and satisfying – enjoyable. Create a psycho-social-spiritual relationship with yourself, your inner self, your outer self, your environment, your social endeavors, and encounters, for we are powerful and grows more powerful as we bring in the light and drive out the darkness.

Religion and religious doctrine work to bring together and morph into one the belief system and the thought system working in collaboration with the physical wholeness, connects our conscious, subconscious, external consciousness and our physical harmonies of each and every part and organ in our body so that everything flows in unison and harmony with each and other which brings about perfection and the perfect balance. The ordinance and ordination of divinity from without and sync to the mandate within and creates unseen spiritual connectivity to the divine source of the universe. Each cell, each atom, each molecule in the universe and on the earth and within the body have a unique form, a unique shape and have so much similarity in the mold that it does not differ from each other in many ways but made on a standard platform. They are similar in un-imaginable ways and functions so closely together that if molecules are all separated, we will not have a body or earth or a floor to stand on, for the density of every element is the compactness that makes it solid or liquid or space.

Therefore spend some time to study the organs, the body, the cells listed in this book and much additional reading related to the body, you and yourself and your connectivity to others, the animal kingdom, the spiritual realm.
Study the following - In You – you will find out what a fantastic body you have, and how to operate it effectively and efficiently

    (1) Heart

    (2) Pineal Gland

    (3) Blood

    (4) Lamanin

(5) Gluon

(6) Thymus Gland

(7) The Components of the Body

(8) lungs, liver, kidneys, Colon, Stomach, Eyes,

(9) Senses: Sight, touch, Taste, hearing and sense of smell

(10)Forces in the Universe

(11)Mind, Spirit, Psyche, and Soul

Get a clear understanding of what they are and how they function, how they work in harmony and dependency of each other, why is so important about "The Blood," which is the life-giving forces of the human Being and all animal being.

Health and longevity, holiness and divinity, life eternal, living life abundantly is a god given gift to all mankind and you need to understand how to keep it that way, for our health, diminishes quickly based on our mind and spirit influences on our physical self and the instructions of keeping it perfect and alive in the scriptures, thus the reason for so much emphasis on the scriptures and the renewing of your mind.

Medical science, science, chemistry, biochemistry are there for our emergencies and upkeep of the things we cannot control, pills, tablets, injections, operations, and surgeries are just an emergency standby for our maintenance when things go south or wrong, but our minds can heal every part, every cell, every molecule within our bodies and keep us healthy all the days of our lives. Man is not just a mechanical being that can be fed fuel, given a few pints of lubrication oil and some grease and keep functioning seamlessly, man is an intelligent, intellectual, spiritual three dimensional (or rather a four-dimensional being), that needs nurturing in multiple ways, which includes a lot of TLC (Tender Loving Care) for full functionality and performance. The quest for a man is to achieve, to achieve and to become greater and greater, better and better than himself and his surrounding and this takes lots of effort and drive, lot of mental, physical and spiritual endurance and motivation to be able to deliver and impress not only himself but his family, friends, neighbor, and colleagues. Physical battles are just a fraction of man's daily encounters which may or may not take a lot or a whole lot of energy from him. Some of the most significant battles are more spiritual and mental, dealing with family, children, friends, environment, meeting the mark, but bigger than all of that is the spiritual battles that he will face and is facing, for according to scripture our struggles are not with flesh and blood but with principalities and powers of the air.

On the Earth, before we were here, Satan fell, kicked out of the Heavens and fell like lightning to earth. Earth became his home and his kingdom for himself and his fallen angels that were under his command. Therefore Hell which is his dwelling place is here on earth. God decided to take it over and created Man to rule over the land and gave man dominion over all living things and the earth itself, therefore taking away that ownership of the earth from Satan to Adam. One of God's mistake was (and as we are aware God do not make mistakes, well he did have to repent for creating Man during the Noah days), was not to give Adam dominion over the spiritual beings. He did not but commanded the Spiritual Realm to bow down to Adam, which they refused to do so.

Genesis 1: 26   And God said, Let us make man in our image, after our likeness: and **let them have dominion over the fish of the sea, and over the fowl of the air, and over the cattle, and over all the earth, and over every creeping thing that creepeth upon the earth.**

27   So God created man in his image, in the image of God created he him; male and female created him them.

28   And God blessed them, and God said unto them, Be fruitful, and multiply, and replenish the earth, and subdue it: and have dominion over the fish of the sea, and over the fowl of the air, and over every living thing that moveth upon the earth.

Psalms 8: 5   For thou hast made him a little lower than the angels, and hast crowned him with glory and honor.

6   Thou madest him to have dominion over the works of thy hands; thou hast put all things under his feet

7   All sheep and oxen, yea, and the beasts of the field;

8   The fowl of the air, and the fish of the sea, and whatsoever passeth through the paths of the seas.

Hebrews2: 5   <u>*For unto the angels hath he not put in subjection*</u> *the world to come, whereof we speak.*

6   *But one in a certain place testified, saying, What is man, that thou art mindful of him? or the son of man, that thou visitest him?*

7   *Thou madest him a little lower than the angels; thou crownedst him with glory and honor, and didst set him over the works of thy hands:*

8   *Thou hast put all things in subjection under his feet. For in that he put all in subjection under him, he left nothing that is not put under him. But now we see not yet all things put under him.*

It takes us: Looking at the passages above, Man had Dominion over the earth and everything living on the earth. This is your God-given rights; it does not matter what happened afterward for man fell due to the misguidance, stubbornness, disobedience, passivity, not adhering to instructions, not taking and standing his leadership ground, listening to gossip, the lust of the eyes (for he should have recognized the Apple being forbidden fruit)

For on earth was One man and one woman, and there were conversations between the Man and The woman and God, and then there was a side conversation between the Woman and the Serpent (figurative physical description) –

1. *("Nachash, Hebrew for "snake," is also associated with divination, including the verb-form meaning to practice divination or fortune-telling. In the Hebrew Bible, Nachash occurs in the Torah to identify the serpent in Eden. ... Tanniyn, a form of dragon-monster, also occurs throughout the Hebrew Bible).*
2. *Fertility and rebirth. Historically, serpents and **snakes** represent fertility or a creative life force. As **snakes** shed their skin through sloughing, they are symbols of rebirth, transformation, immortality, and healing. The Ouroboros is a symbol of eternity and continual renewal of life.*
3. *In **Christianity**, the **snake** is a symbol of temptation. ... Thus, the **snake** could **symbolize** a malicious enemy, betrayal, or deception. **Christians** may find that their **dreams of snakes** relate to trials and tests that they are experiencing in their waking lives or in their relationships with God*
4. *Satan was the actual tempter, and that he used the serpent merely as his instrument. Abrahamic traditions, the **serpent** represents sexual desire.*
5. *"The serpent which now enters the narrative is marked as one of God's created animals (Chr. 2.19). In the narrator's mind, therefore, it is not the symbol of "demonic" power and certainly not of Satan. What distinguishes it a little from the rest of the animals is exclusively his greater cleverness. [...] The mention of the snake here is almost incidental; at any rate, in the "temptation" by it, the concern is with a completely unmythical process, presented in such a way because the narrator is anxious to shift the responsibility as little as possible from man. It is a question only of a man and his guilt; therefore the narrator has carefully guarded against objectifying evil in any way, and therefore he has personified it as little as possible as power coming from without. That he transferred the impulse to temptation outside man was almost more a necessity for the story than an attempt at making evil something existing outside man. [...] In the history of religions the snake indeed is the sinister, strange animal par excellence [...], and one can also assume that long before, a myth was once at the basis of our narrative. But as it lies now before us, transparent and lucid, it is anything but a myth."*
    — Gerhard von Rad, Genesis: A Commentary the Old Testament Library, the Westminster Press, Philadelphia, Pennsylvania, ISBN 0-664-20957-2.

Therefore the interpretation of the significance or the figurative image as described as the Serpent, What the serpent is and what is the apple. What is the tree of Knowledge of Good and Evil? An apple was the fruit and Eve did pick the fruit (Apple) and ate. The apple became a symbol for knowledge, immortality, temptation, the fall of man and sin. The classical Greek word μῆλον (mēlon), or dialectal μᾶλον (mālon), now a loanword in English as melon, meant tree fruit in general but was borrowed into Latin as mālum, meaning 'apple.' If you cut an apple across it displays a Pentagram which represents the spirit embodied by the flesh. The Greek myth in the garden of Hesperides, the golden apple is symbolic of a critical virtue - wisdom, as well as immortality. Thee apple symbolism is very rich and exciting. Indeed, it found in many religions, popular cultures, and legends. Apples can symbolize good (love and beauty), but also evil (sin, temptation, and discord) through the famous name of "forbidden fruit." As a result, the apple became a symbol for knowledge, immortality, temptation, the fall of man and sin.

The serpent is a representative of humanity's desires and wants. It is that aspect of ourselves which is our choices and free will to choose whether to agree with and condone with God's commandments to decide not to acknowledge and follow God and commandments

Satan means adversary and is an independent force working in contrast to God's plan; Satan is instead working within the will of God's plan. Satan is God's creation, used as a force to drive us away from God.
It is the testing force that puts us in the state of choices of a free will to go to the opposite side of God thereby testing our obedience to the will of God and the commandments he has laid out for our lives. Good and evil are two different hands of God in the Jewish philosophy, they are acting on behalf of God, as the tool to test, enlighten and build us towards divinity, putting us through the fires of faith and belief and it forces us to make or break, fight or flight.

The serpent was a test which Eve failed. Eve had a heavenly entity (the serpent) testing her will to obey God's command. The serpent spoke Only Humans speaks as a special gift from God in intelligent communication, in Genesis the Serpent talked to Eve in a communicable language. Another form of clear dialogue could be in mind, like the whisperer into the ears and consciousness of humanity.

Adam and Eve, even though they possess the spirit of God and have an abundance of knowledge from God, were not ready for that entire God had planned for them in his ordination. They were to (1) multiply and populated the earth (2) Subdue the Earth (3) Have dominion over every living thing (4) REPLENISH – which was to re-create what is on the earth and not to consume it all.

God was teaching them daily as he appears in the Garden and as such, they were not ready for the additional gifts and blessings which were –Knowledge of God and Evil and finally the Gift of eternal life from the "tree of Life." That good/evil kind of knowledge was not the same kind of practical knowledge given to them, but a greater understanding of the responsibilities, sovereignty, good morals and a deep understanding of good and evil to ensure they can endure and make responsible decisions for themselves and their entire kingdom of beings and their future generations. In their innocence was the interception of Satan, in the serpent form (*Genesis 3 also makes it clear that because of God's curse on all of creation, the serpent physically changed (to crawl on his belly), which is now a physical description of the Serpent and not the supernatural spiritual form of "the Serpent"*

> *But I fear, lest by any means, as the serpent beguiled Eve through his subtilty, so your minds should be corrupted from the simplicity that is in Christ (2 Corinthians 11:3).*

> 1Corinthians 4:4   *Satan, who is the god of this world, has blinded the minds of those who don't believe*
>
> 1 Chronicles 21: 1   And Satan stood up against Israel, and provoked David to number Israel.

Gadreel mentioned as the third of five "satans" who led other angels into copulating with humans, leading to the creation of the giant-like Nephilim. The others were called Yeqon (or Yaqum, Aramaic "he shall rise"), Asbeel ("deserter from God"), Penemue ("the inside"), and Kasdaye ("Chaldean," "covered hand."

> *JOB 38: 1 Then the LORD answered Job out of the whirlwind, and said,*
> *2: Who is this that darkeneth counsel by words without knowledge?*
> *3: Gird up now thy loins like a man; for I will demand of thee, and answer thou me.*

38 FALLEN AND CAN'T GET UP

Falling Brings clarity and experiences and preparedness for the next move
Get Educated or enhance your education and Skillset
Get connected to Friends and Family
Let go of your pride and ego and open your mouth and ask for some kind of help
Soul talk, self-spirit talk, motivate your inner self to bring about the outer self
When falling on the road, it feels like the way came up and hit you

Ecclesiastes 3:

    To everything, there is a Season

1   *to everything there is a season and a time to every purpose under the heaven:*

2   *A time to be born, and a time to die; a time to plant, and a time to pluck up that which is planted;*

3   *A time to kill, and a time to heal; a time to break down, and a time to build up;*

4   *A time to weep, and a time to laugh; a time to mourn, and a time to dance;*

5   *A time to cast away stones, and a time to gather stones together; a time to embrace, and a time to refrain from embracing;*

6   *A time to get, and a time to lose; a time to keep, and a time to cast away;*

7   *A time to rend, and a time to sew; a time to keep silence, and a time to speak;*

8   *A time to love, and a time to hate; a time of war, and a time of peace.*

Reference- good read: "Born to Win "Muriel James Ed. D & Dorothy Jongeward Ph.D. these are Ph.D.'s they may know more than we do in something

    A time to be aggressive and a time to be passive

    A time to be together and a time to be alone

    A time to fight and a time to love

    A time to work and a time to play

    A time to cry and a time to laugh

    A time to confront and a time to withdraw

    A time to speak and a time to be silent

    A time to hurry and a time to wait.

Study each line and think deep within your subconscious and sub-subconscious what they mean and how they apply to you and yourself. If you cannot help yourself, you may not be able to help anyone. Therefore you are the first; you are number 1, you are

the God of you and God is the first over you. This is not selfish thinking, but for you to lift up anyone else you have first to bring yourself to be lifted up

> *Reframing to your life*
> *Read about the fall of various empires and what the cause is*
> *Become Self-aware*
> *Build self-esteem, self-control*
> *Work with imagery and see yourself rise, in a better job, financially well*
> *Study your time – what you apply yourself to*
> *Reject depression and motivate yourself forwards*
> *Do some soul searching*

Read about the laws of attraction and speaking words with power; it is a god given gift

Speak to your sickness and reject, renounce and cast the illnesses out of your body and mind

Rebuke the Demons of all illness

Speak to your body and control your cells, every single cell, spend the time to talk to yourself, your body, your organs, your brain, and your cells. They are all living beings and have an intellect higher than you do. Do you know these things and how to control yourself? Do you know what are your roles and responsibilities are for each organ and each cell?

Hosea 4:6 My people are destroyed for lack of knowledge: because thou hast rejected wisdom.

We do not know the body that given to us, we do not understand the mind, we do not understand our spirit, and we do not know our purpose, why are we here, why are we a human being? Why am I am a man? Or a woman?

I do not know ME, but I am expecting others to understand and know ME, react to ME as I am hoping them to as per my expectation, but yet I do Not Know ME. I do not know who I am, except by name and heritage, my position and status and how much I want to achieve or gather to sustain myself and family for an extended period, yet I do not know ME. When something goes wrong within ME, I depend on others to define what went wrong, by explaining how I feel, But I do not know ME, my BODY, Myself and what I am.

God made all knowledge available so that we can know our self and know him, for we are the IMAGE of him in spirit and given a body that was created to host HIM and to the US for a higher purpose than just being YOU.

Genesis 1: 26 *And God said, Let us make man in our image, after our* *likeness: and let them have dominion over the fish of the sea, and over the fowl of the air, and over the cattle, and over all the earth, and over every creeping thing that creepeth upon the earth.*

27   *So God created man in his own image, in the image of God created he him; male and female created he them. Matt 19:4 Mark 10:6*

For the Purpose: ***Genesis 1:28*** *And God blessed them, and God said unto them, **Be fruitful, and multiply**, and **replenish the earth,** and subdue it: and have dominion over the fish of the sea, and over the fowl of the air, and over every living thing that moveth upon the earth.*
DO NOT DESTROY THE EARTH. Subdue it, Use It, have dominion over it, let it be for your benefit BUT REPLENISH IT.

Today we cut down the forests for wood to build, but we de-forest and not re-forest. We harvest and not re-plant as we should, We mine for all minerals and devour the earth of its resources and leave it to collapse, we fight for the values of the other man's resources and take it as booty, spoils of war and became a parasite, a leech and suck it out and leave the people without for our greed and avarice and give ourselves compliments of our greatness

Each cell in your body already knows what to do, how to function, what its roles and responsibilities are and when to act with more power and control. Every part of your body has a consciousness, a life and a being of its own and would listen to every word of sound that you utter. The ancient Vedic scriptures stress the utterance of "OM" or "AUM" the universal sound. It is one of the most sacred symbols and should be sounded out loud to cause a vibration to the entire body, same goes for the word "Amen" or "Ameen." It is not just a word; it is a sound that vibrates the entire Head, Brain, Nasal passageways, through the lungs, torso, and core of the body. It sends vibrations that have an internal sonic effect to every organ and cell.

https://en.wikibooks.org/wiki/Hinduism/Religious_Symbols_of_Hinduism

"Hindus consider Aum to be the universal name of the Lord and that it surrounds all of creation. The sound emerging from the vocal cords starts from the base of the throat as "A." With the coming together of the lips, "U" is formed and when the lips closed, all sounds end in "M." The "amen" in Christianity and the "Ameen" in Islam and "aum" may show a common linguistic ancestry within the Indo-European language group, and it is conjectured that the Aum mantra may have traveled from the East to Europe changing its form and context. Judaism contains the first recorded use of "amen" in the context of a response by the congregation to the priest's prayer. Judaism defines the Semitic verb "amen" as meaning "to be trusted."

Om symbolizes the Supreme Personality of Godhead, i.e., Parabrahman. It symbolizes the prana or life breath which runs through one's body bestowed by the Parabrahman. The significance and explanation of Om is given in the Mandukya Upanishad.

Hindus believe that the essence of the Vedas (ancient Indian scriptures) is enshrined in the word Aum. The belief that the Lord started creating the world after chanting "Aum" and "atha" gives this religious symbol a fundamental relevance to the Hindu view of creation. Hence, its sound is considered to create an auspicious beginning for any task that one may undertake".

Sonography – A.K.A ultrasonography - is using high-frequency waves to produce an image for medical analysis, called **ultrasound** waves, and are useful in creating images that are useful in medical science. Sound waves are vibrations that travel through any space, any medium and air and can be very useful in the balance of the body and the nervous system. These are linked to the brain and have a powerful effect on Brainwaves, which influences the entire body and can cause quite a change positively or even negatively and the cells, nerves, etc. receives these sound waves that create a vibration within the body's nervous system. It is so powerful it can shatter hard tissues and disintegrates hard particles, such a cyst in the body and can also be a reverse effect if utilized improperly. Music is one example of the churning of the emotional components and results if variable emotional states, happiness, joy, sadness, depression, anxiety, emotional relationship, etc. The vibration of the universe, atmosphere and of the body can be enhanced or manipulated artificially by electronic music and devices to assist in changing the constant of each Cell and every atom in the environment. Each particle and each cell is always in vibration, a unique vibration and can be altered by sound frequencies (music, songs, instruments and other electronic/magnetic devices, changed and used to create scientific and psychosomatic healing abilities, which has an effect of consciousness and a chain reaction to the physical tiny minute cells. It can bring positive healing and can also be harmful if it is not monitored and used in a positive influential manner, with the right frequency and vibrations. Ancient India has developed methods of reciting mantras and prayers in a musical form, where every prayer or hymn is sung in a very defines note, where the keys include a lot of nasal vibrations of the Upper mouth (palate), which has over 84 different meridian points activated in the chanting of mantras and hymns sends out nasal waves and sounds to all the various parts 0of the body through the nervous system and the bones structure. These sound vibrations are useful in enhancing the body and carries healing of the body, mind, and spirit through the consciousness.   It is the same in the Church, Synagogue, temples through worship songs and music and produces a similar effect.

Sound is a potent energy force and can travel through any medium, water, air, Solids, space and vacuum and can send out a potent effect on anything, for human beings it can affect the emotions, creative force such as expression of love, joy, peace, and happiness and on the other hand can also influence sadness and pain. This can be the methodology of communicating with your body, mind, and spirit positively to alter various state of mind and can create healing powers within, as each cell, each nerve, each organ receives the beauty of sound and vibrations, it tunes itself and normalizes its state and follow a balance as well as an enhanced state of production of more of its functions and create that superpowers within that can fight against bacteria, sicknesses and negative body flows. Our body becomes the transport medium, our bones is a great conductor and so is our nerves.

> *Sidebar:* I have a few friends who are deaf-mute (Persons who are human, created by God); we love music and love to dance to good music. I taught a few on dancing, and asked the question "how do you dance to the music when you cannot hear anything?" Their response through sign language and partial lip syncing, told me that they feel the vibrations through their feet, through their body, arms and air". Vibration, Interpretation of vibration for a "Deaf-Mute" person is the key to their communication

There is a product called "Rife Machines," developed and named after Royal Raymond Rife, which are being utilized to control microorganism in the body, the main focus dedicated to Cancer research and cancer cure. It is proven that the device worked to cure cancer, but rejected by the AMA (American Medical Association). It sends a shallow voltage current and audio-frequency emitting device, capable of sending undetectable current and sonic sound through the body, where the sine wave destroys the cancer virus, further developed a "ray Tube" that zapped cancer virus through a very powerful microscope. Thus proof that sound and vibrations are part of our environment and can be useful in the maintenance of our physical and mental self. It is also documented, but not proven by introducing sine wave uses is 400-480Hz (444Hz) through water via resonant frequencies and is documented in the Vedas for 'AUM" to be 7.83Hz, which is the heartbeat of the Earth. A young person can typically hear from 20 Hz to 20 kHz (20,000 Hz), an older person about 60 years will hear about 15 KHz. A healthy human body vibrates in the range of 62 to 68 MHz

The "Miracle Frequency" is at 528Hz, the ancients used during meditation and sound healing, used audio tones and vibration frequencies to repair damaged tissues and cells within the body, such as the reasons why music is so essential and plays a significant role in our moods, emotions, mental states and has the ability to shrink tumors, shatter cells that are abnormal within the body.

"Jeremiah 51:55: For the LORD is going to destroy Babylon, And He will make her loud noise vanish from her. And their waves will roar like many glasses of water; the tumult of their voices sounds forth."
1 Thessalonians 5:16-18 …. Be joyful always. Pray continually. Give thanks in all circumstances, for this is God's will for your life
Psalms 150:3 Praise him with the sound of the trumpet: praise him with the psaltery and harp.

The sound is vibration, the whole world is a flow of energy, and everything is electromagnetic flow. Breath also has a wave that produces sound. Thus deep breathing and "dragon Breathing' is therapeutic that creates vibration and sonic low resonant audio vibrations that keep the body in tune. The DNA itself is the shape and vibrations of a sine wave in the form our DNA Helex sound matrix. The DNA itself is like a receiver and transmitter of frequency, possibly divine frequency.

Everything on this earth vibrates; the Universe vibrates are atomic material that follows a constant motion, which generates frequencies and sound, sending an ordinary sound wave throughout the universe, the solar system, the earth, and every living organism. We need to be in tune with this vibration, in tune with the sound and the energy it emits and engulfs.

Every atom, every cell is continuously vibrating and can be enhanced by the use of sound and words. We use sound and music to modulate brainwaves and can use words to do the same. The Eastern religions, yogis, sages, seers have developed very great intricate sprayers in mantras that have a useful enhancement to consciousness and induction of healing powers to the body, mind, and spirit. When you say the word "AUM" as is should be pronounced, with the long breath and the position of the tongue and lips, it sends a vibration to the roof of the mouth and vibrates the Brain, Pineal gland (considered the channel to the heavenly dimension) and influenced the body's nervous system. These vibrations may sound very low externally and very low frequency, but internally within the body, it is so powerful that it can be a mighty force that can cause quite phenomena within that is so powerful can be used as a weapon against anything. It is so powerful it can affect both our physical and emotional environment

NASA Scientist declared that the sound of the Universe is "AUM," the sound from the Sun is "AUM," I am not in a state of knowledge more excellent than these scientists to doubt them as they have it recorded and available on YouTube.

The bible is full of prayers and communication with God over every circumstance. The history of the Old Testament depicts practically every normal condition that a person can go through, though not all apply to you personally, it is displaying the secure and robust living in the old and the means and methods of getting by through faith and belief.

The New Testament brought about change, as God renews his covenant and delivers greater more straightforward teaching that is easy to understand and follow; he broke off all the long, tedious process of coming into the presence of God and removed all the barriers towards salvation. Teaching us how to heal, take control, reminds us of our abilities and dominion and gave unto us more power to overcome any circumstance. As stated, he wants you to have an abundant life and not a life of suffering and hardship.

For the healing of your body, you must treat your body with respect and compassion as you are treating another person whom you love dearly (mother, father, brother, sister, son, daughter, etc.), knowing that it is made up of consciousness and conscious cells and particles (God Particle) that have a mind and emotions. Thus the scripture telling you about treating your body "as it is a vessel for the spirit of God to dwell in."

1 Corinthians 6: 19	*What? Know ye not that your body is the temple of the Holy Ghost which is in you, which ye have of God, and ye are not your own?*
1 Corinthians 6: 20	*For ye are bought with a price: therefore glorify God in your body, and in your spirit, which are God's.*
1 Corinthians 3: 16	*Know ye not that ye are the temple of God, and that the Spirit of God dwelleth in you?*
1 Corinthians 3: 17	*If any man defile the temple of God, him shall God destroy; for the temple of God is holy, which temple ye are.*
Romans 12: 1	*I beseech you, therefore, brethren, by the mercies of God, that ye present your bodies a living sacrifice, holy, acceptable unto God, which is your reasonable service.*
Romans 12: 2	*And be not conformed to this world: but be ye transformed by the renewing of your mind, that ye may prove what is that good, and acceptable, and perfect, will of God.*
Romans 12: 3	*For I say, through the grace given unto me, to every man that is among you, not to think of himself more highly than he ought to think; but to think soberly, according to as God hath dealt with every man the measure of faith.*

Speak to your body as it is a friend, trusting that they will fulfill your desires and help you do the things you want them to do. Pray in the spirit and ask the Divine Spirit of God "Jehovah Rapha," the healer to heal your body and take control of each cell within your body. Tell your body to declare healing to every part, be specific for all known sicknesses within, diabetes, heart problems, cholesterol, High blood pressure, cancer, etc Use some methods of imagery, looking at a physiological diagram of your body, focus on each area and talk to it and the spirit of God is within and each part of your body is under that control. If doubtful, I would like you to explain the full functionality of your heart, your brain, your organs, if you have the intellect or wisdom to do so, therefore you must believe that these parts are supreme, and created by some supreme entity that makes them function in such unique manner. Your minds, it is an amazing and most potent tool that is capable of producing transformation within.

Prayers when others are persecuting you: This is one Psalm that calls on God to deal with enemies. David was pleading for God's protection in the midst of a crisis. Sometimes when the enemy steps up the attack, physically and mentally, you need to call on God for protection. It may sound very harsh, but at least you are asking God to step in and take the affirmative action and not allowing you to be the aggressor, for it is for God to seek vengeance and not you.

Psalms 35: 1	*Plead my cause, O LORD, with them that strive with me: fight against them that fight against me.*
Psalms 35: 2	*Take hold of shield and buckler, and stand up for mine help.*
Psalms 35: 3	*Draw out also the spear, and stop the way against them that persecute me: say unto my soul, I am thy salvation.*
Psalms 35: 4	*Let them be confounded and put to shame that seeks after my soul: let them be turned back and brought to confusion that devises my hurt.*
Psalms 35: 5	*Let them be as chaff before the wind: and let the angel of the LORD chase them.*
Psalms 35: 6	*Let their way be dark and slippery: and let the angel of the LORD persecute them.*
Psalms 35: 7	*For without cause have they hid for me their net in a pit, which without cause they have digged for my soul.*
Psalms 35: 8	*Let destruction come upon him at unawares; and let his net that he hath hid catch himself: into that very destruction let him fall.*
Psalms 35: 9	*And my soul shall be joyful in the LORD: it shall rejoice in his salvation.*
Psalms 35: 10	*All my bones shall say, LORD, who is like unto thee, which deliverest the poor from him that is too strong for him, yea, the poor and the needy from him that spoileth him?*
Psalms 35: 11	*False witnesses did rise up; they laid to my charge things that I knew not.*
Psalms 35: 12	*They rewarded me evil for good to the spoiling of my soul.*
Psalms 35: 13	*But as for me, when they were sick, my clothing was sackcloth: I humbled my soul with fasting, and my prayer returned into mine own bosom.*
Psalms 35: 14	*I behaved myself as though he had been my friend or brother: I bowed down heavily, as one that mourneth for his mother.*
Psalms 35: 15	*But in mine adversity they rejoiced, and gathered themselves together: yea, the abjects gathered themselves together against me, and I knew it not; they did tear me, and ceased not:*
Psalms 35: 16	*With hypocritical mockers in feasts, they gnashed upon me with their teeth.*
Psalms 35: 17	*Lord, how long wilt thou look on? rescue my soul from their destructions, my darling from the lions.*
Psalms 35: 18	*I will give thee thanks in the great congregation: I will praise thee among much people.*
Psalms 35: 19	*Let not them that are mine enemies wrongfully rejoice over me: neither let them wink with the eye that hate me without a cause.*
Psalms 35: 20	*For they speak not peace: but they devise deceitful matters against them that are quiet in the land.*
Psalms 35: 21	*Yea, they opened their mouth wide against me, and said, Aha, aha, our eye hath seen it.*
Psalms 35: 22	*This thou hast seen, O LORD: keep not silence: O Lord, be not far from me.*

Psalms 35: 23	*Stir up thyself, and awake to my judgment, even unto my cause, my God and my Lord.*
Psalms 35: 24	*Judge me, O LORD my God, according to thy righteousness; and let them not rejoice over me*
Psalms 35: 25	*Let them not say in their hearts, Ah, so would we have it: let them not say, We have swallowed him up.*
Psalms 35: 26	*Let them be ashamed and brought to confusion together that rejoice at mine hurt: let them be clothed with shame and dishonor that magnify themselves against me.*
Psalms 35: 27	*Let them shout for joy, and be glad, that favor my righteous cause: yea, let them say continually, Let the LORD be magnified, which hath pleasure in the prosperity of his servant.*
Psalms 35: 28	*And my tongue shall speak of thy righteousness and of thy praise all the day long.*

39 PRAYERS FOR HEALING CANCER

Understanding Cancer: Cancer is a weak and confused cell with the incorrect genetic information, unable to perform its intended function. It was exposed to harmful substances or chemicals or damaged by external causes. It could also be related to the body production of ONE lousy cell out of the billions of cells produced continually; this bad cell will multiply and produce other bad cells which then become a cluster of bad, non-functional cells that become a pack of fast-growing hardened cells. These cells are damaged and do not die as regular cells do as programmed by the body, cells produce Carcinogen, a substance that promotes carcinogenesis, the formation of cancer.

Ephesians 3: 20   Now unto him that is able to do exceeding abundantly above all that we ask or think, according to the power that worketh in us,

Father in the name of Jesus Christ of Nazareth, I speak to all the cells in my body to rise up as the God Particle enhances and give you strength and power to fight against all radical cells that are creating any abnormality in my body. I command you all through the power of Jesus to rise up and take authority of my body and all organs, all cells, and elements within my body, dispel those that do not belong there and take away the powers of those that are causing any negative reaction. Raise up your army of T-Cells and fight against any and all cancer cells and make them powerless, reduce their effect on my body, remove them and dispel them from inside, disintegrate them into water and let them pass out as waste from inside to outside. Guard me and my organs, my heart, my liver, my pancreas, my kidneys, my lungs, my brain, my pineal glands, my stomach, my intestines, clean my blood and let the white cells fight against any odd cells and let all my organs function to 100 percent capacity and behave normally.

I give you thanks in advance for all the works that you are doing in me and praise you for healing my entire body. I give power and authority to God and the God particle to take control and make me perfect again. In Jesus name. Amen.

Sickness and Cures in the Vedas: Secrets that were in existence over 5000 years ago

The Atharvaveda is one of the four Vedas dedicated to Life, health and overcoming sicknesses and disease. The Vedas mentioned about 75 plants that are related to the cures of many terminal and debilitating illnesses.

The Atharva Veda (Sanskrit: अथर्ववेद, Atharvaveda from atharvānas and Veda, meaning "knowledge") is the "knowledge storehouse of atharvāṇas, the procedures for everyday life". The text is the fourth Veda, but has been a late addition to the Vedic scriptures of Hinduism

Ayurvedic (Science of Life) Cures through herbal Medicines: A must to add due to the nature of the beast and its ability to cause ultimate death.

Medicines come from the extracts of plants, processes and put into a liquid form or a compressed form with a combination of many other chemical components for off-set of storages and side effects. There are many possible theories of cures integrated from Ayurveda, herbal medicines and other forms of rituals. Cancer cures found in the Vedas over 5000 years ago. This knowledge is investigated more by many large pharmaceutical companies, and are still utilized and applied in the Indian continent (India, China, Asian countries and Indo-Asian cultures all around the world), the knowledge is translated and began to infiltrate the western world where many are choosing these forms of cancer treatment rather than the medical sciences inventions such as Chemotherapy and Radiation. Ayurveda is an ancient Indian system of medicine that utilizes various herbal and cultural methods to cure many ailments and sicknesses. Ayurveda includes strict diets and specific types of food based on the particular disease, first herbal medicines, body cleansing internal and external, meditation and spirituality integrated into a strong belief system, Yoga, psychological, physiological, relaxation and imagery. Massage therapy and chiropractic methods are also applied to create a free-flowing and lose all tensions, muscles and joint for the free flow of blood and oxygen throughout the body. It is all related to a balance of body, mind, and spirit and focusing on the body natural immune system to be activated and enhanced and fueled by any ayurvedic application of herbal and special treatment. Cleansing includes laxatives and enemas, flushing of the body toxicity by consumption of fluids and different drinks, which leads to a clean body, clean organs, sanitary system, removal of toxic contamination in the blood and the entire body. Some of the herbal treatment includes plant products such as from Pomegranate extracts and juice, Mangosteen, Withania Somnifera, Sanjeevani bryopteris, which is traditional Indian plant which can stop the growth of cancer cells. Boswellia Serrata known as Frankincense or guggul is part of the remedy (Frankincense and Myrrh were two costly gifts brought to Jesus by the Wise men-Magi's from the EAST –Persia, India, Arabia).

According to Ayurveda, the body must be in perfect balance (Dosha balance – the entire body/systems/functions and communications). Cells in the body that are off balance sometimes due to the imbalance and the genetic code being influenced by this imbalance due to abnormal fluid levels and the DNA programming these cells start to malfunction or over function (Instead of dying and recreation, they overgrow). This is the advantage of understanding Ayurveda and its path to healing; the balance of mental, emotional, physical and spiritual self is the miracle to a healthy sound body free from any unhealthy radicals.

Many diseases, if it roots cause identified, treated and eliminated.

There are a lot of herbs that can be used to stop or slow down the cancer growth and keep all the cancer cells in check some are:

Amla considered one of the top superfoods that contain some chemical compounds that kill cancer cells.

Tulsi – a form of basil has miraculous healing powers and is also helps in diabetes. Used in much Indian cultural and spiritual worship

Garlic contains sulfur, flavonoids, selenium, and arginine (in the bible as one of the top foods that the Egyptians supplied to the Hebrews to keep them healthy

Turmeric, Curcumin anti-oxidant, anti-inflammatory, and antiseptic abilities

Ashwagandha - a form of Indo-ginseng withaferin which is used to kill cancer cells

Ginger – best for treating many types of infections and diseases.

Soursop (Graviola) contains niacin, riboflavin, folate, and iron. The fruit is strong in antioxidants which neutralize harmful compounds in the body which causes damages to organs and cells; it also has solid cancer and diabetes-fighting compounds. It can reduce tumors and kill cancer cells

Japanese Insulin Plant (costus Igneus): A medicinal plant with Anti-diabetic property

Additional herbal cures: Andrographis paniculata, Annona atemoya/muricata, Phyllanthus niruri/amarus, Piper longum, Podophyllum hexandrum linn. Tinospora cordifolia, Semecarpus Anacardium, Soy Beans, Green Tea, Garlic and onions, Turmeric, tomatoes

Knowing that cancer is a top killer today (second cause of death in the world), more information towards cure and the research of the cure as listed in the Vedas below: **Ayurveda-(Ayus =life, Veda=Knowledge) Three main areas: Charaka Samhita (1100 Plants), Susruta Samhita (1270 Plants), Kashyaya Samhita (Gynecology and Children health)**

The eight division of Ayurveda
(1) Kayachikitsa –   Internal Medicine

(2) Kaumar Bhritya –   *Pediatrics*

(3) Bhootavidya –   *Psychiatry*

(4) Shalakya -   *Otorhinolaryngology, and Ophthalmology*

(5) Shaly -   *Surgery*

(6) Agada Tantra   *Toxicology*

(7) Rasayana -   *Geriatrics*

(8) Vajikarana -   *(Aphrodisiacs and Eugenics*

The third segment focused on the three biological humous or Doha's, the seven body tissues, digestion, and state of mind, etc. The Ayurveda is generally all about medicines, health care and methodologies of keeping the body mind and spirit balanced and intact.

Chemotherapy is the most common treatment, and it has serious side-effects, plus it kills good and bad cells. The combination of Ayurvedic medicines to counter the side-effect of Chemotherapy is the solution. The ancient Indian cures have been successful for centuries, but the knowledge is fading away and getting lost, suppressed and destroyed in conspiracy theories. At this moment Russian scientist has cracked the code for the Vedas Sanskrit SOMA drink which is said to be the drink of the Gods and a cure for all. The Iranians call it Hoama in the sacred Avesta, "divine mushroom" resembles the popular psychoactive species Psilocybe cubensis, Somalata (Sarcostemma Acidum)is another name for the alternative, since the original plans may be extinct.

The bottom line is that cancer is a killer and terminal illness remedied in a few procedures, surgery to remove the cancer cells, chemotherapy, radiation therapy, immunotherapy, hormone therapy, Stem cell transplant and some form of precision medicines. These cures were written and given unto man through the inspired word of God in ancient times and still exist today. Scriptures talk about faith healing and a belief system that causes the mind-body to respond to the supernatural and healing take place through faith. I have witnessed a whole lot of healing in my church alone, cancer, tumors, surgery, heart attacks and many terminal illnesses cured, healed, removed and disappeared, and this is happening all over the globe in many church and temples.

Knowing your enemy is the road to defeating them

Adding more details to understand Cancer fully since one in every three (1 in 3) persons are likely to suffer from Cancer in the next decade, it would be best to understand How? Why? What? And what do we do to counter? Plus all that we can know about and counterattack this silent torturing killer.

Some primary reasons why Cancer is so rampant is due to poor diets and too much fast food and junk foods that are available and are the most consumed. Smoking certainly associated with causing the rise in people living with cancer, other factors include pollution, drugs, Obesity, too much exposure to UV rays of the Sun, being infected by some virus that escalates into a cancer tumor and other reasons could be related to

DNA and hereditary.

   It all starts with the smallest of the tiniest particle that makes up the body, The CELL (about one micron = 1/1000 of a millimeter) in size, is one of God's amazing creation that makes up the structure of the body over 60,000 – 70,000 billion cells in a human body. The code of the cell is still not released to humanity and scientist still trying to understand this tiny 'God Particle".

   A cell consists of a nucleus and Mitochondrion surrounded by the cell membrane, in other words, it is a living being that has a brain, and a body carries all the genetic code of our DNA (Deoxyribonucleic Acid). Imagine this tiny practically invisible nucleus of the cell transmits the instruction in a library of information on "The How to function" and work, act and perform in the processing proteins (food) for the body to function correctly. Here lies the key to our very nature and good health where sugar production and manipulation is the key to maintaining fitness or non-fitness of each cell and the entire body. Proteins transported throughout the body via bloodstreams and distributed adequately and sufficiently as per the needs of each membrane or parts of the body. If the distribution is insufficient, there is an imbalance, and the insufficiency or any error in the creation of protein can result in a cell deformity or cell trying to adapt to the changes and works against the DNA code instructions, thereby creating a new strain.

   The mitochondrion in the Cell creates energy from food, proteins, etc.) And in the process, toxic waste is dispersed as waste, which can trigger tumors by the adjustments made to the genetic codes. (Please note this is ONE KEY to the Conquest over the elimination of Cancer, But still hard to understand and to read as well as detect, but can be superimposed and forced upon by Stem cell process and methodology). When the protection membrane through receptors cannot communicate with the world outside the cell, the cell can try and resolve by responding automatically towards what it thinks is going on, and this could cause negative processes and responses from the surrounding area resulting in an abnormality and harmful tumor effect. It will attempt and will re-write the genetic code to make amends to its understanding of the environment and what needed for survival, a process known as mutation. Another method is that the cell in this process of adaptation or deficiency loses library of genetic codes (just like memory loss) , it will try to act on what memory remains and even morph itself with some other cells, this results in a deformed cell or abnormal cell formation thus cancer (where cancer is abnormal cells that grow and create union with other cells themselves into clusters).

   The body's 60,000 – 70,000 billion cells all COMMUNICATE with each other and know their function and works together in unison for the greater purpose of sustaining and maintaining the body efficiently in good health.

Side Note: If 70,000 billion-minute cells can live in unison, why can't 7 billion human beings do the same? Thus the God's Supreme Being intervention into planet Earth, which he labeled and called "SHEOL" of "HELL" because Satan Fell here and this Earth is his Kingdom and dominion. Therefore we live in Hell and are fighting to get back to a place where God promised us he would take us. Which Makes Planet Earth not the single planet with life forms, but also the worst real estate in the Universe of living beings (because of Logic).

The body itself within the codebook rules possess a process called "Apoptosis" (Definition of Apoptosis : a genetically directed process of cell self-destruction that is marked by the fragmentation of nuclear DNA, is activated either by the presence of a stimulus or removal of a suppressing agent or stimulus, is a normal physiological process eliminating DNA-damaged, superfluous, or unwanted cells, and when halted (as by genetic mutation) may result in uncontrolled cell growth and tumor formation), where cells that are damaged or becomes corrupt, rebellious or dysfunctional are destroyer or put to death, or becomes suicidal. There is a Big BUT here, if these cells refuse to follow the commandment of the genetic codebook, rules, and laws of the code, they follow a path of survival instinct and slowly takes control of itself and forms a possible coup with other cells and /or mutates and over a number of years grow into a distinguishable or visible tumor .

Other means of this dysfunction can occur through a traumatic incident, accident, damage to the body, toxicity by bad food consumption, preservatives, poison, UV rays, Environmental conditions, sicknesses, and infections are on the list to cause cell damage which can result into cancerous cell formation. This is the other process of cell damage called "Necrosis."

Now that you have a bit of a clearer understanding of Cancer, its roots and causes, it takes us back to the mere imagery of how complex our bodies are and the complexity of the functions within. The importance is to understand that each living cell within the body has its very own intelligence, its very own laws, rules, roles and code that it lives by, and all controlled by the ultimate supercomputer of the human body called the Brain. If we put all the instructions and laws of a single cell into text, it would be thousands of lines of instructions. Medical science and scientists are still at an infant stage of understanding One Single cell entirely and even have to assume another 60,000 billion cells within each human body.

This is why it is essential to understand that as a "Human Being" as "a Man (woman), you do not possess a minute or fraction of a fraction, or 1/1000 of 1/1000 the mental faculty or brain power to understand the full functions of the body, mind, and spirit. God has created an amazing being called "Man" (both male and female) [Genesis 1:27 in the image of God created he him; male and female created he them. Gen 1:31 And God saw everything that he had made, and, behold, it was very good].

Let us stress on the following matters in Genesis 1 of the 'Holy Bible.'

Gen 1: 1 God made heavens and Earth, Light <u>"and it was Good."</u>

Gen 1: 7 God made the firmament, divided water <u>"and it was so."</u>

Gen 1: 10 God made the Land, seas, and oceans <u>"and it was Good."</u>

Gen 1: 16 God created Grass, herbs, fruit trees, **"and God saw that it was good."**

Gen1: 20 God made fish and birds

Gen1: 16 God made the Sun and Moon and Start **"and God saw that it was good."**

Gen 1: 21 God created great whales, and every living creature that moveth, and winged fowl **"and God saw that it was good."**

Gen1: 25 And God made the beast of the earth after his kind, and cattle after their kind, and everything that creepeth **"and God saw that it was good."**

Gen1: 26 THEN God decided to make Man: And God said, Let us make man in our image, after our likeness

Gen 1: 27 So God created man in his own image, in the image of God created he him; male and female created he them.

Gen1: 31 And God saw everything that he had made, and, **behold***,* **it was very good**

The Big BUT: Given Free will and dominion and instructions, laws and bylaws and codes to live by, given unto man, but man became his very own cancer (like the rebellious cell who refuses to either change or die). Therefore man has to return to his maker for remorse and rectification, salvation and answers, which includes your cells as well.

Deuteronomy 31:6 Be strong and of a good courage, fear not, nor be afraid of them: for the LORD thy God, he it is that doth go with thee; he will not fail thee, nor forsake thee.

Isaiah 41:10   Fear thou not; for I am with thee: be not dismayed; for I am thy God: I will strengthen thee; yea, I will help thee; yea, I will uphold thee with the right hand of my righteousness.

Proverbs 3: 5   Trust in the LORD with all thine heart; and lean not unto thine own understanding. 6 In all thy ways acknowledge him, and he shall direct thy paths.

2 Corinthian 6:16   For all things are for your sakes, that the abundant grace might through the thanksgiving of many redound to the glory of God. 16 For which cause we faint not; but though our outward man perish, yet the inward man is renewed day by day. 17 For our light affliction, which is but for a moment, worketh for us a far more exceeding and eternal weight of glory;18 While we look not at the things which are seen, but at the things which are not seen: for the things which are seen are temporal; but the things which are not seen are eternal

Mark 11:20   *And in the morning, as they passed by, they **saw the fig tree dried up from the roots**.*

21   *And Peter calling to remembrance saith unto him, Master, behold the fig tree which **thou cursedst is withered away**.*

22   *And Jesus answering saith unto them, Have faith in God.*

23   *For verily I say unto you, T**hat whosoever shall say unto this mountain, Be thou removed**, and **be thou cast into the sea**; and shall **not doubt** in his heart, but **shall believe that those things which he saith shall come to pass;** he shall have whatsoever he saith.*

24   *Therefore I say unto you, What things soever ye desire when ye pray, believe that ye receive them, and ye shall have them.*

Here is a key in the prayer world.
   The fig tree is used analogously in place of Israel
and Sin, But it also signifies the barren, the things that are not productive or may appear as good but does not serve its purpose. In this reference, we are going to refer to cancer as the fig tree. It is there, and you need to speak to it as you talk to the mountain in this reference, the mountain is your burden, the fig tree is a demonstration of what happens as you talk to it and tell it to be removed. The fig tree dried up from the root. Don't you want cancer, diabetes, and high blood pressure, cholesterol to be dried up and removed? Therefore apply the word of God and the method used here to speak to your sickness, speak to cancer. Curse The spirit of Cancer by the power and authority of God and as God dictate

"Whomsoever shall say unto this mountain (Cancer, sickness, disease) be thou removed, with nodoubt and belief and faith it will be removed" Command it to be removed, Speak to your warrior cells to fight against the cancer cells and conquer them, destroy themand cast them out of your body.

There are a couple of lessons to learn from this and a few applications of power.
(1) It becomes sub-consciously injected into your system
(2) your words have power and you are using that voice and ability to command the cells and the body take the appropriate action you are using the power of God within and in the heavens to command it to be removed

(3)Believe in your very own power that you possess and what was given unto you by God

***Bind the cancer cells, bind the Spirit of Cancer, Bind the root of cancer**, bind all cells associated with cancer and cast them out of your body, use your internal energy to generate more power and apply it to the area and the cancer cells, focus and see through imagery that they are breaking up, shattering into little microscopic tine* *pieces and dispelled through excretion. Command the T-Cells, the B-Cells to take authority and fight against these bad cells. Rub your hands together to generate heat and electromagnetic, kinetic energy and place your hands on the area, repeatedly, power flows from high potential to low potential. The high potential is the rubbing of your hands and Laying of those hands on the area shattering and burning away those cancer cells or any other disease. Be proactive get rid of your sickness from within yourself and through the power of the universe, the power generated from you and the power of God through faith and belief.*

***In your prayer and verbiage be creative, be imaginative, be visual, see the sickness** shrink, tell it to shrink and disintegrate, command it to dissolve, command all energies within (all Electrical, electromagnetic, kinetic and all frequencies of power and sound to rise and be strengthened, fight against all bad cells within the body, in the lymph, in the blood and conquer the cancer cells and the disease and cast it out of your body.*

This technique and teaching you apply to every sickness. Make sure you bind any demon that associated with the illness, for that is the weakness and the open door that demons look for to attach themselves to it.
When done with the prayers, make sure you give thanks for your healing, now and in the future and to keep you free.
Many say "I have a brain," but have you seen it? Do you believe you have one? Do you understand the abilities of your brain and the power your brain possesses? So here is the test for you to "Believe" "Believe in faith" that you can be healed, and your brain can understand you and do what you are asking and commanding it to do. You must believe in yourself and your faith in God and the supernatural to bring about the healing. It is done in many places around the world, and you are no exception.

What do you have to lose?, you have some form of illness that needs attention and your time is getting near, your disease is getting maybe worse and worse daily, surrender your heart to God and let the miraculous takes its course, God is a forgiving God, and no heart is hard enough to resist God's supernatural healing powers. Change our heart, change your mind, change your thinking and let the Spirit of God be in control to bring to you the miracles that hundreds and maybe thousands have seen, witness and experience in the day and time.

Hebrew 11.6   *But without faith, it is impossible to please him: for he that cometh to God must believe that he is and that he is a rewarder of them that diligently seek him.*

Psalm 103:1-5   *Bless the Lord, O my soul: and all that is within me, bless his holy name. 2. Bless the Lord, O my soul, and forget not all his benefits: 3. Who forgiveth all thine iniquities; who healeth all thy diseases; 4. Who redeemeth thy life from destruction; who crowneth thee with lovingkindness and tender mercies; 5. Who satisfieth thy mouth with good things; so that thy youth is renewed like the eagle's.*

Exodus 15:26   *And said, if thou wilt diligently hearken to the voice of the Lord thy God, and wilt do that which is right in his sight, and wilt give ear to his commandments and keep all his statutes, I will put none of these diseases upon thee, which I have brought upon the Egyptians: for I am the Lord that healeth thee.*

John 11:25   *Jesus said unto her, I am the resurrection and the life: he that believeth on me though he were dead yet shall he live: 26 And whosoever liveth and believeth in me shall never die. Believeth thou this?*

Matthew 8:2   *And a leper came to Him and bowed down before Him, and said, "Lord, if you are willing, you can make me clean."*

Romans 6:19   *I am speaking in human terms because of the weakness of your flesh For just as you presented your members as slaves to impurity and to lawlessness, resulting in further lawlessness, so now present your members as slaves to righteousness, resulting in sanctification.*

40 PRAYERS FOR HEALING DIABETES

Father, Lord God of Heaven and Earth, Jehovah Rapha, Jesus, As we call upon you Lord and your Holy Spirit, I pray and take authority of all Demonic spirits of the air and in this environment, I take authority of all demonic spirits that are affecting our mental and physical bodies, bind them, rebuke and cast them out into the Lake of Fire to burn in Hell. I bind the spirit of Diabetes in the name of Jesus, I bind the spirit that is affecting our liver, pancreas, and kidneys and cast them out into the lake of fire. I pray and ask you lord by your power and might, as the great physician and miracle healer to bring healing to all those who are suffering from diabetes, high blood pressure, kidney disease, and liver disorder, clean up my pancreas and all organs associated with the condition of diabetes. Restore all my organs in my body to be repaired and restored to the state you made them be –perfect in every way. Let them function correctly and deliver adequate insulin and chemicals necessary to heal diabetes. Heal them lord and make them clean and healthy again. In Jesus Name AMEN.

The rates of diagnosed diabetes in adults by race/ethnic background are:

7.4% of non-Hispanic whites
8.0% of Asian Americans
12.1% of Hispanics
12.7% of non-Hispanic blacks
15.1% of American Indians/Alaskan Natives

The Herbal remedies for controlling and curing or bringing diabetes to the stabilized state are:

Curcumin

Ginseng

Fenugreek

Psyllium

Cinnamon

Aloe Vera: - Lowers blood sugar levels

Bitter Mellon: - A medicinal fruit, the leaves are used as a tea to lower blood sugar levels

Milk Thistle

Holy Basil – Tulsi

Gurmar Leaves

Jamun Seeds and Juice

Banyan Tree bark

Neem (Azadirachta indica) called *'the divine tree' posses a long list of benefits*

and natural cures and listed in many medical informational websites. Neem is processed and sold in every pharmacy and supermarket. Neem is simple to use; the leaves are boiled to make a tea that flushes all organs and is a blood purifier as well

Moringa *oleifera (Sijan or drumstick plant) –*

   Indian subcontinent is called 'the miracle plant" used for "tired blood" (anemia); arthritis and other joint pain (rheumatism); asthma; cancer; constipation; diabetes; diarrhea; epilepsy; stomach pain; stomach and intestinal ulcers; intestinal spasms; headache; heart problems; high blood pressure; kidney stones; fluid retention; thyroid disorders; and bacterial, fungal, viral, and parasitic infections and a ton of other uses.. Now, this plant is processed and sold in every supermarket and every pharmacy. Moringa contains proteins, vitamins, and minerals and an antioxidant protect cells from damage.

Insulin Plant-Costus Igneus – uses are to control blood sugar levels, helps to strengthen cells in the pancreas

Black Seed Oil - another miracle herb that can heal cancer, diabetes, high blood pressure

Isaiah 53:5:	*"But he was pierced for our rebellion, crushed for our sins. He was beaten so we could be whole. He was whipped so we could be healed."*
Deuteronomy 28:1, 6:	*"If you fully obey the Lord your God and carefully keep all his commands that I am giving you today…. Wherever you go and whatever you do, you will be blessed."*
Psalm 41:3:	*"The Lord nurses them when they are sick and restores them to health."*
Psalm 103:3:	*"He forgives all my sins and heals all my diseases."*
Proverbs 3:8:	*"Then you will have healing for your body and strength for your bones."*
Jeremiah 30:17:	*"'I will give you back your health and heal your wounds,' says the Lord."*
1 Peter 2:24:	*"He personally carried our sins in his body on the cross so that we can be dead to sin and live for what is right. By his wounds, you are healed."*

Lord God of Heaven and Earth, I come to you with a childlike faith, believing that you will hear me in my prayer and quest to you to heal me of diabetes, I pray in the name of Jesus you rebuke the spirit of Diabetes and cast them out of my body in the lake of fire or unto the Feet of Jesus Christ. Lord, I submit my entire life and body to you to shine your light upon me and cleanse my body of this sickness and make me whole again, remove this thorn in my flesh and heal me from diabetes. I command all cells in my body to repair my Pancreas, *my liver, and my kidneys and make the organs function as I command my subconscious mind and my unconscious mind to work in my favor to repair **every organ, I** command my conscious mind and my spirit to work and repair all cells, organs and let each and every organ function efficiently and effectively to control the flow of all enzymes, fluids, lubricants, bile and all other fluids within my body be regulated to normal.*

2 Chronicles 20:17 *Ye shall not need to fight in this battle: set yourselves, stand ye still, and see the salvation of the LORD with you, O Judah and Jerusalem: fear not, nor be dismayed; tomorrow go out against them: for the LORD will be with you.*

I pray to the Lord God my creator to reconstruct my inner body and tough my entire body to shine your heavenly light and filter me thoroughly and cleanse me of any and every bacteria, germs, parasites, and cell that do not belong in my body to be expelled In the name of Jesus Christ and by applying the Blood of Jesus upon me. Amen.

In the very same way, you continue daily to rebuke and renounce, cast out all sicknesses from your body for the following, speak in an ordinary voice as you are talking to an enemy with boldness, courage, and power, use simple common words. Be creative and be imaginative, use imagery to visualize the T-Cells and –Cells chewing away at cancer cells, etc. You must let your mind, energies, and spirit work for you through the Supreme Divinity. The bible is full of healing examples and given authority to do much more than were done in biblical times. Sometimes we become too self-centered, too proud or too educated to exercise our God-given talents to perform religious miracles. We can spend time fellowship with friends and family and pray with them whether, in a religious to me or a psychological tone, it will help to draw in the spiritual. The body and its cells are living beings and can be reprogrammed to function efficiently as was created to perform. It is for you to spiritually connect to the organs in the body and speak to your body, your glands, your cells, and your DNA to adjust and make changes as per the way your body was created to function by God. The ancients do this through meditation and speaking to the spirit and innate powers within to subliminally control the functions of the entire body and system to produce adequate cells that strengthen your immune system and fight against the adversity of primitive cells that causes an imbalance within. Prayers are a way of communication in a state of calm to the powers within and the powers above to make amends and regulate your entire system to normality.

*Prayer for Healing for Cholesterol & High Blood Pressure/ **Heart Disease***

Lord God of heaven and earth In Jesus name and by the Blood of Jesus, I pray and ask that you shine your light through me and filter my body, remove all the toxicity from within and cleanse me, remove High Blood Pressure and Cholesterol from within my body and make me healthy again. I need your mighty healing hands to touch me in a mighty way and let the power of miracles of your touch redeem me from all these sicknesses and make me whole again. I am in need of your holy touch; I give you all praise and honor and give thanks in advance for healing me. In Jesus name AMEN

- Exercise regularly
- Eat a healthy balance
- Reduce sodium (salt) in your diet
- Limit the amount of alcohol you drink
- Quit smoking Cut back on caffeine
- Reduce your stress
- Monitor your blood pressure at home and
- see your doctor regularly
- Lose extra pounds
- Get support

Use the template above to pray against any other disease

Prayer for Healing of Addiction/Smoking/Alcohol/Drugs

Prayer for Healing of Ischemic heart disease, or coronary artery disease

Prayer for Healing of diabetes

Prayer for Healing of being overweight

Prayer for Healing of Stroke

Prayer for Healing of Lower respiratory infections

Prayer for Healing of Chronic obstructive pulmonary disease

Prayer for Healing of Trachea, bronchus, and lung cancers

Prayer for Healing of Alzheimer's disease and other dementias, Parkinson's disease, ALS, etc

Prayer for Healing of Tuberculosis

Prayer for Healing of chronic alcohol use

Prayer for – "make your list" with faith and belief it will be done

Catatonia: *a state of psycho-motor immobility and behavioral abnormality manifested by stupor, closely related to schizophrenia and mental disorder and neurological conditions, bipolar disorder, post-traumatic stress disorder, depression, narcolepsy, and autoimmune disorders. It is also similar to encephalitis lathargica and neuroleptic malignant syndrome. Catatonia affects a person's ability to move healthily, either in a minimally responsive or excessive response, excessive movements to even being violent behavior and can last up to 10 days or weeks. Parkinson's disease is closely related and may also be a proponent of catatonia. What it means is that the Brain cells* and secretion (chemicals produced) are out-of-balance and either deficient or carries the wrong responses.

Excessive, unusual movements, agitated actions, frenzy, restlessness, delirium, fevers, rigidity, sweating, abnormal blood pressure and heart rate, psychosis are some of the symptoms and results. It is also psychologically related to the human mind reacting to two opposite and irreconcilable problems by shifting itself off from reality and or confusions of solving one problem that creates another, and the brain locks up.

> http://www.dailymail.co.uk/news/article-3596516/Eighty-children-treated-hospital-outbreak-demonic-possession-Peruvian-school-pupils-say-visions-man-black-trying-kill-them.html
> **"Scores of children at a school in Peru have suffered seizures, and described visions of a man in black trying to kill them in what locals say was a mass case of 'demonic possession.'**

Mark 5: 1 And they came over unto the other side of the sea, into the country of the Gadarenes.
2 And when he was come out of the ship, immediately there met him out of the tombs a man with an unclean spirit,
3 Who had his dwelling among the tombs; and no man could bind him, no, not with chains:
4 Because that he had been often bound with fetters and chains, and the chains had been plucked asunder by him, and the fetters broken in pieces: neither could any man tame him.
5 And always, night and day, he was in the mountains, and in the tombs, crying, and cutting himself with stones.
6 But when he saw Jesus afar off, he ran and worshipped him,
7 And cried with a loud voice, and said, What have I to do with thee, Jesus, thou Son of the most high God? I adjure thee by God that thou torment me not.
8 For he said unto him, Come out of the man, thou unclean spirit.
9 And he asked him, What is thy name? And he answered, saying, My name is Legion: for we are many.
10 And he besought him much that he would not send them away out of the country.
11 Now there was there nigh unto the mountains a great herd of swine feeding.
12 And all the devils besought him, saying, Send us into the swine, that we may enter into them.
13 And forthwith Jesus gave them leave. And the unclean spirits went out, and entered into the swine: and the herd ran violently down a steep place into the sea, (they were about two thousand;) and were choked in the sea.

Mark 5:22 And, behold, there cometh one of the rulers of the synagogue, Jairus by name; and when he saw him, he fell at his feet,
23 And besought him greatly, saying, My little daughter lieth at the point of death: I pray thee, come and lay thy hands on her, that she may be healed; and she

shall live.

24   *And Jesus went with him, and much people followed him and thronged him.*

25   *And a certain woman, which had an issue of blood twelve years,*

26   *And had suffered many things of many physicians, and had spent all that she had, and was nothing bettered, but rather grew worse,*

Many sicknesses and illnesses are related to demonic influences, we have been commissioned to cast out demons from those who possessed, and while praying for a sick person, it is within the spirit to discern and find out if the person is affected by any demons or spirit. This is the reason for the sickness or could be connected somehow. Mark 16:17 *And these signs shall follow them that believe; In my name shall they cast out devils; they shall speak with new tongues;* tells us to follow the high commission and cast our diseases and sicknesses and also demons, this we must be ready and prepared to act upon.

The Bible tells us of the many persons who were crippled and disabled by various spirits

Luke 13:11.   *And, behold, there was a woman who had a spirit of infirmity eighteen years, and was bowed together, and could in no wise lift up herself.*

Luke 11: 14   *And he was casting out a devil, and it was dumb. And it came to pass when the devil was gone out, the dumb spake; and the people wondered.*

Luke 8: 27-33   *And when he went forth to land, there met him out of the city a certain man, which had devils long time, and ware no clothes, neither abode in any house, but in the tombs.*

28   *When he saw Jesus, he cried out and fell down before him, and with a loud voice said, What have I to do with thee, Jesus, thou Son of God most high? I beseech thee, torment me not.*

29   *(For he had commanded the unclean spirit to come out of the man. For oftentimes it had caught him: and he was kept bound with chains and in fetters, and he brake the bands, and was driven of the devil into the wilderness.)*

30   *And Jesus asked him, saying, What is thy name? And he said, Legion: because many devils were entered into him.*

31   *And they besought him that he would not command them to go out into the deep.*

32   *And there was there an herd of many swine feeding on the mountain: and they besought him that he would suffer them to enter into them. And he suffered them.*

33   *Then went the devils out of the man, and entered into the swine: and the herd ran violently down a steep place into the lake, and were choked.*

Demon possession and Sickness associated with demonic possession and influence

- *The demon possessed Gerasene(s):   Mt 8:28-34, Mark 5:2-20; Luke 8: 26-39*
- *A demon possessed mute man: Mt 9:32-34, Luke 11:14-26*
- *A demon possessed a blind and mute man: Mt 12:22-28*
- *The Canaanite or Siro-Phoenician woman's daughter: Mt 15:22-28, Mark 7:25-30*

- *An epileptic boy:*   *Mt 17:15 -21; Mk 9:14-2 9, Luke 9:3 8-43*
- *The man in the synagogue at Capernaum:*   *Mk 1:21-28, Luke 4:33-36*
- *And certain women, healed of evil spirits and infirmities, Mary called Magdalene, out of whom went seven devils*   *Luke 8:2*
- *Job 2: 7 So went Satan forth from the presence of the LORD and smote Job with sore boils from the sole of his foot unto his crown.*
- *Luke 13:11 And, behold, there was a woman which had a spirit of infirmity eighteen years, and was bowed together, and could in no wise lift up herself*

Demon attacks in multiple ways and can cause many undetectable illnesses and sicknesses such as,

Physical disease, Mental impairment, moral interferences, Spiritual, environmental and through natural disasters, outbreaks and devastation losing all your possessions as did JOB in the Bible (but this incident was allowed by God as a test of Job's faith)

> Matthew 12:43-45   *"When the unclean spirit has gone out of a person, it passes through waterless places seeking rest but finds none. Then it says, 'I will return to my house from which I came.' And when it comes, it finds the house empty, swept, and put in order. Then it goes and brings with it seven other spirits more evil than itself, and they enter and dwell there, and the last state of that person is worse than the first. So also will it be with this evil generation."*

Luke 10:17	*"The seventy-two returned with joy, saying, "Lord, even the demons are subject to us in your name!"*
Matthew 4:10	*Then Jesus said to him, "Go, Satan! For it is written, 'YOU SHALL WORSHIP THE LORD YOUR GOD, AND SERVE HIM ONLY.'"*
Luke 11:14	*And He was casting out a demon, and it was mute; when the demon had gone out, the mute man spoke; and the crowds were amazed who He was.*
Luke 4:41	*Demons also were coming out of many, shouting, "You are the Son of God!" But rebuking them, He would not allow them to speak, because they knew Him to be the Christ.*
Mark 3:11	*"And whenever the unclean spirits saw him, they fell down before him and cried out, "You are the Son of God."*
Acts 16: 16	*And it came to pass, as we went to prayer, a certain damsel possessed with a spirit of divination met us, which brought her masters much gain by soothsaying:*
17	*The same followed Paul and us, and cried, saying, These men are the servants of the most high God, which shew unto us the way of salvation.*
18	*And this did she many days. But Paul, being grieved, turned and said to the spirit, I command thee in the name of Jesus Christ to come out of her. And he came out the same hour.*
Luke 4: 33	*And in the synagogue there was a man, which had a spirit of an unclean*

	evil,and cried out with a loud voice,
Luke 11:14	*And he was casting out a devil, and it was dumb. And it came to pass when the devil was gone out, the dumb spake; and the people wondered.*
15	*But some of them said He casteth out devils through Beelzebub the chief of the devils.*
16	*And others, tempting him, sought of him a sign from heaven.*
17	*But he, knowing their thoughts, said unto them, Every kingdom divided against itself is brought to desolation, and a house divided against a house falleth.*
18	*If Satan also be divided against himself, how shall his kingdom stand? because ye say that I cast out devils through Beelzebub.*
19	*And if I by Beelzebub cast out devils, by whom do your sons cast them out? therefore shall they be your judges.*
20	*But if I with the finger of God cast out devils, no doubt the kingdom of God is come upon you.*
Mark 16:17	"And *these signs will accompany those who believe: in my name they will cast out demons; they will speak in new tongues;"*
Matthew 9:32	*As they went out, behold, they brought to him a dumb man possessed with a devil.*
33	*And when the devil was cast out, the dumb spake: and the multitudes marveled, saying, It was never so seen in Israel.*

Do you believe in these miracles? And do you think Jesus performed it in the Bible? Let's also pull up from all the other religious scriptures from the East, West, North, and South, above and below and find the doctrines that define miraculous healings and casting out demons.
Are there any? And if so were the performed by a spiritual Divine Person?

In some Ancient Literature, it states that the Gods and Spirits make themselves known to their patrons by inflicting them with illnesses and disease, and so patrons perform services, rituals and prayer festive to please these entities, which will quiet them rather than exorcize them completely. The bible is one great book of teachings on Casting out all demons rather than pleasing them. Many are affected by angry spirits and angry deities and not to confuse the differences between heavenly beings and human spirits. Human spirits are in abundant existence, as many were not able to transition or refused to transition into the spiritual dimension prepared by God, so they become wandering spirits that roam the area and try to replicate their incident of death merely because they do not believe they are dead and are spirits. What happens is that they try to replicate or relive the episode of when they died so that they can make amends and change the circumstances to avoid the death incident? The process is that they possess some spiritually weak person and repeat the event, thereby creating another death that is similar to the way they died. Vivid examples can crash or suicide, in a car crash fatality occurs, it was observed that similar accidents happen in the same location, which creates more deaths and as such it becomes a cluster of spirits. The difference is that these are spirits and not demons, even though human beings will classify all spirits as demons if they are evil. These are human spirits that exist in the physical plane where humans live, and they cannot be transitioned into the spirit dimension unless they are summoned or cast out to that dimension.

Ancient Greeks will plead to Gods to help in the healing of a sick person, even as they are going through medical treatment. The Bible states that not all sicknesses are caused by demons, God inflicts some for his purpose, maybe to draw the attention of sin, or to persecute someone for committing a grave sin, sometimes for testing purposed such as the incident of Job. There are the seven deadly sins classified as the seven abominations that God hates, this brings about a God-given punishment and associated with sickness.

Ancient scriptures are particular on keeping the body healthy since created by God and host the spirit of God; God did deliver wisdom and knowledge in the various forms of medicine and Leviticus defines the consumption of foods to keep the body healthy. Many Christian faiths are against multiple types of healing, classifying them as New Age, diver's philosophy and the occult, but as we look back into religion from which the new era of Christianity derives, and there are many forms of healing as approved by intellects and God. Where the wisdom of Medicine does come from? And where did the knowledge of alternative medicine come from? Scriptures are particular in the use of herbal medicine and still more specific on the mind healing and altering the state of mind for the betterment of the human spiritual elevation. The Torah, Bible, Quran and the Vedas have an abundance of physical, mental and spiritual healing definitions which includes herbal and alternative methodologies of healing a person. Many psychological sicknesses and thwarted minds associated with demonic influences, schizophrenia, multiple personality disorder, panic, anxiety and many mental disorders associated with numerous somatic illnesses related to demonic spiritual influences.

Multiple disabling disorders associated with influences inked to Para-phenomenal experiences, the occult and demonic forces (somewhat Spiritual influences), where consciousness and cognitive and behavioral processes lead and cause mental deformities and dysfunctions. People become 'zombies,' 'walking dead' or either incapacitated by motion and movement in two ways (1) being a cabbage – bed-ridden of (2) overactivity of hyperactive to being uncontrollable and can be diagnosed as neurological or mental disorders through a misalignment or malfunction of the nervous system in the brain and all through the spinal cord, causing paralysis, weaknesses throughout the body and muscles, poor blood-flow, loss of senses (feelings etc) and multiple-personality disorders, and a very long list of related symptoms, which actually becomes real after being affected by these spirit associated influences. The effects can be devastating, long-term, and fatal and it affects everyone in that circle, family members, friends, neighbors, doctors, school, job, finances and every aspect of life.

A chiropractic diagnosis for the Blood circulation through the Bone structure is essential for everyone. It is a necessity intermittently and should be a part of your yearly check-ups, for a pinch or pressure in a nerve, or passage or vein, nervous system, etc. can cause a slow deterioration in health in multiple ways and can become a permanent or long-term dysfunction or illness. A straightforward situation of daily working on a desk and sitting down all day is a violation of the body's normal functions, we crush and put under pressure all the nerve system which are clustered on your BUTT and do not allow them to run a full circulation as it should.

In any of the above cases, it is always good to make sure that a patient is not affected by any spiritual influences, or any religious controls are removed and cast out.

Medical science states that one-third of all cancer is preventable; one-half of most sicknesses are self-inflicted and can be preventable if we are more cautious and self-aware if we know the body, its functionality and how each part works and process.

41 FALLEN BY LOSS OF JOB, EMPLOYMENT, AND FINANCES

Losing Job can be devastating, it is one way to put you under bondages such as anxiety, depression, frustration, and financial bondage since no money or earnings is coming in. Use the same method of prayer – focus prayer and seek the job that fits your skill set and offer a lot of praise and worship related to the Job, Mention the name of the company, its location, the position advertised and voice all that you can to mention the details of the situation or positions. Speak to God and put yourself under his authority to open up the doors of opportunity and help you find the job that he may have in store for you. Rebuke the spirit of Lack, The spirit of Unemployment and claim job positions in Jesus name.

Do not let frustration, depression, and anxiety get the best of you, for this is how we are weakened spiritually and opens up the doors for darkness, which will grow within us if it does enter and will take us down emotionally. Not only are we at a financial loss, It affects our professional identity, self-esteem, and self-confidence; it also creates separation from your social environment and your work-related relationships. We even lose all security and sense of security with family, friends, and associates, a created sense of failure lurks. Now is the time to be more social, active and more communicative with friends, family, and associates. Get into networking with clubs and employment charters in the area. Staying confident and attentive to social media and job sources are critical at this time. Look forward into the future and allow your mind and God work for you, let love, kindness, and Karma be you seed to sow

> *Dear LORD Jesus, Jehovah Jireh, my provider, I humbly ask of you to look upon my circumstances, as I have lost my Job and my earnings are all gone, I pray and make a petition to you to open up the doors of opportunity in a company that I will be pleased with and a job that I can function well, in an environment where I can function with full capacity and excel in whatever job I am given. I ask of you to watch over me and my family and show me ways to secure job opportunities, and show me ways that I can make provision for my family financially, help me to walk in faith knowing that you will never leave me nor forsake me until the end of time and that you will make a provision and deliver sustenance. I give you all the praise, honor and glory, in Jesus Name AMEN*

Financial hardship could very well be God's way of shaking off all the pride and ego from within you. Many wealthy people are born during economic hardship; It is not the end of the world. Look around and open up your mind to the opportunities that exist around you, One critical thought is, do not allow the temporary situation to be a mental downfall, your mind will work for you, your mind and your inner spirit will have to engage the spirit of God to work for you. Remember every human being have a guardian angel, for we are always under the eye of God, monitoring and observing every act and action we are engaged in, every thought we breed in our minds. Match what kind of money you want with your mental thinking and aim for the stars, if you drop short you might get as far as the moon

Dear Lord, I lost my job and am struggling with financial matters, my debts and credits are overwhelming. I am in dire need for a substantial financial breakthrough; please bless me with an abundant financial breakthrough so that I can sustain myself and family, pay off all my debts and credit cards, loans and any other financial commitments. I know that I did not handle my finances well and asked your forgiveness, I will make sure I do manage my finances as you give me another chance. Please open the doors of Heaven and create a Job opportunity for me, one that I would love and be able to perform well and be appreciated for my works. According to Luke 1:37 For God nothing shall be impossible, you are the great provider, and you own everything please shower your grace upon me so that I can get another position to sustain myself and family. I give you all the Glory and thanks in advance. In the Mighty name of Jesus AMEN - make your prayers simple as though you are talking to a friend, brother, mother or father, be very direct and ask for exactly what you want.

Matthew 7:7	*Ask, and it shall be given you; seek, and ye shall find; knock, and it shall be opened unto you:*
8	*For every one that asketh receiveth; and he that seeketh findeth, and to him that knocketh it shall be opened.*
9	*Or what man is there of you, whom if his son ask bread, will he give him a stone?*
10	*Or if he asks a fish, will he give him a serpent?*
11	*If ye then, being evil, know how to give good gifts unto your children, how much more shall your Father which is in heaven give good things to them that ask him?*
Psalm 34:6	*this poor man cried, and the LORD heard him And saved him out of all his troubles.*

Your faith and belief are your most potent allies against poverty, and Lack for these are two spirits that attack a family. It is the spirit of poverty and Lack, a spirit of poverty and complacency, which is why you will not aim higher than the mere sustenance, so in your prayers and meditation, claim the abundance of wealth and riches and imagine that you do have the plenty. Speak to your spirit and the Guardian Angel and speak to your subconscious to find solutions to our issues. In faith I declare that I am employed and have a great job, I earn over six figures and I am dedicated to giving back according to spiritual laws and as provided by the LORD. Remember God said I came here to give life abundantly. He did not come to make you miserable but expects that you dedicate your life and become rich.

> John 10:10   *"The thief does not come except to steal, and to kill, and to destroy. I have come that they may have life and that they may have it more abundantly."*

Here is a key Karmic value: *Luke 6:38 "Give, and it will be given to you. They will pour into your lap a good measure--pressed down, shaken together, and running over. For by your standard of measure it will be measured to you in return.",* So when you get you give without measuring what you give freely with a good heart, and it will come back to you multiplied, it is the law of God and the law of the Universe

The following are passages and quotes from the Bible to define that God is there for you, but you must have faith and believe it will be done as defined

> Philippians 4:19 *But my God shall supply all your need according to his riches in glory by Christ Jesus. (And this same God who takes care of me will supply all your needs from his glorious riches, which have been given to us in Christ Jesus)*
> Proverbs 10:22 *The blessing of the LORD, it maketh rich, and he addeth no sorrow with it. (The blessings of the lord makes a person rich, and he adds no sorrow to it)*
> 2 Corinthians 9:8 *And God is able to make all grace abound toward you; that ye, always having all sufficiency in all things, may abound to every good work: (And God will generously provide all you need. Then you will always have everything you need and plenty left over to share with others)*

> *Father in the mighty name of Jesus Christ of Nazareth, I humbly pray and ask for your compassion and answer to my prayer. Please give me wisdom and ability to find the Job that you have put aside for me, the Job that you have assigned to me. I seek your knowledge and trust that you will direct me in seeking and finding the Job that is best for me, a Job that I can manage, be comfortable and happy with, that has all the benefits and support I need to be successful in every way. Grant me favors from the hiring manager and the recruiting department to see and assess that my skill set is suited for the Job and allow me to be the candidate appointed for that Job. I give you all the glory and Thanks in advance for the door that you are opening for me. I give you the praise as this j=ob will satisfy my financial needs and supply*

the salary and finances to get me out of debt and provide for my
family, have enough to give to the kingdom and also be able also to
help others in their needs. As I call upon your name which is above
all Names and All knees must bow, I know the supernatural power
that it brings and produces, blessing me with abundance and open-
door opportunities and greater abilities to perform well. I pray that
you stand with me in all that I do and submit myself to you and the
course and path you have prepared for me. I give you all praises and
honor, in Jesus Name AMEN.

Brief Prophetic word - Investments

(1) The growth of the Stocks in the markets about "Clean Energy," any development
from the power from the Sun, Wind, Water, Sea (waves) will be a continuous
growth. The better being Sun and Wind

(2)   GMO food products that will generate food to feed the world, Even though
may not be popular in local Supermarkets, it will generate abundance to feed
the poor and supply needs for poor countries, Investors and going to throw
money into the experimentation and production

(2) Ayurvedic (Knowledge of Living), Herbal medicines, Psychotherapy and Healing
practices will dominate the world as people are beginning to find out
pharmaceuticals are not healing and curing but sustaining sicknesses for life-long
financial gains and the medicines creates more side-effect and sicknesses rather
than cure as the Knowledge of the "VEDAS" (Knowledge) are deciphered, and
scientists are probing more into the more delicate details, knowing that
prevention is the path to cure and the body balance is more important than
chemical input. The popularity of the Ancient Indo-Asia doctrines that are specific
to Health will become more predominant in the studies of the Next Generation.

(4)   Religion will lose its definition as followers are coming to light that God is One
and God is one family and faith had been creating more hatred and division of
people in color, class and creed and division between nations and ethnicity.
Politicians are using religion for purposes of getting nominated, and leaders
of religious organizations are becoming puppets for a politician and
denouncing their spirituality, their ethics and divine laws for the benefit of
favor, popularity and for a biased partisan elect, rather than being spiritually
led towards the higher purpose. Religion has become a privatized business for
many and used for the creation of separation and segregation and the Jesus
movement, The Islamic movement, the Jewish movement became
commercialized for the very same purpose. This will lead to the diminishing of
churchgoers, and church members of the church that is not spirit-filled or
spirit pointed. Outdoor crusades and outdoor revival services and gathering
will begin a new role in believers, and the masses for rallies will be the

NextGen movement. Church will have to work thrice as hard to reap the harvest of the NexGen.

Brief Prophetic word- world affairs Inspired by Scripture:

2 Timothy 3: 1   This also know, that in the last days perilous times shall come.

2   For men shall be lovers of their selves, covetous, boasters, proud, blasphemers, disobedient to parents, unthankful, unholy,

3   Without natural affection, trucebreakers, false accusers, incontinent, fierce, despisers of those that are good,

4   Traitors, heady, high-minded, lovers of pleasures more than lovers of God;

5   Having a form of godliness, but denying the power thereof: from such turn away.

6   For of this sort are they which creep into houses, and lead silly captive women laden with sins, led away with divers' lusts,

7   Ever learning, and never able to come to the knowledge of the truth.

8   Now as Jannes and Jambres withstood Moses, so do these also resist the truth: men of corrupt minds, reprobate concerning the faith.

9   But they shall proceed no further: for their folly shall be manifest unto all men, as their's also was.

10   But thou hast fully known my doctrine, manner of life, purpose, faith, longsuffering, charity, patience,

11   Persecutions, afflictions, which came unto me at Antioch, at Iconium, at Lystra; what persecutions I endured: but out of them all the Lord delivered me.

12   Yea and all that will live godly in Christ Jesus shall suffer persecution.

13   But evil men and seducers shall wax worse and worse, deceiving, and being deceived.

14   But continue thou in the things which thou hast learned and hast been assured of, knowing of whom thou hast learned them;

15   And that from a child thou hast known the holy scriptures, which are able to make thee wise unto salvation through faith which is in Christ Jesus.

16   All scripture is given by inspiration of God, and is profitable for doctrine, for reproof, for correction, for instruction in righteousness:

17   That the man of God may be perfect, thoroughly furnished unto all good works.

(6) A new focus on God – Where people are going to change from belief in religion as specifics but to study God as A reality for what God is and for what God wants for mankind, rather than what man wants for mankind and what man's interpretation of what God wants for mankind. People are going towards gaining more knowledge of the scriptures and writings of God in all forms for they will realize that each religion and the religious ministers of a specific religion only

possess the knowledge of that specific religion and have little or no knowledge of other religions and people, as such they will impress upon the hearts of people ONLY what they are knowledgeable of and will not be able to deliver any answers for others.

(7) Unveiling of much Sin in high places: God will be the architect and orchestrate the unveiling of many sins in many high places such as Church, Governments, False Prophets, propaganda on wars as alternative means to deceive the population. Many aggressive nations will fall to desolation and chaos, including the focal points of religion. God will appoint Nebuchadnezzar and Nebuchadnezzar II over the aggressive power nations, for the purpose of putting them under subjection and unveiling their corrupt farce state of mind and their sinful ways.

(8) Natural disasters will be more rampant all across the world as the world is becoming more in the hands of the evil one and people are more stiff-necked than before being disobedient to God and the laws and commandments of God, God will use these elements to clean the land and to deliver the message to his people and no matter what war you want to fight, no matter what your mindset is, I am God and you will face my wrath and you will come to realize that hate is a sin and an abomination and I am God who brings these storms, not any other. Some examples are hurricanes, wildfires, volcanoes, flash flooding, mudslides, red tide, heat waves, drought, winter storms, Lightening storms, avalanches, etc. These are elements that man cannot strive against and cannot hold animosities against or even have any prejudices in their heart. Some of the purposes is to bring people together regardless of religious beliefs, race, ethnicity, equitable values, color, class, creed or hardness of heart

42 FALLEN BY MARTIAL STATE

Genesis 2:24:   *Therefore shall a man leave his father and his mother, and shall cleave unto his wife: and they shall be one flesh. (Stress ONE FLESH)*
25   *And they were both naked, the man and his wife, and were not ashamed.*

Marriage is a beautiful thing in the lives of people; it is a joyous occasion where two people who love each other are tied by a legal document under the laws of the country pertaining to marriage and by religious rites under the laws of God to be ONE, and that supposedly should mean Body, Mind, and Soul. The bonds are divine and should be treated as such as they were witnesses to the marriage and the sermon that partake, which includes some sacred vows. Here is a typically formatted pledge read by the Pastor or priest in a marriage ceremony.

    God is a family and creates a family and a good relationship, matrimony is sacred to God, and in *Matthew 19.6 wherefore they are no more twain, but one flesh. What therefore God hath joined together, let no man put asunder.* The devil is focused on married couples since marriage is the creation from God for if the family ruined, everything falls apart and so do the worship, focus, and Gods creation.

- *""I, __, take thee, __, to be my wedded husband/wife, to have and to hold, from this day forward, for better, for worse, for richer, for poorer, in sickness and in health, to love and to cherish, till death do us part, according to God's holy ordinance; and thereto I pledge thee my faith [or] pledge myself to you."*
- *"I, __, take you, __, for my lawful wife/husband, to have and to hold from this day forward, for better, for worse, for richer, for poorer, in sickness and health, until death do us part." "I, __, take you, __, to be my husband/wife. I promise to be true to you in good times and in bad, in sickness and in health. I will love and honor you all the days of my life."*

A Hindu Formatted Vow: The Seven Sacred Vows of marriage, which is done in a lengthy ceremony in the presence of family and relatives from both sides, in the presence of Priest or Priests, in and around a Holy fire with Offerings and various incense offerings ceremonially

https://www.culturalindia.net/weddings/wedding-traditions/seven-vows.html

First Vow: *Man- 'You will offer me food and be helpful in every way. I will cherish you and provide welfare and happiness for you and our children'.*
Woman -I am responsible for the home and all household, food, and finance responsibilities.

Second Vow: Man- 'Together we will protect our house and children.'
Woman 'I will be by your side as your courage and strength. I will rejoice in your happiness. In return, you will love me solely'.

Third Vow: man- 'May we grow wealthy and prosperous and strive for the education of our children and may our children live long. Woman - 'I will love you solely for the rest of my life, as you are my husband. Every other man in my life will be secondary. I vow to remain chaste'.

Fourth Vow: Man- 'You have brought sacredness into my life, and have completed me. May we be blessed with noble and obedient children?'
Woman- 'I will shower you with joy, from head to toe. I will strive to please you in every way I can'.

Fifth Vow: Man- 'You are my best friend and staunchest well-wisher. You have come into my life, enriching it. God bless you
Woman - 'I promise to love and cherish you for as long as I live. Your happiness is my happiness, and your sorrow is my sorrow. I will trust and honor you, and will strive to fulfill all your wishes'.

Sixth Vow: Man - 'Now that you have taken six steps with me, you have filled my heart with immense happiness. Will you do the kindness of filling my heart with happiness like this for all times?'
Woman - 'I will always be by your side.'

Seventh Vow: Man - 'We are now husband and wife, and are one. You are mine, and I am yours for eternity.'
Woman - 'As God is a witness; I am now your wife. We will love, honor and cherish each other forever.'

These are VOWS, and not just words uttered informality for the ears of witnesses, but to each other and God is the ultimate witness. The first and foremost through an agreement in the mind and hearts of these two people getting together in preparation for marriage and binding words and their lives together. Every Hindu and all others must revisit the wedding vows they have taken on the day they were married and reminiscence, contemplate on those words all over again and think, go back in time and ponder on the vows you made.

In modern era and modern times we are facing so much hardship, persecution and difficulties in life, we have made vows unto our other half and sealed it with a ring and a kiss and to the heavenly Divinity as a seal that we will adhere to these vows all the days of our lives. We face issues and difficulties in being a person, a person of integrity, humility, compassion, love and harmonious godly feelings for the person I so love and cherish and have deviated from my internal spiritual and honorable words and promises. Marriage is a bond that is forever, everlasting and to be as one through every state in life, whether it is happiness, sadness, hardship, health, and sickness.

ISLAM

> Bride; I, _____, offer you in myself in marriage in
> Accordance with the instructions of the Holy Qur'an
> and the Holy Prophet, peace and blessing be upon Him.
> I pledge, in honesty and with sincerity, to be for you an
> Obedient and faithful wife.
> Groom: I pledge, in honesty and sincerity, to be for you
> a faithful and helpful husband.

There is no perfect relationship, it takes two completely different people, with maybe some similar characteristics and attitudes and a friendly relationship to come together and become of one accord. Both will have to adapt and make changes to many of their single lifestyle patterns and adjust to being a couple rather than a single person. Not only are two people getting together but two whole family lines are merging over this union. It is about two separate minds, body, spirit and soul traditions, which includes social, environmental and cultural differences.

Love is unfaltering and should be a steady momentum sharing of love and emotions, mentally, physically and morally. There has to be a lot of building and multi-changing and challenges in bringing the best of each other in each other, expressions of trust, honesty, integrity, rationally, emotionally, spiritually and physically, it also includes financially and merging into one pathway and goal of common understanding and frequent communication be understood in the purest form to each other.

Have you ever thought of the fact that "your Spouse could have gotten a better person than you?" but choose you to be the better person they wanted as a mate and spouse.

> For a man (*Ephesians 5: 31For this cause shall a man leave his father and mother, and shall be joined unto his wife, and they two shall be one flesh Gen 2:24 Matt 19:5 Mark 10:7 1 Cor 6:16).* It never stated the same for woman   *Ephesians 5:25 Husbands, love your wives, even as Christ also loved the church, and gave himself for it; Ephesians 5:28 so ought men to love their wives as their own bodies. He that loveth his wife loveth himself.*

Ephesians 5:22-33 New International Versions (NIV)

> 22 *Wives, submit yourselves to your own husbands as you do to the Lord.*
> 23 *For the husband is the head of the wife as Christ is the head of the church, his body, of which he is the Savior.*
> 24 *Now as the church submits to Christ, so also wives should submit to their husbands in everything.*
> 25   *Husbands, love your wives, just as Christ loved the church and gave himself up for her*
> 26 *to make her holy, cleansing[a] her by the washing with water through the word,*
> 27 *and to present her to himself as a radiant church, without stain or wrinkle or any*

other blemish, but holy and blameless.

28 *In this same way, husbands ought to love their wives as their own bodies. He who loves his wife loves himself.*

29 *After all, no one ever hated their own body, but they feed and care for their body, just as Christ does the church—*

30 *for we are members of his body.*

31 *"For this reason, a man will leave his father and mother and be united to his wife, and the two will become one flesh."*

32 *This is a profound mystery—but I am talking about Christ and the church.*

33 *However, each one of you also must love his wife as he loves himself, and the wife must respect her husband.*

According to Biblical verbiage and scripture a marriage ordained by God is:

Gen. 2:18-25 "And the Lord God said, It is not good that the man should be alone; I will make him an help meet for him. And out of the ground, the Lord God formed every fowl of the air; and brought them unto Adam to see what he would call them: and whatsoever Adam called every living creature that was the name thereof. And Adam gave names to all cattle, and to the fowl of the air and every beast of the field, but for Adam, there was not found a help meet for him. And the Lord God caused a deep sleep to fall upon Adam, and he slept: and he took one of his ribs, and closed up the flesh instead thereof; And the rib, which the Lord God had taken from man, made he a woman, and brought her unto the man. And Adam said this is now bone of my bones, and flesh of my flesh: she shall be called Woman because she taken out of Man. Therefore shall a man leave his father and his mother, and shall cleave unto his wife: and they shall be one flesh. And they were both naked, the man and his wife, and were not ashamed."

And further instructions: Ephesians 5: 21 – 33 Repeating this to make sure and understood for what it represents. 'Marriages fail because we are not tolerant and build the ego of right and wrong, we are always right, and others are always wrong, therefore I will not submit or be the one to admit my faults and make amends, you will have to be the one to come to my terms or change to please my selfishness'.

Ephesians 5: 21 –Submitting yourselves one to another in fear of God.

22 *Wives, submit yourselves unto your husbands, as unto the Lord.*

23 *For the husband is the head of the wife, even as Christ is the head of the church: and he is the savior of the body.*

24 *Therefore as the church is subject unto Christ, so let the wives be to their husbands in everything.*

25 *Husbands, love your wives, even as Christ also loved the church, and gave himself for it;*

26 *That he might sanctify and cleanse it with the washing of water by the word,*

27 *That he might present it to himself a glorious church, not having spot, or wrinkle, or any such thing; but that it should be holy and without blemish.*

28 *So ought men to love their wives as their own bodies. He that loveth his wife*

loveth himself.

29   *For no man ever yet hated his own flesh; but nourisheth and cherisheth it,*
      even as the Lord the church:

30   *For we are members of his body, of his flesh, and of his bones.*

31   *For this, cause shall a man leave his father and mother and shall be joined unto*
      his wife, and they two shall be one flesh.

32   *This is a great mystery: but I speak concerning Christ and the church.*

33   *Nevertheless, let every one of you in particular so love his wife even as himself,*
      and the wife sees that she reverences her husband.

Spending time to define and understand marriage is essential as preparation in pre-marital counseling as both parties will learn the true meaning of commitment and the sacredness of what marriage really means and how it should work. It is a transformation of an independent free life as a singular being into a merged singularity of two souls, two spirits and two bodies, as soon as one is off balance things starts to shift in uncontrollable chaos if not corrected in time. It is not about one person working to change the other into what they believe they should be and it is not about one person trying to improve themselves to please the other, it is both parties leaving all the old ways and becomes a new person, no longer a single digit but a unique multiplicity which becomes one. It is like a butterfly going through the process of metamorphosis from a caterpillar through the cocoon to a beautiful elevated being that is amazing to watch and floats through the air with gracious movements.

A good marriage the commonality is sex, finances, and money, the material things that they would like to possess, their social and environmental activities, their religious beliefs and their happiness and joy, all sad moments and pains, sicknesses, etc. are common in a marriage, but a successful marriage has a greater focus on the outcome and the product of the union, such as offspring, children and the home where these children will grow up, the advancement of education and provision for the luxuries in life. The keys are sharing everything, from conversations, stories and daily activities at work, sharing information of each other past and history, sharing the same kinds of foods, sports, media favorites, engaging with helping each other with chores, homework, studies etc., being the father and the mother at the same time towards the children, being both husband and wife in times of all and it needs, being humble, listen and acknowledge and make time for each other.

We must pay great attention to the mental states of mind and how it can affect the other person, including on the passing down of the negative traits to the children through DNA and mental and spiritual transfers. The human being was created by a family to be a family, for GOD is plural and not singular, and he created Mankind to be a family and to multiple and replenishes the whole world.

Genesis 1: 28 And God blessed them, and God said unto them, Be fruitful, and multiply, and replenish the earth, and subdue it: and have dominion over the fish of the sea, and over the fowl of the air, and over every living thing that moveth upon the earth.

There are a million reasons why marriage is a good thing for Mankind, therefore treasure it and follow the principles of marriage, in a secular world of rules, rites and laws as well as the spiritual beliefs as designed by the Divine and keep reminiscence your vows, remember it, remember the feeling the day you made those vows and look at your spouse and observe to see and observe and know every part, every line, every mark, notice every smile and every movement and remember what you promised them and look for reasons to deliver those promises

If there is a falling down, watch carefully, be an analyst, e your own mental psychologist and look back at where did things go wrong (not loudly, but mentally by yourself), do not be biased and look at yourself as always right, and do not seek to find the faults and blame the other person, you may be the one that destroyed the relationship without even knowing how, when or why. Sex, money, time, selfishness and differences in views are the leading causes of the biggest downfalls. We become preoccupied with ourselves, creating and adapting differences in feelings, building pride, looking for reasons to grow cold, when family becomes engaged in the relationship in the form of gossip and relating the past ways and discuss the changes, it creates a feeling of wanting to revert. Un-forgiveness and loss of trust, not being adaptable, allowing others to get involved in conversations and discussions, berating and demeaning your other half in the presence of others or discussing private details with others, it becomes un-retractable words, especially if you did not spend the time to know your spouse well.

When there is no "We" anymore and just "Me," no 'US" but "I" and appreciation went out of the door. You must understand that there are much more interested in your marriage than you do and when you realize that there are others who are interested, you become the detective and the investigator, not realizing that your friend at work is wondering how you guys and making your marriage so beautiful and blissful, but their eyes and lips may not be a good thing for you or your spouse.

For a marriage to work you will have to want it to work, you have to make all the necessary sacrifices, changes and adaptations to make it smooth and not bumpy. When this starts to go downstream, you have to think things over.

- Go back to the vows and review, think it over and through again, you need to mean and meet it
- Assess yourself – deep, unselfishly, Love thy neighbor (your spouse) as thyself. List of me??
- Repent and repent openly, sincerely and communicate to your partner how much they mean to you

- Communicate, talk, converse, spill all that is in your heart and let your spouse know you are ready, willing and available to do whatever is necessary to repair, fix and mend all that is broken and will listen to for answers of what needs to be changed in you to adapt to making changes and relationship flourish
- Touching, hugging, petting, massaging – think it, act it, do it lovingly every day
- This marriage is about us, not just I so let us dissolve into each other
- Live, love, laugh, be a comedian, a joker, a clown to create laughter
- Be all that you can be and more in the intimate field, get some boost to spike it up
- Spend time with your other half and understand what they feel, think, want, role play to follow, open up the doors for communication and understanding of how you think and get them to relate to you about them too
- The eyes are the window to the heart, look into the eyes, try to read and feel the emotion through the eyes
- Let the other choose first, dinner, outing, etc
- A marriage is two people, and a problem is also two or more people, it is also about you, figure it out, it is not a one-way street, it flows both ways
- Why did I love you? What were the specials? What were the things I adore about you? Reflect: you will be able to open up the mind and see what went wrong.
- Rebuild the trust and figure out what will make you both reconnect.
- Sacrifices are tough, but to be for the goodness of oneness of marriage and Love
- Reflect on the Divinity and pray together, proclaim what the scriptures

  o *Ephesians 4:2-3: "With all humility and gentleness, with patience, bearing with one another in love, eager to maintain the unity of the Spirit in the bond of peace."*
  o *Ephesians 5: 25 Husbands, love your wives, even as Christ also loved the church, and gave himself for it;*
  o *Mark 10: 6 But from the beginning of the creation, God made them male and female.*
    7: For this cause shall a man leave his father and mother, and cleave to his wife;
    8 And they twain shall be one flesh: so then they are no more twain, but one flesh.
    9 What therefore God hath joined together, let not man put asunder.

_____The happy family begins with a happy marriage, how do you keep it a happy marriage? Assess the relationship and question yourself, it all starts with you, what is the mutual respect look like, what is the love meter reading saying? What is the unison of wife and husband, are you in one accord in everything, is the relationship right, and is it sound, and it is happy? What are the reasons for any lack thereof?
Are you physically, emotionally, spiritually and intellectually a person who acts and

behaves as in a happy relationship and marriage? You have the power to change yourself and your relationship towards a happy one; let it all begin with you. You will need to do a Question and Answer and assess yourself in the relationship and make amends or correction on any areas that you are lacking. Are you making a full contribution towards the family, financially, physically, emotionally and supportive, are you acting and displaying the love that is needed to keeps the love flowing? In a proverb a family that prays together stays together, one of the reasons is that when praying you are voicing the needs and asking for solutions and showing a pure emotion of love letting God and You be the center of the home. Builds a softening of feelings, a bonding of each other and opening the spirit to share and receive whatever the others are facing and seeking and a change in attitude towards earnestness within for the betterment of the other.

A significant influence into the negativity in family relation is job and status, whether the situation is going right or whether it is problematic and brings stress and demeaning state. The status of each party, whether one is in a high position of recognition and respect and the other is in an ordinary job that is of lower rank, the party in the place of high rank may feel and act as if they are the know-it-all and because of the financial comparison have more control within the household and displays the same, becoming a dictator of the house. Regardless of the circumstance of earnings and position, stated in all scripture that the Man is the head of the household, which means all the divine authority flows through him, if this can be recognized, then it put status in place by God's order. If the job and the environment where you work are affecting the household unity and happiness, then change your position, it is better to be happy wherever you are rather than be under a stressful circumstance that creates negativity all around you. Never, Never, Never use negative words to describe your family, job, children or anything that you are next, near of or responsible for, Take the negative words out of your diction and vocabulary, for your words are a creative force. A marriage today, where "One Flesh" seems to be a casual phrase, does not carry its true meaning and direction. Most people want to control people the other party and change them to suit their lifestyle, as it was with Eve, One man and one woman on the Planet and one party gossiped with a stranger and deceived by a stranger, which influenced the entire lifestyle to follow. This is the nature of what today's marriage is becoming and has been for a while with influences from the outside, other sources, family members, demonic influences, etc. and the authority and order of power and blessings are gone, disappeared, taken back and driven out of the dominion that it was ordained to be. We can jump around and blame the world for our faults and mistakes, but it is our fault and our errors that need to be addressed and corrected otherwise it becomes a chain of unfortunate events that follow.

Father Lord God, I come to you humbly, like a child and as a child and ask for forgiveness in every error and mistake I have made in my life, with my mother, father, brother, sister, wife and children and that includes friends, relatives, and associates. Forgive me for my attitudes, my thinking, my native tongue and mouth, my anger and rage, my miss-understanding and lack of understanding. Forgive me for not having compassion and the leniency to listen and comprehend the feelings of my family as they try to express themselves. Forgive me for even being too passive and allow my authority to be tarnished and reduced, rather than taking up my role as a man, a husband, a father, brother, uncle, and friend and stand up for what it means to be a man as ordained by God. My words are simple, direct and humble, I submit myself to your authority and ask that you restore me in the image you created, with all the blessings and dominion of my environment and my family to be a blessing to myself and family and to bring the power of God inside me and to be around my family. I pray that you put a hedge around us and protect us from our mind, own lips and words, protect us from our own selfishness and ways and change us to be more subservient to you and your ways, so that my family will be happy, successful, full of peace and love and be prosperous in everything. Bless my marriage and keep us in unison to one understanding, one flesh and one family. I give you thanks in advance. In Jesus Name AMEN

43 FALLEN BY THE SPIRIT OF AHAB AND JEZEBEL

The spirit of Ahab and Jezebel are two very prominent spirits that affect the Home or organizations, they bring with them the spirit of rejection and opens up doors for despair, depression, envy, inferiority, fear, confusion, and control.

Ahab being a King gave up his dominion to Jezebel his wife, the daughter of a Heathen King and a worshipper of Baal and Ashtoreth, whose religious practices involves worship of Groves, Idols, Sex organs and a long list of a vile cult. Ahab fell under the subjection of Jezebel where Jezebel acted as King and made all decisions, took over the role played by Ahab and Ahab became very passive and under the influence, he no longer has much authority, no control over his household and becomes a subject of the Wife rather than the 'head.'
The wife becomes the King and Head of the house and has all control over decisions, finances, and even the mind of the man. The effect is double-mindedness, lust, insecurity, self-pity, rejection, shamefulness, fear, insubordination, withdrawals, addiction and attracts other spirits to manifest into the physical body and traps the mind. The Ahab spirit and the Korah spirit frequently comes against leadership or anyone that is destined to be a leader

These spirits of Jezebel and Ahab promotes prostitution, sexual pervasiveness and perversion, adultery, and multiple immoralities and roams throughout the bible all the way to Revelations. These spirits are predominant in homes, corporations, government agencies and love the High places for control and authority, to be able to put others into subjection. They are tied to the Spirit of Korah, a rebellious spirit that rebels against Moses, the spirit of Delilah who betrayed Samson

The Spirit of Jezebel also portrays strong will and control of husband and men (or wife if it affects a man) in authority, sexual perversion is one of her traits and will disrespect Husband or leaders for power and influence and will always lead the actual head of household against the will and into idolatry, against religious laws and belief. Spiritual blindness results and even not being able to pray correctly in meditation or focus, refusal to hear the word of God and enslaves any persons within her environment. She is also a Prophet of Lies and False Prophesy. These spirits get you to defile yourself, and your ministry, your self-respect, and your honor are gone, flattery, sexual relationships, un-forgiveness, manipulation of emotions, financial downfall steps in.

1 Kings 18:36-39 And it came to pass, at the time of the offering of the evening

329

sacrifice, that Elijah the prophet came near and said, "LORD God of Abraham, Isaac, and Israel, let it be known this day that You are God in Israel and I am Your servant and that I have done all these things at Your word. Hear me, O LORD, hear me, that this person may know that You are the LORD God and that You have turned their hearts back to You again." Then the fire of the LORD fell and consumed the burnt sacrifice, and the wood and the stones and the dust, and it licked up the water that was in the trench. Now when all the people saw it, they fell on their faces; and they said, "The LORD, He is God! The LORD, He is God!"

The battle against Spirit of Ahab and Jezebel is best handles in strong prayers that involve a group of Spirit-filled people.

One kings 21: 23 And of Jezebel also spake the LORD, saying, The dogs shall eat Jezebel by the wall of Jezreel.

24   Him that dieth of Ahab in the city the dogs shall eat; and him that dieth in the field shall the fowls of the air eat.

25   But there was none like unto Ahab, which did sell himself to work wickedness in the sight of the LORD, whom Jezebel his wife stirred up.

26   And he did very abominably in following idols, according to all things as did the Amorites, whom the LORD cast out before the children of Israel.

Prayer: *Heavenly Father, Lord Jesus Christ, I give thanks and praise for your authority that you have given me to "Trample of Serpents and Snakes" "Luke 10:19 Behold, I give unto you power to tread on serpents and scorpions, and over all the power of the enemy: and nothing shall by any means hurt you "and to battle against witchcraft and the controlling powers of all witchcraft, I bind all witchcraft and all evil, negative attributes that comes up against me and my family and break all spells or spoken word that has been spoken against me, I rebuke the spirit of Ahab and Jezebel, bund them and cast them into the lake of fire, the pits of hell by the power and authority of Jesus Christ. I submit myself to and under the authority of Jesus Christ and give him all authority to manage my life and lead me towards the right direction and achieving the mark that is set forth for me. I declare that I am now free from any hold the Devil, Satan or any of his demons may have had on my life and declare that I am now free. I take back all authority and blessings that were stolen from me and command they return all blessings seven folds, one hundred folds and take all roots that were installed in my out. I command they leave me alone and leave my family alone, for we are covered by the Blood of Jesus Christ and under his authority. I am now free from any spells, free from any attack from sorcerers, witches and witchcraft, any evil spirits and any demonic influences in Jesus Name. AMEN*

- **Fallen into the hands of the Vile and Immoral Person.**

An immoral person will target you, measure you, seek you, assess you, look at your values and try to bring you under their spell. They will trick you so that they can be able to manipulate you and get you under their spell, seduce you like the Spirit of Jezebel to put you under subjection, seduce you sexually and will try to steal your substance, whether it is wealth, money, real estate, valuables, and even your substance. An Immoral woman will take your essence (sperm) and bind you legally to make you pay them for 21 years and more after conceiving a child that they want to be based on your physical and spiritual matter. You become a slave to the system and their behest for whatever they need based on the legal system. It is also spiritual devastation for you, and your spiritual life will be sucked out because of the very situation of being fooled and you being lustfully under the influence and seduction of the immoral woman. Solomon was very careful to teach and warn his son about this situation, even though he was a womanizer and had over seven hundred wives, he could not bear to see his son experience any situation that will lead him against all spiritual God-given talents and blessings, which he had done and gone through in his lifetime.

Proverbs 7-10 Common English Bible (CEB)
Avoid loose women/men/person Apply this to the circumstance and the teaching

7:1   *My son, keep my words; store up my commands within you.*
7:2   *Keep my commands and live, and my instruction likes the pupil of your eye.*
7:3   *Bind them on your fingers; write them on the tablet of your heart.*
7:4   *Say to wisdom, "You are my sister"; call understanding "friend,"*
7:5   *so she might guard you against the mysterious woman, from the foreign woman who flatters you.*
7:6   *When from the window of my house, from behind the screen, I gazed down,*
7:7   *I looked among the naive young men and noticed among the youth, one who had no sense.*
7:8   *He was crossing the street at her corner and walked down the path to her house*
7:9   *in the early evening, at the onset of night and darkness.*
7:10   *All of a sudden a woman approaches him, dressed like a prostitute and with a cunning mind.*
7:11   *She is noisy and defiant; her feet don't stay long in her own house.*
7:12   *She has one foot in the street, one foot in the public square. She lies in wait at every corner.*
7:13   *She grabs him and kisses him. Her face is brazen as she speaks to him:*
7:14   *"I've made a sacrifice of well-being; today I fulfilled my solemn promises.*
7:15   *So I've come out to meet you, seeking you, and I have found you*
7:16   *I've spread my bed with luxurious covers, with colored linens from Egypt.*
7:17   *I've sprinkled my bed with myrrh, aloes, and cinnamon.*
7:18   *Come, let's drink deep of love until morning; let's savor our lovemaking.*
7:19   *For my husband isn't home; he's gone far away.*

7:20   He took a pouch of money with him;   he won't come home till full moon."

7:21   She seduces him with all her talk.   She entices him with her flattery.

7:22   He goes headlong after her, like an ox to the slaughter, like a deer leaping into a trap

7:23   until an arrow pierces his liver, like a bird hurrying to the snare, not aware that it will cost him his life.

7:24   Now children, listen to me, and pay attention to my speech.

7:25   Don't turn your heart to her ways; don't wander down her paths.

7:26   She has caused many corpses to fall; she has killed many people.

7:27   Her house is a path to the grave, going down to the chambers of death.

Proverbs 5-7   New Living Translation (NLT)

Avoid Immoral Women

5:1   My son, pay attention to my wisdom; listen carefully to my wise counsel.

2   Then you will show discernment, and your lips will express what you've learned.

3   For the lips of an immoral woman are as sweet as honey, and her mouth is smoother than oil.

4   But in the end, she is as bitter as poison, as dangerous as a double-edged sword.

5   Her feet go down to death; her steps lead straight to the grave.

6   For she cares nothing about the path to life. She staggers down a crooked trail and doesn't realize it.

7   So now, my sons listen to me. Never stray from what I am about to say:

8   Stay away from her!   Don't go near the door of her house!

9   If you do, you will lose your honor and will lose to merciless people all you have achieved.

10   Strangers will consume your wealth, and someone else will enjoy the fruit of your labor.

11   In the end, you will groan in anguish when disease consumes your body.

12   You will say, "How I hated discipline!   If only I had not ignored all the warnings!

13   Oh, why didn't I listen to my teachers?   Why didn't I pay attention to my instructors?

14   I have come to the brink of utter ruin, and now I must face public disgrace."

15   Drink water from your own well—   share your love only with your wife.

16   Why spill the water of your springs in the streets, having sex with just anyone?

17   You should reserve it for yourselves.   Never share it with strangers.

18   Let your wife be a fountain of blessing for you.   Rejoice in the wife of your youth.

19   She is a loving deer, a graceful doe.   Let her breasts satisfy you always. May you always be captivated by her love.

20   Why be captivated, my son, by an immoral woman,   or fondle the breasts of a promiscuous woman?

21   For the Lord sees clearly what a man does,   examining every path he takes.

22   An evil man is held captive by his own sins; they are ropes that catch and hold him.

23   He will die for lack of self-control; he will be lost because of his great
          foolishness.

Proverbs 31:
1   The words of king Lemuel, the prophecy that his mother taught him.
2   What, my son? and what, the son of my womb? and what, the son of my vows?
3   Give not thy strength unto women, nor thy ways to that which destroyed kings.
4   It is not for kings, O Lemuel, it is not for kings to drink wine, nor for princes
          strong drink:
5   Lest they drink, and forget the law, and pervert the judgment of any of the
          afflicted.
6   Give strong drink unto him that is ready to perish, and wine unto those that be
          of heavy hearts.
7   Let him drink, and forget his poverty, and remember his misery no more.
8   Open thy mouth for the dumb in the cause of all such as are appointed to
          destruction.
9   Open thy mouth, judge righteously, and plead the cause of the poor and needy.
10   Who can find a virtuous woman? for her price is far above rubies.
11 The heart of her husband doth safely trust in her so that he shall have no need of
          spoil.
12   She will do him good and not evil all the days of her life.
13   She seeketh wool, and flax, and worketh willingly with her hands
14   She is like the merchants' ships; she bringeth her food from afar.
15   She riseth also while it is yet night, and giveth meat to her household, and a
          portion to her maidens
16   She considereth a field, and buyeth it: with the fruit of her hands she planteth a
          vineyard.
17   She girdeth her loins with strength, and strengtheneth her arms.
18   She perceiveth that her merchandise is good: her candle goeth not out by night.
19   She layeth her hands to the spindle, and her hands hold the distaff.
20   She stretcheth out her hand to the poor; yea, she reacheth forth her hands to
          the needy.
21   She is not afraid of the snow for her household: for all her household are
          clothed with scarlet.
22   She maketh herself coverings of tapestry; her clothing is silk and purple.
23   Her husband is known in the gates when he sitteth among the elders of the
          land.
24   he maketh fine linen, and selleth it; and delivereth girdles unto the merchant.
25   Strength and honor are her clothing, and she shall rejoice in time to come.
26   She openeth her mouth with wisdom, and in her tongue is the law of kindness.
27   She looketh well to the ways of her household, and eateth not the bread of
          idleness.
28   Her children arise up, and call her blessed; her husband also, and he praiseth
          her.
29   Many daughters have done virtuously, but thou excellest them all.

30   *Favor is deceitful, and beauty is vain: but a woman that feareth the LORD, she shall be praised.*

31   *Give her of the fruit of her hands, and let her works praise her in the gates.*

44 FALLEN BY ANGER AND 7 DEADLY SIN

Anger has a psychological, physiological, psychosomatic, physical and mental adverse effect on your being. It creates a fight or flight response, and many negative emotions are triggered off, from fear, nervousness, excitement and high anxiety. It will instigate the adrenaline glands to pump extra fluids and increases stress hormones, the heart to pump blood faster and could cause high blood pressure and ruptured veins, heart attack, an aneurysm in the brain. Headaches, blurred vision, stroke and much other pressure related ruptures in the system. The increased anxiety, pushing the fight or flight response will automatically create an answer that could lead to your death, committing a serious crime or injury to self or others. The characteristic of anger at most times are uncontrollable and can lead to violence, isolation, depression, rages, and hatred that will scar the memory consistently. It becomes a trigger based on the incident and causes of the event. Suppressing anger is also unhealthy due to its nature; it will accumulate and can lead to one major episode that is disastrous, depending on the body's mental and physical reactions. It is a common emotion in every normal human being, but it varies in each person and on the circumstances as per the trigger, where each person handles anger in a different way, some can control and shun away from rage, others can instantly or over a short period calm themselves down and avoid any complications physically, mentally or environmentally –socially, but whenever wrath strikes it affects the chemical balance of the body, and it does create harm. There is no good feature of rage for the Human mind and body.

The Spirit of Anger there are many signs the defines the presence of the demonic spirit, irritability, tension, egotism, tensions, impatience, elevated voice, sarcasm and hurtful, demeaning words in speech

> **"Ephesians 4:** *Be ye angry, and sin not: let not the sun go down upon your wrath: 27 Neither give place to the devil". Ephesians 4: Let no corrupt communication proceed out of your mouth, but that which is good to the use of edifying, that it may minister grace unto the hearers. 30 And grieve not the Holy Spirit of God, whereby ye are sealed unto the day of redemption. 31Let all bitterness, and wrath, and anger, and clamor, and evil speaking be put away from you, with all malice:32 And be ye kind one to another, tenderhearted, forgiving one another, even as God for Christ's sake hath forgiven you."*

Some actions to take in the management of anger that will help to bring you back to calm are breathing, deep breaths and deep breathing, Understand why you are angry and think first about the repercussions and then let it go, be vocal and let the understanding of the situation out, be very assertive, cautious and avoid any further conflict, aggression, and confrontation with what so ever is getting you in that state of mind.

Remember the risks is all yours: Your heart is at risk, you can get a stroke if it is overwhelming regardless of age, you could bleed internally due to blood pressure and weak veins. Every incident of anger weakens your entire system, your immune system, your cardiovascular system, your stomach, your lungs, your core and intestines, your vision, hearing, thinking, brain (possible cause a brain aneurysm), you are putting yourself at risk against something that can be controlled and managed, and you are opening doors of darkness that can bring evil demonic spirit, you can even react in -a way that may bring you further trouble with people and the law.

Fallen because of Addiction – Alcohol, and Narcotics

One of Satan's demons is the Leviathan, traits lead to confusion, depression, destruction and are closely linked to Alcohol, drugs, and narcotics uses these methods to capture people and put them under subjection by addiction. If you are an alcoholic, you are under the influence of the Leviathan spirit, one of the most robust and trickiest souls in human reality.

> **Isaiah 28:7** *But they also have erred through wine, and through strong drink are out of the way; the priest and the prophet have erred through strong drink, they are swallowed up of wine, they are out of the way through strong drink; they err in vision, they stumble in judgment.*

Alcohol consumption and addiction cause intoxication that puts a whole lot of pressure on organs such as the Liver, Pancreas, kidneys, the digestive system, and the cardiovascular system. It will impact your mind and body negatively, creating that numbness and insensibility that affects your judgments. Alcohol mixed with medication can result in terminal sicknesses or fatality. Effects include speech impediments, drowsiness's, headaches and migraines, vision blurriness and depth perception, consciousness and memory loss. Damage to the heart and muscles related to heart function, ulcers, cancer, the breakdown of the immune system, and will also affect your mental health and stability.

Liver damage will further cause complications such as inflammation in the liver, fibrosis, cirrhosis, and cancer.

> *Prayer: Father in the wonderful name of Jesus, I come to you and present my affliction of addiction in alcohol and narcotics. I am a deep pain to know that I am an addict and confess this sin to you and pray that you hear my prayers. Please forgive me for this indulgence into this addiction, I know that it is not good for me, but as I am mentioning I am addicted and do not have much control over my mind and body*

towards this addiction. I pray that you bind any spirit of alcohol and drugs and cast them out. I pray that you take control of my mind and cleanse me, set me free from this addiction and let me be free indeed. I pray that you take hold of my mind and keep me from wanting to consume and keep away from any of these chemicals as they are bad for my health and my body , and as you have given me this body where the holy spirit dwells, I pray that you cleanse me and remove any negative emotion and mindset towards this addiction and lead me righteously that I can engage myself with you more spiritually and focus on you more to rid myself of this sin. I give you all praise and honor and glory is all yours, in Jesus name AMEN

The old ancients were a consistent user of narcotics and alcohol, it was used in religious ceremonies and practices, and some were classified as a holy article to infuse into the ritual. It is a battle that was fought and the population of all culture battled against for ages. The root of it comes from our ancestors, who were a consistent user and as such the addiction flows through the veins, through the DNA and through to the lineage. Opium and SOMA (though a religious and medicinal) was used over 10,000 years ago; their belief system led them the application due to the enhanced spiritual state they would achieve during rituals, ceremonies and cultural moments. They also believe that their mental faculty gained more clairvoyance and can think more philosophically and being in a genius frame of mind. This may be the good positive reasoning, but the addiction was slowly becoming prevalent. Harmal commonly used by West Indian, Iranian and Andean cultures. Cannabis is old and been around for thousands of years and is believed to be a part of the Indian SOMA drink. Cocoa leaves and the cocoa product are still one of our significant wars on drugs today, but in ancient times its daily use was reasonable. Magic mushroom (Psilocybin) is the standard drug and concoction used in the desert regions as they grow in the desert, supposedly produces a high level of intelligence including hallucinations. Opium has its history in the Asian region, including Europe, Egypt and many parts of the world. It is believed to have been favorite produce cultivated by Sumerians. The Indians used Bhang, Datura (Datura is a genus of nine species of poisonous vespertine flowering plants belonging to the family Solanaceae. They are commonly known as daturas, but also known as devil's trumpets, not to be confused with angel's trumpets, its closely related genus Brugmansia.), Cannabis and a plethora of narcotic producing plants and herbs, most used for medicinal purposes but was also a part of recreational and ceremonial uses. Today there is a near 30% - 50% of Indo related genes that are addicted to some form of an intoxicant, form alcohol to tobacco or other forms of herbal or processed drugs.

This makes it a generational Curse and because it was in full usage by deities, makes it a more profound darker generational curse that we see in today's Indian all over the world. In the Indian scripture of all religion, the drunken dance is part of the culture, and even some of their Gods uses narcotics for hallucination and spiritual elevation to different planes, but that is for Gods, which makes the illiterate man, who do not possess the spiritual powers of heavenly beings to become fools to put themselves in that state as it is far more dangerous to the human flesh and little brain (and mind) in comparison to any being that appears out of a higher plane.

Fallen because of the Seven Deadly Sins – the most hated sins: Pride, Greed, Lust, Envy, Gluttony, and Sloth

1. **Pride:** *Regarding you better than others, egoistically as a narcissist. This is the first sin as created in heaven by Lucifer, being the highest of Angels and the Fairest most decorated and most beautiful*

2. **Greed:** *Pursuit of material things and things of this world beyond what we need or possess*

3. **Lust:** *2 Timothy 2: 21 If a man, therefore, purge himself from these, he shall be a vessel unto honor, sanctified, and meet for the master's use, and prepared unto every good work. 22. Flee also youthful lusts: but follow righteousness, faith, charity, peace, with them that call on the Lord out of a pure heart.*

4. **Gluttony:** *Gluttony is over consumption of food and drinks, it is having the abundance and splurging excessively*

5. **Sloth:** *Excessive laziness and not utilizing all of God's given skills and ability*

6. **Wrath:** *Uncontrollable anger and hate of other people, including prejudice*

7. **Envy:** *Jealousy and a desire for someone else's ability, prosperity, and possession*

   Prayer: Lord Jesus, I come to you to in a humble spirit, bowing down to you and pleading for your compassion to remedy the situation and situations I face with the seven deadly sins that God hates the most and call them 'abomination.' I pray if these are spirits and demons that are influencing me in these areas that you bind, rebuke, renounce and cast them all from all roots inflicted in me and tear them out, cast them all into the lake of Fire and out from me, my environment, my life, my family and cast them away from me, never to return.
   I bind the spirit of Pride, I Jesus name
   I bind the spirit of Greed I Jesus name
   I bind the spirit of Lust I Jesus name
   I bind the spirit of Gluttony I Jesus name
   I bind the spirit of sloth I Jesus name
   I bind the spirit of wrath I Jesus name
   I bind the spirit of Envy I Jesus name
   Bind them all and cancel all powers they have over me, I am now free from any hold they had on my life and render them powerless, I command that by your power in the name

of Jesus to be cast out from my body, mind, and spirit, be cast out of my environment and my family. Me and my family are under the protection of the Lord Jesus, and He has all authority over us. Satan and his emissaries have no authority over us and we are now free. Lord lead me in the path you have prepared for me and protect me from ever encountering these sins. I give you all praise, honor, and glory and Thank you in advance, in Jesus name Amen

45 BLESS THE CHILDREN

For you do not want them to go through any adverse situations. You need to speak blessings over their lives for it is not for them to suffer the sins of their fathers or grandfathers, but to live a life of abundance. This is an old custom and is a living testimony of many wealthy people, who have inherited the blessings of their fore parents.

Bless your children and teach them to carry out the tradition of speaking over them and blessing them that they may e protected and full of abundant life. The world is becoming more stringent and harder; it is becoming infested with evil, drug addiction, crime and violence, weirdness's, natural disasters, wars, and conflicts

1 Kings 21: 29 Seest thou how Ahab humbleth himself before me? Because he humbleth himself before me, I will not bring the evil in his days: but in his son's days will I bring the evil upon his house. (this is what happens when a father sin falls upon the children)

My BLESSING to You My Child

As your father, I am delegated by God Almighty as the Spiritual Ruler over my home and family and by his Authority, I at this moment speak this Irrevocable Blessing into your life. In the name of the God of Abraham, Isaac, and Jacob:

*I bless your entire Life and every aspect of your life in good health, strength, courage, and boldness. I Bless your Relationships that you encounter good people and will be the head all the time and be in good company, always the apple of in the eyes of God. I bless you in your academic studies as you will excel in all your endeavors and achieve the highest level of Education that will put you in an elevated position of responsibility, status, and salary. I bless you with peace, love and joy and prosperity in abundance that you will always be wealthy and have plenty to lend and not borrow. I bless you with supernatural powers to have visions and envision ahead, discerning all evil as they approach and come close to you. I praise you that the Guardian angels will always be your guiding light and will give you the **unction to be a helper to all.** God be with you always, and his spirit dwell in you.*

I bless you with the blessings of Psalms 91

1:   *He that dwelleth in the secret place of the highest shall abide under the shadow of the Almighty.*

2:      *I will say of the LORD, He is my refuge and my fortress: my God; in him will I trust.*

3:      *Surely he shall deliver thee from the snare of the fowler, and from the noisome pestilence.*

4:      *He shall cover thee with his feathers, and under his wings shalt thou trust: his truth shall be thy shield and buckler.*

5:      *Thou shalt not be afraid for the terror by night; nor for the arrow that flieth by day;*

6:      *Nor for the pestilence that walketh in darkness; nor for the destruction that wasteth at noonday.*

7:      *A thousand shall fall at thy side, and ten thousand at thy right hand; but it shall not come nigh thee.*

8:      *Only with thine eyes shalt thou behold and see the reward of the wicked.*

9:      *Because thou hast made the LORD, which is my refuge, even the most High, thy habitation;*

10:      *There shall no evil befall thee; neither shall any plague come nigh thy dwelling.*

11:      *For he shall give his angels charge over thee, to keep thee in all thy ways.*

12:      *They shall bear thee up in their hands, lest thou dash thy foot against a stone.*

13:      *Thou shalt tread upon the lion and adder: the young lion and the dragon shalt thou trample under feet.*

14:      *Because he hath set his love upon me, therefore will I deliver him: I will set him on high because he hath known my name.*

15:      *He shall call upon me, and I will answer him: I will be with him in trouble; I will deliver him, and honor him.*

16:      *With long life will I satisfy him and shew him my salvation.*
     I bless you with the blessings of Moses in

Joshua 1:   *Every place that the sole of your foot shall tread upon, that have I given unto you, as I said unto Moses. There shall not any man be able to stand before thee all the days of thy life: as I was with Moses, so I will be with thee: I will not fail thee, nor forsake thee. Only be thou strong and very courageous, that thou mayest observe to do according to all the law, which Moses my servant commanded thee: turn not from it to the right hand or to the left, that thou mayest prosper whithersoever thou goest.*

Deuteronomy 28:

1   *And it shall come to pass, if thou shalt hearken diligently unto the voice of the LORD thy God, to observe and to do all his commandments which I command thee this day, that the LORD thy God will set thee on high above all nations of the earth:*

2:      *And all these blessings shall come on thee, and overtake thee if thou shalt hearken unto the voice of the LORD thy God.*

3: *Blessed shalt thou be in the city, and blessed shalt thou be in the field.*

4: *Blessed shall be the fruit of thy body, and the fruit of thy ground, and the fruit of thy cattle, the increase of thy kina, and the flocks of thy sheep.*

5: *Blessed shall be thy basket and thy store.*

6: *Blessed shalt thou be when thou comest in, and blessed shalt thou be when thou goest out.*

7: *The LORD shall cause thine enemies that rise up against thee to be smitten before thy face: they shall come out against thee one way, and flee before thee seven ways.*

8: *The LORD shall command the blessing upon thee in thy storehouses, and in all that thou settest thine hand unto, and he shall bless thee in the land which the LORD thy God giveth thee.*

9: *The LORD shall establish thee a holy people unto himself, as he hath sworn unto thee if thou shalt keep the commandments of the LORD thy God, and walk in his ways.*

10: *And all people of the earth shall see that thou art called by the name of the LORD; and they shall be afraid of thee.*

11: *And the LORD shall make thee plenteous in goods, in the fruit of thy body, and in the fruit of thy cattle, and in the fruit of thy ground, in the land which the LORD Sware unto thy fathers to give thee.*

12: *The LORD shall open unto thee his good treasure, the heaven to give the rain unto thy land in his season, and to bless all the work of thine hand: and thou shalt lend unto many nations, and thou shalt not borrow.*

13: *And the LORD shall make thee the head, and not the tail, and thou shalt be above only, and thou shalt not be beneath; if that thou hearken unto the commandments of the LORD thy God, which I command thee this day, to observe and to do them:*

14: *And thou shalt not go aside from any of the words which I command thee this day, to the right hand, or to the left, to go after other gods to serve them*

Thank you, LORD, for blessing my children. I pray you keep them and you bless with

- o *Bless them with Wisdom and knowledge*
- o *Bless them with increased income*
- o *Bless them with Work opportunities*
- o *Bless them with Advancements*
- o *Bless them with Supernatural increase and supply*
- o *Bless them with Multi-million-dollar ideas, inventions, and strategies*
- o *Bless them with writing abilities*
- o *Bless them with Management Skills and Project Management skills*
- o *Bless them with Money management skills*
- o *Bless them with Time management skills*
- o *Bless them with Negotiation skills*
- o *Bless them with Resource management skills*

- *Bless them with Crisis management skills*
- *Bless them with Recession management skills*
- *Bless them with Debt-free living*
- *Bless them with Secret riches and hidden treasures*
- *Bless them with Houses*
- *Bless them with Residual income*
- *Bless them with gifts and financial blessings*
- *Bless them with One hundredfold blessing*
- *Bless them with all bills paid*
- *Bless them with Investment strategies and financial management skills*
- *Bless them with Promotions*
- *Bless them with Visions*
- *Bless them with Dreams*
- *Bless them with and Make them Wealthy and healthy, Full of Love, Humility, Integrity, and power and let your light shine upon them all the days of their lives.*
  In the Name of Jesus AMEN

In the name of JESUS CHRIST of Nazareth, I plead and cover myself with the Blood of JESUS. I pray and ask that you protect me 7 x 24 all the days of my life against any weapons of war, all witches, warlocks, wizards, Satanists, sorcerers, and I break the power of all curses, hexes, vexes, spells, charms, fetishes, psychic prayers, psychic thoughts, all witchcraft, sorcery, magic, voodoo, all mind control, jinxes, potions, bewitchments, death, destruction, sickness, pain, torment, psychic power, psychic warfare, prayer chains, incense and candle burning, incantations, chanting, blessings and hoodoo, and everything else being sent my way and to my family, children and anyone connected to me by bloodline. I break the curse of lust and adultery, fornication and perversion, in the name of Jesus.

In Jesus Name I pray, Amen

> *"May all be prosperous and happy, May all be free from illness, May all see what is auspicious, May no one suffers."*
> *"May there be Peace in Heaven, Sky, Earth, Water, Plants, Trees, Gods, in various Worlds; May there be Peace in all. May there be Peace Indeed within Peace, Giving me the Peace which grows within me.*
> *Om peace, peace, peace"* **-Shanti Path, Upanishads**

Breath is what God gave to us to live and breathe is what sustains us, or we die, therefore according to all religious sect's breath in and make breathing a part of your ritual, work on the perfection of your breathing and study the breathing techniques. Breathing develops harmony with your body, environment and sustains your life and promotes good health. These are enhancements you need to be aware, having fallen down; this alone can open up the phenomena of miracles in your life

Practice the spiritual breathing, as all spiritual vibrations and energies surround us all. Spiritual breathing draws in more of the powers from the air and the Universe. As we breathe in, we inhale pure air and exhale impure air, With mind-frames, imagery of the Holy Spirit and God and healing powers we can utilize breathing exercises to enhance the energies within and fight against sicknesses and weaknesses of the body, build up the immune system, you only have to pray to god, command your inner spirit to connect and control your cells to work for you in the dispersing of radical toxins and destroying radical cells.

"Qigong is an ancient Chinese breathing exercise with meditation which is being developed today for therapy of chronic illnesses in the People's Republic of China. It is claimed to cure gastric ulcers, hypertension, anxiety neurosis, otitis media, and cancer and used as a form of anesthesia."
"Spiritual Breathing: Out and In. ... When we breathe physically, we exhale the impure air and inhale the pure air. In spiritual breathing, we exhale the impure by confessing our sins, and we inhale the pure by giving the Holy Spirit complete control of every area of our life."

Breathing combined with meditation and prayer brings about calmness within, it balances your emotions, reduces high blood pressure, increases your awareness, boosts your immunity, clears up your mind and activates such glands as the pineal glands. It helps to detoxify your body; a toxic, clogged body cannot possess a clear mind. In the practice of Martial arts, we do the "Dragon breathing," breath in deep to your core as that is the location of your central body energies.

So then rise Fallen man and do not let the idea of a fallen being stay within your mental state, get up and rise to the challenge. If you fall seven times, seven times you get up and rise for the 8th, these are the times where true character comes into action, and calamity is a carving of your character, grooming you to a higher, better person.

Proverbs 24:16 *New King James Version (NKJV)*
16   For a righteous man may fall seven times And rise again, But the wicked

shall fall by calamity.

Mark 1:32, 34 *When evening came, after the sun had set, they began bringing to Him all who were ill and those who were demon-possessed...And He healed many who were ill with various diseases and cast out many demons .*

1 Timothy 4:1 *"The Spirit clearly says that in later times some will abandon the faith and follow deceiving spirits and things taught by demons."*

Matthew 12: 43 *When the unclean spirit is gone out of a man, he walketh through dry places, seeking rest, and findeth none.*

44 *Then he saith, I will return into my house from whence I came out; and when he is come, he findeth it empty, swept, and garnished.*

45 *Then goeth he, and taketh with himself seven other spirits more wicked than himself, and they enter in and dwell there: and the last state of that man is worse than the first. Even so, shall it be also unto this wicked generation?*

James 4:7 *"Therefore submit to God. Resist the devil, and he will flee from you."*

A few key points to remember and act upon are

- Forgive yourself for anything you have done against the will of God or any Person
- Love yourself for who you are and for who you plan to make yourself
- Release all the Hype ego from within and humble yourself
- Take an interest in your family, wife, children, family members, neighbors and friends, change your attitude and talk to them, show some love
- Get somewhat involved in the community
- Change your Belief System
- Change the inside of you and your consciousness
- Send out positive energies
- Create your ending, visualize your goal and pray for it to materialize
- Create a 50-30-30 Rule
- Find some well to do or rich friends who can be of some assistance
- Write a book on your experiences, the tips of success in life
- Think, think, think, maybe ideas will flow on an invention discuss in a group
- Network with people who can lead or guide you
- Find work from the Home position while you are searching for a position
- Occupy yourself so that your mind does not get into a rut of depression
- Sell on Amazon and eBay
- Create a Blog on an interesting topic

Our greatest glory is in never falling, but in rising every time, we fall. Confucius

Wake up and live for your breath and life came from a divine source and you have a purpose in life. Living in this world is not just about you and you alone, it is your association with another Godly life form, but you will have to make sure that you are first and foremost in a state of physical, mental and spiritual unison and strength to be able to help anyone else. The blessings will flow from up above through the headship of Jesus Christ unto you and your generations

Shake yourself free; you were given the power to lose yourself from all soul ties and links you may have had in any circumstance, speak to your mountain and set yourself free

Isaiah 52: 1   *Awake, awake; put on thy strength, O Zion; put on thy beautiful garments, O Jerusalem, the holy city: for henceforth there shall no more come into thee the uncircumcised and the unclean.*

2   *Shake thyself from the dust; arise, and sit down, O Jerusalem: loose thyself from the bands of thy neck, O captive daughter of Zion.*

This is one of the great deliverance prayer and statement in the Bible to set you free. Make sure that your prayers are strong and your words spoken over yourself and circumstances are strong and loud so that the Entire universe can hear you declare freedom for all events that are trying to keep you down. If any enemy comes against you Psalms 35 is one of the most excellent prayers against enemies and Psalms 91 is the most significant protection you have. Stress, life's daily pressure, unbelief, doubt, frustrations, overwhelming consistent failures can lead to a depressive state and will allow you to think very negatively. Be Strong and of Good Courage says the LORD to Joshua and Moses, your deliverance is right there on your lips on your tongue and in your mind. This is your life, and you have all legal authority to be in control of your body, mind, and spirit and for your spiritual guidance, the Spirit of God given the authority by you to keep you in all your ways safe, healthy, happy and full of abundant life. Let your pastors and priests are aware of your circumstances to pray for you, they have authority from God to be shepherds and pray over their congregation.

Let go of all pride, ego, fear, unbelief, stop any sinful ways, curses, involvement into any occult, do not be embarrassed over yourself and your prayer life, Built a desire for success and godliness, avoid the negative people around that you entertain and tolerate, shut them down it only talks a telling off once to end it.

When the going gets hard, you need to be prepared to fight against it harder rather than be submissive to circumstances and let it get you into a rut. As pointed out above miracles are happening all around us and you can be the creator of your very own wonder to change your life and your circumstances.

Make a plan on how to get out from these circumstances. Create a Plan A, Plan B, and Plan C and be prepared to launch these action plan against your circumstances, you mind have the power to create, and it works in sync with your words, think it out and voice it, may as well keep it in writing that you review every so often. Hopelessness and discouragement steps in on these occasions, coupled with pity and self-pity, isolation and depression. Bear in Mind all these are spirits of the mind and can also be a characteristic of demons adapting these traits and seeking the doors into your mind and can become very disastrous; a weak mind is like a sponge to negativity and demonic activity.

Prayers and praying are a robust psychological methodology against adversity; you can design prayers into the simplicity of talking out all the issues and the adverse situation you are facing and to finding a solution or attract solutions and people who may be of assistance. Praying directed to God is also led to the mind and spirit, and your very own spirit and your very own mind can work for you to overcome and find solutions. In other words, you are inputting this information into your memory, in the course of praying and speaking it out, the mind and spirit work to bring to you answers and direction to find the solution, it is up to your belief system and your faith in divinity. Build your confidence to know that you are capable of getting out of this situation, have the hope of success over it all, be prepared to step out and be sure that you are going to get out and elevate your standards to a more comfortable and happier zone. It will take a lot of focus, dedication, perseverance, sacrifice, and patience; let your calm and clarity of mind remain quiet and peaceful.

One thing you will have to remember, you are not alone, there millions of people going through very similar circumstances. They face very similar adversity and may even be in the worst position, one of the miracles of God , is as you pray, pray for others who may be in the same both, intercede for them , pray for their family, their job, their finances, their health, their mind (to bring about peace and a sound mind) and pray for their happiness, this intercession has a karmic action and will return to you as you pray for others, bear in mind what you would want for yourself and family.

46 MIRACLES

Now that you have read and understood the prayers in scripture, you must have a great deal of faith and belief to allow your mind and spirit to work these into miracles for you. The references of the many miracles that took place in the Bible are many, and Jesus said that you would be able to perform much more

John 14: 11   *believe me that I am in the Father, and the Father in me: or else believe me for the very works' sake.*

12   *Verily, verily, I say unto you, He that believeth on me, the works that I do shall he do also; and greater works than these shall he do; because I go unto my Father.*

13   *And whatsoever ye shall ask in my name, that will I do, that the Father may be glorified in the Son.*

14   *If ye shall ask anything in my name, I will do it.*

15   *If ye love me, keep my commandments.*

Some prominent Miracles:

- Destruction of Sodom and Gomorrah   Genesis 19.24
- Lot's wife turned into a pillar of Salt   Genesis 19.26
- Aaron's rod turned into a serpent   Exodus 7.10-12
- The Ten Plagues in Exodus   Exodus chapters 7, 8, 9, 10,12, 14
- Parting of the Red Sea   Exodus 14.21-31
- Feeding Millions with Manna   Exodus 16.14-35
- Water from the Rock   Exodus 17.5-7
- The fall of the Walls of Jericho   Joshua 6.6-28
- Stopping the Sun and Moon   Joshua 10.12-14
- Raising the Dead by Elijah   1Kings 17.17-24
- Raising the Dead the Shunammite's son   2 Kings 4.32-37
- Naaman's Leprosy cured   2 kings 5.10-14
- Syrian Army struck down with blindness   2 Kings 6.18-20
- Destruction of Sennacherib's army   2 Kings 19.35
- Shadrach, Meshach, Abednego burning furnace   Dan 3.19-27
- Daniel in the Lion's den   Dan 6.16-23
- Jonah and the great fish   Jonah 2.1-10

Jesus performed the following Miracles

• Two Blind men healed	Matthew 9.27-31
• The dumb Demoniac	Matthew 9.32-33
• A deaf/Dumb man of Decapolis	Mark 7.31-37
• A blind man in Betshaida	Luke 4.28-30
• The Fish net- Great catch Gennesaret	Luke 5.1-11
• The widow's son raised from the dead	Luke 7.11-15
• Man with Leprosy cured	Luke 14. 1-4
• Ten Lepers cleansed	Luke 17.11-19
• Woman freed from Infirmity	Luke 13.11-13
• Water changed to Wine	John 2.1-11
• Official's son fever healed	John4.46-54
• Invalid man healed at Pool (Bethesda)	John 5.1-9
• Man born blind healed at Jerusalem	John 9.1-7
• Lazarus Rose from the Dead	John 11.38-44
• Centurion Servant healed of Palsy	Matthew 8.5-13
• Daughter of Canaanite woman	Matthew 15.21-28
• 5000 Fed	Matthew 15.32-38
• Demoniac in Synagogue	Mark 1.23-26
• Peter's mother-in-law cured from fever	Matthew 8.14-15
• Still the Storm	Matthew 8.23-26
• The devils entered into Swine	Matthew 8.28-32
• Palsied man cured	Matthew 9.2-7
• Jairus's Daughter raised from Dead	Matthew 9.18-26
• Woman cured of Blood Disease	Matthew 9.20-22
• Man's withered hand	Matthew 12.10-13
• Jesus walked on water	Matthew 14.25-27
• Epileptic Boy cured	Matthew 17..14-18
• Blind man cured	Matthew 20.30-34

Disciples performed the following Miracles

• Lame Man at Temple (Beautiful gate)	Acts 3.1-26
• Death of Anaias and Sapphira	Acts 5.1-11
• Peter healed man in the Street	Acts 5.12-16
• Prison Doors opened by Angel	Acts 5.17-21
• Phillip cast of demons	Acts 8.6-7
• Peter healed Eneas Palsy	Acts 9.33-34
• Peter raised Tabitha	Acts 9.36-41
• Peter released from prison	Acts 12.6-10

- Paul healed Elymas blindness   Acts 13.9-11
- Paul healed cripple in Lystra   Acts 14.8-10
- Paul cast out demons   Acts 16.16-18
- Paul raised Eutychus   Acts 20.9-12
- Paul healed Publius father   Acts 18.8-9

These are some of the miracles were performed in the Old Testament and the New Testament. Many done by Jesus himself and as he ordained his disciples to go out in the great commission to perform same

47 THE GREAT COMMISSION

Matthew 28:16   *Then the eleven disciples went to Galilee, to the mountain where Jesus had told them to go.*

       17   *When they saw him, they worshiped him; but some doubted.*

       18   *Then Jesus came to them and said, "All authority in heaven and on earth has been given to me.*

       19   *Therefore go and make disciples of all nations, baptizing them in the name of the Father and of the Son and of the Holy Spirit, 20 and teaching them to obey everything I have commanded you. And surely I am with you always, to the very end of the age."*

Acts 1: 8   *But you will receive power when the Holy Spirit has come upon you, and you will be my witnesses in Jerusalem and in all Judea and Samaria, and to the end of the earth."*

I have searched other scriptures for miracles and miracles performed by other deity and God in other religious texts. I did not find many, I did find the Vedas delivered a great authority of Life, Health and Healing and if we are ordained to such a mission, I believe that we should venture to do so, rather than creating wars and rumors of wars, hatred, animosity, prejudice, and divisiveness. Sometimes your very own heart brings upon you what you harbor in your heart for others, God turns it around upon you and your own, I pray that you clean your mind lest you become a victim of your mind a prisoner of your thoughts

Isaiah 61:1   *The Spirit of the Lord GOD is upon me; because the LORD hath anointed me to preach good tidings unto the meek; he hath sent me to bind up the brokenhearted, to proclaim liberty to the captives, and the opening of the prison to them that are bound; Luke 4:18*

       2   *To proclaim the acceptable year of the LORD, and the day of vengeance of our God; to comfort all that mourn; Luke 4:19*

       3   *To appoint unto them that mourn in Zion, to give unto them beauty for ashes, the oil of joy for mourning, the garment of praise for the spirit of heaviness; that they might be called trees of righteousness, the planting of the LORD, that he might be glorified.*

       4   *And they shall build the old wastes, they shall raise up the former desolations, and they shall repair the waste cities, the desolations of many generations.*

5 *And strangers shall stand and feed your flocks, and the sons of the alien shall be your plowmen and your vinedressers.*

6 *But ye shall be named the Priests of the LORD: men shall call you the Ministers of our God: ye shall eat the riches of the Gentiles, and in their glory shall ye boast yourselves.*

7 *For your shame, ye shall have double, and for confusion, they shall rejoice in their portion: therefore in their land, they shall possess the double: everlasting joy shall be unto them.*

8 *For I the LORD love judgment, I hate robbery for burnt offering; and I will direct their work in truth, and I will make an everlasting covenant with them.*

We suffer for many reasons, our very own mistakes, the mistakes of someone else, some injustice that has met us, but God will keep us safe and will address our circumstances. God is revealing; you don't need anyone to intercede for your blessings, you go directly to God for you have the spirit of God within you

Luke 4: 17 *And there was delivered unto him the book of the prophet Esaias. And when he had opened the book, he found the place where it was written,*

18 *The Spirit of the Lord is upon me because he hath anointed me to preach the gospel to **the poor**; he hath sent me to **heal the brokenhearted**, to **preach deliverance** to the **captives**, and **recovering of sight to the blind**, to set at **liberty them that are bruised**,*

19 *To preach the acceptable year of the Lord. Isa 61:2*

20 *And he closed the book, and he gave it again to the minister and sat down. And the eyes of all them that were in the synagogue were fastened on him.*

21 *And he began to say unto them; This day is this scripture fulfilled in your ears.*

One man is all it takes
One man made a difference in the survival and redemption of the human race and Human Kind,
One man's sacrifice has changed history and saved the world.
One man can also be the cause of the entire destruction and annihilation of the human race (American Scientist J. Robert Oppenheimer and team in the Manhattan Project invented the atomic bomb and so on).
One man- Abraham – the father of faith

One Man – Moses led over two million people out of bondage and slavery

One man became the most significant spiritual teacher

One man created the first computer program

One man led a nation through to independencethrough non-violence

One man led the fight against segregation

One woman "the first lady of civil rights", " the mother of freedom movement"

One man or woman– there are a long list of people, both men and women who played significant roles in influencing the people and being world changers.

Noah, Moses, Joshua, David, Mary, Jesus, Jacob, Joseph, Daniel, Samuel, Elijah, Elisha, Isaiah, Peter, Paul, Charles Darwin, Esther, Debra, Ruth, Martin Luther Jr, Schindler, Mother Theresa, Einstein, Wilberforce, Tesla, Jobs,Lenin, ………

On the other hand: One Man: Pharaoh, Herod, Judas, Saul, Korah, Hitler, Stalin, Pol Pot, Osama Bin Laden, Idi Amin, Ivan the Terrible, Nero, Agripa, Herod, can also be the demise towards mankind and humanity that can cause negative changes to the world

One person could find cures for terminal sicknesses

One Person can ………

One person ….with the right vision

One person can be the one who ………

God is seeking for one man endowed with power and ability to perform what he wants for humanity. The world is full of hunger, poverty, violence, abuse, wars, and rumors of wars, disease, and sickness, and also full of spirituality, both positive and negative, full of demonic activities. Return to spirituality and acknowledge GOD, get back to your spiritual life and the spirit of God will enlighten and lead you in the direction you need to go.

For Jesus came to 'SAVE THOSE THAT ARE LOST."

There is One God and One Salvation and the human race is in danger of itself, and if we are not careful we will be our very own demise, we will cause our own Apocalypse and the end of the world

48 ACKNOWLEDGMENTS

Acknowledgments to the following Web Sites used for Researches, for Quotes and References.

https://www.allaboutreligion.org/origin-of-religion.htm

https://en.wikipedia.org/wiki/Timeline_of_religion

https://en.wikiquote.org/wiki/Vedic_science

The Higgs Boson field: - https://simple.wikipedia.org/wiki/Higgs_field

Sir Francis Bacon: https://en.wikipedia.org/wiki/Scientia_potentia_est

The Human Mind: https://en.wikipedia.org/wiki/Mind

Michio Kaku

www.bible.ca - Body Mind and Soul

Napoleon Bonaparte:

Bernard Shaw

Image: http://www.talentshare.org/~mm9n/articles/man2/4.htm

Bible Used for Scriptural Quotes: NASB, KJV, NKJV, NIV, Blue Letter Bible

https://en.wikipedia.org/wiki/Composition_of_the_human_body

Https://en.wikipedia.org/wlki/DNA

Excerpts from the Internet: Wikipedia

https://en.wikipedia.org/wiki/Pineal_gland

https://en.wikipedia.org/wiki/Satan

Scientific Excerpts from the Internet: Kenneth Locey and Jay Lennon

Peter Dockrill – Lecture 3 May 2016

Quotes from The Bhagwat Gita

Quotes from the Koran

Quotes from the Vedas

Kersey Graves (1813-1883), a Quaker from Indiana

Factbook: https://en.wikipedia.org/wiki/The_World_Factbook

http://www.dailymail.co.uk/news/article-3596516/Eighty-children-treated-hospital-outbreak-demonic-possession-Peruvian-school-pupils-say-visions-man-black-trying-kill-them.html

http://www.answering-islam.org/authors/clarke/worship_same_god.html

Louis Farrakhan quoted the speech at the Million Man March in October 1995,

Muslim writer, Shabbir Akhtar

https://archive.org/stream/WillieLynchLetter1712/the_willie_lynch_letter_the_making_of_a_slave_1712_djvu.txt

The Eurocentrism of Hegel.s philosophy:
http://www.fb03.uni-frankfurt.de/58976054/Racism-and-Rationality-in-Hegel_s-Philosophy-of-Subjective-Spirit.pdf

https://www.biblegateway.com/resources/all-women-bible/Zipporah

John A. Powell, a professor at Berkeley insightful book "Racing to Justice."

http://reluctant-messenger.com/bhagavad-gita.htm

Application bible –New Living Translation

https://en.wikiquote.org/wiki/Vedic_science

* *Huston Smith, A Tribute to Hinduism, page 58*

* *Pierre-Simon Laplace The Celestial Key to the Vedas, page 61.*

* *Tarikh al-Yaqubi, The Foundations of the Composite Culture in India, page 59*

• *Jean-Sylvain Baily, World as Seen under the Lens of a Scientist, page 460*
http://www.markbeast.com/satan/names-of-satan.htm

Gerhard von Rad, Genesis: A Commentary (1973, Revised Edition), p. 87-88, The Old Testament Library, The Westminster Press, Philadelphia, Pennsylvania, ISBN 0-664-20957-2.

"Born to Win" Muriel James Ed. D & Dorothy Jongeward Ph.D.

https://simple.wikipedia.org/wiki/Kalki_Avatar_aur_Muhammad_Sahib#cite_note-3

The Muslim philosopher Ibn Arabi

https://en.wikipedia.org/wiki/Kalki

https://en.wikibooks.org/wiki/Hinduism/Religious_Symbols_of_Hinduism

https://www.biblegateway.com/passage/?search=1+Timothy+3&version=ESV

http://www.discoverehrlich.com/ministryoftheholyspirit.pdf

Haglund, Kristine. "How To Build A Paradox: Making The New Jerusalem." Dialogue: A Journal of Mormon Thought, vol. 49, no. 3, Dialogue Foundation, Oct. 2016, p. 211.

Web source: https://www.biblestudytools.com/daniel/10.html

Kiley, James, and Elisabet Caler. "The Lung Microbiome: A New Frontier in Pulmonary Medicine." Annals of the American Thoracic Society, vol. 11, no. 1, American Thoracic Society, Jan. 2014, p. S66.

"Hindu Wisdom - Hindu scriptures." Insert Name of Site in Italics. N.p., n.d. Web. 24 Oct. 2018 <http://www.hinduwisdom.info/Hindu_Scriptures.htm>.

https://pediaview.com/openpedia/Timeline_of_religion

"Timeline Of Religion - Wikipedia." Insert Name of Site in Italics. N.p., n.d. Web. 24 Oct. 2018 <https://en.wikipedia.org/wiki/Timeline_of_religion>.

Speak To Your Mountain - Sermoncentral.com." Insert Name of Site in Italics. N.p., n.d. Web. 24 Oct. 2018 <https://www.sermoncentral.com/sermons/speak-to-your-mountain-harold-hansen-sermo>.

"Should Not The Shepherds Feed, The Flock? | Standingbehindgod." Insert Name of Site in Italics. N.p., n.d. Web. 24 Oct. 2018 <https://standingbehindgod.wordpress.com/2015/06/29/should-not-the-shepherds-feed>.

https://www.bibleref.com/Genesis/3/Genesis-3-17.html

https://science.howstuffworks.com/environmental/earth/geophysics/fundamental-for...

https://www.arrowheadpride.com/2018/5/21/17373786/another-look-at-a-patrick-maho...

https://www.openbible.info/topics/a_godly_man

https://theblazingcenter.com/2017/11/judge-not.html

https://www.britannica.com/topic/Vedic-religion

https://en.wikipedia.org/wiki/Religious_symbol

https://www.biblehub.com

https://www.sermoncentral.com/sermons/we-are-come-to-worship-him-dr-w-samuel-leg...

https://www.lds.org/scriptures/nt/matt/2.4-6?lang=eng

https://www.merriam-webster.com/dictionary/jehad

http://www.worldquranhour.com/the-greatest-verse-of-the-quran-ayatul-kursi/

https://en.wikipedia.org/wiki/Power_is_knowledge

https://www.importantindia.com/20596/meaning-of-knowledge-is-power-proverb/

http://www.cbn.com/spirituallife/inspirationalteaching/vonBuseck_Foundations_Man...

https://www.webmd.com/brain/features/how-male-female-brains-differ

http://www.columbia.edu/itc/anthropology/v1007/jakabovics/mf2.html

http://lineoflight.com/1910/?p=493:9&n=700&o=-ih,-fl

Makgoba, Thabo. "Water Is Life; Sanitation Is Dignity 1." Anglican Theological Review, vol. 100, no. 1, Anglican Theological Review, Inc., Jan. 2018, p. 113.

https://quizlet.com/187513411/eukaryotic-cells-_-chapter-4-flash-cards/

https://www.studylight.org/bible/kjv/1-corinthians/6-19.html

https://microbenotes.com/dna-structure-properties-types-and-functions/

Arora, Bharti, et al. "Influence Of Atmospheric Pressure Plasma On Biomolecules." Journal of Magnetohydrodynamics and Plasma Research, vol. 21, no. 1, Nova Science Publishers, Inc., Jan. 2016, p. 1.

https://microbenotes.com/dna-structure-properties-types-and-functions/

https://answersingenesis.org/biology/microbiology/laminin-and-the-cross/

https://reliawire.com/laminins/

https://www.chess.com/clubs/forum/view/laminin-a-cell-adhesion-protein-molecule-...

http://www.joshfranklin.org/uploads/1/5/0/9/15093264/6_-_romans.doc

http://www.innerbody.com/image_endoov/lymp04-new.html

https://www.sciencedaily.com/terms/pineal_gland.htm

https://biblehub.com/

https://www.healthline.com/health/pineal-gland-function

https://www.sciencedaily.com/terms/pineal_gland.htm

https://en.wikipedia.org/wiki/Pineal_gland

http://www.crystalinks.com/thirdeyepineal.html

http://www.dla.mil/portals/104/documents/Careers/downloads/BBIFAQs.pdf

http://www.kcm.org/real-help/healing/speak/healing-scriptures-speak-daily

https://epdf.tips/breaking-generational-curses.html

https://www.allaboutgod.com/story-of-lucifer.htm

https://biblereasons.com/satans-fall/

https://wikivividly.com/wiki/Serpents_in_the_Bible

https://en.wikipedia.org/wiki/Satanail

http://angelology.wikia.com/wiki/War_in_Heaven

http://www.ptgbook.org/prophecy.htm?blogpoint00317

http://www.battleinchrist.com/principalities_powers_world_rulers_of_darkness_spi...

https://en.wikipedia.org/wiki/Apple_(symbolism)

http://brandonweb.com/sermons/sermonpages/judges17.htm

https://www.planetminecraft.com/skin/lucifer-554156/

https://en.wikipedia.org/wiki/Satanail

http://markbeast.com/satan/history-of-satan.htm

http://www.learnthebible.org/satans-rebellion-and-fall.html

https://www.kjvbible.org/satan.html

https://www.sciencealert.com/the-largest-study-of-life-forms-ever-has-estimated-...

https://kjvbible.org/angel_dna.html

https://www.lds.org/general-conference/2000/10/ye-are-the-temple-of-god?lang=eng

http://www.religioustolerance.org/chr_jckr1.htm

https://www.douglasjacoby.com

http://www.cbn.com/spirituallife/BibleStudyAndTheology/Discipleship/vonBuseck_Th...

https://www.biblegateway.com

https://www.intouch.org/read/magazine/margin-notes/love-on-its-knees

http://www.kcm.org/real-help/healing/speak/healing-scriptures-speak-daily

https://epdf.tips/breaking-generational-curses.html

https://www.christianforums.com/threads/demons.2145313/

https://www.sacred-texts.com/bib/boe/boe009.htm

https://en.wikipedia.org/wiki/Specific_creation

https://en.wikipedia.org/wiki/Kalki_avatar

https://simple.wikipedia.org/wiki/Kalki_Avatar_aur_Muhammad_Sahib

https://answering-islam.org/authors/clarke/worship_same_god.html

https://www.preceptaustin.org/names_of_god

https://wheelsms.files.wordpress.com/2016/06/el-Shaddai-sermon-notes2.pdf

http://www.myredeemerlives.com/namesofgod/yhwh-tzvaot.html

https://archive.org/stream/WillieLynchLetter1712/the_willie_lynch_letter_the_making_of_a_sla
ve_1712_djvu.txt

http://www.fb03.uni-frankfurt.de/58976054/Racism-and-Rationality-in-Hegel_s-Phil...

http://greatbiblestudy.com/deliverance_prayers.php

http://www.bbc.co.uk/religion/religions/islam/beliefs/jihad_1.shtml

Web source:

   https://www.merriam-webster.com/dictionary/jehad

Jihad | Definition Of Jihad By Merriam-webster. (n.d.). Retrieved from

https://www.merriam-webster.com/dictionary/jehad

http://reluctant-messenger.com/bhagavad-gita.htm

https://www.gotquestions.org/Bible-foolishness.html

http://springs.church/2017/09/08/baptism/

https://everipedia.org/wiki/Serpents_in_the_Bible/

https://en.wikibooks.org/wiki/Hinduism/Religious_Symbols_of_Hinduism

https://www.merriam-webster.com/dictionary/apoptosis

https://www.youtube.com/watch?v=md9aymhFWUI

https://www.theknot.com/content/traditional-wedding-vows-from-various-religions

"Laminin And The Cross | Answers In Genesis." Insert Name of Site in Italics. N.p., n.d. Web. 25 Oct.
2018 <https://answersingenesis.org/biology/microbiology/laminin-and-the-cross/>.

"Laminin And The Cross | Answers In Genesis." Insert Name of Site in Italics. N.p., n.d. Web. 25 Oct.
2018 <https://answersingenesis.org/biology/microbiology/laminin-and-the-cross/>.

"Laminin: A Cell Adhesion Protein Molecule That Holds The ..." Insert Name of Site in Italics. N.p.,
n.d. Web. 25 Oct. 2018 <https://www.chess.com/clubs/forum/view/laminin-a-cell-adhesion-
protein-molecule->.

"Matthew - Joshfranklin.org." Insert Name of Site in Italics. N.p., n.d. Web. 25 Oct. 2018
http://www.joshfranklin.org/uploads/1/5/0/9/15093264/6_-_romans.doc

Arora, Bharti, et al. "Influence Of Atmospheric Pressure Plasma On Biomolecules." Journal of
Magnetohydrodynamics and Plasma Research, vol. 21, no. 1, Nova Science Publishers, Inc., Jan.
2016, p. 1.

Web source: https://www.importantindia.com/20596/meaning-of-knowledge-
is-power-proverb/

knowledge Is Power' - Meaning And Expansion Of The ... (n.d.). Retrieved from
https://www.importantindia.com/20596/meaning-of-knowledge-is-power-proverb/

Romans 1:20 Kjv "for The Invisible Things Of Him From The ..." Insert Name of Site in Italics. N.p.,
n.d. Web. 25 Oct. 2018 <https://www.kingjamesbibleonline.org/Romans-1-20/>.

https://www.healthline.com/health/pineal-gland-function

"Pineal Gland Function: What You Should Know." Insert Name of Site in Italics. N.p., n.d. Web. 25
Oct. 2018 <https://www.healthline.com/health/pineal-gland-function>.

Third Eye - The Pineal Gland A.s.m.r - Youtube." Insert Name of Site in Italics. N.p., n.d. Web. 25
Oct. 2018 <https://www.youtube.com/watch?v=KJx1XMDDHFo>.

"Pineal Gland - Wikipedia." Insert Name of Site in Italics. N.p., n.d. Web. 25 Oct. 2018

: "Satan - Wikipedia." Insert Name of Site in Italics. N.p., n.d. Web. 25 Oct. 2018
<https://en.wikipedia.org/wiki/Satanail>.

Apple (symbolism) - Wikipedia." Insert Name of Site in Italics. N.p., n.d. Web. 25 Oct. 2018
<https://en.wikipedia.org/wiki/Apple_(symbolism)>.

"Names Of Satan And Other Names For Satan - Beast." Insert Name of Site in Italics. N.p., n.d.
Web. 25 Oct. 2018 <http://www.markbeast.com/satan/names-of-satan.htm>.

https://www.sciencedaily.com/releases/2011/08/110823180459.htm
: "How Many Species On Earth? About 8.7 Million, New Estimate ..." Insert Name of Site in Italics.
N.p., n.d. Web. 25 Oct. 2018
<https://www.sciencedaily.com/releases/2011/08/110823180459.htm>.

https://www.sciencealert.com/the-largest-study-of-life-forms-ever-has-estimated-...
"The Largest Study Of Life Forms Ever Has Estimated That ..." Insert Name of Site in Italics. N.p.,
n.d. Web. 25 Oct. 2018 <https://www.sciencealert.com/the-largest-study-of-life-forms-ever-has-
estimated->.

: "Who And What Are The Angels - Kjvbible.org." Insert Name of Site in Italics. N.p., n.d. Web. 25
Oct. 2018 <https://kjvbible.org/angel_dna.html>.

http://www.cbn.com/spirituallife/BibleStudyAndTheology/Discipleship/vonBuseck_Th...
Three Keys To Answered Prayer: Craig Von Buseck." Insert Name of Site in Italics. N.p., n.d. Web.
25 Oct. 2018
<http://www.cbn.com/spirituallife/BibleStudyAndTheology/Discipleship/vonBuseck_Th>.

The Three Parts Of Man - Foundations Of The Faith Q & A ... (n.d.). Retrieved from
http://www.cbn.com/spirituallife/inspirationalteaching/vonBuseck_Foundations_Man

https://www.asitis.com/6/6.html
"Bhagavad Gita As It Is, 6.6: Sankhya-yoga, Text 6." Insert Name of Site in Italics. N.p.,
n.d. Web. 27 Oct. 2018 <https://www.asitis.com/6/6.html>.

Web source: https://en.wikipedia.org/wiki/Timeline_of_religion
"Timeline Of Religion - Wikipedia." Insert Name of Site in Italics. N.p., n.d. Web. 27 Oct.
2018 <https://en.wikipedia.org/wiki/Timeline_of_religion>.

"Daniel 9:24-27 24 Seventy Weeks Are Determined Upon Thy ..." Insert Name of Site in
Italics. N.p., n.d. Web. 27 Oct. 2018
<http://www.ensnaredindistractions.com/Web%20Site%20Designs/Ex-
Designz/webtempcry
stalX8877/CrystalX/Written%20Sermons/Adobe%20PDF%20Files/Bible%20Study/01%20
Seve>.

https://en.wikipedia.org/wiki/Serpents_in_the_Bible
"Serpents In The Bible - Wikipedia." Insert Name of Site in Italics. N.p., n.d. Web. 27 Oct.
2018 <https://en.wikipedia.org/wiki/Serpents_in_the_Bible>.

"What Are The Four Fundamental Forces Of Nature What Are The Four Fundamental
Forces Of Nature ... (n.d.). Retrieved from
https://science.howstuffworks.com/environmental/earth/geophysics/fundamental-
for<https://science.howstuffworks.com/environmental/earth/geophysics/fundamental-
for>.

Web source:

https://en.wikiquote.org/wiki/Vedic_science
"Vedic Science - Wikiquote." Insert Name of Site in Italics. N.p., n.d. Web. 27 Oct. 2018

<https://en.wikiquote.org/wiki/Vedic_science>.

https://www.coursehero.com/file/18579515/Empol-Philosophy/

https://www.webmd.com/brain/features/how-male-female-brains-differ

Web source: https://answersingenesis.org/biology/microbiology/laminin-and-the-cross/ : Laminin And The Cross | Answers In Genesis. (n.d.). Retrieved from https://answersingenesis.org/biology/microbiology/laminin-and-the-cross/

Web source: http://www.crystalinks.com/thirdeyepineal.html : Third Eye - Pineal Gland - Crystalinks. (n.d.). Retrieved from http://www.crystalinks.com/thirdeyepineal.html

Web source: https://www.healthline.com/health/pineal-gland-function Pineal Gland Function: What You Should Know. (n.d.). Retrieved from https://www.healthline.com/health/pineal-gland-function

https://en.wikipedia.org/wiki/Pineal_gland#/media/File:Gray715.png Pineal Gland - Wikipedia. (n.d.). Retrieved from https://en.wikipedia.org/wiki/Pineal_gland

Web source: https://en.wikipedia.org/wiki/Satanail Satan - Wikipedia. (n.d.). Retrieved from https://en.wikipedia.org/wiki/Satanail

Names Of Satan And Other Names For Satan - Beast. (n.d.). Retrieved from http://www.markbeast.com/satan/names-of-satan.htm

. : How Many Species On Earth? About 8.7 Million, New Estimate ... (n.d.). Retrieved from https://www.sciencedaily.com/releases/2011/08/110823180459.htm

The Largest Study Of Life Forms Ever Has Estimated That ... (n.d.). Retrieved from https://www.sciencealert.com/the-largest-study-of-life-forms-ever-has-estimated-Specific Similarities Between - Religious Tolerance. (n.d.). Retrieved from http://www.religioustolerance.org/chr_jckr1.htm

The Book Of Enoch: The Book Of Enoch: Chapter Vi. (n.d.). Retrieved from https://www.sacred-texts.com/bib/boe/boe009.htm

Web source: https://www.sacred-texts.com/bib/boe/boe009.htm The Book Of Enoch: The Book Of Enoch: Chapter Vi. (n.d.). Retrieved from https://www.sacred-texts.com/bib/boe/boe009.htm

Web source: https://en.wikipedia.org/wiki/Kalki_avatar : Kalki - Wikipedia. (n.d.). Retrieved from https://en.wikipedia.org/wiki/Kalki_avatar

Web source: http://www.shieldandrefuge.org/articles/onegod.htm Biblical Passages That Teach - A Shield And Refuge Ministry. (n.d.). Retrieved from http://www.shieldandrefuge.org/articles/onegod.htm

History of Political Thought, Volume 13, Number 2, 1 February 1992, pp. 243-255(13)

49 Conclusion

If 1.6 Billion Muslims, 2.0 Billion Christians, 1.5 Billion Hindus diligently pray for Peace and the blessings of God upon the earth, Stop the violence, stop the persecution, break the yoke of the Devil, make provisions, feed the hungry, fight against crime and violence, break every bondage over the city, country and its people provide food clothing and shelter. I am sure there will be miracles and wonders, but if you trample on each other, then thy will be done on yourself and by others. We focus on religion as dogma rather than what the religion is teaching us to be and how to act towards the calling of God and what God wants us to be, and we allow ourselves to become led by the bullring and be separated from God's true nature and not getting into the realm of God's spiritual dominion, we neglect the Humanitarian aspect of the duties of Man as designed by God and becomes self-centered, egocentric, egoistic and selfish in our thoughts and deeds. The most important message from God is "to love thy neighbor as thyself' which is totally ignored as we become selfishly super-spiritual and ignore our God-Given gift to 'save the lost' and help your fellow mankind from falling. Instead, you will seek your fellow man to either witness to him in delivering the dogma you have embedded in your heart, invite him to church or shun him for not listening to you.

2Chronicles 7:14 if My people who are called by My name will humble themselves, and pray and seek My face, and turn from their wicked ways, then I will hear from heaven, and will forgive their sin and heal their land.

Utilize First Sunday, Friday or Saturday come together in one accord and pray for the Church, the City, The State, The country and the world for all the goodness that we seek and to rebuke and bind all the negativity, there would certainly be miracles and wonders.

Every religious group should join together and create a day of prayer for their country, where they can pray against the satanic Prince over their Country and bind him and all Demonic influences over the country and pray for peace, love, harmony, and prosperity of the country and the people. Pray that God will be the guide and deliver wisdom to the leaders and the people to bring about visions of methods and ways to enhance the economy and prosperity of the nation, To bring healing to the sick and to give wisdom and knowledge to all over their life and their spiritual connection to GOD.

There is a war going on in the spiritual dominion and earth becomes the battlefield and man becomes the pawns for both Satan's kingdom and his emissaries and God and his kingdom. We become the game of chess where the gatherings of souls are most important to both spiritual kingdoms, where one kingdom is trying to prove to the other kingdom that they can rise up above and overtake through winning the souls of mankind. This makes us the greatest being created, for we lack nothing except the true nature of God within, where one kingdom wants us to achieve this Nature of God and the other kingdom does not want us to achieve the nature of God, they would instead put us under subjection no matter the cost and we become either enlightened or blinded depends on who wins first and takes over.

Revelations 12: 15 And the serpent cast out of his mouth water as a flood after the woman, that he might cause her to be carried away of the flood.

16   and the earth helped the woman, and the earth opened her mouth and swallowed up the flood which the dragon cast out of his mouth.

*17   And the dragon was wroth with the woman and **went to make war with the remnant of her seed**, which keep the commandments of God, and have the testimony of Jesus Christ. (The remnants are – the People, you and I and our generations)*

All religions acknowledge Jesus Christ and his existence as God incarnated in these latter days, it is a common understanding that Jesus is a major character that is spiritually connected to God and is part of God, the Prophet of God, the Son of God and God himself manifested in the flesh as Jesus Christ, this acknowledgment is all the religions will result in growing spiritual peace that will spread like wildfire in the hearts of all people. God himself said in the scriptures that "My People are a stiff-necked people" and their hearts are hard and commonly disobedient, no matter how many times they were saved from persecution, they will always be a Stiff-necked people with a hard heart. Why do they possess a hard heart? It is because they are always falling prey into the hands of the Devil in the various forms, even in their worship. This is the reason why many nations suffer at certain intervals every 100 years or 40 years, or at specific biblical numerical, symbolic era, it may look as though they are prospering and getting higher and wealthier, but come a time when God himself puts them under persecution and puts them into slavery and bondage.

This is a calling back to God and Spirituality, a calling to the young generations who are being separated from God and the elders are failing to engage the young millennial as the new generation that needs God and Spirituality more than any generations in the past or any generations to come. This present generation holds the keys to the future of mankind and the survival of mankind from extinction and the earth from complete annihilation as Satan takes control of every leader in country and church and leaders in high places and allow his Prince's over every country, state, city, town, and village to **plunder and devour** (*Job 1:7 The Lord said to Satan, "From where have you come?" Satan answered the Lord and said, "From going to and fro on the earth, and* *from walking up and down on it. 1 Peter 5:8 Be sober-minded; be watchful. Your adversary, the devil, prowls around like a roaring lion, seeking someone to devour.*)

Daniel 10: 10   *A hand touched me and set me trembling on my hands and knees.*

11   *He said, "Daniel, you who are highly esteemed, consider carefully the words I am about to speak to you and stand up, for I have now been sent to you." And when he said this to me, I stood up trembling.*

12   *Then he continued, "Do not be afraid, Daniel. Since the first day that you set your mind to gain understanding and to humble yourself before your God, your words were heard, and I have come in response to them.*

13   *But **the prince of the Persian kingdom** resisted me twenty-one days. Then Michael, one of the chief princes, came to help me because I was detained there with **the king of Persia**.*

14   *Now I have come to explain to you what will happen to your people in the future, for the vision concerns a time yet to come."*

20   *So he said, "Do you know why I have come to you? Soon **I will return to fight against the prince of Persia,** and when I go, the **prince of Greece will come**;*

21   *but first I will tell you what is written in the Book of Truth. (No one supports me against them except Michael, your prince.*

PART II

Transformation and Interconnection
      THE SUPREME GOD OUTSIDE AND INSIDE

(COMING SOON)

ABOUT THE AUTHOR

Bruce Deodat was a high school teacher, coach, mentor, and counselor. Self educated in the field of Clinical Psychoanalysis and Clinical hypnotherapy and Participating Public Speaker, mentor, and trainer. Worked in some major companies as a Senior Manager in The Sugar Industry, an employee at Ziff Davis PC Magazine, Investment Technology Group, Stream Global Services and as a Consultant for Donaldson Lufkin and Jenrette,, IBM, Cisco, Catholic Health Initiatives, Walt Disney Parks and Resorts, Solomon Smith Barney, Xcel Energy, Walt Disney International as Senior Project Manager. Informational Technology Professional as a PMI, ITIL, SCRUM Master and Six Sigma, achieving three Directors All Star Club awards for excellence and performance.
Consultant in the Financial Institutions (Wall Street District), Energy Production and distribution, Entertainment industry, and the Healthcare industries
Venturing in the writer's market
Masters of Arts in Biblical Studies

Made in the USA
Middletown, DE
31 December 2023

46812247R00214